PERFECT COMPANIONSHIP

PERFECT COMPANIONSHIP

Ellen Glasgow's
Selected Correspondence
with Women

Edited by
Pamela R. Matthews

University of Virginia Press
Charlottesville and London

University of Virginia Press
© 2005 by the Rector and Visitors of the University of Virginia
All rights reserved
Printed in the United States of America on acid-free paper
First published 2005

9 8 7 6 5 4 3 2 1

Library of Congress Cataloging-in-Publication Data

Glasgow, Ellen Anderson Gholson, 1873–1945.
  Perfect companionship : Ellen Glasgow's selected correspondence with women / edited by Pamela R. Matthews.
    p. cm.
Includes bibliographical references and index.
  ISBN 0-8139-2335-2 (cloth : alk. paper)
  1. Glasgow, Ellen Anderson Gholson, 1873–1945—Correspondence. 2. Novelists, American—20th century—Correspondence. 3. Women—United States—Correspondence. I. Matthews, Pamela R. II. Title.
PS3513.L34Z48 2005
813'.52—dc22
                                                         2004023804

For my parents and my sister

Contents

Acknowledgments	ix
Introduction	xiii
A Note on the Editorial Method	xxxiii
Chronology	xxxix
Abbreviations	xlv
Ellen Glasgow's Selected Correspondence with Women	
I. 1884–1903	1
II. 1904–1911	17
III. 1912–1926	55
IV. 1927–1938	80
V. 1939–1945	186
Calendar	255
Biographical and Geographical Register	275
Word Division	301
Works Cited and Consulted	303
Index	307

Illustrations follow page 54

Acknowledgments

As with any project that has been years in the making, this one has depended on a great many people. In particular, I want to thank the following people and institutions, without whom this edition would not exist. Any faults that remain are entirely mine.

Staff members at several libraries have provided information, photocopies of letters, answers to queries, short-term work space, and other invaluable assistance, both in person and long distance: Baylor University, Columbia University, Duke University, Goucher College, Huntington Library, Library of Congress, Massachussets Historical Society, Morristown National Historical Park, New York Public Library, Smith College, University of Florida, University of Iowa, University of North Carolina, University of Pennsylvania, University of Texas at Austin (Harry Ransom Humanities Research Center), University of Vermont, University of Virginia, Virginia Commonwealth University, Virginia Historical Society, Washington and Lee University, Wisconsin Historical Society, and Yale University. Extra thanks go to Ray Bonis, Frank Orser, Michael Plunkett, and Nancy Shawcross.

Nancy C. Essig, director of the then University Press of Virginia for most of this project, provided well-timed encouragement and constant support and even located important letters. Nancy also introduced me to Elizabeth M. Berkeley, associate editor for the William James correspondence, for whose expert advice I am very grateful. Anonymous readers of the manuscript for the University of Virginia Press gave me important help more than once, saved me from embarrassing mistakes, and made this a much better edition than it would have been without them. Ellen Satrom and Cathie Brettschneider of the Press have answered countless questions and offered wise counsel.

Research assistants provided invaluable aid at various stages: Matthew Berthold, Amy Earhart, Sara Anna Horton, and Krista May helped with filing, keyboarding, permissions information, proofreading, research, and transcriptions. The students in my Senior Seminar in Ellen Glasgow during the spring 2001 semester rekindled my enthusiasm for Glasgow's letters in ways I did not anticipate and they seemed unaware of. Alicia Clay and Patrick Clay passed along an autograph note from Glasgow from their private collection. I also want to thank Amy Wink and Rebecca Roorda, who shared ideas and materials.

Many colleagues have offered support in various ways. Janis Stout alerted me to the Dorothy Canfield Fisher letters. Glasgow scholars, always a generous bunch anyway, have given sound advice, asked good questions, and answered even more. Special thanks go to Stanly Godbold Jr., Susan Goodman, Edgar MacDonald, Catherine Rainwater, and Dorothy Scura. I'd also like to thank the many Glasgow scholars whose contact has been less personal but whose work has been immensely helpful, among them Julius R. Raper, Blair Rouse, Frances Saunders, Wellford Taylor, Carrington C. Tutwiler Jr. Dr. Francis Foster of Richmond was helpful and encouraging.

Heirs and executors of estates granted permission to publish letters in this volume. I thank the following: John Lovat Dickson, executor of Radclyffe Hall's estate; Helen Glenn Court and Susan R. Rutterberg, great-nieces, respectively, of Isa Glenn and Frances Newman; E. H. Gray, for permission to reproduce letters from Agnes Reese; Messers. Eugene M. Mitchell and Joseph R. Mitchell, nephews of Margaret Mitchell; and Spencer Klaw, Irita Van Doren's son-in-law. Catherine Turney's niece Bettina Salter has been nothing short of inspiring. Institutions generously granted permissions: Baylor University (Texas Collection, Dorothy Scarborough letter); Columbia University (Eleanor Belmont Papers and Daniel Longwell Papers, Rare Book and Manuscript Library); Doubleday, a division of Random House, Inc. (Page Cooper letter); University of Pennsylvania (Agnes Repplier Papers, Rare Book and Manuscript Library); the Mortimer Rare Book Room at Smith College Library (Bessie Zaban Jones Papers); Virginia Historical Society (Lila Meade Valentine Papers, Mss1V2345a and Bagby Family Papers, Mss1B1463b); Washington and Lee University (Special Collections, Leyburn Library, Glasgow Papers MSS 210). The unpublished correspondence of Marjorie Kinnan Rawlings is used with the permission of the University of Florida George A. Smathers Libraries. Permission to publish three letters from Glasgow to Sara Haardt Mencken was granted by the Enoch Pratt Free Library, Baltimore, in accordance with the terms of the bequest of H. L. Mencken. My heartfelt thanks to Michael Plunkett, the director of the Albert and Shirley Small Special Collections Library at the University of Virginia, for permission to publish the letters of Ellen Glasgow (#5060), Mary Johnston (#3588), and Amélie Rives Troubetzkoy; and for granting permission as holder of the letters of other correspondents whose copyright holders are unknown.

At my home institution, Texas A&M University, numerous individuals and offices have been helpful, many financially. I'd like to thank the Center for Teaching Excellence; the Glassock Center for Humanities Research and its director, James Rosenheim (and the center's earlier incarnations, led by Jeffrey N. Cox and Larry J. Reynolds); the College of Liberal Arts, with the deans Woodrow Jones Jr., and Charles Johnson; the Department of English, headed by J. Lawrence Mitchell and then Paul Parrish; the University Honors Program; and the office of the Vice President for Research.

I have depended on many friends for commiserating, inquiring, knowing, listening, and reading; a few of these are Melanie Hawthorne, David McWhirter,

Anne Morey, Mary Ann O'Farrell, Larry Reynolds, Susan Stabile, and Lynne Vallone. Thanks to all of you and to others who have been encouraging in countless ways. Special thanks go to the WC: you know who you are, and although I could have done it without you, I wouldn't have.

My family, Dennis Berthold and Matthew Berthold (and Bijou, the poodle), help me keep my perspective and provide every day the grounding that makes work possible. Dennis has read drafts and listened oftener than should be asked. Matthew helped with research tasks. Bijou walked with me. Thank you, guys, for everything.

This book is dedicated to my parents, Blanche Matthews and Jack Matthews, and to my sister, Lisa Matthews, in appreciation of their love and support over many, many years.

Introduction

In November 1944 Ellen Glasgow wrote to the Danish-born writer Signe Toksvig, with whom she had been corresponding for just over a year and a half: "There aren't many women one would like, if one were a man, to be married to; but . . . you leave the impression of perfect companionship."[1] In her arresting comment Glasgow does more than simply compliment Toksvig for being an ideal spouse: for one brief moment Glasgow imagines Toksvig as her own perfect companion.

This fleeting fantasy in a letter to a female correspondent near the end of Glasgow's life casts an illuminating light on Glasgow's lifelong preference for and dependence on the company of women. More urgent than a simple desire for a close woman friend or two, the privileged position Glasgow grants women often has been lost in the critical discourse, where the critics and historians usually have focused on Glasgow's professional career or on the traditional romance plot—two approaches that are centered on her relationships with men. Reading her correspondence with women shifts the focus to the intimate and casual female relationships that, in my view, gave Glasgow her strongest sense of a self that was fulfilled both personally and professionally.

Glasgow lived in a time of transition between the nineteenth century's acceptance (even admiration) of "romantic friendships" between women and the twentieth century's more complicated awareness that such friendships might be sexual.[2] For Glasgow and other women whose lives spanned this transitional period during which innocence about women's friendships gave way to circumspection, affectional relationships with women often required some combination of denial, subversion, and justification. (In her 1929 novel, *They Stooped to Folly,* and her later preface to that novel for the *Virginia Edition* in 1938, Glasgow indicates her awareness of the cultural shift toward perceiving women's friendships as potentially sexual.) It is impossible to define the precise nature of Glasgow's and other women's relationships during a time that lacked the categories to which we usually assign them today—they were neither the romantic friendships of the past nor the lesbian partnerships of our own time, although certainly there were women who acknowledged publicly their partnerships with women. Given Glasgow's proper middle-class Southern upbringing and her professional ambitions, it seems most likely that her relationships with women ranged from casual acquaintance to close (and long-term) friendship to literal sisterhood to deeply committed attachment—all without an acknowledged sexual component. What seems to me undeniably true is that the satisfactions of

Glasgow's friendships with women outweighed those of her friendships with men and that her primary emotional commitments were to women.

Toksvig was one of more than one hundred women with whom Glasgow corresponded, beginning in 1884 with the ten-year-old Glasgow's "first letter," written to her Aunt Bec.[3] Extant letters suggest that Glasgow's steady adult correspondence began in 1896, when, at twenty-three, she enjoyed her first (and only solo) trip abroad, and ended with her death in 1945.

Simply recovering these letters is noteworthy: in addition to whatever letters inevitably have disappeared over time, others plausibly were destroyed at Glasgow's request, although it is impossible to tell how frequently her correspondents obliged, of course. Her fellow Virginian, writer, and longtime friend Amélie Rives Troubetzkoy, for example, wrote, "*There!* I have kissed your dear letter and destroyed it, as you asked me to!"[4] "Please destroy this letter," Glasgow instructed the editor Irita Van Doren (without success, obviously).[5] Glasgow's niece Josephine Clark admitted many years after her aunt's death that she and her mother, Annie, had not saved Glasgow's letters. Although another sister, Rebe, kept many of her sister's letters, Glasgow's instructions to Rebe had been clear: "Please burn my scrappy letters."[6] Glasgow's companion and secretary Anne Virginia Bennett told Marjorie Kinnan Rawlings that an ailing, elderly Glasgow had made clear that she did not ever want her letters published.[7] That no extant letters to Radclyffe Hall have surfaced, although the letters from Hall clearly indicate reciprocity, may be the result of similar epistolary fates.

Like the correspondents who resisted Glasgow's desire that her letters be destroyed or withheld from others, I have chosen to make these private expressions public, to help ensure their availability to readers. The reasons for doing so are many, not the least of which is the further scholarship and critical investigation that they might make possible. One of the problems in Glasgow studies has been the extent to which Glasgow has controlled interpretations of her personae. From her public statements (in essays such as "I Believe," for example) to her autobiography, she has directed critics' lines of inquiry in what has amounted to a posthumous attempt to dictate representations of her. But changing times and values have made possible a critical and social climate much different from the one Glasgow knew. She needs to be reimagined in order to assess more accurately her central place in late nineteenth- and early twentieth-century American letters. I hope that readers will be convinced, as I am, that these letters move us toward a fuller understanding of Ellen Glasgow the writer and the person.

The 255 letters collected here have been selected from nearly seven hundred known letters in Glasgow's correspondence with other women, her perfect companions. In composing these letters, Glasgow both practiced the craft of writing and, often momentarily forgetful of self-conscious artistry, expressed the ideas and feelings that make and solidify enduring friendships. In the span of almost fifty years during a long and productive professional literary career, Glasgow wrote regularly to friends, sisters, wives of male correspondents, established writers, and other female acquaintances about the things that mattered the most to her and to them.

Why publish letters to and from women only? Foremost, these primary documents, which move us closer to the "real" Ellen Glasgow, are either unavailable in print, no longer extant, published in relatively inaccessible venues, or in need of more reliable scholarly apparatus. Stylistically, Glasgow's letters to and from women correspondents are significant for their subtle differences from those she wrote to and received from most of her male friends and acquaintances.[8] Although there are exceptions, for the most part Glasgow's correspondence with women is less self-conscious, less crafted, and less guarded than her correspondence with men. It is also less often informed by the irony that is one of Glasgow's trademarks as a fiction writer. These qualities more evident in Glasgow's letters to male correspondents—self-consciousness, stylistic care, self-protection, and irony—describe a writerly distance that represents Glasgow's professional relationships with men. Even when personal friendships with men develop (as they certainly do), they customarily begin as literary correspondence with male editors, publishers, established writers, or professors and other literary critics, all of whom have significant power over the publication, distribution, and reception of Glasgow's work. As with most women writers, at least until the late twentieth century, Glasgow depended heavily on the good graces of these professional men for the success of her work.

Glasgow's correspondence with women, in contrast, seems less driven by her awareness of asymmetrical power relationships. Even to women who occupied presumably inferior social positions, Glasgow wrote as an equal. Anne Virginia Bennett, for example, fits this category. Bennett, a nurse, was hired by the Glasgow family in 1910 to care for Cary Glasgow McCormack, the beloved sister who died of cancer in 1911. Bennett's caregiving role in the family might have ended with Cary's death, or with the death of another sister, Emily, in 1913, or even later, in 1916, following the death of Glasgow's father. However, with the exception of a brief interruption while serving as a nurse in France during World War I, Bennett stayed on to run Glasgow's household at One West Main Street, to protect Glasgow from intrusions into her writing time, and to perform secretarial as well as domestic duties. The letters written by most of Glasgow's women correspondents who visited One West Main express warm regards and thanks to "Miss Bennett."

Many commentators on Glasgow's life have maintained that the Glasgow-Bennett relationship was strictly that of mistress-servant, carefully demarcated by lines drawn according to traditional class distinctions.[9] But Glasgow's extant letters to Bennett, usually written during trips away from home, trouble such an interpretation: the letters are those of a domestic partner as much as they are those of an employer. Postcards humorously addressed to "Mr. Jeremy Glasgow" and "Mr. William Bennett," the couple's dogs, suggest a recognition (however tongue-in-cheek) of the women's roles as "parents" to their "children." If the balance of power in Glasgow's relationship with "A. V.," as she called her housemate of over three decades, was more uneven than the classic Boston marriage of the late nineteenth century, it came closer to resembling a traditional marriage than a servant-mistress arrangement. Glasgow, who grew to adulthood in an atmosphere of conventional southern mores that were especially prescriptive when it came to behavior expected of privileged white southern ladies, could do no more than imagine Bennett as her "secretary," or sometimes, a little more boldly, her "companion." She would have been, I suspect, incapable of ascribing to Bennett and herself a lesbian relationship as we understand it today.

The same traditional values that circumscribed acceptable social relationships and sexual mores also limited the range of attitudes toward race, and, in many ways, Glasgow (at least until late in her life) was no revolutionary in her dealings with African Americans. She often sentimentalized her close relationships with African Americans in predictable ways, as shown, for example, in her characterizations of her childhood mammy, as Glasgow called Lizzie Jones, and of James Anderson, Glasgow's cook for all of her adult life. In *The Woman Within* Glasgow characterizes Jones as the self-sacrificing, comforting, and nurturing mammy figure familiar to southern legend, without any recognition of the complexities of Jones's life apart from Glasgow and her family. Anderson, especially in Glasgow's letters, is treated with an equally familiar attitude of noblesse oblige. Glasgow respects both Jones and Anderson, even "loves" them after her fashion. But she articulates her relationships with Jones, Anderson, and others within the stereotypical narratives of a traditional southern world.

Glasgow's correspondence with two African American women, Agnes B. Reese and Elaine J. Dean, in some ways falls into similar stereotypical patterns, as illustrated, for example, when Glasgow sent Bennett to "represent" her at Reese's sister's funeral and Reese thanked her for doing so.[10] But these letters do add another dimension to the complexity of Glasgow's relationships with African Americans and more generally to the complexity of black-white relations just before and during the middle decades of the twentieth century in the South. Reese was the granddaughter of Glasgow's mother's mammy, and letters indicate that Glasgow therefore felt some responsibility for Reese and her family. Reese's sincere letters reveal that Glasgow's behavior was not always condescending or self-serving, as the example just above suggests: six months after the funeral Glasgow quietly sent someone to tend Reese's sister's grave site, an act of unobtrusive "kindness and goodness" that prompted Reese to call Glasgow "an angel of mercy and love" with a "heart" more honorable even than her "talents."[11] Gratitude for Glasgow's "kind heart" is also a theme in the single letter from Elaine J. Dean, who taught English in a Washington, D.C., high school. Dean wrote to thank Glasgow for her novel *In This Our Life,* with its "admirable" representations of African Americans as "respectable human beings with dignity, ideas and opinions."[12] That she preserved Dean's letter suggests that Glasgow was pleased by the appreciation of this African American reader. Letters from Reese and Dean suggest that beneath Glasgow's conventional attitudes lie more nuanced understandings of race relations, perhaps especially between women correspondents who have no illusions about social equality when race is in question.

A strong sense of social equality did prevail in Glasgow's correspondence with white women, even those in positions of professional power. Some (such as Irita Van Doren) were influential editors; some (May Sinclair and Virginia Woolf, for example) had well-established literary careers. Others (such as Nina Hamilton, an English duchess) enjoyed secure social prominence or they were married to men whose professional success conferred status (Ellen Harcourt, for example, was married to the publisher Alfred Harcourt; the husbands of Eleanor Brooks and Bessie Zaban Jones, Van Wyck Brooks and Howard Mumford Jones, helped to define American literature as a scholarly field). To these latter wives of geniuses, as Gertrude Stein's partner Alice B. Toklas wittily labeled herself and other supportive female cohorts, Glasgow often revealed more about herself than she did to their husbands and generally seemed less concerned about the professional figure she cut.

Besides being the impetus for many letters Glasgow exchanged with other women, the subject of friendship forms one of their most common themes. To an early friend, the popular Virginia novelist Mary Johnston, Glasgow wrote that "a little of the same spirit is lighting each of us on our way, and it is this that draws us, I hope, together & will keep us friends until the end."[13] Eighteen months later Glasgow wrote to Johnston: "life to me means love ... of many kinds and degrees." "So love me, Mary, much or little as you can, and I shall love you back in my own measure."[14] In the early years of the twentieth century there were periods when Johnston and Glasgow (and their sisters and cousins) saw each other almost daily. The two friends shared a fascination with mystical philosophies, and eventually Glasgow and Johnston would become active in the founding of the Virginia League for Woman Suffrage (later the Equal Suffrage League of Virginia). Although they saw less of each other over time (perhaps because of Johnston's ill health or perhaps because of Johnston's intense and growing involvement with theosophy, for which Glasgow had little patience), they continued until Johnston's death in 1936 to exchange affectionate short letters characterized by their comfortable tone and intimate knowledge of each other.

In letters to other friends Glasgow indulged in similar expressions of instantaneous friendship. To the Boston writer and salon host Louise Chandler

Moulton, whom Glasgow met through their mutual friend Amélie Rives Troubetzkoy, Glasgow wrote, "My love was with you before we met, it is with you now and it will be with you always." Few of Glasgow's letters to Troubetzkoy exist, but, judging by the warmth toward Troubetzkoy expressed in the same letter to Moulton, Glasgow encloses the three friends in a circle of intensely felt friendship: "It is the liberation and the reconciliation of the spirit that I would make the joy that we hold and feel together, Amelie and you and I."[15]

Glasgow's friendship with the older writer Troubetzkoy (who was married to the Russian prince and portrait painter Pierre Troubetzkoy) had its vicissitudes. Glasgow's existing letters to Troubetzkoy are affectionate and often protective, especially during the latter's years of ill health and depression following the death of her husband, but the tone of the correspondence suggests that the early closeness of these friends was not evenly sustained throughout their lives. Some of Troubetzkoy's letters have an almost pleading tone as she urges Glasgow to visit or wonders if Glasgow failed to receive a letter, and some of Glasgow's intimate that she felt guilty for neglecting her friend. The difficulties as well as the joys that mark long-term friendships are illustrated by this complex relationship. Nonetheless, Glasgow, just before her death, bequeathed to Signe Toksvig a bronze Buddha figure that had been a gift from Troubetzkoy. Enclosed with the Buddha was the small card that had accompanied Troubetzkoy's original gift, suggesting the Buddha's significance as an emblem of friendship and encouragement handed down from one woman to another and then to another.[16]

Sentiments of instant friendship such as those Glasgow used to characterize the circle formed by Troubetzkoy, Moulton, and herself constitute a continuing theme in Glasgow's letters; even much later in her life she often responded to other women with an immediate and urgent sense of mutuality. "Ever since you came to see me, so strong and warm and vital," she wrote to Marjorie Kinnan Rawlings in 1941, "I have felt very near to you, and you have had your own chosen place in my life."[17] Even letters exchanged in relationships that were primarily epistolary (as with the artist Clare Leighton) or entirely so (as with Toksvig) feature expressions of intense friendship. To Toksvig she observed: "I have had in my life ... the sense of a beginning friendship so strong that it seemed to hold the quality of recognition. Your first letter brought this to me."[18] "My friendships run deep," she remarked to another friend, and to still another, she wrote, "I value your friendship more than any words can express. But you know that without my trying to put it in cold typing. And you know, too, that for many years I have loved you dearly."[19] These devotions also came back to Glasgow, in the legendary allegiance of Glasgow's friends or in the expressions of comfort her correspondents claim to feel in her presence.

In addition to (and sometimes concurrent with) these personal expressions of friendship, letters Glasgow exchanged with women often emphasize a sincere

Introduction xix

and earnest professional interest in literary work, with its frustrations and pleasures. The artistic commitment that probably first brought together Glasgow and Johnston, Moulton, and Troubetzkoy (like the mutual admiration for storytelling that prompted Glasgow's childhood letters to her Aunt Bec) also marks Glasgow's other correspondence. That with Bessie Zaban Jones, for example, began in 1930 with a fan letter from Jones. Your books, Jones wrote to Glasgow, "always excite me and move me" as those of "few writers do."[20] Later Jones even acted as a kind of agent when she approached her husband about reviewing the twelve-volume *The Virginia Edition of the Works of Ellen Glasgow*. More directly connected to the profession of letters, Irita Van Doren was perhaps Glasgow's most professionally powerful woman friend. During the years of their correspondence, which began in 1922, Van Doren advised Glasgow about publishers, engaged her in book reviewing that increased Glasgow's literary profile, and obtained sympathetic reviewers for Glasgow's novels. Van Doren's professional support continued even after Glasgow's death when, as the more active of Glasgow's two literary executors, she helped negotiate the posthumous publication of Glasgow's autobiography and aided Marjorie Kinnan Rawlings as the latter prepared to write Glasgow's biography.[21] Glasgow said of Van Doren: "I have admired few women so fervently as I have admired Irita," who is "[b]eautiful in body" and "invincible in spirit."[22]

Glasgow's letters often express a desire for the proximate body and spirit of her women correspondents. "I would have given anything if you could have been with us in that perfect place at that perfect hour," she wrote to Rebe of a magical evening spent in an English churchyard.[23] On another trip Glasgow's first response to the landscape of Tuscany was to wish that Anne Virginia Bennett could share it. "I keep wishing that you could see and smell this place of flowers,"[24] she wrote. The letters, in the hands of their recipients, help bridge the gap between desire for physical closeness and its fulfillment.

Of course, letter writing by definition is about absent others; one of the most common of epistolary conventions is to express a longing ("Wish you were here!") for the absent one's presence. But Glasgow put these conventional wishes into practice as well. Her letters often carried warm invitations to visit her in her Richmond home (or, during summers beginning in 1939, in the houses she rented in Castine, Maine), and she received and accepted similar offers. She visited sisters Rebe in Philadelphia and Lexington and Annie in Norfolk, Virginia; the writer and critic Sara Haardt Mencken in Baltimore; and Irita Van Doren at her summer home in Connecticut. Her frequent visits to New York, where she first met many of her friends, always included a busy social schedule. In England Glasgow went to the homes of the writers Radclyffe Hall, Vita Sackville-West, and May Sinclair. Visits to the house that Hall and her partner, Una Troubridge, shared in Rye, Sussex, especially, provided Glasgow access to an openly lesbian world inhabited by a woman she admired, respected, trusted, and approved.

Glasgow's correspondents routinely expressed an emphatic devotion to her hospitable personality and "warmth" (a word that often is used in others' descriptions of her). After meeting Glasgow for the first time, Marjorie Kinnan Rawlings (who would later die before completing her biography of Glasgow) observed, "You as a person have the vitality, the wit and the irony of your work, but I was not prepared to find you so warm and so beautiful, in spite of the devotion of your friends, which would indicate those things in you."[25] The English-born artist Clare Leighton, in the midst of sorting out her feelings about her failing marriage, thanked Glasgow for her encouragement: "I do thank you for your warmth and for your belief in me. It has helped me more than you know and I shall not betray it."[26] Many correspondents wrote to thank Glasgow for unexpected and thoughtful long-distance expressions of friendship: a card, a small gift, a book, or a print or other illustration.

Many devoted friends visited Glasgow, sometimes with tiring frequency, although in her letters Glasgow rarely expresses displeasure. "I imagined that I came here for complete isolation," she wrote to Rebe from Maine, "but for ten days or two weeks I had an incessant stream of visitors." In the next epistolary breath, however, she adds, "Now I have a letter saying the Saxtons may be on their way. I hope so, for I should like to see them."[27] Even a passing expression of fatigue caused by the strain of visitors "eager to pour out their emotional disturbances" gives way to good-natured humor: "The blessed state of 'all passion spent' certainly invites confidences."[28]

Glasgow's correspondents constantly comment on her unsurpassed talent as host. "[N]othing could mar the perfection of Ellen Glasgow in her home!" the writer Isa Glenn observed after a visit, adding wittily, "It will remain one of the unforgettable scenes—in the secret places of my mind where I store those things that I protect from the wear and tear of life amongst the Intelligentsia."[29] Apologizing for staying longer than she had intended, the *Gone with the Wind* author Margaret Mitchell explained in a letter that her social lapse must have been due to the welcome she felt; "it was because you yourself have that charm of manner which delights the stranger and makes the stranger feel at home."[30] Eleanor Brooks captured in a letter the spell of generosity that many of Glasgow's friends tried to articulate, "We believe that there is some magic about your household, so that if one sets foot in it he is immediately and continuously happy, as long as he is there."[31]

It may be more than mere coincidence, however, that the correspondent Glasgow described as the perfect companion was the one she never met. Despite what most often appears to be sincere affection on the part of Glasgow and her correspondents, there is much to suggest that Glasgow experienced discomfort when she felt constrained by others' demands (or perceived demands) on her. At one point she even complained anxiously about publishers' deadlines, lamenting a contract that omitted the customary "'if and when' clause," which stipulated that she would send a manuscript only "if and when" she completed it.[32] Readers of *The Woman Within* know that in its pages Glasgow sometimes narrates family tensions as personal inconveniences: her father's insistence on religious observance or his strict rules about reading, for example, became to Glasgow personal affronts rather than a stern patriarch's household rules. In one of her earliest extant letters Glasgow complained from England to her sister Cary about the burden of their brother Arthur's expectations: "To be honest, I feel the responsibility of making a pleasant impression for Arthur's sake and it is an untold effort. Sometimes the strain is so great that I feel bruised all over. I am fitted only for a hermitage."[33]

Glasgow's preference for emotional distance from her father and her brother can be attributed, at least partially, to her more general wariness about men and marriage—she apparently preferred distance (emotional and otherwise) from other men, too. Her amorous affairs with men, including two engagements, never resulted in stable love relationships, and she consistently expressed her unwillingness to marry. In part Glasgow's tendency toward self-protection through emotional distance resulted from her experience of the deaths of many loved ones. Some of the people Glasgow idealized the most—her mother; her sister Cary and Cary's husband, George Walter McCormack; her younger brother Frank—were people whose early or tragic deaths separated them from Glasgow in her young adulthood. Finally, the onset in early adulthood of Glasgow's deafness, combined with her embarrassment about it, contributed to her aloofness. The guardedness that existed alongside Glasgow's desire for intimacy was part defensive choice and part enforced isolation.

Glasgow's formidable need for solitude and independence alongside an equally strong desire for recognition and support may help to explain her complicated relationships with her sisters Cary and Rebe, arguably the two people to whom she was most attached. It was only to them, she says, that she read the manuscript of her first published novel.[34] Glasgow characterized Cary as "closer to me than anyone else" and "the most brilliant mind and personality I have ever known," and she described her older sister (hyperbolically) as "the only human being who was of the slightest help to me in my work."[35] Extant letters to Cary support Glasgow's characterizations of their close and mutually satisfying relationship. It was to Cary that Glasgow first wrote of her distress caused by her failing hearing. The two shared an intellectual curiosity and penchant for reading. They were active together in suffrage work and both were writers. Cary, with her husband, Walter, materially encouraged Glasgow's reading and writing through gifts of money and a lending library subscription; and after Walter's suicide Glasgow and her widowed sister read philosophy together. The tone of Glasgow's long letters to her sister during her 1896 trip to England are chatty, filled with news of the people and the London sights; those of her return trip in 1909 are more somber, more focused, for example, on Glasgow's anxieties or the sadness of their brother's death during her absence. It may have been the tragedies of Cary's life—her husband's suicide, her cancer, her life's brevity—that simplified Glasgow's response to this sister she viewed as very nearly perfect.

Glasgow's relationship with Rebe, four years her junior, was more volatile, as might be expected with a sister whose longer life allowed for more variations in their dealings with each other. The first epistolary signs of tension surface after a misunderstanding in which Cary intervened. Following Rebe's marriage in December 1906, Glasgow clearly felt the strain of her younger sister's absence. In one of many similar sentiments at about that time, Glasgow wrote to a friend: "I can hardly write about my missing Rebe—it cuts too deep."[36] The sisters' disagreement in the late spring of 1907 seems to have involved Cary's chastising Glasgow for being less than supportive of Rebe, maybe especially of Rebe's new spouse, whom Glasgow did not care for. The tiff was over in less than a month, and the letters do not (as some have argued) suggest much more than a sisterly squabble.[37] Letters exchanged for the rest of Glasgow's life show the emotional ties between Glasgow and Rebe strengthening, expecially as they watched their family numbers diminish.

But just as a portrayal of Glasgow as emotionally withdrawn from others is incomplete, so a view of Glasgow as the unfailingly gracious host of One West Main Street where she lived for over sixty years also is too simple: the house was a contradictory place for her, one she felt both compelled to inhabit and driven to escape. If the large gray Greek Revival house at the corner of Main and Foushee Streets in Richmond was the setting for her graciousness and almost the only place she could do serious writing, it was also the location she associated most intensely with suffering. There her parents lived out their unsatisfying marriage; there her mother died after a short illness in 1893; there, one year later, Glasgow guided Cary through intense grief following the suicide of her young husband, Glasgow's intellectually supportive brother-in-law, at which time Glasgow described the atmosphere in the house as like "living in a tomb."[38] It was at One West Main Street that, in 1909, the family mourned the suicide of Glasgow's thirty-nine-year-old brother Frank; there Cary died in 1911 after a long struggle with cancer; there Glasgow's father died in early 1916; there, in 1929, Glasgow discovered her beloved Sealyham terrier Jeremy dead following a year of illness. Writing from her new residence in New York City, to which she fled (temporarily, as it turned out) following Cary's death, Glasgow confessed to her childhood friend Lizzie Patterson about an imminent visit home to Richmond: "I dread seeing the place again."[39]

Glasgow's dread can be traced not just to her personal equation of the house with suffering but also to her sense of herself as hypersensitive and hypersympathetic. This heightened sensitivity to suffering had its positive side for Glasgow as a friend, however. Judging from her correspondents' observations, she possessed an unusual ability to transfer her own feelings of persecution into fulfilling another's need for understanding and support. In spite of her biting wit that sometimes left its mark, Glasgow was generous with her empathy, as letters from her women correspondents attest. "You have no idea how your words of praise have heartened me," wrote Radclyffe Hall in 1927. Five years later Hall returned to this sentiment: "I have my letter from Ellen," she wrote, "and when I get depressed & worried and tired I take it out and read it and feel very brave and as though all my troubles were somehow illusions."[40] Amélie Rives Troubetzkoy likewise recognized a letter from Glasgow as the sign of sympathetic understanding: "I felt lonely on my birthday," she wrote, "and then came your lovely message . . . and warmth folded my heart."[41] To Clare Leighton's thanks for encouragement Glasgow responded with a characteristic pep talk: "I have felt always that you would be stronger than the suffering through which you have passed. To this end, you will conquer because you have the will and the heart of a conqueror."[42]

One thing her friends seem often to have comprehended, and sometimes shared, is Glasgow's keen consciousness of suffering in the world generally, her ability to see pain as not only personal but part of a larger cosmic pattern. Troubetzkoy, commenting on the shocking murder of their mutual friend's husband, wonders "what *you* must be suffering my Ellen, with your tender, infinitely compassionate heart."[43] Responding to Leighton's distress over the anticipated beginning of World War II, Glasgow confessed her own "hypersensitivity" ("one of the most real things on earth, not an imaginary affliction") and vividly described herself as "a shell of agonized vibrations": "I am still subject to the anguish that comes from vicarious pain and torment. Even a paragraph in a newspaper telling of the suffering of an individual human being or a helpless animal will cause me days and nights of sympathetic misery."[44] The "power of suffering, both personal and vicarious, has not diminished as I have grown older," she wrote to another correspondent.[45]

Even as a child Glasgow was, in Lizzie Jones's words, "born without a skin"—too sensitive, overly susceptible to pain and suffering.[46] The adult Glasgow seems to have transformed this trait into an ability to put herself imaginatively in the place of others. To Irita Van Doren, Glasgow wrote, only half humorously, of a professional encounter that required her best diplomacy: "It's a nuisance to be forever putting yourself in some one else's place"; "I felt as if I had been born in his skin in some other life."[47] Rather than the more self-involved experience evoked by the idea of one's own skinlessness, she implied, pain is understanding what it feels like to inhabit another's skin. Letters—especially those to her women friends—where Glasgow could both exercise her empathetic capacities and keep them under control, provided an important space for working through the complex meanings of friendship, including the emotional difficulties attendant on feeling others' pain.

Glasgow's letter writing was driven by more practical concerns, too. Conceptualized as conversation (an idea more easily grasped, no doubt, at a time when a letter written one day usually was received the next), letters played a significant role in helping Glasgow negotiate the serious hearing impairment she struggled with virtually all of her adult life. Although in her letters Glasgow only infrequently refers directly to her hearing loss, when she does so the anxiety it causes her is evident. As early as spring 1909, Glasgow wrote to Cary from England that she had declined an invitation to an important authors' dinner because she "felt timid about not hearing."[48] Several months later she wrote Lizzie Patterson from Colorado, "My hearing always stands between me & everything. I can't hear, even with my acousticon the general conversation, & this depresses me terribly."[49] Many years later, and partly in the self-reflective mood brought about by her continuing work on her autobiography, Glasgow wrote to Bessie Jones that her hearing impairment had made it impossible to fulfill a lifelong "eager desire" to travel around the world alone. "For years," she wrote, "I suffered from a morbid sensitiveness that was a kind of tepid Hell, and even now, I have not entirely got over it."[50] Letters provided Glasgow a forum free from the auditory limitations of face-to-face conversation. Reading her friend's latest letter, Glasgow wrote to Marion Canby, made her "feel as if we had talked together as we talked for hours" during a visit.[51] Similarly, Glasgow wrote Jones that her "delightful letter" seemed more like "Another good talk with you before the fire in your living-room."[52]

Glasgow, for whom the companionable exchange of ideas was paramount, was, in a sense, saved by letters. "[O]f all blessings," she wrote to Canby, "I have missed most, and needed most, the intellectual sympathy that overflows from your mind."[53] As far as Glasgow was concerned, that missed blessing resulted largely from the absence of intellectual vitality in her native Richmond and in the South generally. ("The South," she quipped in a letter to Toksvig, "has no delusions about books, because it never reads them.")[54] Her letters enabled relationships founded on a shared conviction that ideas were necessary to a full life, that reading books was important, and that serious intellectual exchange was indispensable. Glasgow used letters to and from distant friends to foster the kind of discussion that she rarely found close to home, both because of her hearing and because of a southern atmosphere more encouraging of gossip than ideas, she believed. Beginning in the late 1930s, when ill health threatened more literally to isolate Glasgow in Richmond, she experienced anew the intellectual vacuum she had always felt in her native city and region, and correspondence with friends kept her in touch with a world of ideas she found necessary. Early trips abroad had provided stimulation for intellectual growth, and later travels had solidified professional friendships with like-minded writers. Even destinations nearer home were essential. New York, as she told Toksvig, is where she had met congenial intellectual spirits, where she had "friends ... who speak my own language."[55]

Letters provided a means of enjoying that language—serious discussion—crucial to Glasgow in thinking through the ideas that resulted in her published writing. The importance of (women's) meaningful occupation, both for her and for her correspondents, is a recurring theme in the letters. Friendships with other women writers were founded partly on a shared commitment to their art. Glasgow wrote to Mary Johnston that, as appealing as Johnston's Bermuda vacation spot might be, "if I had to choose between Bermuda and the power of working, I suppose, in spite of my complaints, I'd pray for the latter."[56] "Yes, I am always at work on a novel," she responded matter-of-factly to what must have seemed an odd question from Bessie Jones. "I really have no life except in my work," she wrote Jones later; "There, and there alone, have I found peace."[57] To Clare Leighton, who had written that she was "working [her] way back to happiness," Glasgow philosophized about contentment, acceptance, work, and inner peace: "all things do not matter overmuch in the end," she observed. "In the past few years I have been able to rise above merely personal disappointments, and *except in the case of my work,* not to care greatly what happens."[58] Even with its heightened sense of drama, this statement genuinely expresses Glasgow's solid grounding in her work. "I ask really so little," she wrote in 1940 to Irita Van Doren after an unexpected layover in Doctors Hospital on her way to her summer retreat in Castine, Maine—"just the strength to go to work and finish my book."[59] In language that appears almost verbatim in her posthumously published autobiography, *The Woman Within,* Glasgow wrote to Toksvig, simply, "I have done the work I wanted to do for the sake of that work alone."[60]

There are many reasons that her writing provided Glasgow with a "refuge of work,"[61] as she put it, among them, a sense of accomplishment, active participation in a world that still limited women's meaningful creativity, and personal satisfaction in doing something well. Her writing also provided the ground for exploring intellectually the beauty she experienced in nature and in the spiritual realm it suggested to her. The same is true of her letters. For Glasgow, as for many writers before and after her, the world of nature, especially of animals and landscapes, inspired contemplation about life and its meanings. This experience of beauty was for her powerful and complex; when she called herself a tree worshipper or described the beauty of Castine as having "saved my life,"[62] she was not exaggerating. Often she found the most satisfaction in places where the beauty of nature united with human creativity: the landscape that pairs nature and art garnered Glasgow's highest praise. "I had never dreamed that such loveli[ness] was left on earth as Fountains [Abbey]," she wrote Rebe from England. "First man did everything, and then nature beautified and softened and embellished the ruins to the last delicate touch."[63] She'd wanted to "see beautiful places," and she had not been disappointed.[64] "[N]ot since Egypt and Greece have I been so completely lifted outside of myself on the wings of beauty."[65] In a later moment of similar transcendence the Tuscan countryside—"a dream of loveliness"—made her feel as if she had "stepped out of life."[66]

"Stepping out of life" aptly captures one particularly powerful cluster of ideas present in Glasgow's letters (and life) almost from the start: her lifelong fascination with spirituality or mysticism. What appear from the letters to be some of Glasgow's most intense (if not always abiding) friendships—early with Johnston and Troubetzkoy and later with Hall and Toksvig—shared a willingness to explore what was to Glasgow the vexed relationship between the worlds of matter and spirit. She wondered in an early letter whether Johnston was "mystic enough" to be interested in *The Imitation of Christ* and the Bhagavad Gita, and she wrote in another letter that she could "almost" see Johnston's "soul ... shining through the delicate flesh. The people I love best," she explained, "I love for this spiritual quality, for it shows me god, somehow."[67] Many years later she confessed her "deep interest in mysticism" to Signe Toksvig.[68] When Glasgow described to Radclyffe Hall a mystical experience during her 1940 heart attack, Hall in responding spoke for their shared sense of a world beyond matter: "I have always felt that there was a great goodness in you, a great and generous & pitiful kindness of heart and spirit.... Such experiences as yours are only given to the worthy."[69] Hall, who knew what it was like to inhabit the precarious and transitional female borderland between an earlier time's innocence and a later time's frankness about female friendship, articulates the possibility of transcending bodily and domestic limitations.

Glasgow's firm belief in a greater-than-individual existence that connects material and spiritual realms explains her equally strong ethical commitment to the world of nature. "I cannot accept a creed that divides man from the rest of creation," Glasgow wrote to Bessie Jones.[70] During a period of recovery following a heart attack, Glasgow gazed from her bed in Maine at a "tall pointed fir outside [her] window." The tree, she wrote to Jones, "has a kinship with something deep down in myself."[71] Especially the animal world commanded Glasgow's allegiance, which is evident not only in virtually everything she wrote but also in her activism on behalf of the Society for the Prevention of Cruelty to Animals (SPCA) (she joined the Richmond chapter in 1893, became its president in 1924, and supported it all of her life). She chastised Marjorie Kinnan Rawlings for "betray[ing] the confidence and the good will of the yellow catch-dog" in *Cross Creek,* and she confessed that Bessie Jones's acquisition of a dog puts "the final touch to our friendship": "Do you know there is always a barrier between me and any man or woman who does not like dogs[?]"[72] Glasgow explained to Toksvig that one of her greatest complaints about both her father and the strict Calvinism she associated with him was their anthropocentrism: "It was the Christian attitude toward animals that estranged me then, and turned me, in later years, toward more humane religions. My father was a sterling character and a zealous Calvinist; but he was without feeling for any creatures other than human beings." She concluded, "May all that have life be delivered from suffering."[73]

Through the years Glasgow also stepped outside herself much more literally through travel. Like other Richmonders of means, she usually spent summers away from the city's brutal heat. White Sulphur Springs, West Virginia—"the White"—was a family destination, and often Glasgow and one or two siblings traveled there or to other mountain destinations. She spent time in the Adirondacks, Colorado, California, and, farther from home, in the European Alps. Sometimes coastal locales were the goal: Atlantic City or Québec City, for example, and later Glasgow's favorite, Castine, Maine. She and various travel companions—sisters Cary and Rebe and friends Carrie Duke, Lizzie Patterson, and Louise Collier Willcox—journeyed much farther afield, too: to Egypt, often to England, to France, Greece, and Italy; as well as more than once to Scotland. And always to New York, her intellectual and creative center. Indeed, for someone who has been so closely associated with her family home in Richmond, Glasgow spent a great deal of her time away from it. Maybe the constant travels away from One West Main Street were precisely a signal of its importance: "place" as idea was so powerful for Glasgow that wherever she went she attempted to create a solidity and security more encompassing than is usually suggested by words such as "holiday" or "vacation." Every place became, in a way, home.

Letters, with their postmarks and addresses, even their stationery and imagined places of composition and receipt, are material and symbolic artifacts of place. Glasgow's letters bear postmarks not just from Richmond but from all over the world. It is as if being somewhere, whether at home or away, meant for Glasgow writing letters. Place depended on writing and vice versa: establishing the sense of a place depended on writing it into existence, and a cogent sense of place enabled writing. In her correspondence one material sign of Glasgow's attachment to place and her sense of its intimate connection to writing is the stationery—most often engraved with her address—that was almost a requirement wherever she went. On a brief trip to Atlantic City she wrote home to Bennett: "I can find no writing paper I am not ashamed to use ... I have notes to write and *no paper.*"[74]

One of the more striking impressions made by Glasgow's collected papers is of the array of writing paper, most of it with "One West Main Street, Richmond, Virginia" imprinted in two centered lines at the top of the page. So important to Glasgow was this engraved grounding in a locale that residence for more than a month seemed to necessitate custom stationery: for the years in

New York City, "One West Eighty-fifth Street" (surely the address cannot be entirely coincidental); and "Appledoor," "Battle Avenue," "Littleplace," "Spruce Knoll," or sometimes, simply, "Castine, Maine," for summers beginning in 1939. Following Cary's death in 1911 there is cream-colored mourning paper with bold black edges and Gothic lettering for the engraved New York address. Over the years papers are shades of gray, pale blue, bright cornflower blue, white, or ivory; patterns are flecked or plaid; textures are smooth or rough; sizes and thicknesses vary, as do styles: small, large, thick, thin, folded, flat. The paper, widely varied in tactility and appearance, mattered a great deal to Glasgow. Whatever surface she covered with her words had to be just right. For locales she passed through while traveling, Glasgow substituted the sometimes elaborate letterhead provided by innkeepers and hoteliers: the Clarendon Hotel, Oxford ("Under Royal Patronage") in 1896; the Antlers Hotel ("Absolutely Fireproof") in Colorado Springs in 1909; the understated Langham Hotel in London in 1927; "On Board S.S. 'Homeric'" in 1930. Using stationery that, like herself, will inevitably travel beyond the place it identifies, Glasgow creates and domesticates her temporary domiciles. Place and writing, for Glasgow, were crucial and inextricable.

Correspondents and friends also expressly identified Glasgow with place, especially houses. On at least two occasions, friends' dreams about Glasgow involved houses and their capacity to serve as emotional safe harbors. In a moving account of her sympathetic dream following the death of Glasgow's dog Jeremy, Mary Johnston wrote, "I was in a house over against your house. It was night time, very quiet, very still, and I looked out of [my] window across to your window ... and I thought, 'Ellen is there, sorrowing for Jeremy.'"[75] Much later Rawlings dreamt of protecting Glasgow by living with her in a dream-induced mansion: "I told you that from now on I should take care of you, and you must not do strenuous things."[76] Especially in her last few years, however, Glasgow protested against the protective instinct she sometimes inspired in others, seeing it as limiting to her independence. "All my life, or so it seems," she observed to Bessie Jones in 1942, "something, usually frail health, has kept me from doing anything I really wanted to do." She continued, "though I have travelled a great deal, I have always been shielded and looked after, and advised and warned and retarded"[77]—unlike her letters, perhaps, which traveled freely. Glasgow wondered if Marion Canby could begin to understand the frustrations caused by her illness: "can you, in your glowing health, imagine a state of mind when so simple an exertion as taking one's measure [for clothing] seems entirely too much?"[78] "[M]y heart compels me to go slowly ... I, who have always hated to go slowly and softly!" she wrote Toksvig.[79]

In one of her most moving book dedications, Glasgow inscribed *The Sheltered Life* to her brother Arthur, "whose affection is a shelter without walls." Perhaps, over the years, the house at One West Main came to seem more like the kind of protection that sheltered her rather than walled her in. For she always did return—to the house itself, to the welcome of its residents and to its visitors. While away Glasgow bought objects for the house she shared with Anne Virginia Bennett—candlesticks, a silver Georgian bowl, china dogs to augment her renowned collection, damask tablecloth and monogrammed napkins—and it was always somewhere near the surface of her thoughts, whether she wrote of escaping the chaos of acquiring new paint and wallpaper or instructed Anne Virginia about furniture polish. When at home Glasgow gave dinner parties and luncheons; played bridge; held meetings; served her famous eggnogs, mint juleps, and old-fashioneds; and, mostly, wrote the novels, poems, stories, literary criticism, and essays for which she is known. Places (especially houses) nurtured both friendship and writing, and all three, Glasgow came to understand, provided protection without constraint.

In a fitting conclusion to a life of writing and friendship, a short letter Glasgow wrote just four days before she died recognizes implicitly the convergence of women's friendship, place, and work. To Marjorie Kinnan Rawlings, Glasgow expressed regret that her failing health prevented a visit to Florida, which Rawlings had repeatedly described as a paradise, especially as a setting for doing the work that brings peace of mind. But that letter also encourages Rawlings to take advantage of the inspirations of both friendship and place in order to do the writing that defines the life of both friends. Glasgow wrote, simply, "Go on with your book. Do not give up. You have great gifts."[80] Both during her lifetime and since her death, Glasgow has been publicly celebrated for her own great gifts of professional accomplishment. Near the end of her life she received prestigious awards—election in 1938 to the American Academy of Arts and Letters, the distinguished inner circle of the National Institute of Arts and Letters; a Howells Medal for Fiction in 1940, in recognition of contributions to American literature; a Pulitzer Prize in 1942; and several honorary doctorates. Today Glasgow's recognitions are more problematic; she is more likely to be viewed as unhappy, a little ungrateful, and even unpleasant to be around. Her quarrels often are featured more prominently than her conciliations and her enmities more than her amities. Her correspondence with other women, however, while not controverting these views, does complicate them considerably. In these letters we see a Glasgow worried about pleasing, happy for the support of her friends, anxious about and embarrassed by her hearing loss, encouraging of other writers, concerned about her failing health, and maintaining through it all a sense of humor. To Glasgow's more public accomplishments—her medals, her awards, and her degrees—perhaps it is time we add her great gifts for perfect companionship fostered through correspondence with women.

Notes

Letters cited by date only, with no provenance or publication identified, are included in the present volume.

1. To Signe Toksvig, November 1, 1944.
2. Lillian Faderman, *Odd Girls and Twilight Lovers: A History of Lesbian Life in Twentieth-Century America* (New York: Penguin, 1991). See especially the introduction and first two chapters. Carroll Smith-Rosenberg's now classic article "The Female World of Love and Ritual: Relations between Women in Nineteenth-Century America," *Signs: A Journal of Women in Society* 1 (Autumn 1975): 1–29 (and later included in Smith-Rosenberg's *Disorderly Conduct* [New York: Knopf, 1985]) also remains useful.
3. To Rebecca Anderson Glasgow, January 7, 1884.
4. From Amélie Rives Troubetzkoy, September 9, 1937 (ViU, Glasgow Papers, Box 18).
5. To Irita Van Doren, September 30, 1938.
6. "Josephine Glasgow Clark," *EGN* 21 (October 1984): 2; to Rebe Glasgow Tutwiler, January 31, 1944.
7. Marjorie Kinnan Rawlings to Irita Van Doren, December 15, 1952 (DLC, Irita Van Doren Papers).
8. Glasgow's letters to men can be reviewed in the only edition to date of Glasgow's correspondence, *Letters of Ellen Glasgow,* ed. Blair Rouse (New York: Harcourt Brace, 1958). Rouse's stated rationale for selection is to publish letters "with regard to biographical, literary, and philosophical relevance," but to exclude correspondence that is "not . . . of a nature to warrant publication" (7). These criteria often meant that more personal letters to women friends were excluded. See my *Ellen Glasgow and a Woman's Traditions* (especially pp. 6–7) for a discussion of the limitations imposed by these criteria.
9. See, for example, Goodman, 119–120; MacDonald, "Remembering Ellen Glasgow," esp. p. 6.
10. From Agnes B. Reese, November 1, 1937.
11. From Agnes B. Reese, May 14, 1938.
12. From Elaine J. Dean, June 26, 1941.
13. To Mary Johnston, February 3, 1905.
14. To Mary Johnston, August 15, 1906.
15. To Louise Chandler Moulton, October 5, 1905.
16. See letter from Amélie Rives Troubetzkoy, [December 25] 1937.
17. To Marjorie Kinnan Rawlings, July 24, 1941.
18. To Signe Toksvig, May 21, 1943.
19. To Bessie Zaban Jones, September 27, 1938; to Irita Van Doren, March 25, 1944.
20. From Bessie Zaban Jones, December 27, 1930.
21. See letters in the Irita Van Doren Papers, DLC.
22. Ellen Glasgow, *The Woman Within* (Charlottesville: University Press of Virginia, 1994), 273. Hereafter cited as *WW.*
23. To Rebe Glasgow Tutwiler, July 30, 1927.
24. To Anne Virginia Bennett, June 1, 1937.
25. From Marjorie Kinnan Rawlings, July 19, 1941.
26. From Clare Leighton, March 13, 1939, ViU.
27. To Rebe Glasgow Tutwiler, September 5, 1939.
28. Ibid.
29. From Isa Glenn, December 2, 1931.

Introduction

30. From Margaret Mitchell, November 11, 1940.
31. From Eleanor Brooks, [February–March 1941?].
32. To Rebe Glasgow Tutwiler, January 28, 1938.
33. To Cary Glasgow McCormack, July 23, 1896.
34. Glasgow, *WW,* 103.
35. Glasgow, *WW,* 187–88, 103.
36. To Louise Chandler Moulton, December 13, 1906.
37. In the most recent biography of Glasgow, for example, Susan Goodman reads the disagreement as more serious. See *Ellen Glasgow: A Biography* (Baltimore, Md.: Johns Hopkins University Press, 1998), 105–7.
38. Glasgow, *WW,* 101.
39. To Elizabeth Patterson, [March 29, 1912].
40. From Radclyffe Hall, August 24, 1927 and June 11, 1932.
41. From Amélie Rives Troubetzkoy, August 29, 1935, ViU.
42. To Clare Leighton, March 14, 1939.
43. From Amélie Rives Troubetzkoy, July 13, 1937 (ViU Box 18).
44. To Clare Leighton, September 20, 1939.
45. To Bessie Zaban Jones, January 8, 1935.
46. Glasgow, *WW,* 5.
47. To Irita Van Doren, August 17, 1934.
48. To Cary Glasgow McCormack, April 28, 1909.
49. To Elizabeth Patterson, September 2, [1909?].
50. To Bessie Zaban Jones, July 20, 1942 (ellipses in original).
51. To Marion Canby, February 24, 1944.
52. To Bessie Zaban Jones, February 7, 1934.
53. To Marion Canby, February 24, 1944.
54. To Signe Toksvig, December 4, 1944.
55. Ibid.
56. To Mary Johnston, July 4, 1908.
57. To Bessie Zaban Jones, December 29, 1933, and January 8, 1935.
58. From Clare Leighton, March 13, 1939, ViU; to Clare Leighton, September 20, 1939 (emphasis in original).
59. To Irita Van Doren, August 1, 1940.
60. To Signe Toksvig, March 26, 1943.
61. To Signe Toksvig, February 4, 1944.
62. To Marjorie Kinnan Rawlings, April 20, 1942; to Signe Toksvig, August 14, 1943.
63. To Rebe Glasgow Tutwiler, July 23, 1927.
64. To Anne Virginia Bennett, July 27, [1927?].
65. To Rebe Glasgow Tutwiler, July 23, 1927.
66. To Clare Leighton, Christmas Eve, 1937; to Anne Virginia Bennett, June 1, [1937].
67. To Mary Johnston, [early March 1905?], and February 3, 1905.
68. To Signe Toksvig, May 21, 1943.
69. From Radclyffe Hall, March 22, 1943.
70. To Bessie Zaban Jones, February 7, 1934.
71. To Bessie Zaban Jones, September 25, 1940.
72. To Marjorie Kinnan Rawlings, April 20, 1942; to Bessie Zaban Jones, September 9, 1936.
73. To Signe Toksvig, August 14, 1943.

74. To Anne Virginia Bennett, September 30, 1935.
75. From Mary Johnston, September 27, 1929.
76. From Marjorie Kinnan Rawlings, July 19, 1941.
77. To Bessie Zaban Jones, July 20, 1942.
78. To Marion Canby, February 24, 1944 (ellipses in original).
79. To Signe Toksvig, October 8, 1944.
80. To Marjorie Kinnan Rawlings, November 17, 1945.

A Note on the Editorial Method

One of the more fascinating aspects of editing Glasgow's letters has been observing the changes in what might be called her style of correspondence over a fifty-year period. By style of correspondence, I mean features of the letters such as Glasgow's changing handwriting (particularly noticeable during her later years of ill health); her increasingly common use of a typewriter, in spite of her explicit preference for handwritten letters; her stationery choices; and even her changing signature (initials only, full signature, and single and double underlinings, for example). Glasgow's handwriting can be fairly difficult to read, particularly because the most common letters are not easily distinguishable—lowercase *n, m, u, v,* and *w,* for example, look remarkably alike, and other letters are similarly indistinct. Depending on the surrounding letters, some formations, such as both capital and lowercase *R* and *S,* change rather dramatically depending on what precedes or follows them. A word's initial letters frequently are formed differently from the same letters occurring within a word. These difficulties (compounded, on occasion, by the poor condition of the copy text) make understandable mistranscriptions of many of these letters in earlier editions; in some cases I, too, have been unable to decipher certain words. I have attempted to reproduce Glasgow's (and her correspondents') texts as accurately as possible, designating any indecipherable words with a question mark inside square brackets: [?]. For a probable transcription of a word, I use square brackets, the probable word, and a question mark: [now?].

Of the more than 700 extant letters between Glasgow and other women, I have selected 255, according to the following principles. Letters written by Glasgow have been given precedence over letters written to her. However, when there are few or no letters from Glasgow to a given correspondent (especially one whose personal importance to Glasgow seems indisputable, such as Radclyffe Hall or Signe Toksvig), representative letters to Glasgow from that correspondent have been included. Occasionally, especially when Glasgow's correspondent is someone whose literary reputation justifies interest in the timbre of Glasgow's relationship with her, a letter to Glasgow is included here (as with Isa Glenn or Agnes Repplier, for example). In general, previously unpublished letters have taken precedence over published ones, with the following qualifications: included here are letters published previously with mistranscriptions or omissions; letters published but not readily accessible to all readers (such as those in the *Ellen Glasgow Newsletter*); and letters previously published but important enough to understanding Glasgow that they bear repeating in a new context.

The readability of Glasgow's correspondence with women has been a primary concern in editing these letters, intended for both scholarly and more general readers. Letters are faithfully reproduced from the original, with the exception of interlineations, crossed-out words, spacing irregularities, or marginal notations. In instances where these occur and seem important as signals of Glasgow's intent or meaning, they are described in the numbered notes following the letter. Misspellings, typographical errors (in typed letters), or grammatical mistakes are reproduced on the assumption that these may be significant in understanding Glasgow's compositional practices or state of mind. Such errors can be useful in determining, for example, the haste with which a letter was written or the degree of comfort Glasgow felt in leaving errors uncorrected. Frequently Glasgow indicates in her letters that she is writing quickly; comments such as "This is just a line" or "I can't read this over" are common. In the letters presented here [sic] is not used, except in Marjorie Kinnan Rawlings's transcriptions, where she uses "(sic)." Two em dashes (——) are used to represent the longer dashes that Glasgow occasionally used for emphasis. A single underline is represented by italics, and a double underline by small capital letters.

I have let stand several idiosyncrasies of Glasgow's usage, and, because these are habitual, most of these do not include numbered notes. Examples are dropped opening or closing parentheses; omitted opening or closing quotation marks; missing apostrophes, especially in possessives; and Glasgow's customary preference for British spellings (*colour* rather than *color,* for instance). She routinely omits periods after titles, such as Mr. and Mrs., and as often as not she omits underlinings for titles of literary works (although she occasionally uses quotation marks). Sometimes Glasgow fills in spaces in her letters (at the beginning or ending of lines, for example, or to mark a separation between segments) with a series of printed or typed exes (x x x). These are reproduced as she wrote them. And finally, she is fond of the Latin expression "Deo volente" (God being willing), which she customarily abbreviates "D. V." These occur in this volume without separate identifying notes.

Each letter is identified (centered, at the top of the letter) as "to" Glasgow's recipients or "from" a correspondent to her. Recipients who are known during Glasgow's lifetime by more than one name are identified by the name most often used in the correspondence: Elizabeth Patterson (rather than Crutchfield, her married name), because most of the correspondence with Patterson occurs before Patterson's marriage; but Rebe Glasgow Tutwiler for Glasgow's sister, most of whose extant correspondence with EG occurs after Rebe's marriage. The biographical and geographical register identifies in cross-references all known variations of names of correspondents, as well as others mentioned in the letters. Unidentified persons are indicated as such in the register. The register also identifies correspondents whose letters are not included here; these correspondents are listed in the calendar.

Letters are arranged chronologically. Glasgow usually dates her letters, as do most of her correspondents; in these cases, the date used is the letter writer's. This practice includes letters written over several days, as Glasgow's letters from abroad, for example, sometimes are. When there is no holograph date on the letter, postmarks are used, when available; these dates appear in square brackets. When there are multiple postmarks, as in the case of international mail or forwarded letters, I have given all markings. When neither holograph date nor postmarks exist, I have provided a speculative date when it is possible to do so with confidence (when, for example, an extant letter just before or after a letter clearly begins or continues a discussion or when external evidence such as a trip or other event suggests a probable date). In such instances the date appears in square brackets with a question mark. Letters dated by librarians but without existing corroborating evidence are similarly treated. Square brackets with only a question mark indicate an undated letter that cannot be dated with any degree of confidence. These letters are listed as undated in the calendar. When two letters have the same date, a letter written by Glasgow is presented before one written to her. If two or more letters of the same date are written by Glasgow and the context does not make clear which was written first, they are arranged alphabetically according to the last name of the recipient. On the rare occasions that letters of the same date are written to the same recipient, the order of the letters usually is clear from the context.

The standard formal divisions of the letters are regularized. The return address—the place of writing, including information on letterhead, when applicable—and date are placed flush right immediately following the line identifying the correspondent. When the return address occurs in printed letterhead, it is presented in small capital letters: ONE WEST MAIN STREET, for example. Dates appear in the form and order as written by the letter writer. Glasgow commonly, although not invariably, writes dates as ordinal numbers, typically using superscript that is underlined (April 22nd, for example). When Glasgow provides the day and/or date (as was her custom), she typically writes them above and to the right of any printed information on the letterhead; her order is preserved. Occasionally Glasgow or her correspondent places the date at the end of a letter; these dates have been moved to the heading and identified with a numbered note describing the original placement of the date. Vertical lines (|), which Glasgow never uses in the text of letters, indicate information given on separate lines in the original, whether handwritten or printed as part of letterhead: Thursday, | April 22nd | One West Main Street | Richmond, Virginia. Any information furnished holographically appears without special designation in this published volume's typeface. Glasgow's occasional prescripts, which she usually wrote at the top of the page above dates or letterhead, are placed as written.

The salutation, flush left and on a separate line (as Glasgow typically writes it), reproduces in style and punctuation that of the original letter. Very occasionally Glasgow omits the salutation.

Some features of the text of the letters are standardized for ease of reading. In autograph letters Glasgow frequently leaves her paragraph divisions ambiguous; in particular, she does not clearly indent the beginnings of paragraphs but, rather, simply begins on a new line that is obviously not continuous with the previous one. (This practice contrasts with her later, typewritten letters, where paragraph beginnings are marked routinely by lengthy indentions.) I have used the standard first-line indention to indicate paragraph divisions. When parts of a letter have been destroyed or erased (or marked through), square brackets (which Glasgow never uses) and italicized print identify the missing material: [*remainder of letter missing*].

If Glasgow's handwriting is sometimes difficult to read, her typewriting is almost worse, as she frequently laments. She customarily omits spacing after commas, for example, often types over partially erased letters, runs off the right-hand side of the page, and routinely omits closing parentheses. These errors, which seem to be characteristic of a hurried or a less-than-accomplished typist, are silently corrected. Readers should assume that postscripts are handwritten for handwritten letters, typewritten for typed letters; individual letters' deviations from this practice are noted.

The formal closing and the signature are indented; vertical lines indicate material placed on separate lines of text in the originals. Glasgow sometimes signed her full name, occasionally only her initials "E. G.," and sometimes her first name. Often she underlined her name or initials, frequently using two horizontal lines (and sometimes using a diagonal single line). As with her letters in general, a single underline is represented by italics, a double underline by small capital letters. Diagonal lines are not distinguished from horizontal lines.

Each letter's provenance and copy text (using abbreviations as identified in the list of abbreviations that appears after the chronology) are provided in an unnumbered note immediately following the letter. Manuscript repositories are identified using the Library of Congress's *Symbols of American Libraries*. A few letters are available only from a previous publication; in these cases the original publication is cited. Following the provenance line, and also in an unnumbered note, envelope markings are provided, when envelopes exist. When there is no note, the envelope has not been preserved. Postal markings are reproduced as marked on the original, as are addresses (including forwarding addresses). Any enclosures mentioned in the text of the letter are assumed to be missing, unless otherwise noted.

Finally, numbered notes identify or clarify information in the letter's text. Persons and places mentioned in the letters are identified in the biographical and geographical register; well-known historical figures and places typically are not identified in notes or in the register, on the assumption that they are easy to locate in standard reference works. Persons or places I have been unable to identify are listed as unidentified in the register. Notes clarify references by Glasgow or her correspondents to her novels (or other work) in progress. The chronology will be useful to readers who wish to know the month of publication.

A few words about Marjorie Kinnan Rawlings's transcriptions of Glasgow's letters to her sister Rebe are in order. Most of these original letters are not extant; in these cases the copy texts are Rawlings's transcriptions. When a holograph letter exists, it provides the copy text; in these cases the provenance line identifies the letter as original. Despite the limitations of someone else's transcriptions, these letters' significance justifies their inclusion. For the most part Rawlings's readings seem trustworthy and knowledgeable, and I have most often treated her transcriptions as accurate. (She had the advantage of being able to ask Rebe Glasgow Tutwiler, who loaned Rawlings the letters, for clarification.) Dates are assumed to be correct. When Rawlings identifies postal markings, including addresses (both the recipient's and the return), I have treated this information as reliable. I have omitted from the transcriptions Rawlings's parenthetical question marks and occasional short notes to herself; these are identified and described in the numbered notes following individual letters.

Every attempt has been made to insure the accuracy of all transcriptions for the letters included here. Whenever possible, the original letter (and its envelope, when extant) has been examined. Transcriptions are of original letters for those whose provenance is Columbia University, the Library of Congress (except for the Moulton Papers, mentioned below), the University of Texas, and the University of Virginia; these account for approximately 70 percent of the letters. When I have not examined the original, I have used an authorized photocopy as the copy text. In two cases—Glasgow's letters to Marjorie Kinnan Rawlings and to Louise Chandler Moulton—I have consulted microform copies kept in the Glasgow Papers at the University of Virginia and in the Library of Congress, respectively. In no case has a previously published letter been used as the copy text; citations of prior publication are provided only as information.

In addition to the almost constant checking that has accompanied the process of gathering and reproducing these letters, the manuscript letters have been systematically proofread against the originals (or copies of originals) on three occasions: after the initial transcriptions, when the manuscript was first completed, and after the final manuscript revisions.

Chronology

1873   Ellen Anderson Glasgow (she later added her mother's family name, "Gholson," following Anderson) born April 22 at 101 East Cary Street in Richmond, Virginia (older siblings are Emily Taylor, Annie Gholson, Joseph Reid, Sally Cary, Arthur Graham, Kate Anderson, and Francis Thomas); Lizzie Jones arrives to take care of infant Glasgow.

1875   Brother Samuel Creed born October 14; dies of diphtheria two weeks later.

1876   Brother Joseph Reid dies of diphtheria at age sixteen.

1877   Sister Rebe Gordon Glasgow (later Tutwiler) born January 31.

1879   On April 14, Francis T. Glasgow (father) purchases for $1,960 Jerdone Castle, a house on 485 acres in Louisa County, Virginia, for family's summer home; acquires new friend in Caroline Coleman (later Duke), whose family farm adjoins Jerdone Castle.

1880   Lizzie Jones (Glasgow's "mammy") goes to work for Patterson family at Reveille (near Jerdone Castle); Glasgow begins friendship with Elizabeth Patterson (later Crutchfield); begins writing poems and stories.

1884   Writes first letter, to paternal aunt Rebecca Anderson Glasgow ("Aunt Bec").

1887   On September 27, Francis Glasgow sells Jerdone Castle for $10,000; Glasgow family moves into Davenport mansion (built 1841) at One West Main Street in Richmond.

1893   Becomes member of Richmond Society for the Prevention of Cruelty to Animals (SPCA), chartered in 1892; Anne Jane Gholson Glasgow (mother) dies October 27 after contracting typhoid fever while vacationing at White Sulphur Springs, West Virginia.

1894   Brother-in-law and intellectual mentor George Walter McCormack dies June 17 (suicide).

1895   Publishes short story "A Woman of To-morrow," the first work to appear in print.

1896   Sails on the *Etruria* to Liverpool (April) to visit brother Arthur in London.

1897   Publishes (anonymously) first novel, *The Descendant* (January); surreptitiously attends all-male state Democratic Convention in Roanoke, Virginia (August); author Hamlin Garland visits in Richmond (October).

1898	Publishes second novel, *Phases of an Inferior Planet* (March); travels to Williamsburg, Virginia (late spring) to collect material for *The Voice of the People* (1900); vacations at Crockett Springs in Montgomery County, Virginia (September–early October).
1899	Sails from New York on SS *Aller* (February 4) for seven-month trip to Constantinople, Egypt, Greece, London, and Paris, with sisters Cary and Rebe; publishes short story "Between Two Shores" (February); sails home on *Kaiser Wilhelm der Grosse* (arrives September 5).
1900	Publishes third novel, *The Voice of the People* (April).
1901	With sister Cary, tours Valley of Virginia to gather material for *The Battle-Ground*.
1902	Publishes fourth novel, *The Battle-Ground* (March); publishes only book of poems, *The Freeman and Other Poems* (August); visits Adirondacks with family; visits Walter Hines Page (publisher) at his home in Englewood, New Jersey (September); brother Arthur marries Margaret Branch in Richmond (October 1).
1903	Sails July 18 for visit to Interlaken, Switzerland.
1904	Publishes fifth novel, *The Deliverance* (January).
1905	Travels to Watkins Glen, New York (January); Cary (sister) has surgery for cancer (March); travels with Rebe to Chase City, Virginia; sails on SS *Bremen* (July 6) to Europe; first meets Louise Chandler Moulton in Paris (October); sails for United States on *Deutschland* (October).
1906	Publishes sixth novel, *The Wheel of Life* (January); travels to Boston (March); to Adirondacks (May), where she first meets Frank Paradise; to Chase City, Virginia; to Hurricane, New York (August); to city of Québec (September); sister Rebe marries Carrington Cabell Tutwiler on December 5 at One West Main Street.
1907	Travels to White Sulphur Springs ("the White") (July).
1908	Publishes seventh novel, *The Ancient Law* (January); departs (July) for Italy: Assisi, Florence, Milan, Naples, Perugia, Rome, and Venice.
1909	Travels to England (early April) with Elizabeth Patterson; brother Frank commits suicide in Richmond (April 7); honored at tea at London home of May Sinclair; publishes eighth novel, *Romance of a Plain Man* (May); travels to Colorado Springs and Rocky Mountains (Woodland Park) with Julia Sully (August–September); instrumental in founding the Equal Suffrage League of Virginia (initially known as the Virginia League for Woman Suffrage), which is officially organized (November 20) at Richmond home of Mrs. Dabney S. Crenshaw.
1910	Travels (May–June) to Constantinople with sister Cary, but trip is interrupted in Naples by Cary's progressive illness; the nurse Anne

	Virginia Bennett arrives at One West Main to care for Cary; Glasgow travels to Warm Springs, Virginia, with Cary (August 3–September 1).
1911	Cary Glasgow McCormack dies August 19 after long struggle with cancer; Glasgow publishes ninth novel, *The Miller of Old Church* (May); moves to One West Eighty-fifth Street, New York City; visits Petersburg, Virginia, the model for the fictional Dinwiddie of *Virginia* (autumn).
1912	Publishes suffrage poem "The Call," in *Collier's Magazine* (July) and in *Current Literature* (November); publishes poem "Song," in *Harper's Magazine* (October).
1913	Sister Emily Glasgow Houston dies March 5 at One West Main Street; Glasgow publishes tenth novel, *Virginia* (April).
1914	Travels with Louise Collier Willcox to England (May–June), where she meets the writers Arnold Bennett, Joseph Conrad, John Galsworthy, Thomas Hardy, and Henry James; sails home (June 18) on SS *Imperator,* dining onboard with Theodore Roosevelt.
1915	Travels with Carrie Coleman to San Francisco (World's Fair) and Santa Barbara, California (July); leaves New York City and moves back to One West Main Street in Richmond.
1916	Publishes eleventh novel, *Life and Gabriella* (January); father dies at home January 29; at luncheon on Easter Sunday, meets Henry Anderson; awarded Presentation Medal of the National Institute of Social Sciences in recognition of services to literature and humanity (presented January 1917).
1917	On July 19, becomes engaged to Henry Anderson, who leaves for Red Cross service in the Balkans.
1918	Anne Virginia Bennett leaves for France (March) as a nurse for the Red Cross; Glasgow quarrels with Henry Anderson on his return from the Balkans and takes overdose of sleeping pills (July).
1919	Publishes twelfth novel, *The Builders,* serially in *Woman's Home Companion* (October, November, December), and in book form (October); speaks (November 20) at Eighth Convention of the Equal Suffrage League of Virginia, held at Jefferson Hotel in Richmond.
1920	Hugh Walpole visits in Richmond.
1921	Adds signature to list of supporters for new Richmond-based literary magazine, *The Reviewer;* publishes essay "The Dynamic Past" in *The Reviewer* (March).
1922	Publishes thirteenth novel, *One Man in His Time* (May); vacations in Ogunquit, Maine; first writes to Irita Van Doren.
1923	Publishes *The Shadowy Third and Other Stories,* only collection of short stories (October).

1924	Assumes presidency of Richmond SPCA; Carl Van Vechten visits; in England, publishes *Dare's Gift and Other Stories* (English title of *The Shadowy Third*).
1925	Publishes fourteenth novel, *Barren Ground* (April); rents house at Barnstable, Cape Cod (summer); receives new Buick sedan from brother Arthur Glasgow at Christmas.
1926	Travels to Napanock, New York (August); publishes fifteenth novel, *The Romantic Comedians* (September). Begins planning (perhaps even writing) autobiography.
1927	Sails for England (June 17) on SS *Olympic;* embarks on return voyage September 14.
1928	Stays in South Poland, Maine (summer).
1929	Publishes sixteenth novel, *They Stooped to Folly* (August); takes motor trip to New England, New York, and Philadelphia (autumn); Sealyham terrier Jeremy dies (September 5) in Richmond; Doubleday, Doran begins publication of the eight-volume *The Old Dominion Edition of the Works of Ellen Glasgow* (1929–1933).
1930	Travels to Chapel Hill to receive honorary Doctor of Letters from the University of North Carolina (June), and there first meets Bessie Zaban Jones and Howard Mumford Jones; sails on SS *Homeric* to England, France, and Scotland (June–September); first meets Radclyffe Hall (June or July).
1931	Stays in Nantucket with Carrie Coleman Duke (July–August); gives welcome address to Southern Writers Conference (October 23–24) in Charlottesville, Virginia, which she helped plan.
1932	Léonie Villard visits in Richmond; Glasgow publishes seventeenth novel, *The Sheltered Life* (August).
1933	Has influenza early in the year; travels to Atlantic City, New Jersey (May); travels to Baltimore, Maryland (June–July) to consult with doctors at Johns Hopkins about chronic sinus infection; travels to Rockbridge County, Virginia, home of her father's ancestors, to collect notes for writing *Vein of Iron*.
1934	Probably begins in earnest to write autobiography (initially entitled "Autobiography of an Exile"; published as *The Woman Within,* 1954); travels to New York and Philadelphia.
1935	Hosts party at One West Main Street for Gertrude Stein (February 5); delivers speech "Heroes and Monsters," in New York to Friends of the Princeton Library (April 25); publishes first book with new publisher Harcourt, her eighteenth novel, *Vein of Iron* (August); declines offer of honorary degree from Rollins College (Florida); travels to New York (September); travels to Atlantic City and Ventnor,

New Jersey (September–October); sells movie rights to *Vein of Iron* (September).

1936 Travels to Ventnor, New Jersey (June); rents house in West Cornwall, Connecticut (summer); travels through Berkshires, Housatonic Valley, Vermont; teaches classes at Bread Loaf School and Writers' Conference (July 30); Allen Tate delivers an ailing Glasgow's prepared talk ("Empty American Novels") to Modern Language Association convention in Richmond (late December).

1937 Declines offer of honorary degree from the University of Wisconsin; James Anderson (cook) hospitalized (April); sails on *Conti di Savoia* (May 15) for Italy; stays in Fiesole at Villa Marsilio Ficino (side trips to Florence) and Ravello.

1938 Awarded honorary doctorates at the University of Richmond and Duke University (April); declines offer of honorary degree from Goucher College in Baltimore; the twelve-volume *The Virginia Edition of the Works of Ellen Glasgow* is published by Scribners (late June); speaks to Dr. John Henry Hobart Lyon's class at Columbia University (October 12); spends twenty-two days in Doctors Hospital, New York, for back injury (October–November); dog Billy dies (November 18); elected (sixth woman member) to American Academy of Arts and Letters (December).

1939 Declines offer of honorary degree from the University of Rochester; Eleanor and Van Wyck Brooks visit (April); awarded honorary doctorate from the College of William and Mary in Williamsburg, Virginia (June); rents "Littleplace" for first summer stay in Castine, Maine; Catherine Turney begins stage play based on *The Sheltered Life;* Glasgow has first heart attack (first week in December).

1940 Declines offer of honorary degree from Middlebury College in Middlebury, Vermont; hospitalized in New York en route to Castine, Maine; spends summer in Castine; has second heart attack in Castine (August 9); awarded Howells Medal (November 14) by American Academy of Arts and Letters (accepted for ailing Glasgow by J. Donald Adams).

1941 Receives special award from *Saturday Review of Literature* (April); spends summer in Castine; publishes nineteenth novel, *In This Our Life* (March).

1942 Receives award for contributions to women's service in public affairs from Southern Women's National Democratic Committee (February); receives Pulitzer Prize for Fiction for *In This Our Life* (May 4); Warner Brothers releases (May) film of *In This Our Life* (directed by John Huston, screenplay by Howard Koch, starring Bette Davis and

Olivia de Havilland); Glasgow spends summer in Castine; has third heart attack (late December).

1943 Begins correspondence with Signe Toksvig; spends summer in Castine; publishes *A Certain Measure: An Interpretation of Prose Fiction*, collection of revised prefaces to the *Virginia Edition* volumes with a new essay on *In This Our Life* (October).

1944 Declines offer of honorary degree from Smith College; the literary executors Frank Morley and Irita Van Doren travel to Richmond to finalize publication plans for Glasgow's autobiography, *The Woman Within* (March); spends summer in Castine.

1945 Has mild heart attack (her fourth) on November 11; dies November 21 at One West Main Street; buried on November 23 in family plot at Hollywood Cemetery in Richmond.

1954 Henry Anderson dies; *The Woman Within* (autobiography) published (October).

1966 *Beyond Defeat: An Epilogue to an Era,* unfinished sequel to *In This Our Life,* published.

Abbreviations

AGG	Arthur Graham Glasgow
AL	*The Ancient Law* (Glasgow)
ALS	Autograph letter signed
ANS	Autograph note signed
AP	Autograph postcard
APS	Autograph postcard signed
ART	Amélie Rives Troubetzkoy
BG	*Barren Ground* (Glasgow)
B-G	*The Battle-Ground* (Glasgow)
BZJ	Bessie Zaban Jones
CGMcC	Cary Glasgow McCormack
CL	Clare Leighton
CLEG	*A Catalog of the Library of Ellen Glasgow* (ed. Tutwiler)
CM	*A Certain Measure* (Glasgow)
CtY	Yale University Library (Yale Collection of American Literature, Beinecke Rare Book and Manuscript Library; Gertrude Stein Papers)
DLC	Library of Congress (Irita Van Doren Papers)
EG	Ellen Glasgow
EGCR	*Ellen Glasgow: The Contemporary Reviews* (ed. Scura)
EGN	*Ellen Glasgow Newsletter*
EGNP	*Ellen Glasgow: New Perspectives* (ed. Scura)
EGRD	*Ellen Glasgow's Reasonable Doubts* (ed. Raper)
EP	Elizabeth Patterson
FU	University of Florida, George A. Smathers Libraries (Marjorie Kinnan Rawlings Collection)
IaU	University of Iowa Library
ITOL	*In This Our Life* (Glasgow)
IVD	Irita Van Doren
L	*Letters of Ellen Glasgow* (ed. Rouse)
LCW	Louise Collier Willcox
MdBG	Goucher College Library (Special Collections, Julia Rogers Library, Sara Haardt Mencken Collection)
MHi	Massachusetts Historical Society
MJ	Mary Johnston
MKR	Marjorie Kinnan Rawlings

MNS	Smith College Library, Mortimer Rare Book Room (Bessie Zaban Jones Papers)
NcD	Duke University Rare Book, Manuscript, and Special Collections Library
NcU	University of North Carolina Library
n.d.	No date (for undated letters)
NjMoHP	Morristown National Historical Park (Lloyd Smith Collection)
NN-B	New York Public Library (Albert A. and Henry W. Berg Collection; Elizabeth Garver Jordan Papers)
NNC	Columbia University, Rare Book and Manuscript Library (Eleanor Belmont Papers; Daniel Longwell Papers)
NYHTB	*New York Herald Tribune Books*
PU-Sp	University of Pennsylvania, Rare Book Manuscript Library, (Agnes Repplier Papers)
RC	*The Romantic Comedians* (Glasgow)
RGT	Rebe Glasgow Tutwiler
SL	*The Sheltered Life* (Glasgow)
SPCA	Society for the Prevention of Cruelty to Animals
ST	Signe Toksvig
TC	Typed copy
TCC	Typed carbon copy
TLU	Typed letter unsigned
TNS	Typed note signed
TLS	Typed letter signed
TSTF	*They Stooped to Folly* (Glasgow)
TxU-Hu	University of Texas at Austin, Harry Ransom Humanities Research Center
ViHi	Virginia Historical Society
ViLxW	Washington and Lee University, Special Collections, Leyburn Library (Glasgow Papers, MSS 210)
ViRCU	Virginia Commonwealth University Library (James Branch Cabell Library, Special Collections and Archives, Belew Collection)
ViU	University of Virginia Library (Ellen Glasgow Collection, Accession #5060; Mary Johnston Papers, Accession #3588)
ViW	College of William and Mary Library
VOI	*Vein of Iron* (Glasgow)
VtU	University of Vermont (Dorothy Canfield Fisher Papers)
WW	*The Woman Within* (Glasgow)

PERFECT COMPANIONSHIP

I
1884–1903

You cannot expect much of me as this is my first letter.
—To Rebecca Anderson Glasgow, January 7, 1884

A few months before her eleventh birthday, Ellen Glasgow, already determined to be a writer, wrote her first formal letter. It was to her paternal aunt Rebecca Anderson Glasgow, whom Glasgow remembered in her autobiography as a superb storyteller and a great reader. Aunt Bec, as she was called, encouraged Glasgow's early reading and, in her capacity as the developing author's first correspondent, her writing. It seems likely that the stationery for this letter, with its charming illustration of a turtle on a sled, was Aunt Bec's Christmas gift in 1883. It would be the first in a long line of customized writing paper.

During Glasgow's formative first trip to Europe in 1896, she not only nurtured what would become an enduring devotion to travel but she also gathered the impressions and observations that enrich a writer's art. She conveyed many of those impressions to her sister Cary, Glasgow's chief confidante and supporter in these early stages of artistic and personal growth. To Cary she also confessed her anxiety as she waited to hear whether her first novel, *The Descendant* (1897), would be published; her pride at her own independence as she negotiated her way around London; and her impatience with their brother's sentimental views of family.

Despite this impatience, family had its significance for Glasgow, too. At this point in her life, female family members—and childhood friends who, like Elizabeth (Lizzie) Patterson, seemed like family—comprised her primary epistolary friendships. Curiously absent from these early extant letters is any mention of cataclysmic family events, notably the death of Glasgow's mother in 1893 and the sensational suicide of her brother-in-law the following year. Such omissions, whether they are the result of letters destroyed, letters never written, or letters not sent, serve as cautionary reminders of gaps that the epistolary record cannot fill, of knowledge that we may never have.

Life did not revolve entirely around family, of course, and during these years Glasgow also began to move into the realm of professional letters. Her first published work appeared—*The Descendant* (anonymously, 1897), *Phases of an Inferior Planet* (1898), *The Voice of the People* (1900), *The Battle-Ground* (1902), and *The Freeman and Other Poems* (1902)—bringing with them the more personal side of public recognition: her first fan letters.

To Rebecca Anderson Glasgow

Home Jan 7th / '84

Dear Aunt Bec

I miss you very much and wish you would come and make us a long visit. I like your stories so much and I have The Wide, Wide, World, Queechy and The End of a Coil by the same author. Frank has Nick of the Woods, but I like to hear you tell them better than to read them.[1]

Sister Cary has gone to Philadelphia on a visit to a Mrs. Mercer, a very rich old lady who has taken a fancy to her, and in her letter she says she is having a very nice time and is going from there to Baltimore where she will meet Sister Annie.

Give my best love to Aunt Maggie and tell her we enjoyed her visit so much that we hope she will come and make us a longer one. Sister Emily is staying with Cousin Lu Harvie I go to school to Mr. Merrill but I have not been able to go for about two weeks because I have been sick. You cannot expect much of me as this is my first letter.

Your loving | little niece | Ellen A Glasgow

ALS ViLxW Glasgow Family Papers, Folder 11

1. Popular novels by Susan Bogert Warner (pseudonym "Elizabeth Wetherell," 1819–85), published in 1851, 1852, and 1880, respectively. *Nick of the Woods; or, The Jibbenainosay*, historical novel published in 1837 by Robert Montgomery Bird (1806–1854).

To Rebecca Anderson Glasgow

March 17th / 85 | Richmond Va

Dear Aunt Bec,

I got your letter two or three days ago, and was very glad to hear form you, and to know that you are well; we have all missed you a great deal and you must come back again very soon—

I have not been to see Uncle Joseph yet, the weather has been bad, and I have had no one to go with me, I will go as soon as Mother is able to go with me. I have read Gold Elsie[1] and liked it very much.

Mrs Richard Jeffery's foot is still[2] very bad, they have it now in a plaster cast, and her Aunt Mrs Mahony says she may have to walk on crutches for years. Miss Virginia was here yesterday and Mother went out to walk with her—all send love and Mother says she will try to write to you soon. Give our love to Aunt Mary and Uncle John.

I am as ever your loving | Niece | Ellen Glasgow

ALS ViLxW Glasgow Family Papers, Folder 11

1. *Gold Elsie, from the German of E. Marlitt [pseudonym]*, juvenile novel (1868) by A. L. (Annis Lee) Wister.
2. EG originally wrote "still is" and corrected it to "is still."

To Cary Glasgow McCormack

Sunday Queen Anne's Mansion | St. James Park, | London, | S.W. [April 28, 1896?]

My dearest C—

I am in London at last and will proceed at the very earliest opportunity to give you a detailed account of myself since I landed at Liverpool. Mr King we discovered on the docks as we were slowly tugged in. Arthur was not to be seen and as soon as we were near enough Mr King shouted he had received a telegram from him, stating that he had just returned from Russia that morning and would meet us in London. We had a terrible time about baggage while the American Special was waiting until the custom officers had passed all the trunks. Then we got into a saloon carriage as they call it and were quite comfortable.

I was exceedingly sorry to leave the steamer as I was enjoying my trip so much for such perfect weather I never saw. People were all quite attentive to me on board and the captain expressed a desire to be introduced to me and to have me come up to the chart room. The first land lights caused a great excitement, and when we came on deck Saturday morning the horizon was a blue wave of Irish hills. The gulls met us off the coast of Wales and followed us into Liverpool, which harbor, by the way is not to be compared to either the New York or the Charleston one. There was a young fellow on board who pursued me to the end and went after my luggage all over the station.

The English country is perfectly lovely between Liverpool and London. All exquisite meadows of the most perfect greens and neatly trimmed hedges. At the London station which is all noise and bustle, especially so they say when an American express arrives, we were met by Arthur and Lafayette Carroll, who is in London. Two cabs conveyed us and our trunk to "Queen Anne's Mansion, St James Park, London, S. W." where we are to stay. The Humphreys have a flat. I have a delightful room with bath adjoining, at a short distance from them. Arthur seemed glad to see me and presented me with 30 P.s, telling me he wished me to make a good impression on his friends. I went to bed very much exhausted about two o'clock, and had breakfast this morning in the Humphrey's drawing-room. We are in the heart of London. Westminster about two blocks away and St James Park at our left. London looks very crooked and dingy somehow, and thoroughly quaint and interesting.

This morning Arthur, Mr. Paddon, Carrol and I went to walk in Hyde Park. It was very interesting. Swarms and swarms of women promenading after church just as they are described in English novels. I have never seen a greater difference than between English and American women. Such flaming colors as they wear I have never behold and such heads of hair. It is most luxuriant and they wear it in heavy bangs and standing about a foot from their heads, surmounted by immense bonnets of pink, blue, white, and every conceivable color. They ought to be exceedingly pretty and dress as we might have done in the time of George the Regent—except more guadily. They look pink and demure.

Mr Paddon and I walked together and had a long talk. I don't think him especially ugly, but what is worse utterly superficial and far more like an American in his speech than like an Englishman. He thinks Longfellow the greatest poet who ever lived and Adelaide Anne Proctor[1] next. I don't find him in the least charming.

Sunday night. It is 1 o'clock. Mr Paddon and Arthur dined with us and have just left. I like him better than I did though I can't understand his being fascinating. This afternoon I took a walk by myself, saw Westminster. There is nobody to take me about so to-morrow I begin by riding on top of a bus by myself along the Strand. My room is thoroughly comfortable, dressing-room delightful. London is so fascinating, but confusing.

Monday. My second day in London and what do you suppose I have done. Knowing that if I didn't find out things for myself I might as well be in Henrico, Va.,[2] as far as seeing London would do, I started out immediately after breakfast by myself. I went to the Army and Navy store on Victoria, bought a guide book. Then I took a bus and road all through the Strand, Clerkenwell, and as far as the Angel Inn at Islington, I sat beside the driver and tipped him in the beginning, whereupon he pointed out every place along the way. At the Angel I descend from my elevation and took a bus going back through Clerkenwell, Oxford St, and Picadilly. I found among other things the Academy[3] and the British Museum. I got down at Hyde Park, walked through Green Park, home. I wish I had some congenial person along with me. If only Frank had come we could have had such a good time. This afternoon I think I'll go along either Regent St. or the embankment. Admit that I have done well to go about so independently. Mr H— is the nicest man I have ever met. There is something very touching about him. He is so unselfish and it is always accepted as a matter of course. I am afraid that I'll miss lots of things in the city. How I'll ever get to the Zoo or the Tower I don't see. The streets are so crowded and how the buses ever get through them is marvelous. I feel very lonely. What about Mrs Walker? I hope she is in London. Give my love to Lelia and tell her that I have just written to Mrs Johnston. I expect to get lost many times, but when I do I'll take a cab and be brought home.

Arthur is thin but in very good spirits. I hope I shan't disappoint him for he wants me to be stylish. The courts are all so interesting to me and the quaint dingy look of everything.

Night. 12 M. I have just returned from the theatre. Mr Woodall I like exceedingly. It was The School for Scandal[4] at the Lyceum, beautifully staged. Thursday afternoon Miss Woodall is coming to take me to the house of commons. They are going to spend the summer in Scotland, somewhere on the coast and have invited me down to see them. I expect to go. Arthur is very nice about everything. If I go to Scotland I am going to get a white and scarlet serge suit. Everything is in bright colors. It is really wonderful everyone says how I get about so readily. This afternoon I walked all along St. James St.; Piccadilly; Bond St. and Oxford St; I must have walked miles. Got home at 6.30, drank a cup of tea in my wrapper, took a bath, dressed, dined and went to the Lyceum. Arthur says that I may travel around some at the first opportunity. But I don't know with whom I can go. The Humphreys will only be here two weeks. After that I leave them. Perhaps Arthur and I will go to live at a hotel. We haven't decided. To-morrow afternoon I go to take tea at the office of an English engineer whom I met on the steamer—on Victoria Street. The shops are fascinating, and so are the streets. I like the omnibuses, but the hansom cabs are unexcelled. I think I'll go to-morrow to the Royal Academy. Then to the Strand and Fleet Street. Westminster I must do soon. This apartment house, or whatever you call it is exceedingly nice. I hate to leave it but I shan't regret some changes. The court is very gloomy and interesting. A wall of buildings ten stories high surrounds a square court, all bricked up. We enter through a high gate way with iron gates. You remember how they are arranged. I have gotten as fond of Scotch marmelade as you used to be. Arthur spoke of getting someone to look up the family records for you. Spoke also very affectionately of you. Poor fellow, he has so much sentiment about his relations. Has gotten Mary Anderson's present. In Russia. From his description it must be beautiful. A belt that costed sixty dollars. A secret, of course. Has a long disk that fastens it. English women have such exquisite hair, but wear it badly. You see them shopping in lawn dresses of the lightest hues. I feel exceedingly somber in my green and red waist. It is one o'c. and I am awfully tired. Good-night. Best love to Father, Frank, Emily, and everybody. Also Paul Pry.[5] Do make Frank take a holiday. Arthur says he wishes he could get Father and Frank over here. London is supreme.

Most devotedly, | ELLEN.

ALS ViU EG Box 14
Publication: *EGN* 5 (October 1976): 2–5.

1. Adelaide Ann Procter (1825–1964), English poet who wrote under the pseudonym Mary Berwick.

2. County in Virginia just east of Richmond.
3. Royal Academy of Arts.
4. Comic play (1777) by Richard Brinsley Sheridan.

5. The interfering, meddlesome protagonist of John Poole's comedy *Paul Pry* (1825). To whom the name refers for EG and her sister is unclear, although the omission of their younger sister Rebe from the list of family members that precedes this comment suggests that she is a candidate.

To Cary Glasgow McCormack

London, July 23 | Thursday. 1896

My dearest C.

Your letter was sent me yesterday and I can't tell you how immensely glad I was to get it. I was in the act of dressing to go to the Royal Academy when it came and as soon as I had read it I went by Arthur's office to deliver a message for Mrs. H. and then took a hansom and went to the Academy. Honestly, I hardly enjoyed it. I confess to a lack of appreciation of modern English art. It is so watery. And besides my artistic instinct is wearing out for I was more conscious of backache than beauty. Saw some exquisite miniatures, and I like watching the people. Yesterday was a gala day in England. The Princess Maud of Wales was married to Prince Charles of Denmark.[1] From early morning vast crowds were gathering and stands for seats were put of all along the lines of the wedding procession. Houses were draped in red and white and silver, the Danish colors, but the decorations weren't as pretty as at our re-union. When I came out of the Academy I couldn't take the most direct way home because of the crowds that flowed continuously along. As far as I can gather it is not loyalty so much as love of entertainment with the people. The afternoon before I took tea with a young Englishman whom I met on the Etruria.[2] Then we went into several shops (his wife was along) and then to Hyde Park. The Queen had just come in to be present at the royal wedding and as we passed Marlborough house we paused with a small crowd that had gather to watch her leave. She was congratulating the young couple, after which she would return to Buckingham Palace. A troop of mounted guards were drawn up beside the entrance, and, some soldiers in scarlet coats a little farther on. Then on a terrace overlooking the street the whole royal family appeared, watching the Queen's departure. The Prince of Wales, Duke of York, Princess of Wales, Princess Maud and others. The ladies wore very high headdresses, white gowns and were quite attractive looking from where I stood. The Princess of Wales very ordinary. In a moment the gates were thrown open and the Queen appeared in an open carriage, outsiders on the horses, and her highland guard behind. She is more exactly like her photographs than anything I ever saw—and very red. That night Arthur took me to the Empire, one of the most celebrated music halls, he says, in the world. The dances were very pretty and the jokes very witless. A less spicy performance I never saw, but I was glad to have gone. Last night I dined with the Woodalls. They are exceedingly pleasant people. I had the seat of honor on Mr Woodall's left—he took me into dinner. The table was beautiful and the dinner delicious. I felt rather tired at first (it is an hour's drive) but after I had mixed an amount of bock and champagne I became considerably vivacious. They think it American and it interests them so I try to talk a great deal. I sometimes wonder what Arthur would have done had I been quite stupid, he watches me so closely.

How I blessed you in my heart last evening when I drew out my opera cloak. I wore my black evening dress and with my usual forte tore a piece of the chiffon on my skirt. The Woodalls have an ideal English home. A brick wall and gateway, covered with creepers, leads up a tiny drive to the house. An immense garden, tennis court and masses of flowers. House beautifully furnished. Drawing-room, breakfast-room, dining-room, library, billiard-room, conservatory, all on the first floor. They are quite wealthy. 6 sons and 5 daughters. I like them all well enough. The eldest daughter was the only girl who appeared but I went into the breakfast-room and saw the younger ones at their dinner. I must stop now and dress as I am going to luncheon with them today and afterward to a cricket match at Lords. I wear my blue and black silk and go in a hansom. I love hansoms but feel extravagant when I ride in them.

10.30 p. m. Arthur has just left and I have put on my wrapper and will add a few lines to this before going to bed. I had planned sending both Frank and Rebe a letter by tomorrow's mail, but somehow I never have a moment's time. I took luncheon with the Woodalls, and sat on their lawn. They have a perfectly lovely garden and the girls are nice, simple, awkward English girls. As far as I can gather girls count for very little in England—except American ones. After luncheon we went to a cricket match at Lords' cricket grounds. I couldn't understand it in the least. It looked to me very much like baseball except more stupid, but there was a great crowd and some tremendous hats. We expect to go down to Scotland to visit the Woodalls some time about the first of August. It is on the coast and you go to Glasgow by train where you take the steamer for the rest of the way. I think Mr Woodall finds me quite amusing as he makes a point of my being there while he is there and insists that I am not to go back with the Humphreys. The girls look upon me as "a wild, strange vision." They want me to spend a little while at their Town house just before returning to America and I may do so. To be honest, I feel the responsibility of making a pleasant impression for Arthur's sake and it is an untold effort. Sometimes the strain is so great that I feel bruised all over. I am fitted only for a hermitage. We are going down the river next week, I believe. Eva has been ill in bed all day. I was awakened this morning by the doctors coming into the passage way of my apartment, looking through the glass door to where I was calmly reposing and addressing me as "Mrs Humphreys." I had to get out of bed while he looked on, don my dressing-gown and explain that I was not Mrs Humphreys.

To-morrow I long to go to the Abbey, the House of Commons in the afternoon. Mr Woodall's brother, an M.P. will show me all over it, but at first we go to the Cadus gallery. But I must have the Abbey in the morning. The next day the natural history museum, and then the zoo. The paleontological display has been moved to the N.H.M. Baedeker says. I wish I could see you to-night. You know Arthur is one of the most romantic persons in theory I ever met. He is still troubled by the fact that we haven't taken the positions in the world our Father took. Mr Humphreys is in Germany and I miss him. Arthur speaks of sending Rebe a lovely present and I try to keep him up to it. He has already bought part of it in Russia. He seems to feel a good deal about "the family," I have just had a note from Mrs Johnston saying she would call on me Monday next. Love to all. Remember me to Robert and Tina. I hope Father and [*remainder of letter missing*]

ALS ViU EG Box 14
Address: Mrs George Walter McCormack | Richmond, Virginia
Postmark: London 2[?] Jul 96

1. Prince Charles of Denmark (second son of Frederick VIII, King of Denmark) married Maud, Princess of Wales, the youngest daughter of King Edward VII of Great Britain. Following Norway's separation from Sweden in 1905, Prince Charles was crowned King Haakon VII of Norway (June 1906).
2. Cunard ocean liner for EG's trip to England.

To Cary Glasgow McCormack

[QUEEN ANNE'S MANSIONS, | ST. JAMES'S PARK. S.W.] [early August 1896][1]
My beloved Cary:

I have just one moment in which to send you a line or two. Last evening we took supper with Arthur and while there decided to go to Oxford to-day to spend Sunday and Monday (Bank holiday) I had a lot of packing to do as I am leaving Queen Anne's for good, which I greatly regret. Upon our return we expect to go to the "Metropole" for a week and then up to Scotland. I am half sorry. I like being here and walking around the crooked streets of London at my own pleasure. I don't care for rushing things. The Humphreys go out to Norwood to day. I am awfully tired as I did all my packing after eleven last night. Arthur's rooms are very nice and he has some beautiful pieces of mahogany. I don't care much for Mr Paddon but Mr Thurman I find very nice indeed.

Arthur gave me his copies of the Woodlanders and the Return of the Native, same edition of my Jude.[2] He is almost enthusiastic about Jude himself, thinks it, as it is, one of the greatest of books, but prefers Tess. I enclose a ludicrous note he received from Mrs Agglesby. It will amuse you. He handed me Judge Wellford's letter. Notice crest! and give it [*portion of letter cut out*] Have been wanting to write to her. It is a glorious day, but I feel all frizzled up and my back aches.

The other day I had a letter from Paris, from a young fellow I had only spoken to twice on the steamer, beginning "May I dare to hope that you will let me write to you." One has such funny experiences. Books are very expensive over here and photographs are by no means cheap. I got me a blue tweed dress to wear walking on the moors in Scotland. I wanted to save my good suit. It is rather becoming to me, a very nicely cut coat and skirt, "plain but neat." I paid two pounds ten for it ($12.00) Mary Anderson's belt is a perfect beauty and weighs tons.[3] (I am so tired that I have forgotten entirely how to spell the simplest word).

Westminster Abbey exceeds anything I have ever dreamed of. The vaulted arches of the transepts, with the tinted light from the windows is as solemn as death—or life. I stood for half an hour at the grave of Darwin, lying beside Hershell with Newton a few feet away and Sir Charles Lyell near his head. To think what that stone, with the words "Charles Robert Darwin, Died Nov. 12, 1882." covers. Hundreds of irreverent feet cross it every day. Hundreds of high pitched voices chatter about the ears of all those mighty dead, when there should be only silence and thought. Henry 7ths chapel I consider a marvel of beauty, and the tombs of the kings I find interesting, but the monuments along the walls of the Abbey proper, seem to me to detract in a measure from the sublimity of the place. The other morning I went to the Temple but I couldn't get into the larger part. How quaint and impressive that pile of buildings is. St Pauls I like from the exterior. The interior of every cathedral I have seen, seems tawdry. I found a beautiful statue of J. S. Mill in the Victoria Gardens, along the embankment. What a marvel of beauty is Waterloo bridge. I wish for more of you all the time. There is not a soul in London with whom I feel at home. I dined with the Paddons the other evening. Was immeasurably bored. Was invited to the Tricobys to spend several days. Had rather take a plunge from London bridge. Don't care for people anyway. Much prefer being by myself as I feel more at home in the midst of a crowded thoroughfare than in any house I have entered. I must stop and continue my packing. The chimpanzees in the zoo are the most interesting persons I have met. They don't have to be entertained. This is such a comfortable place. I should like to stay right here. London is terrible on my shoes, or perhaps it is because I walk so much. I could have gone to Stratford-on-Avon today, but chose Oxford. Arthur is very kind and seems well disposed, but I am always nervous about amusing him, and I can't do it. I don't know him. I always feel much freer when I am not with the Humphreys, tho; Mrs H— is exceedingly sweet and kind. But I have nothing in common with them. Best love to all. With devoted love

I am hastily, | Ellen

ALS ViU EG Box 14
Address: Mrs. George Walter McCormack | Richmond, Virginia
Postmarks: New York 13 August 96, Richmond 14 Aug 96.

1. Despite the confusing (and incomplete) postmarks on the envelopes containing this letter and the next, internal evidence suggests that the letters are in the correct order here. The letterhead address on the first page, but not subsequent pages, is cut out.
2. EG refers to Thomas Hardy's novels and characters in this sentence and the next.
3. EG initially drew a line through "tons," then repeated it.

To Cary Glasgow McCormack

THE CLARENDON HOTEL | OXFORD | August, | 2nd | *1896*

My darling Cary:–

I must send you a line from Christminster[1] to let you know that I think of you all constantly. From the moment I entered the town Jude has walked as a shadow at my right hand. His spirit and Sue's haunt every building.

It is so beautiful! I never imagined a place so expressive of historic and intellectual interests. The very atmosphere breathes medievalism, and I can well understand a student at Christ or Magdalen[2] shutting his eyes to the nineteenth century and relapsing into the third or fifth. I cannot conceive of such surroundings nurturing the scientific spirit of inquiry. Alas, poor Jude! We came last evening and are stopping at what used to be the "Star" inn. I don't quite like it, however. This morning A. and I took a long walk. We went to every college (almost.) The quadrangles and gardens of Magdalen surpass anything I have dreampt of—as do Christ Church and St Johns. It is simply a revelation of architecture and centuries. What fortunate beings are the fellows of these Colleges, and yet it is the past they must absorb—neither the present nor the future. There are bright colored flowers to right and left. So many of the colleges are gay with window gardens of scarlet geraniums or yellow asters. It gives a beautiful look to the meanest street. The Humphreys have gone out to Norwood and I haven't decided what I shall do after coming back from Scotland. Do you know, even here I miss London. There can be but one London in the world. We are going to drive this afternoon. Tuesday we return to London—to the Metropole, I think. I do trust you are all well. Give this letter heading to Rebe. It is quite a religious place, tho; not quite as neat as it might be. There are texts of Scripture and large Bibles in every room. I have the "Star," chamber. Arthur has gotten a present for Rebe that is a perfect beauty. I know she will be delighted, but shan't tell her what it is in order to leave her interest excited. I am going back by myself and I am glad of it, though I shall probably lack the style of my passage over. We are on a busy street and last night I could not go to bed for watching people pass.

10. p. m. We took a glorious drive this afternoon. English country is so exquisitely restful to the eye. The greens are perfect. For the first time since crossing I wore my coat today. Usually a blouse is sufficient and I have been saving my travelling suit. The fare at this hotel is hopeless. We dine at the Metropole tomorrow evening. After returning from drive we took a walk. I have seen at least 16 colleges to-day. I believe New College (which, by the bye is the oldest of all) is the most interesting. The battlements, originally the fortifications of the city, still stand, a mass of creepers. The windows and altar in the chapel are things to dream of. I find Oxford quite different from what I had imagined, but equally beautiful. I thought of you and Anne when I passed the "mitre"[3] this afternoon, and wished for you. Arthur is angelic as far as trying to please me goes. He seems rather depressed, I think, and sick of work, but wants me to see everything. He says to tell you that he is much interested in Needham and wants to buy it. He will give [*remainder of letter missing*]

ALS ViU EG Box 14
Address: Mrs George Walter McCormack | Richmond, | Virginia.
Postmark: Oxford, 3 August 1896[4]

    1. Thomas Hardy's fictional name for Oxford in *Jude the Obscure*. Jude and Sue, mentioned in this paragraph, are characters in the novel.
    2. Colleges of Oxford University. EG mentions several in this letter.
    3. The Mitre, a famous pub in Oxford.
    4. See previous letter, note 1.

To Cary Glasgow McCormack

THE HOTEL MÉTROPOLE | LONDON | September 9, 1896

My dearest heart:—

Two of your letters were sent me this A.M. by Mr Thurman. Evidently it was a mistake about that Cunarder sailing at noon for I had nothing from you last mail, and two this morning. I get so few letters now. You are the only one who writes to me. Rebe doesn't answer my letters. It has been at least two weeks, or more since I heard from her. I always enjoy your letters so much, but can see that your hand is troubling you. It was a great pleasure to me to hear that you were going to the White Sulphur. I suppose, by the way, that you will be there by the time this reaches you. I trust it will do you a vast amount of good. I have been strangely depressed and unhappy for the past few days.[1] I can't stay in the house at all without growing so despondent that it is unbearable. I walk the streets and haunt the National Gallery. I enjoyed the pictures more every time I go, since I have entirely gotten over that fatigue which a lot of new pictures causes me. Now I select a few and sit before them and endeavor to absorb them. This afternoon it was a comparison of Claude and Turner. You remember the two that hang side by side. Claude's superb study of sunlight out of a saffron sky upon shimmering water, an allegorical title which I forget, and next to it Turner's Building of Carthage,[2] the same water effect. They are both grand, but Claude's seems finer to me and most people I believe. Claude's landscapes are simply magnificent, and I must say that I have grown very fond of Turner. Then I studied that sublime painting of Sebastian's The Raising of Lazarus. I don't believe there is a more superbly religious picture this side of Italy. The figure of Christ, you remember, is both beautiful and natural, which is more than I can say of most studies of Christ that I have seen. And every figure, from Lazarus as he unwinds the grave clothes, and rises with that startled, affrighted look, to the wondering disciples are singularly suggestive. On the whole it has pleased me as much as any that I have seen for figure drawing was hardly an art of the masters, and these figures are free and strong, while the color is perfection. I find that Hare[3] calls it one of the finest pictures in England. Of all the madonnas that I have seen there is not one that seems to me more beautiful than Sebastian's Holy Family. It also shows that strength and grace of drawing combined with the wonderful treatment of color. The madonna is full of tenderness, and the child is clinging to her in a childish way, while she has one arm stretched over Joseph who kneels at her feet. It is very beautiful. Do you recall it? I love Andrea del Sarto's Holy Family, but I prefer this portrait even to that. There is an exquisitely voluptuous one of Titian's Venus and Adonis, which for wealth of color and beauty of execution simply enthralls one. The Venus is adorably lovely in form and face. I don't know whether this interests you, but I have nothing else to write of. The National Gallery is so convenient. I am at home in London and it is adorable. I enjoy the gallery more every time I go. If to-morrow is propitious I go to the British Museum again. I wish that was situated at Trafalgar Square. Indeed, you need not worry about me and Japan. I should be only too happy to accompany you. Mr Norcross, of Arthur's firm, who is going to China on business, writes that Japan is a dream from which he dreads to awaken. Everyone falls in love with it who goes. It is growing late. The lights in the reception room are out and I and two men occupy the reading-room. Everyone goes to bed, or upstairs about eleven. I wish for you constantly, and often get tired of everything. Life is very unsatisfactory, "but things are as they are and will be brought to their destined issue."[4] I hope the water at the White will entirely relieve your hand. It is too bad that you should have been troubled with it so long. I don't see how you all have stood this summer. I don't believe people over here know what hot weather means. Suppose you write Mr Patton and ask for news of my book. Of course, it will be another disappointment, but this suspense is so wearing. Nothing makes life very bearable, one may travel from the North Sea to Jericho, and one cannot alter one jot or tittle of one's nature or destiny. I believe that happiness lies not in getting what you want, as in learning to want what you get, "for he is a wise man and hath understanding of things divine who hath nobly agreed with necessity." I have now an abundance of the comforts of life—but a dinner in ten courses is wearying to a lack of appetite, and the more I have the more I want. I enclose for your private edification a poem of little worth. Don't let anyone see it. I really believe there are more Americans in London than English people. The streets teem with them. Everybody has gone to bed, so good night. Love to all.

As ever, | ELLEN

ALS ViU EG Box 14
Address: Mrs George Walter McCormack, | Richmond, | Virginia.
Postmarks: NY 18 Sep 96; Richmond Sep 19 3 P.M.

1. RGT's holograph note at the top of the letter reads: "She is waiting to hear if her first book, 'The Descendant,' will be published—and unhappy until she hears it will be. It was accepted by Harper Bros."

2. EG's description of Claude's painting fits most of his work. The Turner she mentions is probably *Ancient Carthage—The Embarcation of Regulus* (1840), now housed in the Yale Center for British Art.

3. Augustus J. C. Hare's two-volume *Walks in London* (Philadelphia: David McKay, n.d.), which EG owned (*CLEG* 5.69).

4. This quotation and the date "May 1896" appear on the flyleaf of EG's copy of *The Teaching of Epictetus,* trans. T. W. Rolleston (New York: Alden, 1889) and also (with the date "1895") on the page following the flyleaf of her copy of *The Thoughts of the Emperor Marcus Aurelius Antoninus,* trans. George Long (Philadelphia: Altemus, n.d.). See *CLEG* 1.8, 1.16.

To Mrs. [Rush?] Huidekoper

Richmond, Virginia. [September 22, 1897?]

Dear Mrs Huidekoper,

It was a great pleasure to get your note, and very kind you were to write me that you liked "The Descendant." I am delighted that my book made friends with you. Just now, in the glory of autumn weather, I am working heartily. I did not realize how much good my trip had done me until it was over—which sounds unfortunate, but isn't, really.

We are looking forward to seeing Mr Huidekoper and yourself again some fair day. I shall hardly be in New York before May, I think, but may we not hope to see you there?

With kind regards to you both, I am cordially, | ELLEN GLASGOW

ALS ViU EG Box 28
The letter has been pasted onto other pages, perhaps in a book, and then cut out again. No part of the letter itself is missing, but a holograph note can be seen through the back page: "U.S.A. / A Southern woman. The author of some fair novels 'The Battle Ground' _ 'The Voice of the People' etc."

To Elizabeth Whiting

Richmond, Virginia | October 26. 1898.[1]

Dear Elizabeth Whiting,

Among the letters which come to me about my books,[2] there is rarely one that touches me as yours has done—because it is rarely that one expresses one's real self in a real way in this great big conventional universe. If my work has appealed to your heart, I am very glad, for that heart I am sure is a warm and large one—which is perhaps the most gracious gift the gods can give.

So keep on loving my books so long as they are "strong and true," and believe that the writer is always, dear Elizabeth Whiting,

Faithfully yours, | ELLEN GLASGOW.

ALS NjMoHP Manuscript 2520 Reel 18 Frames 652–53

1. The return address and date occur at the end of the letter.
2. *The Descendant* and *Phases of an Inferior Planet.*

To Elizabeth Patterson

January 2nd 1902. | ONE WEST MAIN STREET | RICHMOND, VIRGINIA
Dear Girl:

Many thanks for the dear little copy of some very lovely sonnets.

We so seldom see each now that I begin to fancy we are drifting in opposite ways until there comes, now and then, some realization that the past is quite as strong as the present and much more sacred. You are bound up, my dear, with some of the happiest memories of my life, and the older I grow the more earnestly I feel that the few intense joys of childhood are the best that life has to give. We may become very successful & very wise, perhaps, but the farther we travel from those first years the faster the freshness passes from us and the dimmer grows our memories of the faces we loved best. May the happiest things the fate's have in their hands come to you this year, dear girl.

As always, | ELLEN

ALS ViU EG Box 28
Publication: *L* 34.

To Elizabeth Patterson

Friday. [March 22, 1902?]

My dearest Lizbeth:

I was delighted to get your letter and to have news of the return to health of dear Miss Betty. Do let me know when you get back for I am really going to come out and see your mother—you I expect to come to me.

It must be a heavenly place you are at, and you don't know how glad I am that you should have had this pleasure. I can see you now paddling up those blue creeks, & I wish I could catch a breath of the air, and watch the birds. Your description reminds me so much of my beloved Prince Edward Island.

This isn't a real letter—I haven't time for one—it is just a note to let you know how I enjoyed hearing from you. Did you know I wonder that my thoughts have turned so often of late to those dear lost springs in the big woods? Do you remember, too, those queer bell-like white flowers we used to find—with the blossom growing from the leaf? I have never seen them since.

Best love to Miss Betty—and as ever
Yours, | ELLEN

ALS ViU EG Box 28
Publication: *L* 34–35.

To Ann Seddon Roy Rutherfoord

Wednesday. [late March–April 1902?][1]

My dear Mrs Rutherfoord:

It was a great pleasure to get your letter—as it always is to hear from you—and I was glad that you found so much in "The Battle-ground" that was to your liking. I owe you a debt of gratitude, you know, for much valuable information about the period,[2] and so I find myself insisting upon associating you with the book-life in some peculiar way.

I know Rock Castle is lovely now, and that you are enjoying the *spring days* in the hall, since that is the place of all others that I like to remember you as occupying.[3]

With best love from Cary and myself,
Always yours affectionately, | ELLEN GLASGOW.

NcD

1. EG's best-selling fourth novel, *B-G,* was published in March 1902. This letter's speculative date is based on that publication date and the reference to "spring days."

2. In addition to visiting the geographical locations she fictionalized in her novel (see next note), EG's extensive research for *B-G* included a thorough reading of newspaper accounts and "innumerable diaries and letters" (*CM* 21), some of which may have been provided by Mrs. Rutherfoord.

3. With her sister CGMcC, EG toured the Valley of Virginia in June 1901 (see Raper, *Without Shelter,* 152). This letter suggests that she visited Mrs. Rutherfoord at that time, presumably in her home, Rock Castle.

To Lucy Bramlette Patterson

July 2nd- 1903.

My dear Mrs Patterson,

My favorite quotation varies so often that it is rather difficult to answer your question. However, just now the motto over my desk is the fragment Epictetus preserved from a lost play of Euripides.

"Lead me, O Zeus, and Thou Destiny, whither-so-ever Thou hast appointed me to go and may I follow fearlessly."[1]

Very truly yours, and with best wishes for your good work,
ELLEN GLASGOW.

ALS NcD

1. Variations on this basic principle of Epictetus occur often in editions of his teachings. EG owned and heavily annotated a copy of *The Teaching of Epictetus,* trans. T. W. Rolleston (New York: Alden, 1889), a gift from Elizabeth Patterson in 1888.

II
1904–1911

[I]t is love, after all, that smooths away the edges of personality and makes me *know* another by intuition rather than by knowledge.
—To Mary Johnston, September 15, 1906

These were important years of trial and error for Glasgow, both professionally and personally. Besides adding five more novels to her published oeuvre, Glasgow suffered the deaths of two of her favorite siblings (Frank to suicide in 1909 and Cary to cancer in 1911), and—what seemed almost like a kind of death to Glasgow—the marriage of her younger sister, Rebe, in 1906. Throwing herself into causes and interests she shared with Cary (women's suffrage and a taste for mystical philosophy) helped keep Glasgow close, even after Cary's death, to the sister who was her intellectual mainstay. One consequence of the loss of Cary and the others was an increased sense on Glasgow's part of the fragility of family ties.

Beginning in 1904 Glasgow's deepening friendship with her "fellow craftsman" Mary Johnston brought together issues important to both—mysticism, suffrage, intellectual endeavor—and demonstrated for Glasgow the potential for friendships with women that were also professional relationships. This combination provided a model Glasgow would follow for the rest of her life. If Glasgow had a romantic relationship from 1899 to 1905 with the "Gerald B—" of her autobiography, it did not hinder her expressions of affection to other women in her letters from about the same time.

Glasgow's increasing certainty that marriage was not for her and her continuing literary ambitions during these years suggest that she accepted a belief in the mutual exclusivity of traditional marriage and a professional career. Glasgow's worsening hearing during these years also caused her to worry that she might transmit a hereditary hearing impairment. Whatever the causes, it is clear from these letters that other women provided the emotional and psychological fulfillment—even, perhaps, a suppressed eroticism—that was a source for Glasgow's creative inspiration.

At the conclusion of this period, Glasgow's move to New York City after Cary's death was both a flight from painful associations and a journey toward greater personal and professional freedom. The move, although largely unsatisfying, nonetheless did give Glasgow a greater freedom to shape her life around her work and her women friends and to reject many of the social obligations (such as marriage) she had grown up expecting to embrace. The years 1904–1911 saw the publication of five novels by Glasgow: *The Deliverance* (1904), *The Wheel of Life* (1906), *The Ancient Law* (1908), *The Romance of a Plain Man* (1909), and *The Miller of Old Church* (1911).

To Mary Johnston

March 22nd 1904.

It is a far cry, my dear fellow-craftsman, from the gray skies and the naked poplars outside to the eternal summer of which your letter was overflowing, and I hope that the change has rested you all through———has "rested every hair of your head," as my colored mammy used to say. I have just read "Sir Mortimer"[1] and after the resistless sweep and energy of the first half I should think you needed to stop and draw a long, slow breath. It is full of colour and poetry and quick action and it keeps wonderfully that peculiar golden light as if of a warmer sunshine, which seems to linger on those days when we turn and look back at them. And Damaris is to me the most attractive of your heroines———I like her in that love scene in the garden.

Is your imagination working again, I wonder, and can you really let it be idle———or are you mentally exhausted and aweary of pen and paper as I have been for months? Those systematic hardy workers who go on day after day with never a pause are the ones I envy———they must escape the fit and fever of sudden spurts and inevitable reactions. Intuition tells me just now that Coralie is downstairs, so I'll leave you for her in a while. It was very nice to hear from you——— I feel that I shall be as glad as possible to know you better—to stand within the gate. Yes, I daresay we are different in many ways———it will be interesting, don't you think to learn how different. And the main thing, perhaps we both have.

Faithfully yours E.G.

ALS ViU MJ Box 2
Publication: *L* 43–44.

1. Novel by MJ (Harper & Brothers, 1904), in which the character Damaris Sedley, mentioned later in this paragraph, appears.

To Mary Johnston

February 3rd, 1905. | ONE WEST MAIN STREET

You have been so much in my thoughts, dear Mary, since you went away,[1] and

February 1905 19

there seems a very big slice taken out of our surroundings. We haven't even tried to fill in the blank, but in the midst of our snow storms, we have dwelt fondly upon Eloises postcards, of which Rebe is exceedingly proud. I do hope and pray from the bottom of my heart that those blue skies and palms & the warm air have brought you up again.

I shall never forget the last talk I had with you the afternoon before you went. You looked so much like a little child, and there are moments when one seems almost to see the soul of one's friend shining through the delicate flesh. The people I love best, I love for this spiritual quality, for it shows me god, somehow, & I hunger for him even when I am least positive of his being underneath us all. When I first knew you, do you know, I thought that I could never come quite close to you——that your reserve would be so great, and I am very thankful that I have at last found that there was a way through it. You are different from me in many ways, & particularly in as much as you keep your impulses so firmly in hand while mine so often carry me breathlessly away. And then you have such courage, and suffering, which makes me impatient & ready to rend the heavens, has given you a peaceful and strong composure. Well, well, do you remember the Buddhist proverb—"there are many paths down into the valley, but when we come out upon the mountain we all see the self-same sun." We travel roads that are not quite together, but a little of the same spirit is lighting each of us on our way, and it is this that draws us, I hope, together & will keep us friends until the end. May you lend me a little of your courage, too, dear, when my strength gives out again——

Eleanor Robson has been and gone and I loved her for the sake of something young and tender and pathetic about her. We had a rather nice party, and several times during the afternoon, she turned and said, "Oh, I wish Mary Johnston were here!" Cary and Rebe and I wished just as heartily that you had been——you and Elöise. We did persuade your brother[2] to come, and he has faithfully promised to drop in on our Tuesday afternoons. He reminds me very much of you.

Do send a card, if nothing more privately mine, to tell me how the place suits you now. It is bitterly cold here, but I am working hard and don't mind it much. Next week I'll probably have a few days in New York.

With sincere affection, | Yours ever, | E.G.

ALS ViU MJ Box 2
Publication: *L* 45–47.

1. MJ wintered in Nassau during 1904–1905.
2. Walter Johnston.

March 1905

To Mary Johnston

Sunday. Midnight. | ONE WEST MAIN STREET |
RICHMOND, VIRGINIA [early March 1905?][1]

Dear Mary:

I ought to be in bed, but the spirit is eager to have a word with you, even though the encumbering flesh is rather week. It has been a hard winter in many ways—I don't complain of the cold for I love it—but I have worked like a driven slave and accomplished little, Cary has succumbed at last & after her operation is overruled by a train nurse & to complete the tragedy Rebe and I go to Chase City tomorrow for a fortnight of boredom & mineral water. In the midst of your palms beside your lapping waves think of us, and then thank God for your surroundings.[2]

Well, well, the winter is gone & if I had written to you as often as I have thought of you, my letters would have fluttered like doves—or swans—about your head. But the truth is I was never so pushed for time in my whole life, & except for the hour in which I walk two miles up Grace Avenue, I have hardly had a free minute since you left. Not that it means much, after all, but from a person of inordinate desires & "spacious dreams," I have brought my existence down to the contemplation & the concrete fact——I look neither before nor after, for if I did I'd stand perfectly still——and shriek!

Your letter gave me a genuine pleasure, and we have enjoyed your postcards more than I can say. Yes, I remember Miss Malcolm distinctly, and it *was* funny about Mr Bell. What a small place our planet is, after all. When I reach the Pleides, as I mean to do before my journey's end I hope at least to be allowed a little stellar communication. One star is too small for a whole intelligence.

The best news, of course, that we have had at all is the news of your great improvement. I can't tell you, dear, how delighted, how thankful I am, and I am glad, too, that you have been able to put in again your working dawns. It may be that the book[3] will grow faster than you think, & in all events you have had a pleasant winter. If you only knew how eagerly we look forward to your return you would in charity not seek to delay it. Cary, poor dear, has missed you, I know, and she has, in bed & flat upon her back, taken the keenest interest in the photographs & postcards.

Have you been reading anything, I wonder,——I haven't, that is anything of which I haven't known forever, except two really remarkable novels:— "The Garden of Allah," by Robert Hichens & "the Divine Fire," by a woman writer with a silly name.[4] But the book isn't silly; it is a carefully planned, elaborately worked out & intensely human story of life in London. Beyond this I've kept to Christina Rossetti—what an instinct for words she had!—& to Balzac. Strange combination! Away with me I am reduced to carrying under my arm one of

Anthony Trollope & a dictionary! In my trunk is "the Imitation of Christ," and "The Bhagavad Gita," Are you mystic enough, I wonder, to care for these? If you feel that I am not an undeserving wretch, will you write to me while I am serving my time? The Micklenburg Hotel, Chase City, Virginia. Love to Eloise & to yourself.

E.G.

ALS ViU MJ Box 2
EG's note on the letter's left margin reads: "This is a wretched scrawl, but it carries love to you, and that is better than words."

1. CGMcC's surgery was performed in March 1905 sometime before the twenty-seventh, and in early March, EG and RGT went to Chase City, Virginia. These details suggest that the letter dates from early March.
2. See previous letter, note 1.
3. Perhaps MJ's play *The Goddess of Reason* (Boston: Houghton Mifflin, 1907) or her novel *Lewis Rand* (Boston: Houghton Mifflin, 1908), which MJ began but set aside temporarily because she associated the book so closely with her father, who died in 1905.
4. Best-selling novels published in 1904 by English writers and critics Robert Smythe Hichens (1864–1950) and May Sinclair.

To Isabelle Holmes Perkinson

Friday | ONE WEST MAIN STREET | RICHMOND, VIRGINIA [March 24, 1905?]
My dear Isabel:

It will give me great pleasure to stay with you if I can possibly arrange to come to the University to the installation of Dr Alderman. Just now it is rather uncertain. Poor Cary has been ailing for a long time and she is now ill in the hospital for an operation which I hope will in the end restore her health. So if I come Rebe will be with me in Cary's place. The last day I saw Cary I told her of your invitation and she sent her best love to you.

Affectionately, | ELLEN GLASGOW

ALS NcD

To Eleanor Robson

Saturday | ONE WEST MAIN STREET | RICHMOND, VIRGINIA [April 2, 1905?]
I must tell you how profoundly impressed I am by *De Profundis*[1]—what a wonderful record of a spiritual development it seems to me to be. The book enters into one—and, I think, it has helped to explain something to me which I have never understood quite clearly until now—and this is the meaning of

sorrow, the purpose it is meant to serve in a universe that, we believe, tends to a final good. Here one sees, in this man's life—that pain so great as that was what he needed to give him a finer insight into life—every single, individual throb of anguish seemed to deepen his consciousness of the spirit, and pitiable as it was, one feels that to develop, to become noble, he needed it all—every wrench, every sob of a tortured heart. The book has wrung my heart, too, & yet there is a strange spiritual beauty in it—a hope also, for surely suffering can do great things when it can open so wide a vision to a man who had seen before only pleasure—only the gratification of each passing impulse. Did you feel, as I did, how much more human, how much worthier of respect the released prisoner was than the dilletante man of letters in all his worldly success? Thank you for sending it to me, and thank you, too, for feeling that I had a soul to understand it.

I was so sorry—oh, so sorry that I couldn't be in New York to go to the reception you wrote me of. Now, I fear, I shan't back there until the last of April—for one of my sisters—Mrs McCormack has just gone through a very serious operation. But I do want to see you both so much—and the thought of a meeting is a very fair hope in the future. Do give my love—I *mean* my love to Miss Dwyer, and to you I am, in all sincerity,

Very heartily your friend, | ELLEN GLASGOW

ALS NNC

1. Written by Oscar Wilde (London: Methuen, 1905) while he was in prison for homosexuality. Robson inscribed EG's copy: "To Miss Glasgow—from her friend Eleanor Robson March 1905" (*CLEG* 8.193).

To Eleanor Robson

Hurricane Lodge, | May 29th [1905?] | Hurricane, | New York, | Essex Co:

It is a dear picture, and I am so pleased to have it with me on my table in this mountain camp. I had meant to inquire if you were in New York when we stopped there, but the Nemesis of a winter of pleasure overtook me, and I collapsed physically and was ordered away by my doctor. Here we are freezing, and living upon milk and eggs, and wishing that the energetic spirit did not have to carry the weight of a body that needs building up. It's about time, I suppose, for you to think of sailing, isn't it? We're missing Europe—wishing particularly our dear Tyrol—just now. Why is it, I wonder that even American mountains have a crudeness—a lack of atmosphere? Rebe joins me in love and best wishes to you, and we each send a kiss to dear Miss Dwyer.

Affectionately yours, | *Ellen Glasgow.*

ALS NNC

To Mary Johnston

Thursday. [June–early July 1905?]

My dear, dear Mary:

Though I haven't bothered you with letters there hasn't been a day when I haven't thought of you with tenderness and affection. We have seen too little of each other and yet I seem to know you so well and the place you have in my heart is a very deep and real one.

Since I have heard that you are beginning to grow stronger and better it has lifted a positive weight of anxiety from my mind. Do keep it up, my friend, there is so much in the power of will—I mean in really wishing to grow well—and then you are so much of interest and pleasure to us all.

I can't tell you how often my thoughts will be with you this summer, & I shall think of you particularly whenever I see anything beautiful that you might enjoy with me.

Rebe and I are sailing on the S. S. Bremen, N.G.L. on July 6th, so this is only a brief little note of farewell for a season. When we are both back again in the autumn, I hope—I do hope that we may be very much more together. Meanwhile if you are able to write letters remember that my address is in care of Brown, Shipley, 123 Pall Mall. From the other side I'll send you a letter of more interest I trust.—but just now my brain has gone to cotton wool. The heat has been so intense that I have spent my time in darkened rooms with volumes of philosophy. Spinoza has seemed best to suit the case. Cary writes that you have been "goodness itself" to her, and her trip has been the very greatest pleasure. Give my love to Eloise, and keep it for yourself, you dear, strong, brave girl.

Affectionately yours, | E.G.

ALS ViU MJ Box 2

To Louise Chandler Moulton

Thursday night | HOTEL DE LA TRÉMOILLE, PARIS [early October 1905?]

My dear Mrs. Moulton,

My Amélie has sent me the enclosed little letter to you which I forward at once. It will make me very happy to know you, but she tells me that you have not been well of late so if for any reason you feel that you would rather not see me just now, I shall understand how it is from my very heart. Don't let me be a burden, dear Mrs Moulton, but if you do really feel that you would care to have me come to you for a little talk, send me word and I will run to meet you.

The Deutschland, my boat, sails on Friday, so you can understand what a busy time we are now having—not too busy, though, to drop trifles light as ours for the sake of something really worthwhile.

Believe me | Very earnestly yours, | ELLEN GLASGOW

ALS DLC MSS 18,869 Reel 5 Container 14
Address: Mrs Louise Chandler Moulton, | Normandy Hotel, | 7, rue de l'Echelle, | Paris. Hand-delivered.
Publication: *EGNP* 107.

To Louise Chandler Moulton

October 5th 1905 | HOTEL DE LA TRÉMOILLE | PARIS | 1 West Main Street | Richmond, Virginia[1]

My thoughts have been so full of you since this morning that before going to bed I must send you this little message of love and farewell. It was so beautiful to *me* the way we came together not as strangers but as dear friends who meet again after a long absence, and the sweet familiar recognition was the loveliest thing I have felt for a long time. You brought the spirit very close to me and because of this I know—I feel, oh, my dear friend, with a sense that is above and beyond knowledge that we have come together—as Amélie and I have come— for some wonderful and lovely end. Somewhere—someday the soul that I saw and loved in you I must have known and loved before, and when one believes this the whole universe becomes not a wilderness but a home. Dear, dear friend, may that same One Light which has shone on dark waters for me shine for you, too, and lead us along the same path into that peace which is the one enduring happiness of life. There was so much—oh, so much I wanted to say to you today, but I was not only pressed for minutes, I was also a little shy, for you seemed so much wiser than I and I felt that it was an impertinence to offer you my joy of soul. But you will understand, I know, that it is not I but the wonderful rest that I want you to share and to take—as I want you to share and to take my love. It is the liberation and the reconciliation of the spirit that I would make the joy that we hold and feel together, Amelie and you and I.

What a poor attempt at expressing my thought this is, but it is late and my sister tells me that we must be up early. Don't think me too great a mystic and yet when one meets constantly with wonderful ways of the spirit what else can one be but a believer in and a lover of the unseen. My love was with you before we met, it is with you now and it will be with you always, but mine is so little compared to that love which is both light and knowledge, the love in which we live and move and have our being. The first thrill of joy with which I came to know it returned to me after seeing you today, and this is the surest sign that the spirit of love was with us when we met.

Goodbye, dear newly *found* but not new friend,
Yours always, | ELLEN GLASGOW

ALS DLC MSS 18,869 Reel 5 Container 14
Address: Mrs Louise Chandler Moulton, | Hotel Normandy, | 7, Rue de l'Echelle, | Paris, | France
Postmark: Paris Oct 05
Publication: *EGNP* 108.

1. EG's Richmond address is written at the end of the letter following her signature.

To Louise Chandler Moulton

1 WEST MAIN STREET, | RICHMOND, VIRGINIA. | November 10, 1905.
Dear friend:

Welcome—thrice welcome back to America and to Boston! It seems only yesterday since I left you in Paris—our beautiful coming together is as fresh in my mind as it was that evening when I wrote to you, and you—dear you—have filled so many of my thoughts since then? How is the rheumatism? and how are you? Just now I am working very, very hard, but the day that my book[1] is finished I shall flit into the world again—first to the country for two weeks with a friend who is not well, then to New York and in February, I hope, to Boston. You will be there, then, will you not? If not I will change my plans for I want to see you and to have some long, long talks. Life has opened so much to me of peace and beauty in these last months that the moments pass in a wonderful swiftness. I am content now since I feel that I have had no beginning in time and shall have no end in eternity, but there are hours when I fairly burn with eagerness to pass on to other worlds—to substitute a new and a less earthly body. The eternal self that is in me longs for eternity.

Ah, I *do* want to see you! Amélie writes that she has been ill, but is well again by now.

With much love and with my thought always.
Yours, | ELLEN GLASGOW

ALS DLC MSS 18,869 Reel 5 Container 14
Address: Mrs Louise Chandler Moulton, | 28 Rutland Square, | Boston, | Mass.
Postmarks: Richmond Nov 12 1905; Boston Nov 13 1905
Publication: *EGNP* 109.

1. *The Wheel of Life* (1906).

To Mary Johnston

Thursday | 10 West 30th Street, | *New York,* | ONE WEST MAIN STREET | RICHMOND, VIRGINIA [late autumn 1905?]

My dear, dear Mary:

It was such a distress to me to leave Richmond without bidding you good-bye, but whenever I telephoned they told me your head was aching, and I was afraid to come for fear it would make the pain worse even if you were able to see me. I have been with you in my heart, though, and I want you to know and feel how my love goes out to you. It always seems to me that I should like to take you in my arms and shield you.

Rebe and I are settled here now for about three weeks, seeing doctors, publishers and dressmakers. It has been quite cold, damp and disagreeable as to the weather, and the city seems so full of people, of compressed humanity, that it makes it hard to believe that the world isn't turning entirely to matter. I find it very harassing to one's philosophic vision, & in order to compose my soul I have been reading Spinoza and Plotinus.

Well, well, this scrappy note is interrupted, and I must break off before I've said anything at all. I can't tell you, dear, how I have wanted to be with you. Next autumn let us hope we'll have a chance to talk.

Faithfully yours, | *Ellen Glasgow*

ALS ViU MJ Box 2

To Mary Johnston

EG [late 1905?]

Dear Mary:

Will you receive this brave preacher[1] for the sake of his soul—not his face, which, after all, was only some transient accident of form which he picked up for this planet.

We thought of you constantly—Rebe and I—and this little gift is merely to show you that you held your place in our minds & hearts.

I want so much to see you when you are able.

With sincere affection, | Yours, | ELLEN GLASGOW

ALS ViU MJ Box 2

1. Unidentified. The idea of the impermanence of material form suggests that the "brave preacher" may have been a small statue of Buddha. By the time of this letter, EG owned many books about Buddhism (an interest she shared with MJ), and she is known to have had Buddha figurines.

To Louise Chandler Moulton

March 18. 1906 | ONE WEST MAIN STREET | RICHMOND, VIRGINIA

Dear friend:

The last few days in Boston were very dismal. Our tickets were bought and we were all prepared to leave Sunday when I was taken ill and had to go to bed for several days. On Tuesday I paid a few feeble calls in the neighborhood, but after reaching home I had to give myself a thorough rest. What I regretted most was that the days flew by without my having those long, dear talks with you. The Friday afternoons were charming, but, somehow, I never seemed quite to "get at" *you* on those occasions. Never mind next time will come someday, and then we'll leave out the other people once in a while.

This is just a word before I run in to see some friends who are waiting. Tomorrow I expect to go up to Castle Hill and, indeed, I'll give our Amélie your messages. It *was* good and lovely to see you even in the midst of a crowd. I am so sorry that you are still ailing. May the spring bring you health and peace! Rebe, I know, would send love.

Most affectionately yours, | ELLEN G.

ALS DLC MSS 18,869 Reel 5 Container 14
Address: Mrs Louise Chandler Moulton, | 28, Rutland, | Boston, | Mass
Postmarks: Mar 18 1906 Richmond; Boston Mar 19 1906
Publication: *EGNP* 110.

To Louise Chandler Moulton

April 18. 1906 | ONE WEST MAIN STREET | RICHMOND, VIRGINIA

Dear friend:

So many things have kept me from writing since your sweet letter came to me while I sat with Amélie in her room. First of all, I have been very far from well—merely run down and nervously exhausted—so that even the writing to those I love has seemed a burden. Then I've been away from home almost constantly, and now I've run back for a few days before going off again to Atlantic City. But I've thought of you so much this beautiful Easter—a time which has for me a beautiful symbolism, too. Not as a suggestion of a resurrection of the mere personal life, but as expressive of that endless chain of births and deaths and rebirths through which the soul wins to its freedom and its final union with God. I wish I could talk to you about this——I wish you could feel it in every fibre of your heart as I do today. Of course, one can't always feel so exquisitely alive to the enfolding spirit, but when one does—ah, when one does, the whole universe is but a home in which one cannot lose one's way because of the friendly faces of the stars.

There is a verse in the Wisdom of Solomon which I love to repeat in the silence at night: "For to know Thee is perfect righteousness; yea, to know Thy power is the root of immortality."[1]

Lovingly yours, | *Ellen Glasgow*

ALS DLC MSS 18,869 Reel 5 Container 14
Address: Mrs Louise Chandler Moulton, | 28, Rutland, | Boston, | Mass
Postmarks: Richmond Apr 18 1906; Boston Apr 19 1906
Publication: *EGNP* 110–11.

1. *Book of Wisdom* (Apocrypha) 15.3.

To Rebe Glasgow Tutwiler

Monday. | THE MECKLENBURG, CHASE CITY, VA. [spring 1906?]
My precious Rebe:

We got up at six o'clock and found it very cold, after the thermometer stood at 94 for two days. After a mean early breakfast we went out to the stables, where they put me on a new horse because Morgan's back[1] was sore. I began to think I was quite ready to be a walkaway when this one got quite gay from the cold & pranced & shied along. After a little, tho; she quieted down, but I had to go slowly most of the way because of this sore place. For two days now I've kept a cloth saturated with Witch Hazel or Hinds on it & now I am sitting on a handkerchief soaked in Pond's extract. It is too bad I should have got knocked up.

You might put your velvet dress away and take your white suit to New York. I know that my things have moths in them at home. I think now that we'll leave next Tuesday (tomorrow week), then Cary goes for a week to Va. Beach, & I want to go on the 15th. I suppose the only way to meet you is for me to stop at Philadelphia—but I have no clothes. I'll go first to your apartment any way & get my hair waved there, and if Jean really wants me I might stay two nights with her. Otherwise, if you can get me a room, I'll stay the night there, tho; I think we might as well go on to New York on an afternoon train. Let me know what you think I'd better do. I want to get some spring clothes. What do you think of going to the Burlington? Or had we better go to the Seville? If you are laid up at the Burlington how would you get your meals?

With dearest love, | Yours, | E.G.

TC of ALS FU
MKR note: "Postmark not readable | Pencil notation: *1906*"
Address: Mrs. Cabell Tutwiler, The Colonial, Philadelphia

1. MKR's transcription reads, "Morgan's buck (back)"

To Mary Johnston

Hurricane Lodge, | Hurricane, Essex Co., | New York. | Aug 15. 1906
My dear Mary:

Your letter was one of the most delightful and surprising happenings of the summer! What a marvel of recuperation you are—and I can assure you that I have ceased entirely to picture you as an invalid—imagining instead a very lively and elastic little lady who has a good deal of work and play and sweetness and trouble before her yet. Dear, you must set your face forward in earnest and keep always with me in this "small old path" of the *Upanishads,* "difficult to tread as the raw edge of a razor." As for me I can only tell you of the joy—the real joy that your letter has brought me. Tears were in my eyes when I read it—tears of tenderness, of happiness for you. I took up my pen to answer it at once and then—ah, then—well, that is about myself and less interesting to me and far less smooth in a way than your road has been these last few weeks. It's strange, Mary, isn't it that I who have comparative health and strength to work and play and wander about the earth and make friends and enemies; yet I choose (who can hold also to a hardly bought philosophy even in tragic moments)—that I who have all these things should possess so little of the natural happy instinct for life that today at thirty-two[1] I could lie down smiling and give it up and pass on to one of the Universal lives I see beyond x x x

But forgive me, dear, forgive me—I didn't mean to say such things to you and I am ashamed. They sound as if I were unhappy and I am not—oh, far, far from it. For the last year I have been happy for the first time in my life—happy not in the outward shadow part of me, but in my soul which is clear and radiant out of a long darkness.

x x x Ah, I am with you in your feeling about work, and with you, too, in having spent a summer staring (with newly sharpened pencils beside me) at a spotless sheet of paper. *Dolce far niente*[2] is not to my mind but very much indeed to my manner during these last weeks. Day steps after day into the abyss of wasted time. People come and go and instead of an impressionable mind, I seem to present merely the waxen smile of polite features. I've even detached myself in vain from metaphysics—Kant and Bradley stand half read on my desk, and my best beloved Fichte I haven't dared open for a month—Yet in spite of everything the eccentric whirl of a summer hotel sweeps me from my mooring, and, for sheer lack of concentration I cannot write. Our cottage is nice, but the hotel is abominable, and driven to desperation at last, we are going to pack up shortly and depart for Montréal and Quebec. The Adirondacks hold no more illusions for me. My four years dream of a camp here has been washed away in rain. I've been here almost three months and we have had barely ten perfect days and nights. Last night the stars were magnificent—Pegasus and Andromeda faced me brilliantly when I lifted my shade, so I went down and had a friendly re-union with the constellations,—but the chances are that they will hide themselves very soon again. Have you watched Venus, I wonder, this summer, as closely as I have. She sets now just over our finest mountain & [?]³ in her footsteps the great bear swings into view. I get a wonderful peace and the most exquisite pleasure from my friendship with the stars. x x x

What you say of Italy stirs my pulse, but for me it is not possible because of my bank account and the manner by which I must set about increasing it. Yet for you I hope the plan will work itself into a fact. Richmond will be really Richmond in October—will it not? Then we must arrange to see each other when we can, and you must lose quite the "submerged sensation" you sometimes feel. I've had it often myself and I know the curious soul-loneliness it brings. I want to draw you, dear brave heart, not only back to work and play but back to me. There's so much of the child in me yet, and life to me means love just as it does to a child—love of many kinds and degrees, but each and all helping us in our way and bringing the journey's end a little nearer the knowledge of God. So love me, Mary, much or little as you can, and I shall love you back in my own measure.

Ever yours, | ELLEN GLASGOW
Love from Rebe to you both. Kiss Eloise for me.

ALS ViU MJ Box 2
Publication: *L* 52–54.

1. EG's age at this time is thirty-three, but confusion over her birth date as recorded in the family Bible caused her to believe until late in life that she was born in 1874 (see *WW* 5–6). The mistaken year, 1874, is engraved on EG's gravestone.
2. An Italian phrase (perhaps originating with Pliny) meaning "sweetness in doing nothing" (that is, blissful relaxation in idleness).
3. Blair Rouse transcribes this word as "immediately," which appears from the original letter to be inaccurate.

To Mary Johnston

CHATEAU FRONTENAC. | QUEBEC, CANADA. | September 15th 1906
My dear Mary:
Your letter was forwarded to me here, and if I had had the necessary time, I'd have been charmed to meet the people you spoke of—but Rebe and I have both been "invalided" since coming to Quebec, and, to tell the truth, we've done little but eat and sleep and sit about in neighboring hospitable squares. In this way the only acquaintances we've made have been certain sociable dogs that attach themselves in our train and invarialy accompany us back into the château.

Now our visit here is about over—on Monday we leave for New York, and then—if dressmakers and the gods agree!—we hope to see Richmond about the 2nd week in October. Do you know I shall be really glad to return to those dusty streets and that dismantled house.[1] I want to work—work—work for at least six quiet months. x x x

Your letter, dear, was like a song of joy, so overflowing with vitality and a high heart for life. I know—*I know* it all, for a year ago I passed through exactly the same awakening of myself, though from different causes. Mine was not physical, but spiritual—mental—what you will! For a year I was so dead that I couldn't feel even when I was hurt because of some curious emotional anaesthesia, and, like you I had to fight—fight, a sleepless battle night and day, not for my reason but for my very soul. Then at the end of a year—at Brennerbad[2] last summer I came out triumphant and for three whole months it was as if I walked on *light,* not air. I was like one who had come out of a dark prison into the presence of God and saw and knew him, and cared for nothing in the way of pain that had gone before the vision. Of course, dear heart, the exhileration, the first rapture of the mere rebound to physical or spiritual health cannot be permanent, but, I think the strength of the victory and the memory of it, are build into the eternal process of one's spirit. We suffered in different ways, but we both suffered[3] to the death—each of us saw at the end of her road the mouth of hell—and each of us turned and struggled back to life—you along your steep path and I along mine. It is something to be thankful for that now at last our roads may run a little while into one. The old sorrows, the old temptations, the old fights are like so many steps by which we go on and upward and always, I hope, to something bigger and higher than we knew before. Ah, Mary, Mary, as I walked about just now in this glorious weather, it seemed to me that I could look back not only without bitterness, but with thankfulness upon the way I had come. The exaltation may soften and pass into quiet, but the peace of the soul does not and cannot surrender to the old anguish again. x x

I can't say more, dear, but this much I must tell you that if my letter gave you an impression of dejection or restlessness it reflected me very falsely. I was born with a terrible burden of melancholy—of too much introspection—but for a whole year, for the first time in my life, I have not known a single instant of the old depression. I am perfectly willing to die, but I can say now, as I never could before, that I am equally willing to live until I come to where my road turns again. The sense of—eternity—of immortality that is not a personal immortality has brought me not only reconciliation, but the kind of joy that is like the [rush?] down from the battle of the senses I have come at last into what Whitman calls "the Me Myself,"[4] that is behind and above it all. x x x

I wonder if you will understand what I've written—but I don't wonder about your sympathy, for I know that I have that always just as you have mine.

Our temperaments, our inheritances, our attitudes even may be different—but it is love, after all, that smooths away the edges of personality and makes me *know* another by intuition rather than by knowledge. Goodbye for a time—when we meet you will be settled in your home,[5] and I shall be so much interested in everything about it. We must take up our afternoons early in the autumn.

Yours always with | love, | ELLEN

ALS ViU MJ Box 2
Publication: *L* 55–57.

    1. EG may refer to the household rearrangements necessary after her sister Cary's surgery in 1905, when Cary's room was moved downstairs.

    2. Brennerbad, in the Austrian Tyrol near the Italian border, is misidentified as Mürren in Godbold (74) and Bremerbad in Goodman (101). EG stayed at the Grand Hotel.

    3. The death in 1905 of MJ's father, to whom she was very close, apparently precipitated her serious illness. EG's sister Cary's surgery for cancer was in 1905. Many EG scholars also believe that a love affair with the "Gerald B—" of EG's autobiography was brought to an end in 1905 with "Gerald's" death.

    4. The concluding words of section 4 of Walt Whitman's "Song of Myself" (1855, 1891).

    5. MJ traveled in Europe during the summer of 1906; EG refers to her return to Richmond and in the following sentence to the afternoon gatherings of the Glasgow and Johnston sisters.

To Rebe Glasgow Tutwiler

Friday. | ONE WEST MAIN STREET | RICHMOND, VIRGINIA
[December 7, 1906]

My own Darling Child:

    I don't realize yet that you have gone away[1]—perhaps because I've had to think about food and things every moment. But I never knew what you were or how much I loved you until these last days. You have always been the most perfect thing on earth and I love you with every bit of my heart. Poor Frank was very ill, but is up now. I'll write a letter soon. Give my love to Cabell—and you be happy and cheerful and wear your pretty clothes. Goodbye, very precious love.

    Ellen.

TC of ALS FU
Address: Mrs. Cabell Tutwiler
Postmark: Dec. 7, 1906

    1. Rebe Glasgow married Carrington Cabell Tutwiler on December 5, 1906, and moved to Philadelphia.

To Louise Chandler Moulton

December 13*th* 1906.

It was very sweet and good of you to write me, dear, true friend. All summer I had you in mind, but there were many worries, and I worked so hard to get well again that there was little time left for any pleasure——even for writing to those I love. Now in the midst of the excitement of my sister's wedding I have been reading your beautiful book.[1] How dear it was of you to send it! She has, of course, told you this herself by now.

I am so sorry you are no better for your "cure." Is the rheumatism still so painful? And what are your plans and prospects for the winter. Oh, I only wish that I could come to Boston within the next few months—but it doesn't look to-night as if that would be possible. When I *do* come I shall probably bring another sister.[2] She is an invalid now, but when she is well, we hope to go North together and I am sure you will find her as delightful as I do. I can hardly write about my missing Rebe—it cuts too deep. Yet she has promised to go to New York with me in May and to spend next summer in Virginia. Would I might say Europe!

Amélie is at "Castle Hill"—or will be within a week. I haven't seen her since she landed, so, of course, I am eager to be with her as soon as possible. It seems an age since I last saw her dear, lovely face. And now, dear, I must stop and go down to my sick sister. You have always been so sweet and kind to me that it touches my heart when I think of it. I do hope that I may see you before many months.

Most affectionately yours, | ELLEN GLASGOW

ALS DLC MSS 18,869 Reel 5 Container 14
Address: Mrs Louise Chandler Moulton, | 28, Rutland, | Boston, | Mass
Postmark: Richmond December 15 1906
Publication: *EGNP* 111–12.

1. Unidentified. The volumes Moulton is best known for were published before 1900; her collected poems were not published until 1909. *CLEG* records no books by Moulton that Glasgow owned, but this one seems to have been a wedding gift to Rebe (the "she" referred to two sentences later).
2. CGMcC.

To Rebe Glasgow Tutwiler

[December 14, 1906]

My own darling child:

This is the first moment I've had to myself since you left and I am missing you more than I can say. I hope you are well and happy now, and not too tired to go out when you are asked. The house seems very empty without you. Cary never comes to the table, but it didn't seem to matter much tho. I never spoke there. Mr. Paradise has just gone and I've just come back from the station. He had a beautiful visit—everybody liked him & he fitted into the situation without any effort. After you went I don't know what I should have done if he hadn't been here. He wasn't like the man at the Hurricane somehow, for on this visit he seemed to say always the right thing & everybody found him very entertaining. Julia came over to dinner & missed her train talking to him, & Cousin Archer fell so in love with him that he came every day and insisted on taking him to walk yesterday afternoon & down to the capitol at nine this morning. I am sorry he is gone, but, doubtless, I can now get back to work. Yesterday morning he, Lulie[1] & I (Lulie came down because Amelie was away) went to the Confederate Museum—& the day before Carrie & Mary went with us to the tobacco factory. I did very little to entertain him—only asked Cousin Archer & Gov. Montague in to a beautiful supper one night—raw oysters, sweetbreads, pheasants, salad, ham, ice cream, sherry, champagne. They enjoyed themselves very much, I think. Cary came in, but I missed you—as I always shall. Betty Glasgow is downstairs now, & Gordon Paxton (horrors!)[2] spent a night. Your service is nice, but we have not opened it. I want to know what Arthur sent you. Today there arrived pictures (gorgeous) of their new house[3]—just bought it—including basement there are seven stories. I wish you could peep into your room now for on the rug there reposes a little waif picked up by Berta. He is the sweetest & most grateful little dog—slept in my room on a blanket by the fire & behaved beautifully all night. After being washed he is too pretty, but Joy has almost killed him, so Coralie has found him another home. I've sent you a collar for him & he'll look very presentable. It's so dark I must stop. Goodbye, my own darling child.

 Your | Ellen

TC of ALS FU
Address: Mrs. Cabell Tutwiler, The Colonial, Philadelphia
Postmark: Richmond, Va. Dec 14 1906

 1. MJ includes a question mark after this name; it is probably Julia (see following letter).
 2. MKR: "the word 'horrors' is crossed out—typist's note."
 3. Moncorvo House, in London.

To Rebe Glasgow Tutwiler

Sunday [December 16, 1906]

My darling child:
 Julia spent last night here, and my work has suffered so from many distractions that I feel as if I should never settle down to it again. Things drift along in

an aimless way—Freeman & Patsy giving fresh illustrations of imbecility every day, & the whole house embedded in dirt. The people I gave the little dog to telephoned a moment ago to say he had run away & I looked out of the window & there he was! He is now asleep under my bed, having come from 1000 West Grace. Joy falls on him tooth & nail whenever he sees him. He is a dear little fellow & so pathetic.

I wonder what you are wearing today & how are you looking? Mr. Winter wrote Julia: "So pretty Rebe Glasgow is married. I meant to send her a present, but missed the date." Julia says she can have your slips[1] made for you if you wish her to. Everybody says you were lovely at your wedding—& so you were. This is just a line. I feel as if I had been beaten all over—but I *must* get to work. It is very hard. I can't tell you how I miss & love you. You are the dearest thing God ever made.

Your | Ellen
Love to Cabell.

TC of ALS FU
Address: Mrs. Cabell Tutwiler | The Colonial | Philadelphia
Postmark: Richmond Dec 16 1906

1. MKR inserts a question mark after "slips."

To Rebe Glasgow Tutwiler

Thursday [December 20, 1906]

My own Darling Rebe:

I have worked hard all the morning, & this is a little moment before dinner. A hard storm & bitter cold is just over, & Cary has been distractedly distributing Christmas presents for the last few days. Lizzie Jones comes Sunday to pack your box (only eatables) which goes off Sunday. I hope you will enjoy the things. Little Brother[1] is in his new home again. I hope he will stay—he was too sweet. Nothing goes on here except that I miss you every minute. I hope you will go out & wear your clothes & make friends. I know you looked lovely in your velvet. Wear it when you can. This is just[2] a line—my hand is too tired to write. I am midway of the third chapter, very slow. My massage was begun again, so I have hardly a moment to call my own. I get in a panic terror for fear I can't write the book,[3] after all.

Goodbye, darling. Take care of yourself & be happy.
Your own devoted, | Ellen

TC of ALS FU

Address: Mrs. Cabell Tutwiler | The Colonial | Philadelphia
Postmark: Richmond, Va. December 20 1906

1. The stray dog mentioned in the previous two letters.
2. MKR transcribes this word as "not," a probable mistake attributable to EG's handwriting. EG commonly uses the phrase "just a line."
3. AL.

To Rebe Glasgow Tutwiler

Sunday. [December 23, 1906]

My own Precious Rebe:

This letter will reach you Xmas Eve, so I wish I could make it full and interesting, but I'm afraid it will fall far short of all the love and good wishes that it contains. Lizzie comes this afternoon to pack your box, and I'm so sorry there wasn't more I could put into it. Mrs. Coleman promised me faithfully to get dried tongue, but it never came, & everything somehow seems to be sweet & injurious. There has never been a quieter Xmas. Coralie & I have filled six stockings for poor children, & accompanied by Joe and Patsy we go down to 27th Street to deliver them tomorrow afternoon. I am giving Carrie & Cary each one of my new blouses made by Mrs. Gordon, Julia fifteen yards of black crepe de chine for a dress, Amélie a dressing saque, Mrs Rives a balsam pillow, (on which Lucy *sewed* the linen cover slip, because she didn't have time to work button holes, she said) Lutie[1] two pairs of gloves, & that about completes my output. Coralie & Louise I gave scarfs & Anne those tortoise shell pins I got in Florence. The Coleman's are coming to dinner, & I suppose Father will eat mince pie & be ill as usual. Nothing has happenend for two days except that poor Mr. Cross had pneumonia & died in three days. Two days after his funeral I sent a note addressed to him to Fouquereaus; then the only other incident was Jas. Johnston's beating a man for whipping a horse. Anne remarked: "I always said there was good in Joe."

It's very cold here. I wonder what you are doing, & how you occupy yourself all day. Have you met any people you really like? Here I go on the same old way with hardly a minute to call my own. If I can get off the last of March I want to go to Chase City—the first two weeks in April probably, then to New York the middle. I've told Carrie you are going with me, but you mustn't do it unless you really want to. I am going to try to get Mary's cottage at the Warm Springs, so you must come down whenever you please. Cary & I will probably go the 1st of July & stay through September. I hope you'll come the 1st, if possible, for I think it will do you good. Emily enclosed a letter from Robert, & Cary sent him your address. He said he would die for father at that minute. Cary said she'd like to have him back, but I said: "God forbid!" I hope you are enjoying your clothes & going out every day in the fresh air. Try while you are in Philadelphia. I can't tell you how I miss you, but if you are happy, it is all right & I am glad & thankful. Four chapters of my book² are finished—5 more in the rough, but I want to do twenty before I go away. Father has an economical fit; we've had rabbits for a week un- [*bottom of this sheet cut off*] the quality of the butter he gets. Arthur sent us each $25—mine, I hope, can go to the S.P.C.A., & father has subtracted five of Cary's, for reasons known to himself. I wonder what your Xmas days will be like?—it's equally tiresome the world over, I suppose. Dr. Willis & Dr. Van der Hooy³ have been to supper, the latter looks a mere college boy. Let me know if you hear anything of your Dr. Clarke—& find out sometime the name of the [*bottom of sheet cut off*] So busy your things couldn't get packed till after Xmas.

Your own | Ellen.

TC of ALS FU
Address: Mrs. Cabell Tutwiler | The Colonial | Philadelphia
Postmark: Richmond, Va. Dec 23 1906

1. MKR inserts a question mark here and following "Fouquereaus" near the end of this paragraph.
2. *AL*.
3. MKR inserts a question mark here.

To Rebe Glasgow Tutwiler

Friday [January 18, 1907]

My darling child:

It takes a greater than I—yea, a greater being than the Preacher to express the emotional & material cataclysm of the last five days. After the exodus of Patsy, who departed regretfully but cheerfully, (bearing with her, as we discovered afterwards, the majority of the bed linen, including Carys,) and of Freeman (who was angelic) and Maria (who took everything with her that Patsy had left behind, particularly kitchen things) we hoped in our vanity that we should get a life of quiet. But to reckon without Providence is a small fatality compared to reckoning without Domestics. Caroline & Ella both found the condition of the rooms back there one of dirt & destitution, so I myself—in my own person— had Mrs. Dahl calcimine light green all the walls of kitchen, stairway, & laundry, paper Caroline's room, put matting on the floor, & have ordered oilcloth for the floor of the kitchen & pantry (that's expensive, too.) Everything that *could* be seized & carried back for rear decorations has been; curtains from sitting-room last year, blue felting left over from my room, steamer chair, bureau out of dressing-room, & Cary's tall black lamp, which she finally found courage to retract. The renovation is so complete that we feel as if we'd have to sell everything in the front part of the house to pay for the re-furnishing of the back. But, thank heaven, things will be clean & decent there, as they have never been before, and our servants promise to be excellent ones. Personally, I prefer Bryce (Carroll Bryce), the butler, tho Caroline is very nice & said by Nita[1] Patterson to be a treasure. Ella, the girl who can't stay, is really invaluable, & she may go to the Warm with us. But I shall be in New Jersey when it is over, & fear Father will be, also.

More than this I've bought a set of the British Encyclopaedia, from Mc-Donogle, last edition, & a beautiful set of Thackeray from Lamiot, half calf. They are in your black book case in the sitting room, that is they *will* be when they come. Added to it all I've worked very hard & finished about one fourth of the book.[2] I'm too tired to write more, but I love you devotedly every minute. I want to see you terribly, but I hope to get more work done before the second week in April, when I go away to N. Y. So glad you'll stay in town for a year.

Your | E. G.

TC of ALS FU
Address: Mrs. Cabell Tutwiler, The Colonial, Philadelphia
Postmark: Richmond January 18 1907

1. MKR inserts a question mark here, and just after "New Jersey" and "Lamiot" in the next few sentences.
2. AL.

To Rebe Glasgow Tutwiler

Wednesday. [May 22, 1907]

My darling little child:

Your letter has made me cry, for I know I oughtn't to have written what I did to you—but conversations like that with Cary somehow seem to make me lose all my balance. If I have ever loved anybody I have loved you, & I thought I had always been as good to you as I was able to be during all these years. I suppose it's silly to get upset by what Cary says, but she made me feel that I never wanted to see any member of my family again. Of course you are the only one that has ever come in any vital way near to me, & it was because I cared more for you than for myself that I was always eager for you to marry, because I realized that my work took up so much of my time & you had nothing in your life that corresponded to it. I shall always love you in this way, but I have a terrible temperament to deal with, & I have always felt satisfied simply to know that you were well & happy however far off you were. For years you were the only thing that kept me alive & yet I know that because of my own absorbing wretchedness, I never was as great a pleasure to you as I might have been. However, that's over, & you are, I think, the dearest & sweetest human being on earth. Be as happy as you can, but if you ever need me, I will come through fire & water to help you.

Cary has decided not to go to the White Sulphur—so father has taken half of one of the Florida cottages—two rooms with a bath & a maid's room. I shall go up the 20th of June (He makes reduced rates if we take it from then) with the Bishop's Mary (whom I've got for a maid) and either Louise Willcox or Lucy Coleman—who will stay with me until you come. I think it would be excellent for you to ride a pony, but you would have to have a linen skirt. If you send me your waist & hip measure I'll try to get Mrs.[1] [*blank space*] to make you one. Also length of your short skirt.

It is terrible that you should feel so badly. I hope the White Sulphur will suit you, but there is no necessity to stay unless we like it. If it doesn't we can go somewhere to a more bracing climate. You know I love you, my darling little sister.

Ellen

TC of ALS FU
Address: Mrs. Cabell Tutwiler, The Colonial, Philadelphia
Postmark: Richmond, Va. May 22, 1907

1. Perhaps the Mrs. Gordon mentioned in EG's letter to RGT, December 23, 1906.

To Rebe Glasgow Tutwiler

Thursday. [May 23, 1907]

My darling Child:

I am distressed that I have hurt you, and yet I don't suppose under the circumstances that I could have helped it. In New York I did feel a change (I thought you seemed to enjoy everybody else more than me,[1] but I reconciled myself to it, though not so pleasantly as I might have done, I suppose. Then I had that talk with Cary, and I felt suddenly that I'd never been any use to anybody & this made me want to get away from there for good. Life is very difficult here; it wouldn't be perhaps for another person, but I'm too nervous to fit into it. I cried over your letter yesterday, & my eyes have filled with tears whenever I've thought of it—but if I could feel that you are perfectly well and cheerful I shouldn't mind so much if I had to give you up. What worries me is the thought that you are sick. I love you better than I've ever loved anybody in my life, I know.

Miss Morris is going to make you a riding skirt if I can get her. You must try to find some health somehow. Goodbye & God bless you. You are the best thing on earth.

Yours | Ellen

TC of ALS FU
Address: Mrs. Cabell Tutwiler, The Colonial, Philadelphia, Penn.
Postmark: Richmond, Va. May 23 1907

1. The missing closing parenthesis is MKR's.

To Rebe Glasgow Tutwiler

Friday. [May 24, 1907]

My precious child:

It was a dear, sweet letter from you this morning, and I think it wonderful the way you have made yourself so calm and bright about life and all the little worries of living. You've in a measure made your disposition, too, and that's more wonderful, still. I think you have developed and perfected yourself during these last three years with the utmost strength and wisdom.

I can't write much—it's hot and glary[1] and I've been to the dentists four afternoons & must go again. The day I got home I split one of my teeth (a dead one) straight through. The rooms look very nice—my pottery is on the top of one of my shelves & the lamp shade looks perfectly lovely when it is lighted. The two little chairs are simply charming. I hope the Bishop's Mary will prove a comfort, but I am afraid to it *to* much.[2] The last Mary (that is the Mary before the Mary I have now) went off with one of my best shirtwaists I'd never worn—& heaven knows what else. But the B———'s[3] Mary is at least reliable. He could not afford two servants, so as she couldn't cook he had to give her up—& Carrie got her for me.

Try to keep well—& if I can I'll try to get to feel really at home with Cabell. Men, however, are so different from women that I don't know how it will be. But I'll try for your sake.

Devotedly, | Ellen

TC of ALS FU
Address: Mrs. Cabell Tutwiler, The Colonial, Philadelphia
Postmark: Richmond, Va. May 24 1907

1. MKR inserts a question mark.
2. MKR inserts a parenthetical note: "sic—I am afraid to hope it too much?" The underlining in "to" is MKR's.
3. MKR inserts "(sic)."

To Rebe Glasgow Tutwiler

Tuesday [June 4, 1907]

Darling:

I haven't sat down for three days, & I'm going to Norfolk today to attend the Colonial Dames Day[1] at Jamestown. Yesterday was one of the great experiences of life. Cary has risen to the occasion like a veteran, entertained on her post[2] for three days—After the parade, & we shouted and wept ourselves hoarse, we had a whole Company of Texans, the Higher (Higbee?) Guards of Fort Worth Texas to dinner—filled the sitting-room & dining-room with tables—gave each man (23) a julep, fried chicken & coffee, ice cream & a cigar. Coralie (they were General Joe Johnston's men) Mary, Clarke, Sallie Anderson, the Colemans & John Armstrong Chanler (who has been here every day & all day during the re-union) came to serve, & all said it was one of the occasions that could never be forgotten. Such appreciation you can't imagine. They wept & sang in the hall before leaving, "God be with you till we meet again!" And before falling into the parade, they came here & presented arms to me out in the street. The Commander of the Texas camp—a charming man called in the afternoon to thank us, "because" he said, "we had done for the privates what everybody else did for the Colonels & Captains," I'd give anything if you'd been here. Coralie never enjoyed herself so much in her life—& it was so touching & pathetic. I'll try to get Father to send you the papers. Can't write. Cary has been wonderful, but I fear will succumb. I am almost dead—but it is in a good cause.

With devoted love, | Yours, | ELLEN

TC of ALS FU
Address: Mrs. Cabell Tutwiler, The Colonial, Spruce & 11th St., Phila., Penn.
Postmark: "From Richmond," "Mailed June 4, 1907" (MKR notes)

1. In a letter to RGT dated May 30, 1907, EG says she is at this time being inducted into the Colonial Dames, an organization founded in 1890. Its members must trace their lineage to a pre-Revolution officer or official (in contrast to the Daughters of the American Republic [DAR], which requires that members trace their heritage to any person living in pre-Revolutionary America).
2. MKR inserts a question mark here, and just after "Clarke," below. The Higbee Guards were Confederate veterans.

To Mary Johnston

White Sulphur Springs. | Greenbriar Co., | West Virginia, | *July 20. 1907*
Dear Mary:

Could you imagine me, not sauntering in muslin at midday, but rising, half asleep at 6 o'clock to ride ten miles through rain or sun as the weather might be? Yesterday I came home drenched to the skin, but after a resort to the bottle which Mrs Gamp was disposed to patronize,[1] I rallied my forces and was ready to don white muslin and a sunshade by the time the storm was over. These rides really save my health and preserve my sanity—if not wholly, at least sufficiently to enable me to escape suspicion of being the feeble minded atom which this climate, combined with this idiotic manner of life, has made me. Everybody up here except myself (and Coralie who is with me now,) has a baby——and as a consequence we two are rather left out of subjects of conversation. Even the excitement of watching our offspring, with bated breath, on the floor of the ballroom is denied us. It's a sweet enough old place here, and our cottage is very comfortable (possessing two bathrooms and a Virginia creeper on the porch)— but in spite of these attractions, if the good Lord permits, I intend to spend next summer somewhere in the British Isles. Lets be together—then the fun would be doubled, wouldn't it? All that you write me makes me the more anxious to set sail; and I am regretting particularly on this oppressive day, the fleeting plans I had made about Wales. But it's far better, after all, that Cary should go. Her condition was really very serious, and the long sea trip means so much pleasure and health to her. She expects to spend five weeks up high in the Italian Alps, sailing back on the "[Gaelic?]" which touches at Palermo and The Azores. She preferred the Southern passage so much, else she might have made my journey to Betts-y-Coed.[2]

No, I've written very, very little—who could when one's brains have degenerated to cotton wool? Of course you haven't written either—but wait till October! Since I got here I've been reading the D'artagnan romances, Spenser's Hymns on the Heavenly Beauty, and the comedies of Steele. A queer mixture certainly. As for you—well, read from the book of mankind and select passages to quote, please, at tea-drinkings on your return. Oh, for the plum cake and tea in Devon! and oh, for the cream & strawberries! and, oh, for the digestion which could partake of them sans peur et sans reproche.[3]

With the love of us three (Rebe, Coralie & E.G. to Eloise and yourself), and a special kiss of greeting to my Mary.

Your very | loving, | E.G.

ALS ViU MJ Box 2

1. Mrs. Gamp, from Dickens's *Martin Chuzzlewit,* says, "leave the bottle on the chimley-piece, and don't ask me to take none, but let me put my lips to it when I am so dispoged" (chapter 19).
2. Bettws-y-Coed, Wales.
3. French for "without fear and without reproach."

To Mary Johnston

July 4th 1908, | ONE WEST MAIN STREET | RICHMOND, VIRGINIA

Dear Molly,

My first act of patriotism on this historic day will be to send a long intended letter to you. Outside a noisy demonstration is being cheerfully carried on by the small Irishman next door. Inside Joy has retired beneath the bed, while the glorious Fourth reverberates across "Emma," that lies blandly upon my window-sill. My chief consolation the past week has been the entire set of Miss Austen and Harriet Martineau's autobiography. Did you ever read the last, I wonder? The early chapters are a trifle pedantic, but she seems to me to have possessed *moral* courage in a higher degree than any man or woman I ever read of. She was too, one of these rare soul, who love truth for its own sake, not for any earthly reward or any spiritual justification or luxury. Just now I am debating what volumes I may take away with me, considering them less with regard to their mental quality than to the weight of the paper on which they are printed. I've laid aside Wilhelm Meister because its in two light volumes, & "The Golden Treasury" because it can fit into my hand bag. Webers "Modern Philosophy" I bought to go with me, he turns out to weigh a great deal too much for a mountain climber, so I'm leaving him behind. I'll take either Spinoza or the Bible according to the space, and that will make up my summer reading unless there happens to be a set of Anthony Trollope at Borca as there was at [Schmadribach?].[1] Berta & Cary & I spent last afternoon discussing our various hotels and our panama hats. I wish we could walk in upon you today while you are gathered together on your cottage porch, where you are doubtless perusing the Constitution of the United States. Thank your fate that you are beyond firecrackers so you aren't tempted to the immoral wish that Columbia was still enslaved and the Bunker Hill monument in the quarry. I am told by the Times-Despatch that $10,000,000 worth of fireworks has been sold to celebrate the Day. If this isn't liberty, pray, what do you want?

x x x x I am so glad, so heartily glad, that dear Coralie is with you—and by you I mean the three of you, of course. My heart has been so sore for her, but it seems to me if there was ever a sorrow that was lovely and sacred it must be hers. She was so unfailing and so unselfish.

It must be very beautiful in the Warm Springs valley today, & until I arrive at Borca, & stand face to face with the Dolomites, I shall think of you with envy. How does the book come on?[2] My ten rough chapters have just gone to the bank, & I am trying to get the weight off my flattened wits. Yours will come out before we return, will it not? I shall demand it when it when I leave Boston of the first bookstore. And by then *you* will be thinking of Egypt. I only wish I were thinking of Bermuda for next winter—however, if I had to choose between Bermuda and the power of working, I suppose, in spite of my complaints, I'd pray for the latter. When all is written Voltaire said the last word for the philosophy of contentment when he remarked, "Let us cultivate our garden."[3] That's my motto. Happy or unhappy, what does it matter when one can cultivate ones garden?

Dear love to you one and all, and will you tell Coralie that I shall think of her whenever I see anything beautiful. Please write to me, my Molly, to the steamer, König Albert, July 18th Hoboken, you know.

Ever your | E.G.

ALS ViU MJ Box 2
Address: Miss Mary Johnston, | The Warm Springs, | Bath County, | Virginia
Postmarks: Richmond Jul 4 1908; Hot Springs Jul 5 1908

1. Near the Jungfrau and Mürren in Switzerland, where EG traveled in 1905 (see *WW* 165).
2. *Lewis Rand* (Boston: Houghton Mifflin, 1908). EG's "rough chapters" in the next sentence are from *The Romance of a Plain Man;* EG routinely deposited drafts of her work in progress in a bank vault.
3. From Voltaire's *Candide.*

To Rebe Glasgow Tutwiler

Hotel Subasio | Assisi [Italy] | 5th of August [1908]

My darling Rebe.

I wanted to send you a line from Assisi, but I am so tired I can hardly hold a pen in my hand & in an hour we start back to Perugia. We drove down yesterday morning just as you & I did, stopping at the Etruscan town & Portmoular[1] Perugia is more beautiful than I remembered it, & the Porta Agusta still the most impressive thing there. But Assisi! We saw so little of it & the town itself is a perfect poem—a dream of colours, all shot with pearly lights & warm cream & brown tones against a sky as blue as Egypt's. The friar, by the way, who showed us over Portmoular was the one you & I had seen at Saint Damien's[2]—do you remember the rather affected one who ran Sabatur? In the afternoon we drove to Saint Damien's—as interesting & more beautiful than I remembered it. Then a brother Minor, with an exquisite head & face like a young Giotto Saint Francis took us over, & as he spoke only Italian we had as interpreter a Florentine friar—Padre Jeroni, who has a monastery at San Mineat[3] He was delightful. We gave him our cards & are to see him in Florence in September.

As for the church[4] it is, as I thought three years ago, the gem of Italy. Nothing more beautiful can be imagined—all soft opalescent lights inside & the outside makes one catch one's breath when one sees it against the blue sky. The Giottos are beyond words, & also the Madonna of [blank space] surrounded by saints. It seems like a dream that you & I have had together. That will never be again, but someday you & Cabell must come, & you will enjoy that more—if you can stand the Hotel. Pillows of wood, coffee of sweet potatoes, eggs seasoned with le trèfle incarnat[5] Berta counted 43 flea bites on her yesterday. In Naples the mosquitoes were dreadful, but not since. Cary, by the way, in her excitement over Portmoular, wrote herself "Cary Glasgow", as she now stands. She and Berta enjoy each other & everything together. Berta thinks her thoughts & waits on her assiduously. As for me, I, of course, would have a better time if I had a fourth person, who was congenial, to pair off with me. I see everything by myself, but the astrologer told me that to be always alone was inevitable[6] fate of one with my horoscope. Did I tell you about her and what she said? Berta says there are 143 flea bites now—that was several days ago.

In an hour we return to Perugia—tomorrow to Florence. It will be lovely to see Florence again, but I am a wreck. Cary perfectly indefatigable— She & Berta starting now at 2 P.M. for Santa Clara's fount[7] I hope to rest at Bosca, but my back is almost broken. However it is the experience of a lifetime. Nothing in Italy compares with it. But oh! for a cup of tea! We really got fairly good tea at Bergani's in Perugia. It is much better than the Padua. This place is unspeakable, but superbly situated—exactly like the food at Leone's.

I hope you are well & settled. Oh, such figs! In Naples we got a delightful luncheon at Gampeyli's restaurant & had luscious purple figs packed in ice. We drank Cevvieto[8] wine for dinner every night. The Table d'hote at Bergani's is excellent.

With love always. | ELLEN

TC of ALS FU
Address: Mrs. Cabell Tutwiler, Pocono Inn, Mt. Pocono, Buck Hill Falls, Monroe Co., Pennsylvania

    1. MKR inserts "(sp?)" after this and a question mark after subsequent occurrences of "Portmoular," MKR's mistranscription. The place is the Porziuncola, which EG in *WW* (175) spells Portiuncula, a small chapel in Assisi restored by St. Francis and the place of his death. The "Etruscan town" may be the nearby Cortona.

    2. MKR inserts a parenthetical question mark here and after "Sabatur," probably a mistranscription for Salvatore, an ancient church in nearby Spoleto. San Damiano is a church in Assisi identified with St. Francis.

3. MKR inserts "(sp?)" here; perhaps the church of San Miniato al Monte in Florence.

4. The basilica of San Francesco, which contains Giotto's frescoes of the life of St. Francis. MKR's blank space two sentences later may refer to a fresco by Cimabue of the Madonna and saints.

5. Crimson clover, sometimes used as an herb. MKR transcribes this phrase as "Le trifel Incarnot" and adds a parenthetical question mark.

6. MKR adds "(sic)."

7. MKR adds a parenthetical question mark here and one after "food" near the end of this paragraph. The "fount" is probably at Assisi's church of Santa Chiara (Clara), and Bosca, in the next sentence, is MKR's mistranscription for Borca di Cadore in northeastern Italy (see next letter).

8. Probably MKR's mistranscription for Orvieto, a well-known wine from the nearby town of the same name.

To Elizabeth Patterson

August 13th 1908. | MILAN | PALACE HOTEL DES DOLOMITES | BORCA-CADORE

Dearest Lizbeth,

We have had a beautiful trip so far, and I have wished for you often. These mountains you would adore—they were originally coral reef, geologists say, & when the sunshine strikes on them they flash back tones of coral & rose & mauve that make one catch ones breath from the beauty. Italy was lovely too, & when we left the boat at Naples we went up to Rome, Perugia, Assisi (the gem of Italy) Florence & Venice. In three weeks we expect to go back to Florence & Venice before we sail.

I hope you are having a good summer—you and dear Miss Betty. Will you send me a line to the steamer S. S. Canopic reaching Boston Sept. 28th to say if you can meet us at the Hotel Seville in New York on the 30th of September. My address over here is care Thomas Cook & Son, Piazza San Marco, Venice, Italy. How you would love Venice! Someday we may see it together.

I can't write more—I must lie down, but I wanted you to have this line about New York. There's so much I'd like to tell you.

Love to Miss Betty and yourself—a heartful.

Yours, | ELLEN

I'll send you some more postcards, but if I can't write again, I'll telegraph you as soon as I leave, & will you leave Richmond the night of the 29th or come the morning of the 30th, as you like.

ALS ViU EG 5083 Box 28
Address: Miss Elizabeth Patterson, | "Reveille." Forwarded: East Gloucester | Mass; c/o | Steven's Cottage.
Postmarks: Hotel Dolomites, 14 Aug 08; Richmond, Virginia Aug 27 1908; Gloucester, Mass Aug 28 1908

April 1909 47

To Cary Glasgow McCormack

Dorking, April 28. | 1909

My dearest Cary,

I have thought a great deal about your being in Richmond in all this terrible time.[1] I wish you could get away. Rebe writes she will take Joy at any time.

The air here is glorious & I have grown much stronger, with fine appetites—both of us. Never in my life before, however, have I felt *old*. My face has suddenly developed so many lines & furrows. This English spring is enchanting & the country—just blossoming—looks like fairy land. Yesterday we drove to Box hill—a famous place where box grows wild all over a hill—the only place in England where it does grow wild. On the way we passed George Meredith's home—a simple, small, but pretty house set close to the road in a clump of trees. In a strip of green by the woodside his donkey was grazing, & Lizzie got out & took a snapshot—of the donkey. Every day at twelve he takes a drive in his donkey cart.

The dowager Duchess of Marlborough had a superb place here—such lanes, such trees. "She was a fine, 'andsome girl of fifty-five—Lily, Duchess of Marlborough," remarked our driver. "I can't see why she pegged out."[2]

Later—we have just returned from a three hours drive & eaten a hearty luncheon served in my room. Everything is very expensive in this inn. We pay [?] 50 cts a day for one little handful of fire. In London 18 pence for a very large, bright one. I don't wonder that we are the only guests here.

The drive was beautiful. Such greenness! I went attired in Josephine's coat, my old blue skirt & a dilapidated hat—but I feel like a different creature. When I left London I was very low.

The climate here is wonderfully invigorating, but I grow restless, so we go back on Saturday & on Sunday I shall try to go to Mrs Clifford's.

The afternoon before we left we went to a "tea party" at May Sinclair's, and I wish I could describe it. Lizzie dreamed of funerals all that night. We were nicely dressed—I in my brown satin & I've bought a lovely brown hat at Liberty's, large, with a plume & some soft shaded roses & chiffon strings. Liberty's hats are exquisite. As we stood outside the studio door Lizzie said, "There's not a sound—we've come too early"—& then we entered. In a circle of chairs arranged in the centre of the room there sat about 20 women & two men—all drinking tea & eating bread & butter in a funereal silence. She greeted us in a whisper & placed us with our backs two inches from the stove where we sat with the perspiring rolling from our faces, in a silence as profound as that about us. In the middle of the room a rather handsome, freshly coloured girl sat all alone on a high chair, with a stolid & angry look on her face, drinking tea & eating plum cake as hard as she could—& nobody addressed a word to her from the beginning to the end of the performance. Behind her a very large man entered & stood perfectly still, clenching & unclenching his fists. At the end of 20 minutes an idea siezed him & he darted over, took up a plate of plum cake & handed it about. Everybody looked insulted when he offered it & I tried to look as insulted as the rest. All the time May Sinclair darted about in her hushed, undecided way, serving tea—looking like a frightened mouse & not opening her lips during the entire occasion. One person was introduced to me & one to Lizzie, & then somebody got up & played on the piano. Kate Douglas Wiggin sat down by me & we made a little stir, at which everybody looked alarmed. She is an impossibly conceited person & kept telling me that Mr Killman, her publisher was coming there to see her. A little later, when he came, however, he made straight as an arrow for me & dragged May Sinclair up to introduce him. He never spoke to Mrs Riggs, & was really quite attractive. He even smiled when I told him that if I'd seen him sooner I shouldn't have run away from him— & a smile is an uncommon sight in merrie England. They take their pleasures sadly, yet I suppose they take them just the same. Lizzie has discovered the grave of an old gentleman who did penance when he was over a hundred for having an illegitimate child.

We tell ourselves daily that we can't judge a great nation by a few people we have seen—& we are going back doggedly to try it a little longer. I feel old & sad, & I have not as yet had one moment's satisfaction, but I can't give up yet. Every now & then I remember something so terribly pathetic about poor Frank—& it is so hard to go on just the same. I am trying desperately to keep up an appetite & not break down again in London.

The climate there is simply maddening. I can't walk even a few blocks & to go to a gallery was more than I could do. When I go back, I hope to keep up strength enough to stand meeting people. I was so horribly anxious before— & that was why I declined the authors' dinner. May Sinclair said they were very anxious to have me, but I felt timid about not hearing. Miss Nicholls sent me four introductions that sound very nice—a different class, I think, & I understand now why Americans pursue the fast aristocracy. Even genius doesn't seem to liberate a person from the thrall of class.

I must stop now & sleep. This war in Constantinople[3] has made me uneasy about Mr Poynter. I couldn't help feeling a little sorry for the Sultan.

Please send this letter to Rebe. I haven't been able to write to her.

Love to father & Annie, & my best love to you. Try to keep well,

Your devoted, | E.

I forgot to tell you that the funniest thing about the tea was—it was given to me! I know it would have been very embarrassing to May Sinclair to know that I found it out—but it leaked to me through an old lady in the street who stopped me & said, "You were the guest of honor. I looked at you admiringly all the afternoon & wanted so much to be introduced." And there we sat not speaking to a soul with our backs two inches from a stove. It was one of the most painful occasions of my life. I was so embarrassed that I was positively as awkward the English.

Our rooms in London were lovely & 5 guineas a week—food not good, really, but eatable & very reasonable. A large fire in both rooms—on the first floor, two blocks from Claridges, in an old fashioned house, with beautiful woodwork—panelling & ceiling. The color of our sitting-room is green, & it is a really charming room. We have a butler—Barrows, who devotes most of his time to us. He is very efficient, but we mistrust him & were in terror at leaving all our belongings in his charge. It is raining hard now, & I am afraid to go out as I'm not very well.

I don't know how long I can stand London, but it depends, I think, upon the people. I need some mental distraction horribly—& if I can't find it I'll go distraught. If Julia can meet me in N.Y. I may come back in July & go to Colorado if I have the money. I don't know. My plans are vague, but I can't sit down & think. It is acute agony to write with this pen, ink & paper. I must stop & send this to be posted. We have just had tea—thin bread & butter, very good—& delicious raspberry, which Lizzie eats—not I. Twice a day I indulge eagerly in bread puddings. I've fattened a good deal, but will lose it in a day, I fear. I shall try though to lead a regular life & walk in Hyde Park, two blocks away. Please take care of yourself.

Your devoted E.

ALS ViU EG Box 14

1. Frank Glasgow committed suicide in Richmond on April 7, 1909, just after EG reached England.
2. That is, died.
3. A revolution in Turkey in 1907–1908, led by the Young Turk movement, destroyed the Sultanship of Abdul-Hamid II. The resulting confusion, besides contributing to the general mood of disintegration throughout Europe and the East, allowed Austria to annex Bosnia and Herzegovina.

To Elizabeth Patterson

THE ANTLERS | COLORADO SPRINGS, COLO., | Aug 13 1909

My dearest Dear,

So far our[1] trip has been pleasant, but not exciting. In Denver people sent us hampers of flowers & took us automobiling about every day—all people from the East. Husbands with delicate wives or wives with delicate husbands. Mr Alston was very, very nice to us. He looks ill & very unhappy, & I think, on the whole, it would have been painful to you to see him.

Here we are now at Colorado Springs. Mrs Ellwanger appeared last night & today we have a large luncheon given us by the most important woman (they tell us) in the place. More delicate wives, I presume. As soon as I'm well—in a week—we'll go off to the mountains—but write me here. I miss you every day. Let's go away together again soon. I am still asserting that you are an angel. Julia is fine, but so much older than either you or me—& preaches the doctrine of middle age to me in season & out. She says it makes her middle-aged to look at me because I'm so hopelessly young. Oh, well. I'm still very sad, my Elizabeth. What is the use? And to what end is it all?

Dear love to your mother. Where are you? How is she? Will you go with me when I need you? There is nobody like you.

Devotedly. | Ellen

ALS ViU EG 5083 Box 28
Address: Miss Elizabeth Patterson, | Route 2, | Richmond, Virginia; forwarded: Clifton Springs | N.Y.
Postmarks: Colorado Springs, Colo. Aug 13 1909, 12:30 p.m.; Richmond Aug 16 1909; Clifton Springs 19 Aug 1909 7:30 p.m.; Richmond Aug 1909

1. EG was traveling with Julia Sully.

To Elizabeth Patterson

August | 17th | 1909 | THE ANTLERS | COLORADO SPRINGS, COLO.
Dear Precious,

Your letter came yesterday, & I was so sorry to hear that dear Miss Betty is not well. Clifton, I hope, will set her up again for the winter.[1]

Nobody can take your place. I am missing you all the time, & the further I get from England, the more I realize what beautiful patience and sympathy you showed me every minute. I don't believe anybody else in the world would have been—or could have been—as understanding as you were then. Will you go again with me next year—& we'll see things & go down into Devon—unless we go to Constantinople instead! So keep up your French, please!

I wrote you to Richmond a few days ago, but suppose you will get it. Julia is fine—& *so* much older than you or I. When I get unhappy, however, it frightens her so.

Dearest love to you both.

Always your | Ellen

ALS ViU EG 5083 Box 28
Address: Miss Elizabeth Patterson, | Clifton Springs, | New York
Postmarks: Colorado Springs Aug 17 1909 12:30 p.m.; Clifton Springs Aug 20 1909 8 a.m.

1. EP's mother was in the sanitarium at Clifton Springs, New York.

To Elizabeth Patterson

Care B. C. Day, | Manitou Park, | Woodland Park, P.O. |
Colorado. | Sept *2nd* [1909?]

Dear Angel,

I was so glad to have your letter, but so sorry to hear of Stephie. That disease, however, is sometimes quite curable. People have it & get over it very often, & she is so young. I hope your mother is much better & that will justify Clifton. It must be a terrible place. x x x

Here we are 8000 feet high in the Rockies in an atmosphere that is a mingling of sage & pine & ambrosial sunshine. We simply love it, & mean to stay till the 15th of September unless it closes over our heads. As it is everybody has left now except the people at our table—all exiles except ourselves. Julia enjoys every minute of it, but I have been very, very unhappy at times. My hearing always stands between me & everything. I can't hear, even with my acousticon the general conversation, & this depresses me terribly. Life is over for me, my Lizzie, & the shade of the old woman at Verrey's[1] looms larger every day. *That* is my end.

People have made a great deal over us, & when we go back to Colorado Springs the end of September, we leave a number of acquaintances. But what, after all, does it amount to? Passer le temps[2]—nothing more.

Oh, yes, darling, we must go off again & you must stand by me. Other friends are good & dear in their way, but I wrote Cary a few days ago that no one had ever been to me what you were in England. I love you more & more whenever I look back on it.

How I wish you were here now in this enchanting air. The hotel is very comfortable, though only a mountain lodge in the midst of a prairie, & we pay 20.00 a week a piece. It is just rough enough to be picturesque, & my breakfast is brought every morning by a charming cowboy—in a sombrero. He has a smile as broad as the plains, but as for young Lochinvar, I fear, he has long ago ridden out of the West. With a hug to you both.

Ever Your | Ellen

ALS ViU EG 5083 Box 28
Address: Miss Elizabeth Patterson, | The Sanitarium, | Clifton Springs, | New York
Postmark: Woodland [?], Sep [?]

1. Verrey's is a French restaurant in London; EG apparently refers to an experience shared there by her and Patterson during their trip to England earlier in the year.
2. French for "passing the time" (literally, "to pass the time").

To Cary Glasgow McCormack

Manitou Park, | Woodland Park, P.O. | Colorado. Sept 3rd [1909]
My darling Cary,

It is very hard to write because I have no blotter & the paper is giving out. The place is more attractive than ever, but we have daily fears of its closing. Mr Howe (the multi-millionaire) & his son & retinue leave today. He told me last night he'd gladly stay a month except for guests who were coming. He is one of the saddest people, who likes to sit around & listen to our conversation. His simplicity is very nice, & he has a kind heart & is a gentleman all through. The little boy is a perfect Paul Dombey[1]—as good & gold, with perfect manners, & never surly. When the child grows up he will be the richest man in Chicago, & yesterday he came to me, as I was passing, & ask if I thought he might keep a hickory stick he had found, or if it belonged to somebody? Just now as Julia sat at the table with him, his thin little voice piped out "Miss Sully, don't you think it very interesting about the North Pole?" His father timidly presents us with cocktails, prepared by his valet, every night.

The funniest thing of all I've forgot to tell you. Last Sunday Bob, the stage driver sent me a Denver paper with a full page account of myself, ending "Now that Miss Glasgow has come, the Rocky Mountains will have their *Boswell!*" The Boswell of the Rocky Mountains is the name for me at the table.

It is really interesting out here, because it is so utterly different from anything I've ever seen. Ask me when I get home to describe the deserted village to you. It's too long to write. Yesterday we drove for five hours over the worst roads I ever imagined to find an old gentleman whom Bob informed us is a collector of prints. He'd come to live here because of a blighted romance, they said, when he was very young & had lived in a log cabin on the mountain ever since—entirely alone. He was an Englishman & an Oxford man. We found him at last, buried absolutely alive, a fine looking old man, wearing peasants' clothes, & without a human being within miles & miles. He showed us a box of perfectly worthless pictures, with a dazed look as if he hardly knew we were there. We discovered from pictures that his people were English publishers of the Smith, Elder days, with a house in the Strand—named Akermann. Why he came & hid himself here nobody knows. I must stop—J is waiting.

Devotedly, E

ALS ViU EG Box 14
Address: Mrs George Walter McCormack | 1 West Main Street | Richmond, | Virginia
Postmark: Woodland Park, 3 Sep 1909

1. The sensitive young son in Charles Dickens's *Dombey and Son* (1846).

From Ruth McEnery Stuart

Summit, New Jersey, | Thursday, Dec 8th [19]10

Isn't it too bad, you dear Ellen Glasgow, that I have such luck—again!

I've been down at Atlantic City this week, utterly *hors de combat* from the stress of things in New York and resting formally—but now I'm here for the night with my good friends the Hamilton Mabies whom I wish you knew and that they knew you—and I'm to read here tonight to a club and shall be back "in the old town" tomorrow—D.V. That is, I—or my "remainders" will be there, for truly, tho' I'm putting up a brave bluff, I don't feel in the least equal to the evening's "*chore.*"

I ought to be in bed with a family and flowers and indulgences.

But nevermind. I've had them all and now I have you, for one thing, and the comfortable feeling that there's a real friendship for us—just waiting.

I don't know whether you will have gone your way by now, or not—but, if not, I'll love to see you before your flitting.

I'm going for a few days to a little hotel where I hide for a little turn, occasionally, the St. Albans, 349 West 58th Street, Telephone 787 Columbus. Call me if you are in town, do. And give my love to that choice Mrs. Wilcox whom I hope to see, if she is with you.

I'll go in late in the forenoon, probably.

Ever affectionately | (when I see you and when I don't) | Ruth McEnery Stuart

ALS ViU EG Box 18

To Lila Hardaway Meade Valentine

ONE WEST EIGHTY-FIFTH STREET | November 30th 1911[1]

Dear Lila,

I know it has looked to you as if I were never going to answer your letter, but as the dreary days have gone by, one after one, it has seemed to me a physical impossibility to take up a pen. It has taken me months to get at all settled, I have been really ill since I left Richmond, and all together the simple daily living has taken every bit of strength that was in me. Yet, though I may have seemed unappreciative of your letter, I was, in reality, so pleased to have all the good news of the work and to hear from you directly. I wish I could help you just now with the finances, but, after all, however, one may feel about a cause,[2] one's doctors and one's landlord have to come first in the matter of money, and my expenses have been so very heavy these last few months, that I am beginning already to wonder how long I shall be able to live here. However, all years aren't moving years, I suppose, and after a while I hope things will run evenly.

I should like so much to see you. Aren't you and Ben coming to New York before Christmas? So far I have met, of course, very few people, but most of my friends are ardent suffragists, and I hear a great deal from them about the details of the movement. I was very much interested to hear from Mr Munce of the Men's League in Richmond. Does it mean that they are really working for it, or is it merely nominal?

With a great deal of affection to you both,

As ever yours, | ELLEN GLASGOW

ALS ViHi
Publication: *EGN* 21 (October 1984): 5.

    1. The date is written at the end of the letter following the signature.
    2. Women's suffrage.

Cary Glasgow McCormack. EG: *"She possessed an insight into the future that was almost clairvoyant, that precious and radiant sister of mine." (To Lila Hardaway Meade Valentine, September 17, 1920; photo courtesy of the University of Virginia Library)*

Mary Johnston. EG: *"You looked so much like a little child, and there are moments when one seems almost to see the soul of one's friend shining through the delicate flesh. The people I love best, I love for this spiritual quality." (February 3, 1905; photo courtesy of the University of Virginia Library)*

Rebe Glasgow Tutwiler, ca. 1900. EG: *"Do take care of yourself. You are really all I have, and you are bound up with my childhood and with my memories of Mother, who seems to come nearer to me as I go on." (August 21, 1941; photo courtesy of the University of Virginia Library)*

Photograph (ca. 1905–1910) inscribed by EG to "My dearest Lelia," whose identity is unknown, serves as a reminder of how much we cannot know about EG's life. (Editor's private collection)

Amélie Rives Troubetzkoy and her dog. EG: *"Though we never see each other, I have always the feeling that time has been scarcely more than an illusion between us." (August 23, 1937; photo courtesy of the Virginia Historical Society)*

Anne Virginia Bennett with "The Lambs," Jeremy (left) and Billy (right). EG: *"She has shared my compassion for all inarticulate creation, and even turns that compassion upon me." (WW 216; photo courtesy of the University of Virginia Library)*

One West Main Street, Richmond, Glasgow's home for most of her life. (Photo courtesy of the University of Virginia Library)

Irita Van Doren, ca. 1947. EG: "Beautiful in body, and invincible in spirit, all her defeats in life have been victories." (WW 173; photo courtesy of the Library of Congress)

Radclyffe Hall with Fido, ca. 1939–41. To EG: "*In ones life there is always* the dog." *(September 29, 1929; photo courtesy of the Harry Ransom Humanities Research Center, University of Texas at Austin)*

Marjorie Kinnan Rawlings with Pat at Cross Creek, ca. 1939. (Photo courtesy of the University of Florida Libraries)

Signe Toksvig, ca. early 1940s. EG: "It is a rare pleasure indeed to find a writer or a friend who speaks my own language and who, stranger even than that, has approached life by the road I travelled long ago, when I was very young." (August 14, 1943; photo courtesy of the University of Virginia Library)

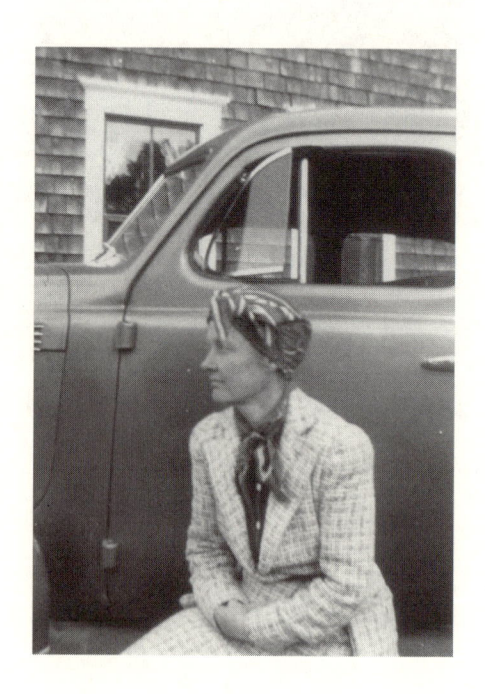

III
1912–1926

[I]f only women would stand firmly together, I believe they could stop—or better still *prevent*—such a horror [as the war].
—To Lady Kentore, January 26, 1915

Relatively few letters exist for the difficult years following Cary's death in 1911, when Glasgow moved to New York City and discovered that it was almost impossible for her to write anywhere but at her family house in Richmond. She carried some of New York back with her when she returned to Richmond in 1915, however, in her heightened confidence in her literary identity and her reinforced ties to the publishing world that gave her her greatest sense of professional belonging. Whether in New York, Richmond, or one of the distant places to which she traveled, Glasgow from about 1912 on carried with her a stronger sense of herself as a writer.

During her trip to England in 1914, Glasgow met some of her (mostly male) literary idols. But the letters Glasgow received following her voyage were as likely to be from the women married to the writers she met (Jessie Conrad and Ada Galsworthy and F. E. Hardy, for example) as from the writers themselves. Her circle of women friends and acquaintances began to expand beyond the borders measured by geographical proximity to Richmond. Glasgow's first extant correspondence with Irita Van Doren, her future literary executor, dates from 1922; she first corresponded with the writer Agnes Repplier in 1924 and with Blanche Knopf, the wife of publisher Alfred Knopf, in 1925.

The mutually respectful relationship between Glasgow and Irita Van Doren began in 1922, when Van Doren was on the advertising staff of the *New York Herald Tribune* and before she assumed her editorship in 1923. Although their friendship was more than merely professional—they shared, among other things, a similar sense of humor, and they visited each another on several occasions—Van Doren advised Glasgow about publishers, engaged her in book reviewing that increased Glasgow's literary profile, and obtained sympathetic reviewers for Glasgow's novels. Later, as the more active of Glasgow's two literary executors, Van Doren helped negotiate the posthumous publication of Glasgow's autobiography, in which Glasgow observes, "I have admired few women so fervently as I have admired Irita," who is "[b]eautiful in body" and "invincible in spirit" (*WW* 273).

Nearer home, too, Glasgow's quotidian relationships with women remained central, even in the time of two important events involving the men in her life: her father's death in 1916 and her engagement to (and subsequent breakup with) Henry Anderson in 1917. Anne Virginia Bennett, Glasgow's secretary and companion; Rebe Glasgow Tutwiler, her younger sister; Carrie Coleman (Duke) and Elizabeth Patterson (Crutchfield), childhood friends who remained significant figures in Glasgow's life; and Mary Johnston and Amélie Rives Troubetzkoy, who, with Glasgow, formed something of a Virginia women writers' circle, all remained steady presences in Glasgow's daily existence. Also during this time Glasgow assumed the presidency of the Richmond Society for the Prevention of Cruelty to Animals (SPCA), a position she took very seriously.

By the end of these years Glasgow's reputation as a major novelist was firm. After *Virginia* in 1913, *Life and Gabriella* (written, unlike any of her other novels, mostly in New York) in 1916; *The Builders* (1919); *One Man in His Time* (1922); and *The Shadowy Third and Other Stories* (1923), her only published collection of stories; *Barren Ground* and *The Romantic Comedians* in 1925 and 1926 received the kind of critical attention that ensured Glasgow's literary reputation for the rest of her life and career. A comment in a letter written to her sister on Christmas Day 1926 suggests that Glasgow was already thinking seriously about, and perhaps writing, the autobiography that critics have assumed Glasgow did not begin until 1934.

To Elizabeth Patterson

ONE WEST EIGHTY-FIFTH STREET [March 29, 1912]

My dearest Dear,

The jonquils arrived in perfect condition, and are now enriching my rooms with their gold. They are beautiful beyond words—it is too dear of you to send them.

It seems a thousand years since I saw you. I am planning to spend a few days in Richmond about the 5th of May, but when the time comes, I may not be able to make up my mind to go back. I dread seeing the place again.

How are you, my dear one? Do send me a line now and then. I feel as if I should never see you again.

Devotedly ever | your Ellen

ALS ViU EG 5083 Box 28
Address: Miss Elizabeth Patterson, | (Reveille) Route 2, | Richmond, Virginia; forwarded: Madison | Florida; care | Mrs [N?]. H. Dial
Postmarks: Richmond Mar 29 4 P.M.; Richmond Va Apr 2 1912 12 m; Madison Apr 4

To Lila Hardaway Meade Valentine

ONE WEST EIGHTY-FIFTH STREET | July 1st 1912[1]

Dear Lila,

The day after your letter came I began to answer it. Then something interrputed, and—well, all these weeks have passed and still I have not written.

I wish very much that I could send you a larger cheque. Thirty dollars seem so little—but just now I really cannot do any better. I have fallen wofully behind in my work; my expenses appear to grow heavier every day, and there are innumerable calls on me that I simply cannot disregard. To my prime interest the S.P.C.A. I have been able to give nothing of late x x x and now this endeth the first complaint—. It was ever so good to see you—you and dear Ben, who are both very dear to me. I wish I could promise definitely to go to Norfolk. If I can, I'll certainly do so, but it all depends on how I get through the summer. You and Mary are wonders. I can look on and admire, but I can't in the least hope to emulate you. I suppose a part of it is that you both have your roots still clinging to life, and I haven't. I've been plucked up, root and branch, and so I really haven't much heart in anything—not even in Woman's Suffrage. I used to have once, but I haven't now.

With much love to you both.

As ever yours, | ELLEN

ALS ViHi
Publication: *EGN* 21 (October 1984): 5.

1. The date is written at the end of the letter, following the signature.

To Elizabeth Patterson

ONE WEST EIGHTY-FIFTH STREET [July 3, 1912]

My darling Lizzie:

This is just a line to tell you that Miss Bennett is going back to nursing next week, and to ask you to tell anybody you know who may want a nurse that she is the best one who ever lived. Berta Wellford will always know her address.

What are you doing, sweetest? And how is life treating you? I was so sorry not to see you again in Richmond.

With much love to your mother.

Ever and ever your devoted | Ellen

TC of ALS FU
Address: Miss Elizabeth Patterson, Route 2, Richmond, Virginia
Postmark: 3 July 1912.

To Julia Sully

Sunday | ONE WEST EIGHTY-FIFTH STREET [November 23, 1913?]
Dearest Dear,

I have hardly had a moment's breathing space, or I should have written you. I have got really quite thin again, & feel very nervous. It was nice to have your letters, and to hear that you are better. I have planned for you to come to me as soon as Berta leaves in February.

Will you please tell Lizzie—I don't know her address—that I expect her the very first of December. Ask her just to write me or wire me the train she will come on. I don't suppose she will wait for me to write to her, do you? At any rate, if she is waiting for that, show her this letter.

I have seen Mr Winter. He seemed to know I was back, & came without my telephoning him. Looks well & is very cheerful.

Devotedly, E.G.

ALS ViU EG Box 28

To Rebe Glasgow Tutwiler

Hotel Curzon | Curzon Street, | Mayfair, | London. W. [May 31, 1914]
My dearest Rebe.

I was so glad to get your letters, but we've lived in such a rush that I haven't had time to answer them. We have met crowds of people, mostly fashionable ones—very few of them literary, but most of them seem to have read my books. Here is a forget me-not—from Stoke-Poges churchyard, put beside the tomb of Grey.[1] It is a lovely place, very quaint & picturesque. We lunched at Windsor (where everything is closed because of the militants),[2] & went over to Stoke Poges by bus. It was a good way to spend that Sunday.

Margaret has been very sweet to us, & has invited a number of people to meet us at luncheon. On Tuesday she asks us to luncheon again, & on Wednesday we go there in the afternoon to hear John Powell play. We have been out so much I can't begin to remember where, but the thing I am looking forward to most is a dinner John Galsworthy is giving me—he and his wife. We have been to one awfully stupid luncheon at the Pages—all Americans & all uninteresting ones—& we dine there again on Tuesday. Yesterday we saw Shaw's Pygmalion—perfectly delightful—

I have bought at lovely dress & cape of brown crepe from Jays,[3] whose things are ravishing. It is the prettiest gown I ever had. We are trying to change our passage to the Imperator, sailing June 18th. I'd rather not have to stint & stay a little shorter time.

Dearest love. | E.G.[4]

TC of ALS FU
Address: Mrs. Tutwiler, 430 West Chestnut Ave, Phila., Pa.

    1. The poet Thomas Gray (1716–1771), whose "Elegy Written in a Country Churchyard" (1751) is said to be set at Stoke-Poges.
    2. MKR inserts a parenthetical question mark here. The "militants" are women's suffrage protesters. At a demonstration by the Women's Political and Social Union (WSPU) on 21 May 1914, during which Emmeline Pankhurst was arrested, two hundred women attempted to break through a cordon of fifteen hundred police officers at Buckingham Palace (see Tickner 207). Mrs. Pankhurst had been released on May 29, 1914, two days before EG's letter.
    3. MKR's transcription reads, "Jacys (sp?)." The mistaken "at" earlier in the sentence is MKR's.
    4. MKR's transcription reads, "E.B. [x'd out] E.G. (sic)."

To Rebe Glasgow Tutwiler

King's Arms Hotel, | Dorchester. | June 6th 1914

Dearest Rebe,

Here we are in Hardy's[1] country, & we are going to drive over to see him at four o'clock.

Then we drive across Egdon Heath to Markham, where we spend the night, going tomorrow to Salisbury & Canterbury & then back to London. We are having a beautiful time, but it takes so much money. The 2600. I allowed myself is almost gone in one month, & for this reason we are sailing home on the 18th on the Imperator. On Friday Arnold Bennett has asked me to tea—on Thursday Galsworthy gives me a dinner. Next Sunday Joseph Conrad has asked us to luncheon at his country home & we have just been invited to meet Henry James. Every minute of our time is filled before we sail, & we've had to decline so many outside invitations. Tomorrow Lady Hadfield gives me a luncheon—she was Miss Wickersham, an American.

Margaret has been very sweet—sweeter than I ever knew her to be. You must come over when I get to New York. I got Cabell an Irish tweed coat, very warm—of brown. For myself two gowns from Jays—one a spring gown—one a winter suit. Their things are ravishing.

Devotedly | E.G.

I like W. B. Maynell[2] so much. He sent me an inscribed copy of the Guarded Flame.

ALS ViU EG Box 14

    1. Thomas Hardy.

2. EG misspells Meynell, and MKR mistranscribes it as Maxwell. The inscription in EG's copy of Meynell's *The Guarded Flame* reads: "To Miss Ellen Glasgow in a slight token of homage from her brother-in-letters W. B. Meynell June 1914" (*CLEG* 17.269 [listed erroneously under "Maxwell"]; see also 17.259).

To Mary Johnston

November 1st 1914. | ONE WEST MAIN STREET | RICHMOND, VIRGINIA

Dear Molly,

I've just finished "The Witch",[1] and it is very fine, I think. You have a wonderful power of re-creating a period, and I feel the Elizabethan Age as vividly as if I were dreaming about it. It is a book of great beauty and nobility of thought.

It seems years since I saw you. Are you well? Are you happy? Are you working again so soon? I know the country is lovely in this weather.[2]

About the 26th of this month I expect to go back to New York. I am somewhat over half through a book,[3] but the flesh and particularly the hands grow weary.

With love to the three of you,

As ever yours, | ELLEN GLASGOW

I like Joan thoroughly. She is the finest of your women characters, I think, and I see her always against the background of the forest.

ALS ViU MJ Box 2

1. *The Witch* by MJ (Boston: Houghton Mifflin, 1914). Joan, mentioned in EG's postscript, is a character in the novel.
2. That is, at MJ's home, Three Hills.
3. *Life and Gabriella*.

To Lady Kentore

January 26th 1915. | ONE WEST EIGHTY-FIFTH STREET | New Year

Dear Lady Kentore,

How lovely of you to remember me and to send me the charming card at new year. The verses brought a glow to my heart because I feel that you really meant them for *me*.

Ever since I got your letter last summer, I have wanted to write to you, but I have been working very hard, and so many, many things came between me and my letters. It was a great disappointment to leave London without seeing you again "last year!" I said to myself, and I am still saying just as eagerly "next year!"

This terrible war has seemed to bring us closer than ever to England. Though our government is neutral, there is no question whatever about the feeling of our people, and many of us wish with all our hearts that some protest had been made against the invasion of Belgium. There are a great many Germans over here, and they are so very noisy that it is almost impossible for the American voice to be heard above the uproar, but noise, after all, is not an argument, and will convince only fools!

The sober minded among us feel that England is fighting our battle as well as her own, and that our future hangs on her victory. We are confident—almost too confident, I fear, that you will triumph. But the end is far off, and the waiting is almost as painful for us as for you. To sacrifice the noblest to feed cannon, and to leave the infirm and the maimed to father the race seems all horribly wrong, doesn't it? And if only women would stand firmly together, I believe they could stop—or better still *prevent*—such a horror. Well, peace or war, England has my heart, & I hope soon to be in London again.

Very sincerely yours, | ELLEN GLASGOW

And not a word have I written about the woman question. Your letter was full of interest.

ALS ViU EG Box 28

To Katharine Baird Hopper

Richmond, Virginia, | May 3rd | 1915

My dear Miss Hopper,

No, I have never read a book on negro sorcery. My knowledge of the negro comes from life, not from books, and when I start to write of negro characters then I simply shut my eyes and dream myself back into my childhood. I heard their innumerable tales of conjuring from my old colored mammy and other negroes—and only a year or two ago one of our servants, a young colored girl, came to me with a story of having been "conjured by de cook" of a neighbor.

Thank you very much for your letter and for your appreciation of my books.

Sincerely yours | ELLEN GLASGOW

ALS MdBG
Address: Mrs. Katharine Baird Hopper | 3618 Duvall Avenue | Baltimore, Maryland
Postmark: Richmond, Va. May 5 1915

July 1915

To Rebe Glasgow Tutwiler

San Francisco, California | Fairmont Hotel | July 27th 1915

My darling Rebe.

We are having a beautiful trip, and California is a land of perfect enchantment.[1] I have hardly a minute in which to write because there is so much to do and people are so nice to us. My reception at the Virginia Building was so delightful. The Commissioner appointed me officially assistant hostess there during my stay, & gave me a pass to the Fair grounds. Miss Heth[2] is very sweet. We are going there this afternoon to a reception given by a Mrs. Damon Mansfield. The invitation reads, "The California Branch of the Society of Americans of Royal Descent request etc." Did you ever hear of anything so [blank space] in your life?

Carrie says she wrote you last night all about our time here, so I'll send you a note instead of the letter I intended. She told you about the trip to Mount Tamalpais, and the play of a Mid Summer Night's Dream in the [blank space]. It was perfectly lovely, & you never saw anything so beautiful as the redwood trees. But Carrie wrote you about it, and also about the day we spent at Senator Phelan's place[3] last Sunday. The flowers in his garden were wonderful—hollyhocks almost up to the second story window, & daisies so big that they seem like caricatures. I'll write to you again in a day or two when there is something to tell that Carrie hasn't said. She is lunching at the Exposition now with a man she met at one great[4] dinner—quite a case. When I saw her shoes adorning her feet with pale grey stockings, I told her the symptoms were serious. I declined the luncheon so Carrie went off gayly alone.

I'd love to live out here—for the air & the flowers. One can have such an adorable garden. I wish you were here. What of your trip to xxxxxxxx Have you decided when you go?

Maine[5] [blank space] I have been beset by photographers & reporters, but eluded all except one, who rose up in the lobby as I came out from lunch, & with whom we spent eleven hours the next day, leaving the hotel at 2 o'clock & returning at one. He took us up Tamalpais, & it was a beautiful excursion.

I hope you are well. Love to Cabell & dearest love to you.

Your devoted | Ellen

TC of ALS FU
Address: Mrs. C. C. Tutwiler, 430 West Chestnut Avenue, Chestnut Hill, Philadelphia, Pennsylvania

1. EG and Carrie Coleman attended the 1915 world's fair—the Panama-Pacific International Exposition—in San Francisco. Situated on what is now known as the Marina district (with Mount Tamalpais and the Presidio overlooking the fairgrounds), the fair, as its offi-

cial name indicates, commemorated the completion of the Panama Canal and the 400th anniversary of Balboa's "discovery" of the Pacific Ocean. Every state had a building; Virginia's, where EG was honored, was a replica of George Washington's home at Mt. Vernon.

2. MKR inserts parenthetical question marks after "Heth" and "Mansfield."

3. Villa Montalvo, built in 1912, in Saratoga, California.

4. MKR inserts a parenthetical question mark here. In the following paragraph, the row of exes is MKR's. Underneath them can be seen "Warm? (?)"; EG's original letter probably said "Warm Springs" or, more simply, "the Warm," a common shorthand name for Warm Springs.

5. Presumably this refers to the Maine building. MKR places the word flush left.

To Elizabeth Patterson

Sunday. [December 27, 1915]

My precious Lizzie:

Nobody on earth but your dear self would have thought of sending such an enchanting Christmas surprise. The delectable basket took me straight back to some of those happy days of my childhood & yours. I cannot tell you how I appreciate your sweet thoughtfulness & love. It made the sad day a little less sad for me.

I am coming early to the party; I shall stay late, and I shall try very hard to look festive. On the fourth of January, I am going away. Will you send me sometime this week the names of all those people I met at your house last evening? A happy year!

Devotedly ever, | Ellen

ALS ViU EG Box 28
Address: Mrs. E. M. Crutchfield, | 1632 Monument Avenue, | Richmond, Virginia
Postmark: Richmond Va, Dec 27 1915, 3 P.M.

To Rebe Glasgow Tutwiler

Sunday [December 27, 1915]

My darling Rebe.

The chemises are the loveliest things I ever saw. It was so sweet of you to make them, but I feel that you ought not to have gone to so much trouble and taken so many fine stitches. I am ever so glad to have the charming picture of Cabell—it is very attractive. I showed it to Margaret & she thought it charming, & his hair perfectly beautiful—

Arthur spent the morning with me on Christmas Day & was nicer than I've almost ever seen him, but almost as depressed as I am—Carrie & I expect to start off on the 4th of January. We shall be only a few days in New York (D.V.) at the Hotel Seymour, 50 W. 45th Street.

I hope you had a happy Christmas—
Devotedly Ellen

TC of ALS FU
Address: Mrs. C. C. Tutwiler, 430 W. Chestnut Ave., Chestnut Hill, Philadelphia, Pa.
Postmark: Richmond, Va. Dec. 27 1915

To Rebe Glasgow Tutwiler

ONE WEST MAIN STREET | RICHMOND, VIRGINIA | Saturday
[November 4, 1916]

My darling Rebe,

I was so distressed to hear that you are worried again. I know just exactly how you feel about it, and the kind of panic that makes your heart stand still, but, my darling, I am sure that a thing like that doesn't mean anything unless it goes on for years. Annie has that sort of trouble every now & then, & always in the autumn. I believe you tax yourself too much when you are not well & it invariably makes you feel it next time. Try to be careful. I am so glad you are going to Atlantic City. Do wear your colored clothes now. I think the white furs will be so pretty with the black velvet hat. I hope you you will get some pleasure out of life this winter. Nobody deserves it more than you, for I think you are one of the noblest characters I have ever known, & life ought certainly to give you a little satisfaction at least— Then you are looking so well & lovely now. I thought you were as pretty as you could be when you were in New York with me, & I want you to dress becomingly & go about more. When the house is straightened out[1]—if it ever is—couldn't you leave Cabell with Minnie & come down for a week, & let me give you a dinner?

The confusion has almost put me out of my mind, & it seems to go on forever. I am sitting in the midst of bedlam trying to write this letter. The worst part is that I haven't a particle of interest in the house, & don't care a hang what it is like. There hasn't been a minute this last month when I didn't wish I were dead. Goodbye, my darling. Take care of yourself.

Ellen

TC of ALS FU
Address: Mrs. C. C. Tutwiler, 430 W. Chestnut Drive, Chestnut Hill, Philadelphia, Pa.
Postmark: Richmond Nov. 4 1916

1. EG's house was being remodeled.

To Lila Hardaway Meade Valentine

ONE WEST MAIN STREET | RICHMOND, VIRGINIA |
September the seventeenth, | 1920[1]

Dear Lila,

This autumn is so full of memories of Cary and you and Ben and the beginning ten years ago—was it *really* ten years ago?—of the splendid work that you have at last brought to victory[2]—this autumn is so crowded with these old associations that I must tell you once again how fine and wonderful I think you have been through it all from the very beginning. It took a long sentence to say this, but it isn't a word too long to hold all my meaning.

Do you remember that day in the first *hope* even of the League when Cary and I came to ask you to start such a movement in Virginia? We were the first, I know, to suggest it to you, and we spoke of it because Cary had said, "There is only one woman in Richmond who has all the qualities needed to carry the League to success, and that woman is Lila Valentine". She possessed an insight into the future that was almost clairvoyant, that precious and radiant sister of mine.

Well, on this beautiful autumn day, so like those days, I feel that I wish to remind you of this and to tell you also that in all the years since then I have watched your faultless leadership with admiration and sympathy—and a deep affection for the friend who was even more the friend of my beloved sister. I have grown weary at times of the fight, but never of the fearless and gracious spirit you shed over it.

Always sincerely yours, | ELLEN GLASGOW

ALS ViHi
Publication: *EGN* 21 (October 1984): 5.

1. The date is written at the end of the letter, following the signature.
2. The Equal Suffrage League of Virginia (initially known as the Virginia League for Woman Suffrage) was founded officially in November 1909, with Valentine as president and EG and MJ as vice presidents. The Nineteenth Amendment granting suffrage to women was ratified on August 26, 1920.

To Irita Van Doren

February 26th 1922 | ONE WEST MAIN STREET | RICHMOND, VIRGINIA
Dear Mrs Van Doren,

It was a great disappointment not to see you and Mr Van Doren again before leaving New York. I had looked forward to another delightful talk with you both, but after the bad weather came, I was ill for about ten days and went out very little except to the doctor's. The next time I am in New York, I hope I shall be more fortunate—and it may be then that I shall see the house and garden below Washington Square.

Meanwhile, if you should come South, won't you stop by Richmond on the way, and give me the pleasure of having you in my home and showing you the Virginia that is real?

With very kind regards to you both

I am | Sincerely your new friend, | ELLEN GLASGOW

ALS DLC

To Rebe Glasgow Tutwiler

March 20th 1923

My darling Rebe,

I have just had your letter. I suppose I could come the last week in April. I won't have any money, but the trust fund comes May the 1st.

Get seats for two matinees. I would rather see "The Lower Depths", and "The Cherry Orchard" or the Three Sisters—" I don't care about Tsar Fyodor".[1] Any of the others I'd prefer. Try to get seats not too far away for I am getting near sighted. If you can get the seats for two or three matinees. Berta did not see Chekhov, but she said "The Lower Depths" was the finest. Hugh Walpole told me a piece of acting in "The Three Sisters" was the finest thing he'd ever seen on the stage. I have the Chekhov books & I'll get "The Lower Depths"

If possible I'd like to come on April 23rd & go to New York for a day to see Dr Thompson & get glasses.

I am sending this in a hurry. Let me hear what you do.

Devotedly | E

TC of ALS FU
Address: Mrs. C. C. Tutwiler, 9000 Crefeld, Phila., Pa.

1. Plays by Maxim Gorky, Anton Chekhov, and Aleksei Tolstoy, respectively. The punctuation here and in this paragraph's final sentence is MKR's.

From Agnes Repplier

MISS AGNES REPPLIER | 920 CLINTON STREET | PHILADELPHIA, PA. | March 30th 1924[1]

Dear Miss Glasgow,

You *did* give me a charming time in Richmond. I was sorry to say goodbye to you, and to feel that you were slipping out of my life for an indefinite time.

But if you have a sister in my part of the world,[2] you must sometimes visit her. And when you visit her, you will surely spare at least a few hours to lunch with me. Perhaps this spring, perhaps next autumn? No later than that, I trust.

Do you plan to have your book[3] out by Christmas? I'll send you mine if I can lay hands on it before I sail. I could not bear to have you buy another another of my books, after seeing the row of them upon which you have already wasted your substance.

Remember me kindly to Miss Bennett; and please bear me in your mind, or, better still, in your heart, until we meet again.

Faithfully yours, | Agnes Repplier

ALS ViU EG Box 17

1. The date is written at the end of the letter, following the signature.
2. RGT, who lived in Philadelphia.
3. EG's "book," *BG,* would not be published until 1925. Although Repplier's 1924 novel, *Under Dispute* (referred to in the next sentence), is not listed among the books in Glasgow's library, Glasgow thanks Repplier for sending it to her (see next letter). The other five books by Repplier that Glasgow owned—*Books and Men* (1916), *Compromises* (1904), *Counter-currents* (1919), *The Fireside Sphinx* (1901), and *A Happy Half-century and Other Essays* (1908)—were signed by Repplier during this visit to Richmond (*CLEG* 17.273).

To Agnes Repplier

September 5th | 1924 | ONE WEST MAIN STREET | RICHMOND, VIRGINIA

Dear Miss Repplier,

I wonder if your summer abroad is over, and if my letter may reach you in Philadelphia? It was very good of you to send me "Under Dispute," and it has given me the delight that I find in all that you have written. The sparkling freshness of your style is as enchanting as ever, and your wit and wisdom are apparently inexhaustible.

I hope you had a pleasant summer and that we may see each other in the autumn.

Sincerely yours | Ellen Glasgow

ALS PU-Sp
Address: Miss Agnes Repplier, | 920 Clinton Street, | Philadelphia, | Pennsylvania
Postmark: Richmond Sep 6 1924, 2:30 PM

To Irita Van Doren

September 15th, 1924 | ONE WEST MAIN STREET | RICHMOND, VIRGINIA
Dear Mrs Van Doren:

It is very pleasant to have word from you, and to know that you are to edit, with Mr Sherman, the new Literary Supplement.

No, I'm afraid I can't review Mrs Peterkin's stories.[1] A Northern critic, who has not been brought up with negroes, will be able to do it with so much more authority—at least in print. To tell the truth I read several of these stories in The Reviewer, and the negroes seemed to me to belong to a world I'd never seen. This, however, will not stand in the way of the book's success. I am sure that most Northern readers will feel perfectly at home in this world of dubious colour.

I am so glad that Mr Van Doren is to lecture in Richmond next winter.[2] His was the only name that I selected; and I hope that you will come with him, and that you will both stay with me.

I have been hard at work for two years on a novel which I feel that you will like.[3] By the spring, I hope. I can get it out; but I am not sure. It has been a long piece of work, and it is not finished yet. As soon as the last word is written I shall start straight for New York, and I am looking forward to the pleasure of seeing you both.

Sincerely yours, | ELLEN GLASGOW

Will you tell Mr Van Doren that this new book of mine is the kind of book he told me I ought to write (it has, in fact, been in my mind for the last ten years) and I hope he will review it somewhere.

TLS DLC

    1. *Green Thursday: Stories* (New York: Knopf, 1924).

    2. Carl Van Doren lectured in Richmond on March 30, 1925, the year in which he published a book on James Branch Cabell.

    3. *BG*.

From Irita Van Doren

BOOKS | THE NEW YORK HERALD TRIBUNE |
225 WEST 40TH STREET, NEW YORK | Tuesday—March 10, 1925[1]
Dear Miss Glasgow,

A letter which I dictated last week, and cast aside as being in a number of respects unsatisfactory must have been sent to you by some too kind person in the office, though, as I remember, I had not even signed it. Please forgive the results.

I'm so sorry you are not well and wonder if we should burden you with a visit just now. At least can't we arrive at some later and more convenient time? I haven't looked up train schedules yet, but surely you needn't have us on your hands all day Saturday. I'll see what can be done about it.

The prospect of seeing you and of meeting various people in Richmond whom I've long wanted to know is delightful. It is most kind of you all to take so much trouble.

I am writing today to Miss Sully from whom I had a note about the date for Carl's lecture and about the Sabbath Glee Club.[2]

Mr. Longwell was in Saturday and we talked over all his publicity plans for "Barren Ground." They seem excellent and most comprehensive. I didn't quite like the tone of some parts of the blurbs for the jacket. He agreed with my suggestions and promised to make the changes of which we spoke. The advertising copy he is preparing this next week and promises to let me see it before it goes out. The reviewing schedule is excellent:

Mr. Cabell	The Nation
Carl Van Doren	The New Republic
Stuart Sherman	"Books"
Frances Newman	Saturday Review
Hugh Walpole	Literary Review
Hergesheimer	Sun

The reviews will be prompt and the effect ought to be good. I advised Mr. Longwell to go out to Chicago, a tier list city in the book business, and see Krock and Fanny Butcher, Harry Hansen and Llewellyn Jones and get them personally interested in the book.[3] He will probably go and stop by Indianapolis on the way back.

If Emily Clark could get a review in the Philadelphia Ledger it would be well. Mencken will probably cover the Baltimore Sun as well as the Mercury.

But I'm probably only repeating news you've already had from Doubleday's. They are anxious to have you come up the first part of April for a few select luncheons and dinners. How do you feel about it?

I'm looking forward most eagerly to our visit.

Cordially | Irita Van Doren

ALS ViU EG Box 19
Address: Miss Ellen Glasgow | One West Main Street | Richmond | Virginia
Postmark: New York, N.Y., Mar 10, 1925, 6 P.M.

    1. The date is written at the end of the letter, following the signature.

    2. Richmond's Negro Sabbath Glee Club occasionally performed during functions at EG's home.

    3. The journalist Arthur Krock did not work in Chicago, so IVD may mean that Longwell will visit Krock on the way to Chicago.

To Irita Van Doren

March 11th 1925 | ONE WEST MAIN STREET | RICHMOND, VIRGINIA
I am so grateful to you for looking over the adver*tisements*
Dear Mrs Van Doren:

Oh, please come on that early train Saturday, the 28th! It is much the best train, and I am making some plans for Saturday. I shall be quite all right, I hope, by then—only I was explaining why I couldn't be at the station. But your visit will do me good and I am looking forward to it with the greatest pleasure. Let me know if you can possibly stay over Monday. One day I want to take you down to Westover on the James,[1] and that fills a whole morning or afternoon. If you can stay until Tuesday morning or even until Monday night, we can plan something for Monday morning and leave the whole afternoon free for Dr Van Doren's lecture. When I hear positively how long you can stay, I will make all arrangements, and your time will not hang on your hands

You are wonderfully helpful about my book. I am naturally delighted that Dr Van Doren will review it for the Nation and it is the best possible news that Dr Sherman will himself review it in *Books*. I read the splendid review of Arrowsmith[2] (one of the very finest I ever read) and thought, "If he would only do mine!" Thank you a thousand times.

Yours ever | Ellen Glasgow

ALS DLC

    1. Home on the James River of the colonial Virginian William Byrd (1674–1744).
    2. Novel (1925) by Sinclair Lewis.

From Louise Collier Willcox

516 Warren Crescent | Norfolk, V^a | April 12. 1925.
Dearest Ellen:—

Now you have done what I have looked for ever since The Descendent—written a great, flawless novel. I can't find a criticism to make. I've just finished it with a sort of breathless sensation of having had a great experience. The barren countryside lives & breathes & becomes a personality—as land only does in one other book I know—Hardy's 'Return of the Native'. All the characters live & breathe and are closer & nearer to you than the people you know best—the indomitable Dorinda, Ma with her dreams of Africa, Joshua, the inarticulate Nathan, the good & great, thwarted by nature from manifesting his spirit, John Abner, & Jason,[1]—so like so many of us—overcome by life. Apart from the fundamental conception & the throbbing life in the book, it is a masterpiece of beautiful writing,—writing that begins well & works up to a wonderful climax of serenity & nobility. It is a wonderful achievement & will live as long as there is such a thing as English literature or interest in human development. I did not know it was published until Mary Reid drove me down town yesterday & left me in a book-shop while she went to market. What a trememdous amount of life you have put into it. Well,—you've made a great masterpiece. It makes other modern novels—& I've read dozens of them as I've lain here this winter—seem flimsy & cheap. How much is left of you, I wonder, now it is done. So much vitality has passed into it, I wonder if you have any left? Can't you come down for awhile? And could you be content with a quiet visit? Just golf and quiet bridge at night? I couldn't go to or give any parties—even if I would. But I go downstairs once a day now, & sometimes twice & I'm much better off than I was. Young Westmore is helping us on a bit now & Christine is off our hands financially. She has signed a five year contract as a prima donna in Italy & can only be lent to this country on a % basis during that time. This month she is guest prima donna at the Opera House in Venice. Westmore climbs steadily: he is a director of the Seaboard Air Line R. R., then Florida Northern & Western R.R., of the Dodge Motor Co, the Goodyear Tire & Rubber Co. & a member of its controlling executive committee, Director of the N.Y. Public Utilities, Light & Heat, the Land Co. of Florida, Equitable Office Building Corporation, Farmer's Manufacturing Co. Detroit Metropolitan Corporation, Detroit Properties Corporation, Newport Land Co. & heaven knows what else & has just had his thirtieth birthday! He will be a millionaire I suppose in time—but I shant be there to see. The babies I brought into the world are out now more or less dominating life,— & West & I are here growing old & feeble but with a certain amount of peace.

I am going to send your book to poor, old Mr. Paradise. It will mean so much to him just to feel he once knew the person who could do it. I feel a little breathless myself at the thought that I know you—excited as if I had met & had a talk with Shakespeare.

Now, I suppose your ambitions are satisfied. I wonder about your reviews. I have not seen any yet. I wonder if it will be recognized for what it is—or will slowly become a part of the consciousness, an heritage of humanity. It ought to be translated at once into French, German, Russian & Swedish. It has the age of the race & the youth of America in it.

Annie Clephan is coming here from England from May 5th to 12th. She is a delegate to the International Women's Council in Washington & spends a week here before she goes on to Boston for something or other. Before or after that, I'd love to have you if you feel like coming.

Well, my dear, you have achieved great things. You must be as near happiness as one gets to be in this life. I've always thought you would do a great book—but I never quite expected this! I love the way the eternal element, the meditative, subconscious strain of thought & perception is traced throughout in Dorinda. The book is only tragic because it so relentlessly presents the fragmentary, evanescent sense of life. I can't get over saying: it's wonderful! wonderful!

Had I known it was so near publication I should have asked John Farrar to let me write about it in the Bookman.[2] But better writers than I will do it. Whatever it took out of you to write it—it is worth it all. People will be reading it for generations & knowing what life was in the barren lands of old Virginia & what the human spirit eternally is. And to think you could do it! It ranks with the best of Tolstoi & Hardy. I've got to stop now & think it over & over.

Love ever, | Louise.

If you'll send me any notices, I'll return promptly.

L.C.W.

ALS ViU EG Box 20
Address: Miss Ellen Glasgow | 1 West Main Street | Richmond | Va
Postmark: Norfolk Va Apr 12 1925, 7:30 P.M.

1. Characters in EG's *BG,* the novel LCW praises in this letter.
2. LCW did not review *BG* for *Bookman.* She did write a letter to *The New Yorker* (April 26, 1925) praising *BG,* and she reviewed it (along with three other novels) for the *Virginia Quarterly Review* (July 1925).

To Irita Van Doren

April 21st, 1925 | ONE WEST MAIN STREET | RICHMOND, VIRGINIA

Dear Mrs Van Doren:

If I haven't written to ask news of Anne, it has been simply because I felt that you had too many calls upon your time to be troubled by letters.[1] I have thought of you, however, almost every day, and I hope with all my heart that things are going well with you and your little girl. When she is better I wish that you would bring her down for a little visit to us. It might amuse her to see Virginia and we should be so glad to have you both at any time except the first four days in May when the house will be crowded.

On the eleventh of May I hope to be in New York, and perhaps if you can't come before that time, we might make some other plan. It will be delightful to see you again, and I feel that I can never thank you enough for the help you have been with my book. Nothing that has ever been written about my work pleased me so much as the article by Dr Sherman.[2] He was so splendidly generous, and for the first time I feel that some one is looking beneath and discerning the spirit in my work as a whole. It is a discouraging experience to write for twenty-five years without having anyone understand what you are trying to say. However, this makes me feel that it is worth while.

Though I have not, like James Cabell, a a particular and private hell named Beyond Life in which I can comfortably roast my enemies, I can at least stand by my friends, and if you or Dr Sherman ever need me to help you in a special case, I shall try to sharpen my rapier. There is probably nothing that I can do; but I wish you to feel that, if the time ever comes, you may call on me to render whatever service I can.

Every one was enchanted with Mr Van Doren's lecture. His visit made a bright spot, but we missed you very much.

Affectionately yours, | ELLEN GLASGOW

TLS DLC

1. Van Doren's ten-year-old daughter had suffered a serious eye injury while playing.
2. Stuart P. Sherman, "The Fighting Edge of Romance," *NYHTB,* 9 April 1925, sec. 5, pp. 1–3; rpt. *EGCR* 241–45.

From Agnes Repplier

920 Clinton St | Philadelphia | May 10th 1925[1]

Dear Miss Glasgow,

It was very good of you to send me "Barren Ground," and I have read it with the rare pleasure that only studies of conditions give me. Above and beyond all, I love primitive conditions and the progress of the seasons. "The Growth of the Soil," which is a bit spun out, "Maria Chapdelaine," which is flawless, and "Barren Ground," which rings true—these are the books which make for understanding.[2] The close of "Maria Chapdelaine" and the close of "Barren Ground" are equally satisfactory. Emotions are transitory but sunrises and sunsets are for all time. "Likewise there is a wind upon the heath."[3]

I hear of you sometimes from your friend, Mrs. Balch, whom I should like to see oftener than I do. The worst thing about work is that it crowds out companionship. I am off to New York to-day, to read a paper to-night, when I want to have supper with Cornelia Frothingham. Don't forget me as the months speed by. I am ever and always your friend and ardent admirer,

Agnes Repplier

You are such a profoundly intelligent writer.

ALS ViU EG Box 17

1. The date is written at the end of the letter, following the signature.
2. Novels published by Knut Hamsun in 1921, the French writer Louis Hémon in 1916 (posthumous), and EG in 1925, respectively.
3. From *Lavengro: The Scholar, Gipsy, Priest* (1851) by the English writer George Borrow (1803–1881): "There's night and day, brother, both sweet things; sun, moon, and stars, brother,

all sweet things; there's likewise a wind on the heath. Life is very sweet, brother; who would wish to die?" (chapter 25).

To Agnes Repplier

June 17th 1925

Dear Miss Repplier,

It was a great pleasure to know that you like Barren Ground. There is no one writing today whose good opinion I would rather have than yours. Your books are always close at hand and I dip into them very often for refreshment and enjoyment.

I spent only one day in Chestnut Hill. Next time, I hope to stay longer and to see you while I am there.

Affectionately yours | ELLEN GLASGOW

ALS PU-Sp
Address: Miss Agnes Repplier, | 920 Clinton Street, | Philadelphia, | Pennsylvania
Postmark: Richmond, Jun 18 1925 1 AM

To Blanche Knopf

October 24th, 1925

Dear Mrs Knopf:

I was so glad to have your letter, for I had thought of you so often during the summer, and your card pleased me very much.

It is lovely of you to send me Katharine Anthony's book.[1] This is one of the autumn books that I am most desirous of reading, and I am looking forward to it with the keenest anticipation.

Just now I am recovering from a sharp attack of influenza; but I hope to be in New York the very last of November for a stay of ten days or two weeks. Seeing you and Mr Knopf will be one of my greatest pleasures if you are in town. I should like also to see Mr Stallings again and finish a conversation we started last spring.

Is there any hope of your coming to Richmond this autumn?

With kindest regards to you both,

Affectionately, | Ellen Glasgow

TLS TxU-Hu

1. *Catherine the Great* (New York: Knopf, 1925).

To Blanche Knopf

October 38th,[1] 1925

Dear Mrs Knopf:

"Catherine The Great" is a brilliant and fascinating biography. Miss Anthony has made a dim moment in the past live again in the sunlight. It is impossible to tell you how much I enjoyed the book.[2]

Affectionately yours | ELLEN GLASGOW

TLS TxU-Hu

1. Probably 28th.

2. A line has been drawn through this final sentence by an unknown hand. In EG's next letter to Knopf (November 5, 1925), she gives permission to "use my opinion" of Anthony's novel, thus suggesting that the first two sentences of the present letter were used by the publisher to promote *Catherine the Great*.

To Rebe Glasgow Tutwiler

Richmond, Sunday, December 27th [1925?] | Monday

My darling Rebe;

I began this letter yesterday, but something broke in upon it, and now I am struggling to get packed and ready to leave tomorrow for New York.

We were delighted with the presents, and I am very glad to have the Life of Keats.[1] It ought to be in my library, and I am sure I should never have bought it, it is so expensive. Cabell's box of candy is delicious. Thank him for me, and the Sealyham cards are too sweet for words. Thank Carrington too.

I had, I think the nicest Christmas since I was a child and we used to lie awake and wait for poor Mother to get up. I think of her so often at this season, and Christmas Eve I went out to Hollywood and fixed your wreaths, which were perfectly beautiful. The section certainly looked as if it were remembered; but it is a very sad time of the year.

Well, I had one glorious present. Arthur gave me a Buick sedan, the larger size at $1765. My Essex was about wearing out, though it turned into a very good little car, and gave splendid service all summer. Do you know that they only allowed us $215 in exchange, and it was such a bargain that Carrie bought it today. Every one told her it was an opportunity.

Arthur looked at several cars, but he favored the Buick. Every one has some particular preference, and the Branch's advised him to get a Buick. I had rather liked the Chrysler; but he decided on the Buick, and it is a really beautiful car, very graceful and not nearly so small as the Essex. The color I like very much, a grayish blue, and it is a decidedly smart looking car. I hope you will come down later in the winter and ride in it, as I have kept Nathaniel ever since we went to Cape Cod. Arthur told Beulah B. that as long as his sister would have a chauffeur, he thought he would have to give her a better car. I got some other very nice presents, and I gave myself a robe for the car and a set of open work things for luncheon, a runner and mats. I need a lace one very much.

Christmas morning I took a large turkey (James roasted it) to the Afro-American Home for Old Folks. It was so pathetic to see those old colored people and they have so little done for them, and are not in the Community Fund. They sang for us, some of them over ninety, and all the old school. Then I went to look at Lizzie Jones' grave. I had always felt so badly that I had never seen how it was attended to. I found it entirely obliterated. No one would know that any one was buried there, and I remembered the way that old woman used to walk that long distance to the end of her life and the years when she went to Hollywood every spring and planted flowers while I was in New York, and the other years when she worked there with Mother and Cary. I engaged a man to make a mound over it and I am going to have a marker put over it. Lizzie Peterson[2] says she will help about it, and we will get one for about fifteen dollars. A.V. is going out to Evergreen Cemetery (that is where Lizzie is buried) on New Year's day to see about it.

Carrie came in Christmas Eve (the day after Arthur left) and stayed with us until today. We had a nice Christmas and she is certainly wonderful.

I must stop now and pack. Thank you again for the three lovely presents. Devotedly always.

Ellen

What is it you have to show me. I wish I could stop by, but I ought to come home to get to work.

TC of TLS FU

1. Probably Amy Lowell's two-volume *John Keats* (Boston: Houghton, 1925), which was in EG's library (*CLEG* 8.158).

2. MKR's mistranscription for Patterson. Lizzie Jones was also Elizabeth (Lizzie) Patterson's childhood caregiver.

To Irita Van Doren

September 26th, 1926 | ONE WEST MAIN STREET | RICHMOND, VIRGINIA

Irita dear,

I am really very regretful, but, in the circumstances, I think it would be better for some other writer to review *The Ninth Wave*".[1] I had intended to devote the first two days after my return to doing an interpretative review of the book. This, however, was before I had read the flippant and (as it seems to me) inadequate notice of my book in The Century,[2] and since reading this, I have lost the impulse that would have made the writing possible——at least in this weather.

I do not mean, of course, that Carl has not the right to use any tone or manner he pleases. I am speaking merely of my own reactions and of my temperamental inability to approach the book in the right attitude of mind. I feel sure that any one of the many writers, good or bad, whom Carl has so generously helped in the past, would be in a better position to write a review of his first novel.

I am rushing this off to you because I deeply regret the delay.

My affection to you always. I hope you will be able to run down this autumn.

As ever, dear Irita, | ELLEN GLASGOW

TLS DLC

1. Carl Van Doren's first (and only) novel (New York: Harcourt, 1926).
2. "The Benefit of Malice," in "The Roving Critic," *Century Magazine,* 112 (October 1926), 764–65; rpt. *EGCR* 281–82. The review of EG's *RC* by Carl Van Doren ("The Roving Critic") generally is favorable, although the tone is somewhat sarcastic. What may have irritated EG most is a comment in the final sentence: "like most of Miss Glasgow's books," the novel is "somewhat longer than it had to be."

To Irita Van Doren

October 21st 1926 | ONE WEST MAIN STREET | RICHMOND, VIRGINIA

Dear Irita,

I am distressed that you should have had this great sorrow,[1] and my heart goes out to you in tenderness.

You are to me one of those tranquil and luminous spirits that should be spared all grief and anxiety. Yet you are not spared these—perhaps because you are so magnificently above them.

Do let me know whenever you and Carl can come to me? Is the first of November too soon?

Until Christmas the weather is usually good. What of the last week in November or the first week in December?

Affectionately always | *Ellen*
Hugh Walpole will be with me this week end.

ALS DLC

1. EG's reference is unclear. Two recent events in IVD's life may help explain, IVD's daughter Anne's eye injury in 1925 or the death of her friend and colleague Stuart Sherman in August 1926.

To Rebe Glasgow Tutwiler

Christmas Day 1926 | ONE WEST MAIN STREET | RICHMOND, VIRGINIA
My darling Rebe:

This is the first minute I have had free, and I have a million things to tell you. First of all, I am wild about my bag. It is just the kind I like, and I think it is ever so much prettier for having the blue in it. This shade of blue goes with everything, even red. I can't tell you how pleased I am to have it, and it was so sweet of you to send it after the lovely presents you sent.

Poor Anne Virginia has been very sick in bed for four days, with dreadful bronchitis, and no voice at all. She was delighted with those lovely handkerchiefs. And I must tell you that Jeremy deserted everything for the squeaking dog you sent. He has played with it all the morning, and is lying now with his head on it before the fire.

Carrie and Lucy are spending the day—or taking dinner with us. Carrie is now making cocktails.

I was very much pleased, too, with Cabell's books. They are lovely, and the box of cards from Carrington is both useful and ornamental.

I will write you again tomorrow, or today. I have so much to tell you. My presents are lovely and I got really a great many, including flowers. Poor Anne Virginia has been ill in bed for four or five days, with dreadful bronchitis and cold all over. I had to work awfully hard getting things the three days before Christmas. I never went in so many shops in Richmond at one time, and today, as a result, I have developed a dreadful cold, too.

The chief thing I did was to arrange a Christmas for The Afro-American Old Folks Home. Everybody thinks of children, but these old colored people are so pathetic and so neglected. They are not in the Community Fund. I got Mrs. Pratt to contribute half but her brother-in-law was killed and she had to go out of town. A. V. was in bed unable to speak and but for Lucy Coleman I don't know what I should have done. She filled 26 little tin boxes with candy, nuts and fruit, and to each one we tied a little purse containing two brand new quarters of a dollar. Then I gave them two turkeys (cooked by James, with a can of gravy, and a bread box of rolls, and two enormous pound cakes. Jane Williams is in that home now. I pay half her fee (they take her for three dollars a week, and she looks so much better cared for. Her adopted daughter Mary Ellen pays the other half. Carrie, Lucy and I went there yesterday and took all the things. I feel that that was really worth doing. You never saw such joy at our coming. They sang for us, some negro spirituals. A blind old woman leads the music.

Then just as I was getting into the car, I saw a little very pretty fox terrier puppy wandering [*one or two lines missing from bottom of page*][1] following said they had never seen him before, so I took him up and carried him to the shelter. I hope he won't die from exposure. He is well bred and his tail has been cropped, evidently a pet that got lost. There are eighteen dogs at the Shelter besides that puppy and three others we got from the pound on Christmas Eve. One, a beautiful hound we got a home for at once and a small female poodle went in half an hour. People were coming all the time, usually asking for fox terriers for Christmas gifts.

A. V. was delighted with her handkerchiefs. She will write when she is able, but now she can do nothing. She got very nice presents, and Henry sent her a perfectly gorgeous basket of red roses and white heather. I never saw a lovelier basket. Glasgow gave her a beautiful black brocaded hand bag, and he gave me a handsome portfolio from Florence.

I have whole chapter to write about him.[2] I [*Last line or two of page missing. Evidently another missing page or more. Letter ends here.*]

TC of TLU FU

1. This note and the second, identifying missing sections of the letter, are MKR's.

2. MKR inserts "(sic)" following "have." "Him" seems to refer to Henry Anderson (mentioned in the previous paragraph). If so, then this sentence appears to refer to EG's controversial exposé of Anderson in the chapter entitled "Fata Morgana" in her autobiography (*WW*), and it suggests that EG may have been at work on her autobiography (or at least been thinking seriously about it) long before 1934, the year it is usually assumed she began writing it. The missing page or pages of the letter, which was loaned by RGT to MKR, would be explained by RGT's withholding any of EG's subsequent discussion in this letter of her "chapter" on Anderson.

IV

1927–1938

[I]t is intellect, after all, that counts as one goes over the hill of life.
—To Anne Virginia Bennett, August 25, [1927]

During these years of Glasgow's mature career she consistently enjoyed the professional recognition and personal benefits that accrue to the successful writer: awards, honorary degrees, attention by other professional writers, and the ability to travel more extensively than ever (she took her last trip to Europe in 1937). Her mental and emotional health, and her physical health during the first years of this period, seem to have been more stable than earlier, as well. In 1927 her effusive letters to her companion and to her sister detail an extended trip enjoyed by an enthusiastic traveler throughout England; even the grammatical errors common in these letters suggest a breathless and hurried enjoyment. Gone are the despondent moods of the younger Glasgow during her first trip to England more than thirty years earlier.

In the midst of these relatively happy years, however, in 1929, Glasgow's beloved Sealyham terrier, Jeremy, died. Glasgow's letters and those to her from concerned friends confirm the depth of Glasgow's feelings for her dog and the sincerity of her loss. She had difficulty recovering her mental equilibrium and wrote to Anne Virginia Bennett that she could not "see anything ahead." Jeremy's death and the epistolary expressions it occasioned, nonetheless, did have the benefit of strengthening Glasgow's bonds with women friends new and old. Mary Johnston's moving note of sympathy and the English writer Radclyffe Hall's long letter to a friend she had not yet met are two such examples.

Initially, Glasgow's impetus for writing to Radclyffe Hall in 1927 may have been professional respect: Hall had received two prestigious literary prizes, although the fame—and infamy—that would become synonymous with Hall's name after the obscenity trial for *The Well of Loneliness,* her 1928 lesbian novel, was still to come. Glasgow seems to have proposed, in a letter now missing, a meeting in England; Hall's response expresses regret that she will be out of the country. Three years later Glasgow accepted Hall's invitation to visit her and her partner, Una Troubridge, at their house in Rye, Sussex. Glasgow regretted missing Virginia Woolf, whom she wanted to meet, in 1927, and she was delighted with her visit to Vita Sackville-West, Woolf's sometime lover, that same year. In 1935 Glasgow hosted Gertrude Stein and Alice B. Toklas in her home. Glasgow's evident comfort in lesbian company adds an important dimension to understanding the depth of her preference for women's companionship. The correspondence between Glasgow and Hall lasted from 1927 until the year of Hall's death in 1943. Of Hall, Glasgow wrote, "few human beings can equal her in charity, in loyalty, or in magnanimity" (*WW* 260).

Other new friends acquired during these years, notably Clare Leighton and Bessie Zaban Jones, were mainstays for the rest of Glasgow's life. Glasgow met the English artist Clare Leighton on New Year's Day in 1936, probably in New York City. Younger than Glasgow by almost thirty years, Leighton looked to Glasgow for encouragement, particularly (and ironically) in her relationships with men. Leighton's letters suggest that she later left England for the United States at least partly in order to escape a spouse who was abusive (whether physically or psychologically or both is not clear). Glasgow often served as the older and wiser counselor who assured Leighton not only that she was right to leave but also that she would regain her happiness and stability. In what appears to have been Leighton's subsequent emotional entanglement in the domestic troubles of friends, Glasgow advised distance and the cultivation of self-possession. Glasgow's letters to Leighton are patient, encouraging and attentive to Leighton's feelings. Their correspondence ended only with Glasgow's death.

Books, especially those by Glasgow, formed the initial mutually engaging topic between Glasgow and Bessie Zaban Jones, the wife of the American literature scholar Howard Mumford Jones. Glasgow and Bessie Jones met in June 1930 in Chapel Hill, North Carolina, when Glasgow received an honorary doctorate from the University of North Carolina, where Bessie worked and her husband taught. After a subsequent fan letter from Jones to Glasgow, the two faithfully exchanged letters for the rest of Glasgow's life about the idea of work (as distinct from Glasgow's work in particular), about the particularities of place (the South, New England, Cambridge and Harvard), and of home and houses. In a late letter to Glasgow, Bessie Jones wrote that she was "enriched" by Glasgow's "clear vision" in her fictional depictions of women's lives (February 27, 1945, ViU).

Three of Glasgow's most highly regarded novels were published during these years: *They Stooped to Folly* (1929), *The Sheltered Life* (1932), and *Vein of Iron* (1935). Between 1929 and 1933 Doubleday, Doran published the eight-volume *The Old Dominion Edition of the Works of Ellen Glasgow*, introduced briefly by the author in each volume; in 1938 the twelve-volume, signed *The Virginia Edition of the Works of Ellen Glasgow*, with its more extensive prefaces, was published by Scribners. Glasgow probably began in earnest to write her autobiography, *The Woman Within*, which would not be published until nine years after her death. She received during these years the first—and several subsequent—of her honorary doctorates.

From Zona Gale

Portage, Wisconsin | April 14. 1927[1]

My dear Ellen Glasgow—

I have been so rejoicing in the lovely wood-cut, with its Christmas greeting.[2] And I wish so much that I had something at all approaching it in beauty to send to you for an Easter greeting. But since I have not—for that would not be easy—I want to send you this word of thanks and appreciation. And, too, my greeting and remembrance for this magic time. It *is* remembrance, you know, for once Gelett Burgess brought me to your apartment in New York.

I hope that I may see you again sometime. Meanwhile, like every one else, I can read you—and congratulate you on the fine work and on the delight which you are giving out. My warm admiration and thanks go with this.

Faithfully yours, | Zona Gale

ALS ViU EG Box 14

1. Both place and date are written at the end of the letter, following the signature.
2. EG sent a reproduction of Julius J. Lankes's engraving of her house as a holiday greeting for 1926–1927 (see Taylor, "Ellen Glasgow in Woodcuts," 9).

To Rebe Glasgow Tutwiler

June 26th 1927 | MONCORVO HOUSE, | ENNISMORE GARDENS, | LONDON, S.W.

I can't read this *over*!

My darling Rebe:

Well, here we are![1] This is Sunday morning, and it is now twelve o'clock. At 10.30 I got Carrie out (for she would spend all her mornings in bed if I left her to her inclinations) and we stole through a sleeping house like thieves in the night. Outside, it was cold and bleak, and the street was tenanted only by a decrepit crossing sweeper, who parks his broom, Margaret says, in this house & has coffee here every morning. We walked to the corner (Prince's Gate) found a taxi, and drove through a sleeping London to the Foundling Hospital. Alas! It is no more as we remember it. Only the charming walls & trees remain, but the children have all been moved to the country, and a large sign "for Sale in freehold lots" ornaments the gate. From there in a pouring rain, & shivering with cold, we drove to Westminster Abbey, but it was too crowded, & no seats were left. Then we came home, found the maid in our room, & she suggested a fire, a suggestion which I gratefully seconded. Now, with a small but active blaze, two grams of aspirin & dry stockings & shoes, I am trying to shake off the chill.

To go back to where I left off, we had a comfortable but uninteresting trip, & went into a rough sea in the channel. The day steward (a delightful Irishman sent our table steward (whom we became really attached to) to the dock & to the train with us, & we had no trouble of course. Davis, the table steward reminded me so much of Gian-Luca, and we have arranged to have him on our return voyage. He says he has been a waiter ever since he "was little," & that he has learned how people differ as only a waiter can learn, & that it isn't often anyone finds two such "nice ladies." He came to the train & shook hands with us at parting, with that sad & wistful look so like Gian-Luca. Just as we left Southampton the sun came out & we saw England in the sun, but it has been really cold & we long for warm clothes. At Waterloo we got out & started off with a porter before I saw Arthur looking for us. Then we came on his luxurious car & left his man to bring on luggage. They were having a dinner party of young people for Marjorie & we were glad when our trunks arrived too late for us to dress & we had dinner on trays in our room. Nobody could have been nicer or more cordial than they have been to us; and I think Arthur enjoys showing us his beautiful things. He has a great many very fine things, & the house is very comfortable & the food delicious. He showed us all the guest rooms and let me take my choice, and running strictly true to form, I chose the best & most luxurious, with bathroom attached & Carrie in an adjoining room. After that we heard that John and Beulah are coming this afternoon—but anyway we were here first & are most comfortably installed. We are perfectly independent & do exactly as we please, which makes it easier for everybody. Yesterday at ten o'clock we went to Mrs Hemming, I had a facial treatment, we both had manicures, & both made appointments for a course of treatments. Carrie too has caught on. Then I had my hair "set" next door, & we came in just at luncheon time to find the Duchess of Hamilton was expected to lunch—no one else—& she is a perfectly lovely person, the most unearthly creature I have ever seen. She dresses exactly like the member of a sisterhood, with her only ornament a chain & jet cross; & she is in mourning for her youngest daughter, who died of pneumonia just a month ago. She has the most ethereal personality, & her whole life is given up to work for animals & against vivisection in particular. She came to discuss some plans for an international humane congress with Margaret! A perfectly unaffected and guileless spirit, the duchess seems, with great sweetness & sincerity, & wearing the the rustiest black with grace and indifference. I did not care the faintest bit what I had on, though I had just come in from a hairdresser. Anyway, no one could be more devoted in her feeling for animals, & that was a bond. She, however, is a vegetarian, does not wear fur, & appears to be as consistent as Mary Johnston, which is the most one can say. She is the only one of Margaret's friend I ever felt drawn to, & I wish you could meet her. I don't know what this bond is.

In the afternoon Arthur & Margaret rushed us out to Wentworth golf club for tea. Magnificent trees, & perfectly beautiful borders of flowers. We took a walk there, had tea, & A. & M. took a turn in the dance. When we got in, it was half past six, & we spent an hour going over the house with Arthur. I enjoyed very much seeing his beautiful tapestries. They are really superb & I think the ballrooms is the loveliest room in the house, though his own little library has some very fine thing. A head of a child on the mantel by Donatello that is simply enchanting, some exquisite hangings & chairs, & a beautiful very old bookcase. He has some very attractive pictures, two delightful Hopners and a head of a boy (said to be by Romney) which I think is my favorite.[2] We had dinner just ourselves last night. The food is delicious & we have a glass of wine with every meal. Nothing has given me the feeling of uplifted spirits like escaping from prohibition!

I must say that we are made welcome in every way, & both Arthur & Margaret are as cordial.

Princess Alice on the 8th but as we don't dance, I think we'd better go before it occurs.[3] Now, it is almost lunch time, so I must stop. There are lots of things I want to tell you that I can't write. Please send this to Anne Virginia— I'll write to her next & you all can exchange. I hope you can read it. I've written so fast.

Devotedly— E

ALS ViU EG Box 14

1. Carrie Duke accompanied EG on this trip.
2. John Hoppner (1758–1810) was an English portrait painter patronized by George III; George Romney (1734–1802) was the popular English portrait painter of *Milton and His Daughters,* among others.
3. Presumably a ball at AGG's home, to be attended by Princess Alice, Countess of Athlone (1883–1981), a granddaughter of Queen Victoria. AGG and his wife Margaret often entertained royalty.

To Rebe Glasgow Tutwiler

July 23rd, 1927 | HOTEL MAJESTIC, | HARROGATE.

My darling Rebe,

Never must you come to England, or to Europe again, without visiting this country, and seeing Fountains Abbey and Durham Cathedral! I had never dreamed that such loveliest was left on earth as Fountains. First man did everything, and then nature beautified and softened and embellished the ruins to the last delicate touch. It stands today, against a perfect background, and it gives you the loveliness that is a pure distillation of ecstasy. Never have I spent such a morning, & not since Egypt[1] and Greece have I been so completely lifted outside of myself on the wings of beauty. The whole time I was longing for you. So few people could really *feel* what it gives, but I know that you could, and you must come over for the sake of Bolton and Fountains and the great Northern cathedrals. I have not seen many of the English cathedrals yet, but I have seen enough of them to know that there aren't any churches in the world to compare with them, and I feel at present that the Northern ones are more beautiful than in the South of England. Yet each in its own distinctive way is exactly what it should be, and is perfect in its surroundings. Well, Carrie and I had waited all this time for a cloudless and a free afternoon on which to see Fountains Abbey, a day like that perfect summer one we spent at Bolton. At last we awoke one morning to bright sunshine, & I said, "this is the day. We must go before a cloud comes in the sky." We hastened to dress and drink our water & have breakfast, but by half past nine, when the car was at the door, the sun had gone under, and we had a gray morning, though fortunately no rain fell while we were there. After we once reached the Abbey, we forgot whether the sun was shining or not, for such perfect loveliness did not need sunshine. You, who love ruins, would adore it, and it is useless to try to find words that can make you realize what it is. The size of it is almost Egyptian, and the nobility of it is also. We wandered from ruined nave and chapel and cloisters and court and innumerable rooms, like "The House for Strangers" and "The Infirmary" and "the Chapel of Nine Altars," until when at last I looked at my watch, it was past luncheon time. We had been there three hours and it had seemed not more than half an hour. I don't know why so few people have told me about the Yorkshire Abbeys. Partly, I suppose, because most Americans don't stop between London & Edinburgh and partly because there are so few persons who really know what beauty is—especially the beauty in ruins. But if I had seen nothing over here, but Fountains, Bolton and Durham, it they would have repaid me for the trip,—and you simply must come here next year.

 I don't know why I felt so strongly that I must see Durham. Nobody had ever told me what it was, but something in me urged me not to go away until I had seen it. The distance was too great for a day's trip, so we planned that we would go by train & spend the night at the Royal County Hotel. I had just been told by the doctor that my blood pressure was very low again, and he was giving me hypodermics of arsenic & strychnine;[2] but I decided not to tell him of our plans, but to go up one afternoon after a Nanheim sulpher bath & return the next day in time to take another. Well, we went, and I wouldn't take anything in the world for having seen the Cathedral. We got to the hotel, had tea, & then went out to the walk up hill, just as closing time came. The Cathedral is the most sublime building you can imagine jutting out like a great promontory, built of solid rock on solid, dark, grim, and more like a fortress than a church. Less perfectly beautiful than York, it is more impressive in its way, and the only word that describes it, is that one *sublime*. There is something barbaric and menacing about it, and it was a defense in the border wars against the Scots as well as a church. At its feet, under the rocky cliff winds the River Weare,[3] one of the loveliest rivers I have ever seen. Fortunately, after we went inside, we find a verger, who had come to close but was persuaded to stay & take us over. The enormous columns in the nave reminded me of Karnak.[4] Carrie & I stood clutching each other and saying, "Why did no one ever tell us? Why did no one ever tell us how magnificent it is?" I have never seen Carrie so awed by anything building or place. She says all the churches in Italy seem superficial and tawdry beside York and Durham. And outside, after seeing the most beautiful altar and scene you can imagine, (the second one presented as a thank-offering after the Battle of Neville's Fields,[5] we wandered over the emerald green turf, and read the old tombstones & then down the hill to the soft feathery trees by the river. That night, we saw almost the only bright sunshine we had seen in England shining through our shadeless windows on the white bedroom wall at ten o'clock in the night! The next morning we came home taking a slow train, after an excellent breakfast of Yorkshire bacon and toast.

Tomorrow, if it is fine, we are to motor to Whitby because it is the loveliest drive across the Yorkshire moors. The trip takes one day, but the doctor told me yesterday that he wanted me to take a day's holiday from treatment. We had tickets to a Pageant of English Literature, but at the last minute I felt too tired to go. I sent Carrie alone, not feeling that I ought to risk having a headache tomorrow.

She has just gone, & I must stop now and go to bed. There are so many things to tell you, for I have never mentioned so many places—& especially I have not told you of the wonderful wildflowers, & especially the poppies among the wheat. Every wheatfield has great splashes of red, like a dragon's blood, & the poppies and wild foxglove grow in masses along the stone walls, & even in among the stones. At Fountains the ruins were grown with wildflowers, high up in the towers & arches were sprays of snapdragon, foxglove, & red poppies, & grasses grow all along the top of the walls. Best love. I was so glad to have your letter. I'll write to A.V. in a day or two.

Devotedly Ellen

ALS ViU EG Box 14
Address: Mrs. C. C. Tutwiler | West Outlet Camp, | West Outlet, Maine
Postmark: Harrogate, Yorks., 24 Jul 1927

1. EG had traveled there with CGMcC and RGT in 1899.
2. Doses of arsenic and strychnine were accepted treatments for low blood pressure and nervous disorders, respectively. EG had suffered from nervous exhaustion during the early months of 1927; her trip to England was planned, in part, as treatment.

3. Usually spelled Wear.

4. In Egypt, on the site of ancient Thebes.

5. The altar is the Neville Screen, presented to the cathedral by the Neville family in celebration of the English victory over the Scots in the Battle of Neville's Cross, 1346.

To Anne Virginia Bennett

HOTEL MAJESTIC, | HARROGATE. | July 26th 1927

Dearest A.V.

I wrote Rebe about Durham and Fountains Abbey, and the high points in our trip so far (and I think always will be) are York, Fountains, and Durham. I'll try to tell you about Whitby, but before I begin, I must arrange a small business trifle.

Will you write to Mrs McCormack, 1401 Stockley Gardens, Norfolk, & ask her what my niblick[1] cost, and send her the money. Alas, the golf clubs & bag I bought at Selfridges have never been unwrapped. The little time I've had free from cure, I've wanted to see something beautiful! We rent the cheapest little two seater car we can get, & with a very good driver who knows the country well, but the car is the only reasonable thing here. I never realized that things would be so expensive over here, & there are so many extras—belonging to the cure. The doctor also is very expensive, but very good.

The way we came to this hotel (a really excellent one in every way) was quite funny. A few nights after we came to Harrogate Margaret told us that Sir Archibald Weigal; the great nephew of the Duke of Wellington and Lady Weigal, who has the even rarer distinction of never going out to dinner unless she was accompanied by two physicians and her secretary)—were coming to dine with us that evening. According to Margaret's credulity Lady Weigal (the heiress of one Blundell-Maples, who made an enormous fortune out of a shop, I think) had had to miss it. The way this velvet turf spreads under the thickest trees, and down to the very edges of the rivers, is perfectly marvellous. And as for the roses that we imagine cannot live without sun, they surpass any I have ever imagined for richness, color and beauty. We are collected seeds of rare flowers, but I suppose they will never put up. Here, everything that is scattered to the winds appears to blossom. I wrote Rebe about the poppies in the wheat, & the wild foxglove & snapdragon by the woodside.

Sunday we had a glorious day. The doctor told me not to take any treatment. So we motored 150 miles to Whitby Abbey & back. Whitby is one of or, I believe, is really the oldest seaport in England, & it is said to be the place on the North Sea where the Saxons landed. There is a great Saxon Abbey there, which was ruined by the Danes in 800 or so, and then refounded by some Norman Baron under William the Conquerer. It is a wonderful ruin, & still dominates the land as well as the sea. For my part, nothing is comparable to the ruined abbeys of Yorkshire, & no churches ever built by man approach the English Cathedrals in sublimity and beauty. The drive home was one of the loveliest we have ever taken. Over glorious moors, & by a place called the Hole of Halcum[2] [*remainder of letter missing*]

AL ViU EG 5083 Box 28
Address: Miss A. V. Bennett, | 1 West Main Street, | Richmond, | Virginia, | U.S.A.
Postmark: Harrogate Yorks., 26 Jul 1927, 7:30 P.M.
Publication: *L* 82–83.

1. The number nine iron golf club.
2. EG perhaps means Hutton-le-Hole, a small Yorkshire village.

To Anne Virginia Bennett

HOTEL MAJESTIC, | HARROGATE. | July 27th [1927?]

Dearest A.V.

I have written to you and Rebe so constantly that I have not had a minute left for anybody else, not even for Henry, who has been a faithful correspondent. When I get back to London, I shall probably have even less time, & on the moor trip, I'm afraid I can only send postcards. Rebe seemed so interested in it all, and I thought frequent letters might relieve the monotony of the summer in Richmond. I was disgusted to hear that Josephine had been disagreeable about dogs when she visited Rebe, and I hope Rebe will adhere to her resolution not to ask her again. It's funny that she never shows that side to us. I wonder why it is?

All this brings me back to those adorable Sealyham puppies! When Carrie and I were lying down upstairs before tea, we kept saying, "If only we had Little Anne curled up by us!" I am resisting an impulse to take one, or two, because one would be so lonely, back with us; but I suppose it would be a mistake. It is a long trip, and I think Jeremy and Billy are better off without a companion. Henry would want one, but I am not sure the puppy would have a good home, and anyway it would be hard and expensive to carry one over, though I am sure Mr Tweedie would give it the best of attention on the Olympic. However, there is a duty on dogs now.

When we first came here there was a nice English woman who came to the pump room[1] every day with an enchanting dog, full of personality, who was taking the cure with her. His name was Chummy, and she said he had started to be a Sealyham, but had changed his mind and decided he wouldn't! She was perfectly crazy about him; and had refused to leave home unless he came with her. On the train she told them that if they put Chummy in the back, she would go too, so they left him in her compartment. At the Crown Hotel, she paid 22 shillings a day for herself, and two shillings, sixpence for Chummy, and they had, she said, quite a large room and bath together. She is the only person (discounting antique dealers) that Carrie has spoken to since we came here.

In her spare times Carrie (she has stopped the baths) haunts the antique shops, and already, I believe, she has spent almost all of that "tentative" letter of credit. She has bought some very good things, among them a fine Chippendale dining-table and a Chippendale grandfather's clock. I haven't bought but one thing, & that she paid for and will let me take from her. I am afraid of running out of money, living and the cure, all, are so costly. But I found one really charming old portrait very reasonable, & we decided the Miss Grovenor might easily be Esther our great, great grandmother.[2] If I have any money left after the motor trip, I shall try to get one fine piece of silver, an urn or bowl for flowers, but I am not counting on it.

The last two days it has poured, but tomorrow, if it is fine, we are to motor, in the afternoon to Helmsley Castle and two ruined abbeys. Rebe shares my passion for ruined abbeys, so I shall write her after I've seen them. There are Rievaulx and Byland Abbeys, and I am planning another trip to Richmond Castle, and Saint Agatha's and Mount Grace Priory—all ruined of course! England has certainly reason to be grateful to Henry VIII. who destroyed abbeys and created ruins! My feeling for them has become so overpowering that I am altering my northern trip in order to include Tintern Abbey, the third of the Cistercian order, and one of the most romantic.

When I broke off yesterday, I donned my raincoat, purchased the day after I arrived & worn frequently, & hurried down to the Royal Baths, & this morning, before breakfast, we did the same, only the Royal Pump House was our earlier goal. However and wherever situated they are all Royal. At 11.30, I sallied forth again, and while I lay in the effervescent Manheim sulphur bath, the attendant dried my wet stockings. Every bath attendant is exceedingly nice, and I imagine superior to those at Continental places. This afternoon, as the shops in Yorkshire close on Wednesday afternoon, Carrie and I had tea in our room and after that "lounged around and suffered"[3] from cold, until I dressed and came down to the fire in this very cozy, though ugly, writing-room, which I usually have alone.

Squeeze the lambs for me. I think of them so often, & I have already bought them two little balls from Harrogate, "made in England for dogs." At Selfridges in London, I am going to the toy department. That is a huge shop, the biggest in London, & very good. I don't think Rebe would have been in it. I got a splendid golf bag there, which I have never even unwrapped. Whatever time we had free, I wanted to see beautiful places. Nothing ever built by man in the way of a church can compare, in my feeling, with the English Cathedrals. I love them more and more, each one is perfect in its place, but I cannot imagine that any quite equals York in beauty. When we leave here Tuesday, we plan to stop at Lincoln and Ely.

Best love. I hope you keep well, and did I ever tell you how pleased I was to have the cable the other day?

As ever Ellen

ALS ViU EG 5083 Box 28
Address: Miss A. V. Bennett, | 1 West Main Street, | Richmond, | Virginia, | U.S.A.
Postmark: London W. 1, Aug 15, 1927, 2:45 A.M. Either this letter was posted with a later one, or the envelope is the incorrect one.

   1. The Royal Pump Room was built in 1842. The sulphur well is still in operation.
   2. Esther Cook Gholson was EG's maternal great-great-great-grandmother.
   3. A paraphrase of one of EG's favorite quotes from Brer Terrypin in the Brer Rabbit stories by Joel Chandler Harris.

To Rebe Glasgow Tutwiler

HOTEL MAJESTIC, | HARROGATE. | July 30th 1927

My darling Rebe,

The most wonderful windfall from the blue occurred this morning. Just imagine it! I had a letter from Arthur, a very nice one, telling me that he was taking his car to Vittel, but that Margaret was [*portion of letter torn off*] her car and chauffeur, [*portion of letter torn off*] of my motor trip and until I sail. Doesn't that make a difference? I must say Margaret has certainly been nice to us, for after all she could have taken her car too, if she had wanted to, or have had the chauffeur clean the house, as Miss Shepstone told me they always did (washing the crystals,) etc), while the family was abroad. The only [*portion of letter torn off*] he saw. I did not, as Beulah would have done, resent the fact that I did not see more of it. Nothing could have been more satisfactory to me than the freedom from being companioned in which we lived in London. Now, staying when we return at the Hotel Langham, in Portland Place (we decided to go there because it is reasonable and Dr. Wilmer stays there) it ought to make the greatest difference to have the car to take us on trips. If nothing prevents, we want to go to Rochester and Canterbury for the day, & I've planned an afternoon drive to Chigwell, where the old Maypole of Barnaby Rudge is, and on to Epping Forest. I must say that Carrie has seen more of Yorkshire (thanks to my ingenious discoveries) than anybody in Virginia & most people in America who have been over here. When I saw how innocent and helpless the [*word marked out*][1] about what to see and how to see it in London, I realized that travelling with me (in spite of diminished luxury) must have its advantages.

Since I wrote you we have had two wonderful trips. First, we motored to Richmond and saw the old Castle on its river bluff, and then just before sunset we went out to Saint Agatha's or Easby Abbey, three miles beyond Richmond. When you come here, as you must, don't fail to go there, for it is an enchanted and enchanting spot. If possible go as we did at the hour of sunset. Even more than Stoke Poges this churchyard seemed enfold in the spirit and the hour of Gray's elegy.[2] A small, very old church, still in use, is just under the ruined Abbey, and an old churchyard overgrown with ivy and grasses, "Where heaves the turf in many a moldering heap." On one side there were fields like emerald velvet, where sheep were still browsing by one of these lovely English rivers, fringed by immemorial willows. On the other side "the ivy-mantled tower" and the perfect ruin all overgrown with foliage and small purple flowers like bluebells that grew in between the stones and along the top of the highest tower. I have never seen anything more divinely soft and hauntingly look mellowed as it was of "the light that never was on sea or land."[3] I think I should have sat there until dark if the keeper had not kept returning to close the gates. It was a long way from home. We reached here at 10.30, and it was still light. I would have given anything if you could have been there with us in that perfect place at that perfect hour. It is incredible to me that any other county in England should be so beautiful, so satisfying, or so full of varied interest as Yorkshire.

Yesterday we went off for the whole day, and like all our other experiences here it was a flawless experience. First we went to Coxwold, saw the old fifteenth century church where Sterne was "perpetual incumbent" and the charming old house where he lived & wrote "The Sentimental Journey" and "Tristram Shandy."[4] Then to Byland Abbey, another ruin of great beauty and impressiveness. Again & again I reflect that England owes a debt of gratitude to Henry the VIII. who destroyed abbeys & created ruins! After a lunch of Bass Ale & Yorkshire ham and eggs at the Byland Abbey Inn, we motored to one of the most magnificent places in England—the ruins of Rievaulx Abbey. Even more beautiful than Byland, it makes description impossible. There are only two others that surpass it: Fountains & Bolton because of its park. Rievaulx as architecture is as fine as anything I have seen, & the remnant of it is superb against its green hills & forest. But for the natural beauty of its surroundings Bolton (though smaller than Byland Fountains, & Rievaulx is the most beautiful. The French Park at Fountains is not appropriate, & since it is off from the ruins one need not see it at all. Simply for the beauty and impressiveness of the buildings and the artistic effect of what is left, Fountains is the most beautiful. Indeed, it's as beautiful as anything I have seen in my life.

This is my last letter from Harrogate and from Yorkshire. Tuesday (God permitting) we go to Lincoln, spend the night at the Saracen's Head and go the next day to Ely, where we have engaged a room at *The Saint*. I shall try to send some postcards, but I shall scarcely have time for a letter.

Sunday—I am just back from a spray and effervescing sulphur bath, and this afternoon we shall stay in our rooms and pack. We leave (D.V., at 9.30 Tuesday morning, but our trunks and bags go straight to London, while we stop at Lincoln and Ely. I shall be sorry in a way to go, for this has been one of the pleasantest and most restful months I ever spent. Nothing has, so far, happened to mar the freedom and the peace of it, and I think I have enjoyed Yorkshire more than any place I have been to abroad. This is largely owing to the fact, I suppose, that I have come to the time when I enjoy places more than people. Places really give me more than people, and because of this I have been able to open my mind to this beauty and interest as I was never free to do when I travelled before the war. Then, too, all those wonderful places, like Egypt and Greece and Italy were a kind of tormenting delight (their perfection hurt) and there was a torrid intensity in the very atmosphere. But this country, the moors, the fields, the streams—all this is pure refreshment. Even the rivers, as Carrie said yesterday, look as if they would refresh you not drown you if you were to fall into one of them. Yet, curiously enough, I have no wish to come back again. I should not try, if I could, to repeat the experience, and never have I wavered in my resolve to make this trip my last one. Perhaps this is one reason why I have been able to get so much satisfaction from the things I have seen.

Did I tell you, or did A.V. tell you how lovely your miniature is—the most beautiful of all, I think.

I am resisting an impulse to bring back an adorable Sealyham puppy—sometimes I think I'll bring you Little Anne, and then I decide that it would not be wise. But, oh, if you could see them! I've got Cabell a dark rug of elephants' hair because of his cars.

Lovingly E.

ALS ViU EG Box 14
Address: Mrs C.C. Tutwiler | 9000 Crefeld Street | Chestnut Hill | Philadelphia, Pennsylvania, USA
Postmark: Harrogate, Yorks 31 July 1927, 6:45 PM

1. The name "Branch" is faintly legible.
2. The English poet Thomas Gray, whose poem "Elegy Written in a Country Churchyard" (1751) is the source of the quotations in the next three sentences. See EG to RGT May 31, 1914.
3. "The light that never was, on sea or land, / The consecration, and the poet's dream," from "Elegiac Stanzas Suggested by a Picture of Peele Castle in a Storm" by William Wordsworth (1770–1850).
4. Laurence Sterne (1713–1768), the English clergyman and author, lived in Coxwold,

in North Yorkshire, and was "perpetual incumbent" because he received perpetual stipends for his clerical appointments. The house EG refers to probably is the one in Sutton-on-the-Forest.

To Anne Virginia Bennett

LANGHAM HOTEL, | PORTLAND PLACE, | LONDON. W. I. | August 7. [1927?]
Dearest A.V.

Here we are in London again, with the difference (oh, what a difference!) of having a car of our own. I was so glad to find your letter here, and so glad too that you are having the hall done before my return. I think now since we have the car (though of course I'll have the expense of running it and Hasley's board on the trip of two weeks, but I can manage all right, and shan't need any more money. But everything costs so much that I have no temptation to try it but once. There are so many ways I could spend all that money more permanently.

If you have time while the house is being cleaned, will you try to straighten my drawers in my study as well as in my bedroom. When I get home I must settle down to work as soon as I can.

I felt splendidly the last week or so at Harrogate, but since reaching London I have ached all over from exhaustion & lost my appetite. We both feel hematous & weak & get tired so quickly. I suppose I've overdone it, but I hope to get back my strength on the boat, if not before. I know now why people take "an after cure."

It is damp & very chilly here today, so I suppose what they call "the heat wave" is broken. Ever since we came the papers have been writing about "the heat wave" "London gasping with no relief in sight" because the thermometer "has not fallen below 58 degrees for several days"! All the time, while London panted, Carrie & I have shivered if a window were open at our back and never gone out without a coat & a woolen robe over our knees.

We came to this hotel because we heard it was good, & Arthur said Dr. Wilmer always stayed here.

The rooms are nice, and more reasonable than most (fifteen dollars a day) but the food (extra of course) is very poor & that may be one reason I don't eat much. We try to go out, but I have never enjoyed restaurants as Rebe does— & I get so tired I'd rather have my meals at the hotel, especially dinner. Tuesday, if it is fine, we hoped to motor (a day's trip) to Rochester & Canterbury— & Wed or Thurs. to Waltham Abbey, Epping Forest & Chigwell to see Dickens' Maypole Inn. The 17th, we intend to start for our moors trip, & I have lengthened it to include Tintern Abbey, Gloucester, & Oxford. I don't care particularly about going to Oxford, but Carrie has never seen it, and I thought she ought not to miss it. I am eager to be off, but I cannot believe that any other part of England will seem so beautiful to me as Yorkshire.

Our first disappointments came with the interiors of Lincoln & Ely. I had heard so much of Lincoln's being the most beautiful cathedral after York that it was a blow to find the nave low & small & out of proportion with the enormous exterior, which is fine and wonderfully impressive. Ely, too, is beautiful on the outside, but absolutely spoiled by modern (1850) mural decorations within. The marvellous octagon roof, which must have been very impressive in its original state, has been painted to look like the interior of an Italian church. Anything less in harmony with the structure of the building or the English Gothic architecture it would be impossible to imagine. As for the town, we did not care for Lincoln and were glad to leave. This may have been because we went to the wrong hotel, the Saracen's Head when we ought to have stayed at the White Hart close by the Cathedral. We hated the Saracen's Head. It is modern & pretentious and entirely bad. On the other hand Ely is a charming, sleepy, perfectly typical English Cathedral town, & the Lamb is an old inn that you love from the moment you enter it. We enjoyed it very much, the food was all good & typically English—

The first rain Thursday brought us to London & Hasley met us at Liverpool St. Station. He is splendid & so much interested in everything that we see & wherever we go. He told us we must certainly see "the churchyard where the elegy was written,"—[1] He said he had learned a good deal about "little old shops" from the daughter of Mr Pierpont Morgan, who was "always looking for them."

Our first two days we spent looking for a coat for you. We went everywhere, & I changed my mind twenty times. At first I thought I'd get a gray or brown tweed, but the gray did not look smart, & the tweed they make now is very loosely woven & bulky and made Carrie & me both look so large that I decided not to get it for you. Finally, after going back three times & spending hours there, I ordered a black coat of the best black material, rough, that I could find, and Jay is now making it. We are going Friday to see it tried on a very nice woman who says she is five feet seven, which as well as I remember is your height. I selected the only coat that seemed to me to have any room about the hips. They are all made so straight & tight and narrow. Then I put all the trimming into a very good big collar of Persian lamb, the best black fur they had. I certainly hope it will fit you and that you will like it. I gave a great deal of time and thought to trying to get the best one, & I am sure black will be much more becoming to you than the light tweed, which does not give in to the figure at all. The darker shades of tweed are not worn & all were ugly. But this black rather woolly material was the only pretty black I could find——

I also bought, or rather ordered, for they have to be made, Jeremy & Billy paraphernalia. They don't have fancy things here, but I hope they are well made. There wasn't any pretty blue, it was too gray, so I got Billy a very pretty green instead. He will have to get his blue in America. I got Dimple a little plaid collar, though they said the plaidie's were for Scotties especially.

My back aches so I'll have to stop. Sunday is as dreary in London as in New York, but we'll go to the London Museum after lunch. I hope I'll feel better after a while.

Tell Rebe again her miniature is, I think, the prettiest that I have seen—I like it best of all. It is really beautiful. Love to lambs. As ever—

E—

ALS ViU EG 5083 Box 28
Publication: *L* 83–86.

1. Here, two lines referring to AGG and Margaret Glasgow have been marked out. See note 2 in previous letter for Gray's "Elegiac Stanzas."

To Rebe Glasgow Tutwiler

August 7th [1927] | LANGHAM HOTEL, | PORTLAND PLACE, | LONDON. W. I.
My darling Rebe,

I was so glad to have your last two letters since I came to London. I hope you got all of mine for I have written very often—oftener than I ever wrote, I think, in my life. When I left Harrogate I felt splendidly, but I have been dreadfully tired ever since I reached London, and my back aches whenever I begin to write. I am very much pleased to have the news about Princeton, and I hope Carrington will make us proud of him there. Today I went to Selfridges and we selected the ties. I hope you will like them. Yes, I know you will be pleased with the miniature. It is perfectly lovely. Beulah is at Tucker Hill[1] now. She took it over.

I wrote A.V. about Lincoln and Ely, and that the interiors of both were disappointments to me. Tomorrow, if it is fine, we expect to motor to Canterbury. I am very eager to see how that Cathedral compares with the Northern ones. You, when you come to England again you must spend at least ten days at Harrogate & motor over Yorkshire. I cannot believe any other part of England will ever appeal to me as strongly. We found a splendid dinner & a very reasonable garage, & we went everywhere in a little two seated car that never gave us the slightest trouble.

Sunday C. & I went to the London Museum & Saturday we went to the Tate. There are some beautiful things in the Tate, but so much sentimental stuff, & I have got to the state of mind that abhors the English Pre-Raphaelites. I liked the Whistler things & the Romneys & Hoppners & all that generation of painters, but the Victorian painters, with their eternal illustrations made me very tired. The National Gallery was finer far than I remembered it. I enjoyed that more than ever before, I think. Today it was pouring, but Hasley came in the car & took us out to the shops, where we saw a good deal and I bought a number of small presents.

Then we went to Simpsons in the Strand (because I was tired of French mixtures) and had a perfectly delicious lunch of English roast beef (exactly right) and vegetable maison & pickled tomatoes and Bass ale. Following this we had the most heavenly stewed raspberries & cream. The berries were stewed just a little & had more flavor even than fresh ones. After lunch we came home because a man (a Mr Hartley I met at Hugh's) was coming to tea. Now, we are going to bed without any dinner, and (I for one) with an aching back.

No, we are not going to Paris. We have so little time, & neither of us would leave England for anything, especially since we have the car and Hasley. I think it is a much better plan to go to only one country and see that as thoroughly as you can. The mistake I made in the past was to take in too many, & the reason I've enjoyed this trip so much is that I've not rushed from place to place, but have stayed long enough to absorb the atmosphere. There is a great deal in England that I shall have to miss, but I am seeing as much as I can without rushing. Our motor trip ought to cover two weeks, and I've added in Tintern Abbey & Gloucester, because abbeys and cathedrals give me more pleasure than anything except moors and rivers and country roads.

It is too bad that you should have that trouble with your cook. I hope it won't be as hard finding another as you expect. By this time you are preparing to leave, I suppose, & I hope you will find Louise well. Oh, I wish you could see Sally & Little Anne & Simon and Budrau!

Everyone I wanted to see has left London now,[2] and as far as that goes, this trip has not been so satisfactory as my last one. But I feel less and less like seeing people.

I suppose you will find at home the book I sent you about the Yorkshire Abbeys.

Devotedly, ever | Ellen

ALS UVA EG Box 14
Address: Mrs C. C. Tutwiler, 9000 Crefeld Street, Chestnut Hill, Philadelphia, Pennsylvania, U.S.A.
Postmark: London W.1 1927, Aug 9, 11:15 A.M.

    1. Unidentified.
    2. EG received a note from Virginia Woolf on the same day as this letter (August 7), expressing regret that she would not be in town to meet Glasgow. On her "last" trip, in 1914, EG met many writers.

To Rebe Glasgow Tutwiler

Aug. 11*th* [1927] | LANGHAM HOTEL, | PORTLAND PLACE, | LONDON. W. 1.
Darling Rebe,

It is a fine morning and we are starting at 9.30 for a day of motoring:—Waltham Abbey, St. Albans, Epping Forest, and Dicken's old inn The Maypole (King's Head) at Chigwell. By the way, I've got some delphinium seeds for you from Dicken's Garden at Gad's Hill. We stopped there on the way home from Canterbury, and saw the house (a dreadful place inside) and the pretty garden, where there is still kept planted in flowers and ivy the graves of his bird and two cats. The boards at the graves read (all marked by him "This is the grave of Dick, the best of birds," and on another of a cat, "Haroun," dates. "Thou, O Lord, will save both man and beast." Why don't you have the walk marked over Jock's grave? It would make it so interesting. After visiting the house we went to the Leather Bottle inn (his Chig haunt) and had an excellent dinner. "Werry good vittles," as Mr Weller would say, "and a werry pleasant time was enjoyed by all, including the vidder."[1] Well, at twenty I might have had a thrill from it—but not now!

As for Canterbury! Only York is more beautiful, and I wonder if York is *really* more beautiful? Perhaps the interior and the detail work of York is more perfect. But the surroundings of Canterbury are matchless. The cloisters are a dream of loveliness, & the crypt is the most beautiful one I have ever seen—the most beautiful, it is easy to believe in the world, and the purest English gothic. You may have been here. I cannot remember.

Later. Awaiting dinner at 7.30. Broad daylight. I had to leave for our trip, & we had a lovely day. St. Albans Cathedral is different from any other (each one is distinctive) and it has a beautiful interior, as well as the longest gothic nave in the world. From there we went to Waltham Cross and I saw the best preserved one of the "chere reine" crosses.[2] Then to Waltham Abbey, which is really a church, and the oldest Norman building in England. Built by Harold before William the Conqueror. After that we had lunch (rather poor) at the Old Thatched Inn at Epping, and then took a walk in glorious Epping Forest. If we had not seen Burnham Beeches we should have thought it even lovelier, but Burnham Beeches is simply the enchanted forest. It is something I dreamed of seeing—beeches as large as California redwood, & as expressive as olive trees, or more so. It was almost impossible not to believe in fairies and dryads. Such an ineffable green light, and the leaves draping the gnarled old boles like streaming veils of chiffon with the sunlight filtering through. We walked miles. It was all so beautiful that it hurt, & such a revelation of the spirits of trees. An enchanted forest, if there ever was one. Did you go there from Stoke Poges? If not, don't fail to go next time. We intend to spend a whole afternoon there when we come back to London. The waiter has just come up to lay the table, and a bottle of Sauterne is waiting for the Salmon and lettuce and rice pudding. We have had these delicious English rice puddings for the last three nights. Tomorrow we lunch with May Sinclair, but Saturday we plan to return to Simpsons for some of his roast & stewed raspberries. We had two invitations for lunch Friday—our only invitations so far, for everybody is away. The first day of our trip I think we'll stop for lunch with Frank Swinnerton, & Mrs Conrad found out I was over here & asked me to visit her, so I may stop for tea with her. I had a lovely letter from the Duchess of Hamilton asking us both to come & pay her a visit. I hope we can arrange to motor there for a night, but I am not sure. Having the car makes all the difference in the world, and I *do* wish you were here to enjoy it with us. You would so delight in these places, especially in Burnham Beeches & Canterbury,—there is no feeling that we are being extravagant in using it. Hasley is the best driver I ever saw. He handles this great big car as if it were a pram, but sometimes he goes so fast through the shires that he makes me nervous. I told him it would kill me if we ran over a dog. Coming home from Canterbury a truck in front of us ran over one, & we stopped but there was nothing to do. I hope the poor thing was unconscious. Carrie got out, & the people all seemed very kindly, & said they had sent for "the humane [Ritter?]." Wherever there is a village in England there seems to be a branch of the humane society. I have never been in any country where animals as a whole appeared to be so well cared for and considered and it is the only place I ever travelled where my heart was not constantly wrung by dreadful sights.—

Our dinner came. We ate the salmon & embibed the Sauterne, and are waiting for the rice pudding. We have dinner in our sitting-room & lunch out somewhere. There is great confusion in the dining-room downstairs, & the food here is not very good. Day before yesterday we lunched at the Pall Mall (table d'hote & only fair) & Saturday we are going (D.V.) to one of the Soho restaurants.— The rice pudding came. We have eaten that & I am so tired I must stop. I'll try to write Sunday, though we are planning to go that morning to the Jeffrey Museum[3] at Horton, Shoreditch.

I wish I had Little Anne or Sally or Budrau or Simon here now to take home to the lambs. There are so many dogs over here & all so adorable. Today we saw a number of fluffy ones & a lovely old English sheepdog. The Sealyham is the fashionable breed now, & people in America don't know what they are like.

Best love, | as ever your | devoted | Ellen

ALS ViU EG Box 14
Address: Mrs C. C. Tutwiler, 9000 Crefeld Street, Chestnut Hill, Philadelphia, Pennsylvania, U.S.A.
Postmark: London W.1 Aug 12 1927, 11:15 A.M.

1. Words spoken by Sam Weller in Charles Dickens's *Pickwick Papers*.

2. "Chère reine" ("dear queen") crosses were erected at various sites in England by Edward I in honor of his wife, Eleanor of Castile.

3. London's Geffrye Museum of Furniture and Decorative Arts, which is located in a row of eighteenth-century almshouses.

To Anne Virginia Bennett

Aug 14. [1927?] | LANGHAM HOTEL, | PORTLAND PLACE, | LONDON. W. 1.
Dearest A.V.

We have just been laughing over the pictures you sent of Sealyhams & Scotties. As the days pass my hope of taking one home diminishes. We have had an interesting time in London, though one day at Canterbury (I wrote Rebe of this) and above all *Burnham Beeches* have been the cream of it all.

Today Mrs. Clark & Dr. C. expect to arrive, & I have told Hasley to drive Mrs Clark all day tomorrow. Carrie & I can go to places perfectly well by ourselves. This is Sunday, & nothing is open until 2 o'clock, so we will wait & go to the Geffrey Museum at Shoreditch. I never heard of anyone who went there; it is a wonderful museum of all Jerseyham in an old almshouse (1600). Yesterday we went to the Wallace Collection, which I much prefer to the Tate. There is an incomparable Rembrandt there, and the most beautiful Bonheur (to me) that I have ever seen. I sent you a colour print of that enchanting picture by Sir Joshua Reynolds, & I sent little Jane Duke one of the equally lovely "Miss Bowles." We had lunch at Simpsons in the Strand, gave up Hasley (we gave him every Sat. afternoon & Sun. off in London) and went to the National Portrait Gallery.

In the morning I tried to find the Shelter of the Dumb Friends League, but by mistake I drove miles to the Animal Rescue League, in the poorest part of London, a little house founded by one woman, & now run by three women. It was a poor small place, but it does more work than any. 51,000 animals were put to death there last year. They are able to keep any or find homes, but they send some dogs to the Home at Battersea Park. It made us rather sick, but I'm glad I saw it. It is just as well sometimes to see what some people have to endure (including animals) and yet live on. Those poor women! Yet the animals in London are the best taken care of I have ever seen, and it is the only country I ever travelled in where the heart is not wrung constantly by the sight of the work animals. Beside Virginia, England is a paradise for dumb things.

I am not, by the way, very well pleased with Jeremy's and Billy's paraphernalia. It cost me $16.25, but I believe I could have got it better and certainly cheaper at Abercombie's.[1] The English don't make fancy things. This came from a leather place where they made only dog collars, etc, and I suppose it will wear.

But it looks small (though it took the man an hour to get the measurements) and on the whole, I am disappointed in it. Carrie and I found some interesting (and reasonable) antiques, I hope, in Bloomsbury, by the British Museum, but as a rule everything, including cloth (& especially clothes of silk) is very dear. They tell us that antiques have gone up thirty per cent in the last year—& we can well believe it!

Tuesday, starting early, we are (unless something prevents) going to motor down to Fern, the country estate of the Duke of Hamilton. The Duchess wrote and asked me to visit her and bring "my nice friend," so we are going down for two nights and a day before we start on our motor trip. It is a hundred miles to Fern, and it is down beyond Shaftesbury, in or near the New Forest.

We expect to return to London Thursday, & get ready for our motor trip early Saturday morning. That day we have promised to lunch with Frank Swinnerton at Cranleigh, his cottage, in Surrey, and to take tea with Mrs Conrad, at "The Old Farmhouse," near Godalming. I think it is interesting to do these things. I see the people and the way they live. A few minutes ago the telephone rang & Mrs Conrad called up from Godalming to make sure that we were going to stop to see her. It was sweet of her to write to me, as soon as she heard that I was in England, for I did not let her or any one else know. I wrote to Virginia Woolf, and she asked me to come to see her when she got back to London, but that won't be till October the first. I am sorry to miss her.

Day before yesterday we lunched with May Sinclair. She was very nice, but, oh, so pathetic. I don't know what has happened to her, but it must have been a stroke of paralysis. She can't turn her head or move one arm at all, & she has become very fat, after being so little & thin. It is tragic to see her and remember what a gift she once had, what power and vigour and insight! She told us we must motor through Cotswold after we leave Tewkesbury, & to Stow-on-the-Wold, so we have included that in our trip. She lives in an attractive corner house, with a brick wall & green gate, in Hampshire, and she has a black cat, which she seems to love more than anything in the world.

Yesterday it poured all the afternoon, but the sun is out now, & I hope it will stay clear. I went to the Irish Linen stores a day or two ago, & bought the only reasonable thing I've seen in London, a perfectly beautiful damask table cloth, four and a half yards long, & 2 1/2 wide. It's a famous hunting pattern with birds and trees & ferns on it, as fine as any I ever saw. When they told me they had sold the last dozen napkins I was overcome, but after long looking they found one dozen that had been ordered by somebody & not yet sent, & they let me have it because I would not have time for them to order one from Ireland. Wasn't that lucky? They are having my monogram embroidered on the cloth & napkins. Also having it hemmed and laundered. Carrie has bought some very good things, & some lovely samplers & also some china. I got a pink lustre tea set for four pounds at Harrogate, 12 cups & saucers & plates, & very cheap. I have seen some perfectly beautiful things, & I am looking at a Georgian bowl. If I have any money left after our trip, I'll get something. Also I have my eye on Rebe's present, but I am waiting to see if I find anything on the trip I like better. If I do, I'll buy this for myself if I can afford it when I return.

We went to see your coat yesterday, & I think it is much the best thing I could get. I hope you will like it & that it will fit.

Devotedly— Love | to the lambs— E.

ALS ViU EG 5083 Box 28
Address: Miss A. V. Bennett | 1 West Main Street | Richmond, Virginia | U.S.A.
Postmark: Harrogate Yorks.

    1. EG probably means Abercrombie, the well-known London department store.

To Anne Virginia Bennett

Aug. 19th [1927] | LANGHAM HOTEL, | PORTLAND PLACE, | LONDON. W. 1.
Dearest A.V.

I have thought all day how much Cary would have enjoyed this English country and motoring over it.[1]

We came back yesterday from a lovely visit to Fern, the English country place of the Duke of Hamilton. I wish we could have gone to their old castle in Scotland, but they go there only for a few weeks in Sept, and by that time we shall be out of England. I have never known anyone so unselfconscious and so full of sympathy for animals as the Duchess. She reminded me so often of Cary in the things she said and felt, for she is very intelligent and well-read. She has a keen sense of humour. The sun came out just as we got to Fern & we had the only two good days they had had this summer. It was an interesting experience, for we had a glimpse of English country life at its best. We went all over the estate, from the flower garden to the stables and the pasture for cows, & saw all the wonderful fruit raised under glass, figs such as I had not eaten since Cary and I were in Naples—large purple Turkish ones, & peaches, all raised in hot houses, under glass. It was all very lovely because every one there was so nice, among them Miss Lind-af-Hageby, to whom I have become much attached.

The Duchess has nine dogs as daily companions, besides 3 border terriers that live in a large paddock in the woods. She offered me one of them, but I'd rather have a Sealyham, if any, and I am still longing to take home Sally or Anne. The child she lost is buried there at Fern, in a fairy glade where she said she wanted to be. It is all so terribly tragic and heart breaking. She talked to me about the child, & I saw that this one youngest child was closer to her and more sympathetic to her than anyone in the world had ever been. Miss Lind said that at first they thought it would kill the duchess. For two days after the child died so suddenly of septic pneumonia she would not believe it had occurred. When you talk to her intimately she impresses you, for all her vitality, as a heartbroken person, and as unworldly as any human being could be. I wonder what the bond is with Margaret, but it must be the very best influence M. could have over her. Her manner with servants alone is so different from any Branches.

One of the dogs at Fern, a beautiful Irish terrier was rescued by a policeman from a bag as she was being taken into a medical laboratory. The dogs, two Irish terrier puppies, were stolen one evening as they were playing with some children in a square in London, & the rest running a policeman stopped a man as he was going into the laboratory of some college here, & said, "What have you got in that sack?" The man said, "potatoes." Then the policeman, who had suspected for some time that he was selling stolen dogs, opened the bag and the two puppies, half suffocated, rolled out, & the policeman recognized them from the description of the lost dogs. The bottom one in the bag has been more or less ill ever since (it happened only last spring) and was at a veterinarian, but the one I saw was as sweet as could be. They had had a big meeting about it, & Miss Lind told me it had done a great deal for the anti-vivisection movement.

We are starting tomorrow at 9.30 on our trip, and I must stop & pack. The first day we have lunch with Frank Swinnerton at Cranleigh and tea with Mrs Conrad at Godalming. The day after that we have tea with the Thomas Hardys at Max Gate Dorchester. I had a very sweet note from Mrs Hardy. We do not expect to be back in London until Sept 2nd, and we sail, if nothing prevents, on the 7th. That ought to bring us, again if nothing prevents, to New York on Sept. 13th (Tuesday).

I bought today a perfectly beautiful pair of old Sheffield candlesticks. They cost three hundred & seventy-four dollars, but Carrie got the dealer to come down, by degrees, to 290. They are very fine & rare with the hall mark & a crest engraved on them. I bought, also, several days ago, an old Georgian bowl for the center of the table. I hope it will be as lovely as it seemed here—the best thing to fix flowers in we could find. We have just come back from the British Museum, where I went because I couldn't find the Rosetta Stone on my last visit. Two blocks away from the Museum there is a fascinating curiosity shop kept by an old lady named Mrs Webster. She had something I wanted for Rebe, but I hesitated because Carrie could not get her to reduce her price. She said she bought it at Christie's[2] and paid more than she asked me. Finally, I waited until the day before we were leaving London & went back & paid her what she asked. It was more than I had intended to spend, but I think it is a gem, & it will look lovely in Rebe's home. It now lies on Carrie's bed in company with a number of samplers. Jay is keeping your coat until we return to London, & also a hat for me.

I am hoping that the motor car will diminish the cost of the trip a good deal, but of course I have to pay for the board of Hasley & the car. I hope I shan't have to cash a check till I get to New York. I am delighted to think of the pink hall. The next money I have I am going to buy myself a Sealey mattress.

Best love to the precious lambs. As ever

E.

ALS ViU EG 5083 Box 28
Address: Miss A. V. Bennett | 1 West Main Street | Richmond, Virginia | U.S.A.
Postmark: London W.1 Aug 19 1927 10:15 P.M.

1. The date, August 19, was the anniversary of CGMcC's death.
2. Christie's auction house.

From Radclyffe Hall

LE GRAND HOTEL | BAGNOLES-DE-L'ORNE | Normandy. France. |
August 24th,[1] 1927.

Dear Miss Glasgow.

I feel that I must write and tell you how deeply I regret being unable to be present at the luncheon which is being given in your honour by Mrs. Evans, this as I so very much want to know you personally, having already met you through your books. But as you will see by the above address, I am far away in Normandy, five hours by train even from Paris. However, were it not that I am in the very middle of a tiresome "Cure" I should certainly return to England rather than lose the opportunity of meeting you.

I expect to be back in London about September 22nd. Is there any hope that you will be in London or indeed anywhere in England at that time?[2] I shall be in Paris on September 19th & 20th for two days, and if you should happen to be there yourself, perhaps we could lunch together on my way through? If you will write to me at Bagnoles de L'Orne when you get this letter, there is just the chance that we may be able to meet after all. Supposing that you are not going to be in Paris but are going to be in England on my return, I could motor to see you even if you are out of London, so perhaps you will let me know your plans.

And now, in case we do not meet this time, I want to thank you for your magnificent support of "Adam's Breed"—my first book to be published in America.[3] You have no idea how your words of praise have heartened me, because I feel that praise from such a writer as you are is no mean thing. My book is fortunate indeed to have found such a sponsor, and your opinion has greatly lessened my disappointment in the fact that it did not, on its first appearance, receive as cordial a reception in the States as Mr Russell Doubleday and I hoped it would do. As I am half American (my mother was a Philadelphian) I am still hopeful that Americans will come to like my work; indeed I have a personal feeling in the matter, having spent many happy times in America, and this is yet another reason why your kindness has deeply touched me.

Yours sincerely | *Radclyffe Hall.*

ALS ViU EG Box 15

1. This superscript "th" is punctuated by a dot under each letter. All other superscript dates in the letter have double underlines.
2. EG sailed for the United States on September 7, 1927.
3. EG had signed a petition protesting the censorship of Hall's work. *Adam's Breed* was published in 1926.

To Rebe Glasgow Tutwiler

KING'S ARMS HOTEL, | DORCHESTER, | Aug 24. 1927

My darling Rebe,

This is the fifth day of our motor trip, and I have not had a minute for writing. Now it is before nine in the morning. Carrie has gone to an antique shop, & I am waiting for the car at ten. If Carrie were by herself she would never see anything except antique shops in mean streets.

The first three days were very stormy. We left in a pouring rain Saturday from London. It poured all day long, & after a delightful lunch with Frank Swinnerton (he is much more interesting than his books) and a rather dreary tea with Mrs Conrad at Godalming, we spent the night at the very attractive inn at Burford Bridge. There is a really beautiful garden behind the inn, with wonderful fir trees & roses. In spite of the rain we stopped on our way from Godalming, at the Silent Pool, which is simply the most beautiful thing in the way of fresh water I have looked at. Did you see it? I hope so, but I never heard you mention it. After a raining day & night, we left in the rain for Winchester. The cathedral is rather disappointing without (not so perfectly symmetrical an exterior as Salisbury) but the nave is, perhaps the most perfect of all. We took a lovely walk across the marshes trying to find the hospital of St. Cross but the rain drove us home. The next day we drove through the New Forest, between gleams of sunshine & hard sheets of rain. Nothing could spoil that. It was & is drowsily lovely—those enchanting fairy glades of bright green in the midst of the ancient oaks & beeches. Tuesday was, a glorious day. That was, yesterday & we had a most interesting visit to Sherborne. Did you go to the old Almshouse? It was founded in the days of Henry VI. 1437, & I found it intensely interesting. 12 old men in their coats & 6 old women in red capes have lived there since 1437. The prior, the head of the old men took us over, a Mr Phillips, who seemed to be in every way a gentleman. I gave him a present and he insisted upon giving me one in return, a little old glass bowl from his bureau. I am going to send him some Virginia tobacco. After lunch I stopped & bought some tobacco for the men & four pounds of candy for the old women & took it to them. It was so pathetic & so interesting. A beautiful picture (triptych) painted in the early fifteenth century, & some wonderful old pewter & old stained glass. I find the old English almshouses so very interesting. We went to another (Thomas Hardy told me about it) in Dorchester. That was a very old building, but tragic in its distribution—1 old woman & six old men, & the old woman complained of the old men to us exactly as if she had been married to all of them!

We had a charming tea yesterday with the Hardys. He doesn't seem to have aged at all in 13 years, and is without doubt the nicest old man I ever saw. Age has not clouded his vision in the least, nor has it deadened his sensibilities. He has all of our sympathy for animals. It was an extremely pleasant afternoon, and I am so glad we went. Mrs Hardy is a very nice woman, but I missed the darling wire-haired terrier Wessex.

Now we are off to Lyme Regis, Honiton & Exeter. I have added Tewkesbury, Gloucester (after Tintern Abbey) into our itinerary. Also the Cotswold, which everyone says we must not miss, Chipping Camden, Moreton-in-the-Marsh & Stowe-on-the-Wold. One of the most interesting afternoons we spent was the Sunday before we left London when I took Carrie to the Geffrey Museum (the most picturesque place in London (old almshouses) Charterhouse Square, & then we got out & walked over to Lincoln Inn Fields, St. Mary-in the Strand, & St. Clement Danes, past it the Inns of Strand.

I must stop, & go. Dearest love,
Devotedly | Ellen

ALS ViU EG Box 14
Address: Mrs C. C. Tutwiler, | 9000 Crefeld Street, | Chestnut Hill, | Philadelphia, Pennsylvania, | U.S.A.
Postmark: Dorchester Aug 24 1927 8:30 P.M.

To Anne Virginia Bennett

August 25th [1927] | IMPERIAL HOTEL | TORQUAY
I am so glad to think of a nice painted hall!

Dearest A.V.

We spent last night here at this very good hotel. Torquay (pronounced Tor-*kee*), is a beautiful place on the Devon Coast, with the most glorious air. We have had a good deal of rain, but today, & the day we spent in Dorchester could not have been better. Saturday morning we left London in a pouring rain, and pushed hard and fast for the first two days of our trip. We had a delightful lunch with the Frank Swinnertons in their charming antique cottage (500 years old) at Cranleigh. There is a lovely garden in front of it, but the rain poured so we could barely see it. When we got there they had a big wood fire in the immense old stone fireplace, and Mrs Swinnerton, who is very sweet & much younger than he is) took off our wet clothes just coming from the gate, where he met us bareheaded, had got us dripping, and gave us a delicious glass of sherry. I don't think I ever enjoyed a lunch more. After restaurant fare it seemed so good and homelike. They waited on the table themselves. Everything was ready & the table all waiting when we arrived, except the hot dishes, which he took in from the kitchen door and carried or served. It was all so sweet and informal, and he is very delightful to talk to, so much more interesting than his books.

Later—I was writing before breakfast, and Carrie was not dressed. She came down & we went into the dining-room & had breakfast (the first Devonshire Cream) at a table looking out on a beautiful view of sea and rocks. It is heavenly outside, and I am going out to sit in the sun until eleven o'clock, when we go on to Two Bridges, where (God permitting) we shall spend the afternoon & night. I want to take a walk on Dartmoor and to spend a night there. If they can't take us, we'll try Tavistock—& go on tomorrow to Tintagel.

Tea with Mrs Conrad was rather dismal. She has become enormously stout, and so very complacent, poor soul, clinging to the shadow of fame which he shed over her. On the contrary, the Hardys were lovely & simple, & seemed so glad to see me. She is very shy, but a thoroughly nice sensible woman. I missed Wessex, the wire-haired terrier, and they said their hearts ached whenever they thought of him. He died of old age a few months ago, and he was a puppy of six months when I saw him in 1914. I never saw so attractive a man of his age as Thomas Hardy, which proves that it is intellect, after all, that counts as one goes over the hill of life. He is far more modern and advanced than most men of 25, and age has not deadened his sensibility in the least. I was so glad I went after hesitating to do so. It must be the last time, and I shall like to remember how he was when I saw him so near the end of life. He is profoundly civilized and sympathetic about animals, just as he is in his books—and especially in Jude.

I wrote Rebe about Sherborne, a lovely little town, which she saw, I think, and about Mr Phillips, the prior of the old men in the almshouse. It was very touching, & I am going to send him some Virginia tobacco, if I can pay the duty, as soon as I get home. Two weeks from yesterday, we sail. Embrace the lambs.

Love, E.

ALS ViU EG 5083 Box 28

Address: Miss A. V. Bennett | 1 West Main Street | Richmond, Virginia | U.S.A.
Postmark: Torquay Devon, 25 Aug 1927, 3:15 P.M.
Publication: *L* 87–89.

To Rebe Glasgow Tutwiler

BEDFORD HOTEL | TAVISTOCK. | Aug 26*th* 1927

My darling Rebe,

Yesterday was one of the most beautiful days of our trip. We left Torquay on a glorious morning, when the sea was as blue as Indigo and the view from the terrace of the Imperial Hotel was [?] [?]. Our run across Dartmore to Two Bridges, where we had lunch, was a delight, and I decided that we must spend the night here at Tavistock and take a walk on Dartmoor late in the afternoon. I have never had a more wonderful week. Hasley drove us out after five o'clock, and we got out and wandered for two hours or more all over the heather and gorse. We went up a tor (little mountain) named "Gibbet Tor" because they used to hang people there. Years ago, no one remembers when, somebody cleared a space on the spot, & put up a mound of stones, & it is supposed to bring you luck to add a stone to the mound when you go up on the tor. We had not heard this, but we picked up white stones on the way & added them to the pile. On the way back Carrie met a woman who told her. The air was the most glorious and bracing I ever felt in my life—finer than sea air, and it is still this morning, when I am writing before breakfast, while Carrie is dressing.

Nothing in nature, not even the mountains or the sea, is as sympathetic to me temperamentally as moors, and you could conceive of nothing more majestic and impenetrable than Dartmoor while the sun sank below its rim and the shadows of the clouds moved slowly over its face. From purple, as vivid as heather, just as Hardy describes Egdon Heath, it changed to brown—and russet black and then to a kind of brown & violet darkness. I wish you could have been with us. I know how you loved it last summer, and as I told Carrie nobody else in the world but me would ever have insisted upon spending the night in Dartmoor and being there at sunset. The air is so pure and uplifting, without a trace of dampness, that you feel as if you were on top of the world, and can see the roundness of the earth. And the sheep and wild ponies make it that much more lonely and forsaken.

I have been glad to get your letters. I believe you have written oftener than anyone, & I got up early so as to be able to write you a letter from Dartmoor. After breakfast we go on to Tintagel, and we are going to spend tonight there, D.V. Tomorrow night (D.V.) we stay at Biddeford instead of Lynton, because Hasley has a son at school in Biddeford. In such a little while we sail.

Best love E.

ALS ViU EG Box 14
Address: Mrs C. C. Tutwiler | 9000 Crefeld Street | Philadelphia, Pennsylvania | U.S.A.
Postmark: Tavistock 26 August '27, 10 A.M.

To Rebe Glasgow Tutwiler

Aug 31. 1927 | THE LYGON ARMS, BROADWAY | WORCESTERSHIRE

Darling Rebe,

It is eight o'clock in the morning, and I am waiting for breakfast. This is an enchanting little village, and this hotel is really a thing of beauty, very artistic in every detail. The dining-room is the most attractive I've ever seen in an inn. We went from Tavistock, to Bideford (dreadful place & hotel) but Hasley has a son there, and then by Lynton & the adorable Exmore, to Glastonbury. I loved the Pilgrims Inn,[1] one of the best we seen, with *really good* coffee. Those ruins are very beautiful, & my only regret was that the abbey was closed on Sunday. However, we visited the Almshouse (I always do) and made the acquaintance of an unusual old woman, who had a lovely rose garden——a Mrs Curtis, with a daughter crippled from tuberculosis in the same tiny room with her. Seven old women live there in that row of little rooms, each with its own little garden attached. She had grown all her roses from slips, and she was to grow a new salmon coloured one and name it for me. The chapel notice said they received only 12 shillings six a quarter as an endowment. The town must help. I gave her a quarter allowance, & Carrie gave her something too. It was so pathetic, but full of human interest. The next morning before we left we went to the Abbey, but the visit had to be very short. I wanted to stay, for it was very lovely. This, I think, was the Abbey you saw and the only one. We went to Bath & Wells from there. Wells I thought lovely without, but disappointing within, and Bath has one of the loveliest naves, I think, in any Cathedral. Only York, Winchester, Exeter, & Bath have had satisfying interiors. After York (pure perfection) the interior—especially the naves of Winchester and of Exeter are the most beautiful. Exeter gave me a glow, it is so wide and rich and human in its feeling. But each Cathedral is individual & beautiful in its own way. Gloucester has the most perfect cloisters and an exquisite Lady chapel, but the nave is disappointing. I love the Abbey churches, the ones at Sherbourne & Tewkesbury are wonderfully.

My greatest disappointing is the Wye Valley, called the "loveliest river scenery in England." The Wye does not compare to many Yorkshire rivers, and Tintern Abbey is not comparable in any way to Fountains. It is a lovely ruin, but it is impaired now by the disfiguring preservation which is going on everywhere in England. The situation is flat, and very poor because there is no park around it. You go in and pay for admission right at the Abbey door. After the marvelous situation of every Abbey in Yorkshire, especially of Fountains, Bolton (most beautiful woods & park) and Rievaulx, it was a sad disappointment to find no trees around it, & the ruins scraped of every flower and leaf!

Tomorrow we hope to reach London in time for some letters. Tonight we spend at Oxford. I am delaying my start a quarter of an hour in order to go to the bank to get the money for some Georgian serving spoons I saw here last night large, heavy serving spoons 2 pounds 10. a pair.

Love as | ever E

ALS ViU EG Box 14
Address: Mrs C. C. Tutwiler | 9000 Crefeld Street | Philadelphia, Pa. | U.S.A.
Postmark: 31 Aug 27, Worc.

1. Now called George and Pilgrims Hotel, a stopping place for fifteenth-century pilgrims en route to Glastonbury Abbey nearby.

To Anne Virginia Bennett

Sept. 1st [1927] | LANGHAM HOTEL, | PORTLAND PLACE, | LONDON. W. 1.
Dearest A.V.

We have just this minute got back to the Langham, and on the way up we stopped by Brown, Shipley & I found three letters from you, 2 from Rebe, & 2 letters and a cable from Henry. This is just a line and the last I will write before sailing. You will probably get it the day before I land, which I hope will be Tuesday, the 13th. I shall have to stay several days in New York, but hope to reach home Saturday the 17th at 6.25. I am crazy to see the lambs.

This trip was simply perfect, not a delay, not a mistake, not a stop even, for oil or gas. We went more than 1200 miles, & Hasley is a marvel. He is the best chauffeur I ever saw, & so intelligent in other ways. He made our trip a different thing, & if we had been multi-millionaires we could not have travelled better. All the same I am thankful to get back to a sitting-room.[1] We are having late tea, with an omelet, & *no* dinner. Though our trip was wonderful, and we went to so many lovely places, I have seen nothing that could compare in beauty and interest to Yorkshire. The month we spent in Yorkshire was the best and most satisfying part of the whole summer. For sheer beauty the South and West of England is surpassed by the North, and Tintern Abbey does not in any way equal Fountains. Nor does the valley of the Wye compare with the loveliness of Wharfdale and the scenery around Bolton Abbey.

I found a lovely letter here from Radclyffe Hall saying that if she was not in the midst of a cure, she would come all the way to England to see me (she is in Normandy), and one from Lady Hadfield asking me to visit her on the Riviera.

Well, I am so tired I must stop. I am so glad the hall will be finished before I return. I picked up a few little things on my trip, and I am going to buy covering for the Sheraton sofa in the drawing-room at Liberty's.

Love —E

ALS ViU EG Box 28
Address: Miss A. V. Bennett | 1. West Main Street | Richmond, Virginia | U.S.A.
Postmark: London W.1, Sept 2 1927, 11:15 A.M.

1. Just before "sitting-room" the words "*private toilet &*" are scratched out.

From Radclyffe Hall

Grand Hotel. | Bagnoles de L'Orne. | Normandy, France. | September 4th 1927.
Dear Miss Glasgow.

Thank you so much for your most kind letter. It is a real sorrow to me not to have met you—but I have a feeling that it is only a pleasure delayed. I have written to my publishers—Carroll & Co—and told them to send you my other serious book: "The Unlit Lamp," I don't know whether it will appeal to you as much as "Adam's Breed" but I think it may interest you. I have instructed them to send it to the Langham Hotel by hand, in the hopes that it may reach you before you sail. Yet once again I have to thank you for your wonderful words of praise—I love to think that you have seen Gian-Luca's forest now; and that you remembered him in connection with it has made me very proud. Thank you also for giving me your address in Richmond. If I do come to the States, I shall surely come also to Richmond Virginia in order to see you. I once went to Richmond for a few days and loved the old town so much. Wishing you a prosperous voyage.

Yours sincerely | Radclyffe Hall.

ALS ViU EG Box 15

To Rebe Glasgow Tutwiler

Sept. 6. 1927 | LANGHAM HOTEL, | PORTLAND PLACE, | LONDON. W. I.
Darling Rebe,

I had thought that my letter from Broadway would be my last one from

England, but I seem for the first time in my life to have acquired the habit, and whenever I have a spare moment, I turn to the desk. One thing is "sure and certain," when I reach home I shall not look at a piece of letter paper or address an envelope with my own hand for at least six months. This, I suppose, will reach you after we are in America, for we are sailing early tomorrow morning, if God and the fates permit.

Our motor trip was quite perfect—almost the only perfect thing I ever knew. The car was luxuriously comfortable, and Hasley was a miracle of efficiency and intelligence. We went over 1200 miles without so much as a single minutes' delay or a wrong turning, even on the side trips which were not included in the itinerary. Not once did we have to stop on the way for gasoline, oil or weather or the slightest repair.

The country we saw was all beautiful, but with the exception of Dartmoor nothing meant as much to me as the Yorkshire landscape and ruined abbeys. After seeing so many counties, and almost every famous part of England (except the Lakes, which we missed) there is no doubt in our minds that Yorkshire is the most beautiful, as well as the biggest county in England. It takes time to see the North, where distances are greater, but it is the most beautiful, the most enchanting, and the least commercialized part of England. There was no sign of commercialization at any Yorkshire Abbey. The entrance fees are all paid far away from the abbey ruins, but to go into Tintern was like entering a museum, and the ruins were so scraped & scoured and riveted together that they were a little too reminiscent of an exhibit in an archeological institute.

After Broadway, we spent a night in Oxford, and late that afternoon Carrie and I took the circular walk at Magdalen College, with Addison's Walk entirely to ourselves at sunset and afterwards. The next day we saw the Colleges and motored up to London in the afternoon. Since we came back we have been twice to the Natural History Museum, because I wanted her to see her ancestors, and understand, as I told her, why she looked as she does. It is fascinating place. Did you go there. I imagine Carrington would adore it. Then we went a second time to the National Gallery, which is my favorite of all the London galleries. We spent another whole afternoon there.

At 11. o'clock this morning, we are motoring down to Knole to go over the place with Mrs Nicholson (Miss Sackville-West, the writer). She is a daughter of Lord Sackville, who owns Knole, and first we are to lunch with her at her home in the Weald, a mile or two away. Everyone tells me that Knole is the most beautiful country place in England. It was given by Henry VIII. to Lord Sackville & has been in the family ever since, and unchanged for over four hundred years.[1] The garden is the same & even the varieties of flowers & trees & shrubs. There are 365 rooms in the house, and (I do not admire this particularly) one room was furnished in silver furniture for King James I. when he came for a visit. However, this is all out of a book somebody gave me, and I can tell you more after I've had my excursion. Mr Evans, a delightful man, who is one of the firm of Heinemann is going down with us, and he telephoned Miss Sackville-West that we should like to visit the place. Then she asked us to lunch with her, very kindly, and offered to take us over Knole which is as big as a village. She was born there and lived there until her marriage.

Our special train leaves at 7.55 tomorrow morning, so we must have breakfast at 6.30. I hope you can come down to Richmond very soon, for we are too burdened and too rushed to stop over. I wish we could, but I am obliged to stay at least three days in New York, & we shall not be able to go down till Sat. 17th. I hope you will like what I am bringing you. After looking everywhere I decided this was the best. You were so good about writing.

Best love, —E

ALS ViU EG Box 14
Address: Mrs C. C. Tutwiler | 9000 Crefeld Street | Philadelphia, Pa. | U.S.A.
Postmark: London W.1, Sep 6 1927, 1:15 P.M. "By S. S. Olympic, sailing Sept 7."

1. Knole was given not by Henry VIII but by Queen Elizabeth I to Thomas Sackville in 1566.

To Helen McAfee

January 31st | 1928 | ONE WEST MAIN STREET | RICHMOND, VIRGINIA
Dear Miss McAfee,

I was very glad to have your letter ten days ago, and to hear that you will see England in June. I had an enchanting summer there last year, and after motoring from north to south and east to west, I look back with the greatest longing to beautiful Yorkshire and the ruined abbeys of the north. I hope you can go there. Fountains Abbey, Dartmoor, and a visit to Thomas Hardy, the youngest old man that ever lived, were the high points of my summer.

Yes, I think it is time for me to begin work on that article. As soon as I have rounded a difficult part of my novel,[1] I shall honestly try to turn in the direction of criticism. The truth is that I have too many ideas and too little industry.

Sincerely yours, | ELLEN GLASGOW

ALS CtY
Address: Miss Helen McAfee | *The Yale Review* | Yale Station, | New Haven, Connecticut.
Postmark: Richmond Feb 2 1928 1 P.M.
Publication: *L* 89–90.

1. *TSTF* (1929).

To Irita Van Doren

February 8*th* | 1928 | ONE WEST MAIN STREET | RICHMOND, VIRGINIA

Dear Irita,

Yes, I shall be charmed to have you the week end of the 18*th*. Let me know what train to meet, and just how long to plan for ahead. I hope Carl can come too.

I hope I can write an article or two for you, but I've had a hard time with my work this winter and I am sadly lacking in industry. I doubt if I am able to write four articles, especially as the Yale Review appears determined to have that paper on Southern Literature———.

However, we'll talk it over,

Affectionately Ellen

Love to Carl & Miss Paterson.

I have some ideas for an article on "Woman Myths as Invented by Men,"[1]—if you could give me a free hand and a few books———

ALS DLC

1. Published as "Some Literary Woman Myths," *NYHTB* May 27, 1928, pp. 1, 5–6. This article evolved into the preface for the *Virginia Edition* of *TSTF.*

From Frances Newman

HOTEL ALGONQUIN | NEW YORK | April fourth [1928?]

Dear Miss Glasgow

Mr Messner, of Boni and Liveright, says they sent you the galleys of Dead Lovers are Faithful Lovers[1] this afternoon. He is very sorry to send you anything so inconvenient to read, but there have been some delays, and the book won't be ready to bind until early next week, and I suppose that will be too late for you. I would have loved to see you, but Mrs Cabell told me how tired and busy you are, with your book and the articles both.[2]

If you saw the interview with me in the Times-Dispatch, I hope you realize how unfair to me the "re-write" of it in the News-Leader was. Of course, I shouldn't have thought of saying what I thought you "ought" to write. I only said I was glad you had let your wit have its way in The Romantic Comedians, and that I hoped you would again. I do cherish that book.

Affectionately yours | Frances Newman

ALS ViU EG Box 17

1. Novel (1928) by Newman.

2. The book is *TSTF.* EG published two articles in May 1928, both in *NYHTB*: "Impressions of the Novel" (May 20, pp. 1, 5–6) and "Some Literary Woman Myths" (May 27, pp. 1, 5–6).

To Irita Van Doren

ONE WEST MAIN STREET | RICHMOND, VIRGINIA [July–August 1929?]

Irita dear,

Dan Longwell has just been here, and he tells me how kind and helpful you have been in the matter of "They Stooped to Folly." Thank you ever so much. I do appreciate it, and I have the confident feeling that you will keep them from doing anything that seems in the least cheap. I do wish the announcements to have dignity and distinction, and I am just a little apprehensive.

Yes, it sounds very nice about Isabel Paterson, though I had counted on Burton Rascoe's reviewing the book somewhere. But I know Mrs Paterson's will be illuminating.

It looks now as if I shouldn't be able to get away until August, and I fear you will have flown. However, if I miss you then, I shall expect to see you in September. Certainly, I am willing to have the drawing—if only it won't be a caricature! My last photographs made me vow never to sit for a portrait again, and it seems to me that most of them are very dreadful. That one of Evelyn Scott,[1] for example, I thought a horror. The ones I like best are the red chalk drawings. Who does these? Perhaps Dan could find out, and I remember some of these were in Books. It may be, however, too late when I come.

With love and many thanks, | Ellen

TLS DLC

1. The poet and novelist, born Elsie Dunn (1893–1963), author of novels including *The Narrow House* (1921) and *The Golden Door* (1925).

From Mary Johnston

THREE HILLS | P.O. WARM SPRINGS | VIRGINIA |
September the twenty-seventh, 1929[1]

Dear Ellen,—

I have read "They Stooped to Folly" and I think you have done a very good piece of work.

I am so sorry about Jeremy.[2] I dreamed of you the other night. I was in a house over against your house. It was night time, very quiet, very still, and I looked out of window across to your window and saw that it was lighted—not a shiny light, but a light turned low, and I thought, 'Ellen is there, sorrowing for Jeremy'—then the dream changed. But it was a very 'real' one, and has left a vivid sense of the night and the lighted window and you.

Ever affectionately yours, | Mary Johnston

ALS ViU EG Box 16

1. The date is written at the end of the letter, following the signature.
2. Jeremy died on September 5, 1929.

From Radclyffe Hall

Hotel Pont Royal. | Rue du Bac. Paris | September 29th 1929.
Dear Ellen Glasgow.

I was so glad to get your letter, but deeply sorry to hear of the loss of your Jeremy. I also have lost a beloved dog—one Rufus a sable Collie. It was during the war but I still remember and always will. I had many dogs before him and have had a few since, but in ones life there is always *the dog,* so you see I know just how badly you are feeling. I much liked Jeremy's obituary in Richmond Times Despatch, and my great regret is that I never knew him. I hear from my London literary agents that they have received the copy of your book which you have so kindly sent me.[1] I expect to be returning to England fairly soon so have asked them to keep it for the present, as I don't want it to get knocked about in the post and out here they are so awfully careless. As a matter of fact I have already read it and was just going to write to you on the subject. I think the style a very perfect thing. With your writing I always have the feeling that you are one of those writers who are only content to say a thing as beautifully as it can possibly be said, and I rejoiced while I was reading. The character drawing is wonderful also. I shall look forward to the Old Dominion Edition when it is finally published.

And now to return to Jeremy again. I am one of those who firmly believe that animals have an after life, and so Jeremy is probably still very near you.[2] Don't be surprised when you open your eyes at some distant time on a pleasant new country, (not so awfully unlike old Virginia) to find Jeremy waiting to greet you. It *must* be so if we survive death—at least this is my personal conviction.

I want to come over to America quite soon. I am often very home sick for the bigness of it. But I have not been there for a good many years, and am scared to death by the prices. I am told that New York is terribly expensive, and that is where I should have to be for the greater part of my visit. If and when

I do come across the ocean, however, I shall surely come down to Richmond Virginia because I so very much want to meet Ellen Glasgow.

Yours sincerely | *Radclyffe Hall.*

ALS ViU EG Box 15
Address: Miss Ellen Glasgow. | 1. West Main Street. | Richmond | Virginia. | U. S. America.
Forwarded: c/o Mrs. Tutwiler, | 9000 Crefeld St., | Chestnut Hill, | Penn.
Postmarks: Paris R. F. 29 07 1929; Richmond Va Oct 14 1929

1. Probably *TSTF.*
2. In April 1932, Hall inscribed a copy of her novel *The Master of the House* (1932) as follows, "To dear Ellen who feels as I do that no conception of God can be even partly satisfying unless it envisages His love for His whole creation" (*CLEG* 17.262–63).

To Anne Virginia Bennett

Wednesday | 9000 CREFIELD STREET | CHESTNUT HILL | PENNSYLVANIA
[October 16, 1929]

Dearest A.V.

We got here late last evening after a trip through New England (the weather was perfect & the autumn foliage magnificent. But I felt badly (though better in some ways) & I have a stabbing pain in my heart all the time. When I wake in the night & think of Jeremy, I feel as if I should die. Never have I slept so poorly, I think.

I know it is far harder on you because he was much closer to you than to me, & I don't see how you get any peace. But life has to lived as long as you can't die, & I must at last, I suppose, get my mind on something else.

These are very short notes.

We expect J. tomorrow.

Will you have a man rub up the dining-room table, feet too. You remember how sticky [Nens?] made it before? Rebe says Old English Wax polish is said to be the best.

And will you ask Carrie to telephone about my dyed coat. Also to attend to the desk.

I am perfectly miserable, & I can't see anything ahead.

Lovingly | E.

ALS ViU EG 5083 Box 28
Address: Miss A.V. Bennett, | 1 West Main Street, | Richmond, | Virginia
Postmark: Philadelphia, Pa. Oct 16 1929 11:30 A.M.

To Irita Van Doren

Monday | ONE WEST MAIN STREET | RICHMOND, VIRGINIA
[January 20, 1930?]

Irita dear,

I am so glad to hear from James Cabell that you may be able to run down to see me this winter. It will be just what I need to pick me up, for I have been far from well and in that bleak state of mind when one confronts, without an illusion, the ever-present futility of things in general. It sounds, as I describe it, as if it were a very unpleasant state——and it is! All the work of my life seems to have shrunk to the size of a pea.

But, in spite of this, if it is worth your while to come, I shall be simply delighted to have you, and my nephew[1] will be charmed to take you to dances.

I have been thrilled by Blair's book.[2] She has that rare gift a genuine artistic perception.

My love to you always— | Ellen

ALS DLC

1. Carrington C. Tutwiler Jr. or Glasgow Clark.
2. *Free* (New York: Harcourt, 1930), a sequel to the popular *Condemned to Devil's Island* (New York: Harcourt, 1928) by Blair Rice Niles.

To Irita Van Doren

Friday | ONE WEST MAIN STREET | RICHMOND, VIRGINIA [June 6, 1930?]
Dearest Irita,

I have thought of you constantly, and it is a relief to know that you are over the worst of this trouble.[1] If only you can get the children out of town, I feel that the summer will be a good one.

All the details interest me because of my deep affection for you.

I shall be in New York only one day before sailing on the Homeric, Friday, June the 13th. As this day will be Friday I suppose you will be at the farm. Otherwise, won't you come to see me in the afternoon? If I do not see you, remember that my bankers abroad are Brown, Shipley & Company, 123 Pall Mall, London.

Can you, by the way, send me the address of Sylvia Townsend Warner? She asked me to let her know, and promised to tell me of a place in Dartmoor. With much love always

Ellen

Emily has asked me to review her book in the autumn.[2] Does this seem to you all right? I am one of the subjects, you know.

If you think I should do it, will you keep space in *Books* (a short space) for me?

And please read my essay on James Cabell in The Saturday Review.[3]

ALS DLC

    1. Perhaps IVD's daughter's "illness," for which EG expresses concern in another letter ([May 20, 1930]).

    2. "An Experiment in the South," EG's review of Emily Clark's *Innocence Abroad,* was published in the *NYHTB* on March 22, 1931, 1–6.

    3. "The Biography of Manuel," *Saturday Review of Literature* 6 (June 7, 1930): 1108–9.

To Anne Virginia Bennett

ON BOARD S.S. "HOMERIC." | Tuesday. 16. [June 1930]

Dearest A.V.

The sea has been as smooth as possible, with just the faintest motion today, & it has been very warm. We found our room G.7. very large & the nicest except one, I had ever been in; but the next morning the purser moved us up to a beautiful room on A. Deck, & we have had luxurious quarters. I suppose this is ocean travel at its best, but its best is extremely irksome to me. Physically, I may be stronger, but my state of mind is worse, if anything, than it was on land. I am so miserable that I cannot take the slightest interest in anything, & I go to sleep & wake up either in tears or in a panic. I don't believe it will ever be different, for I am like the man in the Indian fable who walked to the edge of the world & looked over into nothingness.[1] After that nothing made any difference. Of course, I might be much worse, for I am not in physical pain— only this queer sensation in my heart. Something happened to me that day I got back & saw Jeremy lying there, as if the roots of my life dried up & withered. I am weeping now, & a man is on the other side of this desk in the library.

Carrie has not yet got up, though she has started. She can lie about more than anybody I ever saw, for hours just doing little figures with a pencil. She is much too fat and has a fine appetite. I have eaten more, but the food is not very good. Even Bass ale doesn't seem all my fancy had painted it. The boat, however, is the nicest, I think, of all—or rather I like it better than the Olympic—I like the arrangement of it. Our steward is splendid & all the service is good.

To my amazement, we did not sail until nine or ten o'clock Saturday morning. There was the worst fog of years, & all the boats sat in the harbor. We kept saying, "This is the slowest boat, & then looked out & saw the dock & the gangplank. I got 8 beautiful boxes of flowers, & three other presents, 11 in all. But, oh, the notes! I'd rather not get presents than write notes. That Anne Carsall Moore sent me beautiful flowers. [Tanner?] West blue delphiniums. Stewart Bryan & Henry both sent me orchids. I've worn them every night. H. sent other flowers & the orchid found with them.

I worry about your being there all summer. I know it will be dreadful. But, honestly, I look forward with relief to the time when I am in Hollywood with Jeremy. I may feel better when I can move about. Hug Billy.

With dearest love Ellen

ALS ViU EG 5083 Box 28
Address: Miss A.V. Bennett, | 1 West Main Street, | Richmond, | Virginia | U.S.A.
Postmark: Southampton Paquebot, 22 June 1930

1. Unidentified allusion.

To Rebe Glasgow Tutwiler

ON BOARD S.S. "HOMERIC." | June 18 [1930]

I have not half the patience to read this over.
My darling Rebe,

After being very warm it has turned too raw and bleak to sit out, and having had rather mean China tea, there is nothing to do until dinner. This is a very steady boat. Everything about it is as nice as can be except the food, and that is the worst I remember on any big Atlantic liner. The cabins are splendid. The one we had engaged was the nicest I had ever had with a bathroom as large as the one at the Chatham, but the morning after we sailed the purser moved us up to an imposing cabin on the promenade deck—the nicest stateroom, I think, on the ship. (This pen is very difficult to write with. It scratches like a hat pin.) So I suppose we are having ocean travel at its best, and it has extremely few attractions for me! I have never liked anything about it.

We came on board about 8:30, and I found eleven packages in my cabin—eight boxes of beautiful flowers. People were certainly nice. We have had flowers on our table in the stateroom. and I've worn orchids every night. Both Henry & Stewart Bryan sent me orchids. Mrs. Campbell Clark sent me a beatiful basket of flowers, Emily Balch[1] & Mrs. Meade Clark sent me red roses, and in all I had 8 boxes besides the gorgeous rose-coloured bag from Mrs. Pratt, two pair of evening stockings from Josephine and some books from the Brickells. We went to bed about midnight, & kept saying all night "This is the steadiest boat I ever felt." We were still saying that Saturday morning when we looked out & saw the dock and the gangplank. The boat had never moved because of the thickest fog in years, & it was almost lunch time before we started. I couldn't have ale the first day (after all I'd talked about it!) because we were not a mile out (to say nothing of three!) when we went down to lunch.[2]

I hope you will enjoy your crossing more than we do. Fine as our cabin & everything else are, we find it all very irksome. The steward is splendid & waits on us like a lady's maid, but I get dreadfully restless and nervous if I lie down, as Carrie does—almost all the time except when she goes by herself to the pony races—I may be better physically, but my state of mind is as depressed as ever, and I do not take the slightest interest in going to England again. Life seems to have worn on my nerves until I cannot escape any part of the past. Yesterday was the anniversary of Walter's death & I lived over all the horrors again. But I believe that Jeremy's loss has shaken me deeper than everything else. I don't know how or why, but it was just as if the last living roots of my being died and withered away when I came home from Maine and saw him. If I had not gone away it might have been easier. I don't know,—but that moment seemed to epitomize all life to me. Nothing has mattered since—all I have wanted is to have everything over. My head aches and I must stop. I hope you will have a good trip and enjoy it every minute.

Devotedly, | Ellen

TC of ALS FU
Address: Mrs. Cabell Tutwiler, Woods End, 9000 Crefeld Street, Chestnut Hill, Pennsylvania
Postmark: Southampton Pacquebot 22 June 1930 (MKR note)

 1. MKR mistranscribes this as "Boldi (Baldi?)."
 2. EG refers to the restrictions of Prohibition in the United States.

To Anne Virginia Bennett

Saturday | ON BOARD S.S. "HOMERIC." | June 21. [1930]

Dearest A.V.

For the last two days there has been a high sea, & we have had racks on our table. Neither of us has been ill, but the voyage is so irksome that I always wonder why I think Europe is worth it. I am now, as usual waiting for Carrie, who has not dressed. Then we will have lunch (Bass ale for me, brandy for her) and "lounge around" like Brer Tarpin until tea time.[1] Today she will have no pony races, as the people land at Cherbourg at four o'clock. Tomorrow we leave harbor just at 7.30 and land immediately afterward at Southampton.

I wish I could take some interest, but I can not care about anything. Life seems to have got into my nerves. I suppose I am better physically, though I have not had the energy to walk round the deck even once. I just sit in my chair and let existence wash over me. The food is very poor, but it doesn't make any difference at all. I have no appetite. But for ale at lunch and some light wine at dinner, I should eat nothing. The stimulant does help a little, however—

I have not spoken to a soul, but Carrie has made an acquaintance or two at the pony races (wooden ponies, of course) One of these happened to be a Mr. McKee, who was once famous as "Baby McKee," because he was born in the White House. This may have been before your day, but I remember it as a child. He is now on the stock market, & thinks very highly of United Corporation. If Beverley Munford ever sells the bonds & U. C. is low, buy some for me. Arthur did not approve of it, but he did not approve of United Gas Inc. either unless it was *very* low.

I hope you and Billy are well. The other night (the 18th) I woke up with the queerest sense of Billy & you. I may have been dreaming, but I started awake just as if Jeremy or Billy had jumped on me. For a minute I was afraid something had happened to Billy. It was one o'clock, which would have been about four hours earlier, or more, in Richmond.

I hope Berta will come to stay there. I don't like to think of you being alone. If she does, try to see Judge Haddon. Hug Billy. With much love.

Ellen

ALS ViU EG 5083 Box 28
Address: E. Glasgow | 1 W. Main Street, | Richmond, Va, U.S.A.
Postmark: [South]ampton [P]aquebot | Jun [3]0

1. See EG to AVB, July 27, [1927?], note 3.

To Anne Virginia Bennett

OLD ENGLAND LAKE HOTEL, | WINDERMERE, | Aug 24th [1930]

Dearest A.V.

I started to write you the day I left Edinburgh, but after a letter to Rebe on the Empress of Scotland, my back began aching. I am certainly stronger than I was, & I eat my meals (though I am rarely hungry) but everything tires me, and I feel hopeless about going to work again.

After a beautiful motor drive yesterday to Grassmere, Derwentwater & Ulswater (all the loveliest of the Lake country) I woke with a bad headache, & had to take two doses of Pyromidone before I could get up in the bitter cold. Today is fair, but with a strong wind & bitterly cold. There are several good fires, but English people are closely banked around them.

In Edinburgh the weather was dreadful, as it has been indeed the whole summer everywhere. The first day, after the duke[1] sent us in in his car, we had lunch, rested (I cannot really rest) and then went out to drive around old Edinburgh. I cannot remember whether I wrote you this or not, but we went in the dripping wet wearing Mackintoshes & rubbers (galoshes) to Greyfriar's churchyard[2] & saw the grave on which that blessed Bobby had slept every night for fourteen years, from his puppyhood until his death. Canting piety, of course, would not allow him to be buried in the grave. The keeper said the old Sexton had buried him secretly under a big rose bush in the center of a flowerbed, but I distrust the Scottish religion. There is a sandstone slab over the grave of "John Grey, ould Jock" erected by American lovers of Bobby"—but where is Bobby. The fountain is just outside at the end of greyfriar's bridge, & the statue was modelled from Bobby a few months before he died. But, oh, human nature! And, oh, dog nature!

We left a day sooner than we expected to because of the rain & the cold. It was, however, worth a visit to Edinburgh just to see the War Memorial.[3] I had heard it was the finest in the world, and I am convinced of it—I, who dislike war & memorials of war as much as anyone could. But it is amazing that so immense a conception should have sprung from the Scottish imagination & from a race that was nurtured on the dry bread of Calvinism. Every creature that shared in the war is included, from Man to the carrier pigeon, & there is even a stone roundel of the mice that helped the men in the tunnels & little birds in cages——all "the tunnellers friends" The face of the dog in the bronze frieze is the almost the most beautiful of all—filled with a kind of earnest wonder. Beside him there is marching "the carrier pigeon service," a man carrying a pigeon basket & holding a pigeon in his arms. The stained glass windows depict symbolical figures, like Blake visions, which are very fine and intricate. Indeed, my only criticism would be that the memorial invests war with a kind of romantic glamour. There is nobility & heroism, but no cruelty and brutality which are the seeds of war in reality.

The next day we had a long motor trip, in flashes of sunshine & torrents of rain to Dryburgh (where Scott is buried) Melrose, Abbotsford, & Jedburgh. It was nice for Carrie to find an aisle in the beautiful new Abbey at Jedburgh called "the Jerdon Aisle." Francis Jerdone came from there in 1741, & must have added the "e" in America.[4] The caretaker had the most exciting time of her life, all in the pouring rain. She brought a large mop & brushed away the moss from the tomb.

Dryburgh was the loveliest place, & we had sunshine there. But nothing we have ever seen in England can compare with Fountains Abbey. And to think that I was never able to see it again! It may be just as well, for all I can do this summer is to think a place is lovely, but to feel no response emotionally to the thought.

The Lake country is the most beautiful part of England we have seen this year. I still love Yorkshire best, but we could not go back to any of the places I loved. Illness & the wet cold weather prevented any real pleasure at Harrogate.[5]

Tomorrow we go back to London, & I shall be as glad to return as I was to leave it. I have been glad to miss the heat & that terrible drought. All the stories of ruined crops & people killing their cattle wring the heart——but I cannot say that I have had one hour of genuine pleasure—or even one moment. The best, I think, was when I came unexpectedly upon that field of flaming poppies. Though I am much better, I am still too easily exhausted & too drained of emotional strength to enjoy anything. And I think always of Jeremy, & the pity & terror of life. A girl at Dryburgh had a charming blue Bedlington terrier, & she told us his name was "Jeremy." "I wouldn't be without him for anything in the world," she said.

Did I write you that Carrie met the Sealyham again at Harrogate—the one that was so like Jeremy. He was with a woman & two little girls, & when C. told them the man had offered to sell him to us, the woman's eyes blazed, and she said "Sell this dog. He'll sell him over my dead body. We adore him," and she added, "You can't trust men."

I was so pleased we heard of him again because it had worried me, & I had said several times, "Perhaps there is somebody else in the family who really appreciates him."

I must stop. It is so bitterly cold in here.

Love to Billy.

Devotedly— Ellen

ALS ViU EG 5083 Box 28
Address: Miss A.V. Bennett, | 1 West Main Street, | Richmond, | Virginia. U.S.A.
Postmark: Windermere Westmoreland 24 Aug 30 4:30 P.M.

1. Probably the Duke of Hamilton.
2. Church and yard in Edinburgh, on the site of a fifteenth-century friary. Glasgow's attraction was to the legend of Greyfriars Bobby, the dog who faithfully watched over the grave of his owner, border shepherd John ("Jock") Grey (d. 1848). In the third sentence from the end of this paragraph, the omission of one set of quotation marks is EG's error.
3. The Scottish National War Memorial (1927) at Edinburgh Castle.
4. Carrie's family had owned Jerdone Castle (near Richmond) before selling it to the Glasgows.
5. EG had spent a month in a Harrogate "nursing home" for exhaustion before going on to Edinburgh (see *WW* 258–59).

To Sara Haardt Mencken

THE BERKELEY | LONDON, W.I. | September the fourteenth | 1930[1]

Dear Sara,

I send you my love and every blessing it is in the power of affection to bestow. You have always seemed to me to be one of the few real persons born into this shallow-hearted literary generation. Never have you asked of life more than you are willing to bring to it.

Mr Mencken is wise and fortunate, I think, in his love;—or, it may be, those who love wisely are always fortunate. May the future bring to you both all the fine and lasting gifts of the gods that watch over us.

After a long illness and a summer that has been more trying than pleasant, I am sailing for home in a few days. Perhaps the autumn may find you in Richmond.

With kind regards to Mr Mencken and the heartiest good wishes,
I am to you as always,
Affectionately, | ELLEN GLASGOW

ALS MdBG Rare 816 G548Jro
Publication: *L* 105.

1. The full date is written at the end of the letter, following the signature.

From Radclyffe Hall

THE BLACK BOY, | RYE, | SUSSEX. | November 12th 1930

Dearest Ellen.

The library bookcases now having been completed, all our books have come here from London and among them the four volumes of your collected edition.[1] Thank you a thousand times for the words you have written to me in the books—and believe me they will be treasured, but this I need not tell you.

Una & I hope to spend a peaceful Christmas in our ancient little house—after many storms a lull will be a real blessing.

I have arrived at the last quarter of my new book[2] and am working hard and fairly fast as I usually do towards the end. Meanwhile we often talk of you and Carrie and of the joy we felt in your visit to Rye[3]—although it was all too brief.

We do sincerely wish you a happy Christmas, dear Ellen, and all good things in 1931. If thoughts can give them to you then surely they will be yours. And please pass many good wishes on to Carrie from us both.

Yours affectly | *John*
PS I remember that you always call me Radclyffe.

ALS ViU EG Box 15
Address: Miss Ellen Glasgow; letter hand-delivered or included in another envelope.

1. The first four volumes of EG's *Old Dominion Edition*.
2. Probably *The Master of the House* (1932).
3. In late August 1930.

From Isa Glenn

Hotel Peter Cooper | 130 East 39th Street | New York City |
17 November 1930

Dear Ellen Glasgow:

Your letter found me in bed, threatened with my annual attempt at illness, Pneumonia—which I have to write with a capital because I am so afraid of it. I am up today, undoubtedly largely because of the great encouragement your letter gave me. You were charming to write it! Mr. Knopf has telephoned me that you have, in addition, given him permission to use it in advertising the book:[1] and that is angelic. Thank you a thousand times, my dear.

I'm glad you liked Carey's ponderously evolved solution of the Mona Lisa smile.[2] I decided that that would be the most poignantly horrid thing he could say; and of course it only goes to prove that if a woman controls herself (and they always say that they want us to control ourselves) it goes over the man's head. They—the men—are very nice, and very appalling, and, I've no doubt, are indispensible to us?

Do you know what, of all your work, I find sticking in my head when you are mentioned? The exquisite pattern of THE ROMANTIC COMEDIANS: the Judge, again at the cemetery on the 1st page, and again feeling the naughty sap rising. It is amazing, and pathetic, and brings forth laughter that is the true laughter because it is mixed with a lump in the throat. The lump in the throat, I suppose, comes from our sense of being blanketed with futility.

If I've spelled anything wrong, please remember that I am running a race against the chill in my room, now I am out of bed. Isn't it idiotic, to be so afraid of a disease?

Thanking you once more, and eternally, | *Isa Glenn*

TLS ViU EG Box 15
Address: To | Miss Ellen Glasgow | 1, West Main Street | Richmond | Virginia.
Postmark: Gra[nd Central?], NY Nov 1930

1. *A Short History of Julia* (1930).
2. Carey Gordon, the male protagonist of *A Short History of Julia*, compares the smile of the female protagonist Julia de Graffenried to that of Leonardo da Vinci's famous *La Giaconda*, popularly known as the Mona Lisa.

December 1930

From Bessie Zaban Jones

1503 Cambridge Road | Ann Arbor, Michigan | December 27, 1930.[1]
Dear Miss Glasgow—

This autumn, when I was reading some of your books and re-reading others, I wrote you a letter—a genuine piece of "fan" mail, to tell you how your books always excite me and move me as few writers do. And especially so now, when your wonderful evocation of the South is such a sweet pleasure to our homesick hearts.[2] I am very sorry now that I was too timid to send the letter, for your beautiful Christmas greeting makes me think you might have cared to hear from us. I have not seen your house in the brick, so to speak, but I shall judge that Mr. Lankes did the block of it con amore, for it seems to me one of the most attractive things he has ever done.[3] We are going to frame ours and display it prominently and proudly in our new house (which hasn't begun to be built yet!)

Another reason for regretting not sending my letter to you is that it contained the warmest invitation to you to visit us. I hope it is not too late to give *that* to you here, for we should love to see you again and soon, and Richmond looks a little remote to us just now for that unless we can lure you to Ann Arbor. Do you ever venture to these foreign parts? Even if you don't, may we offer ourselves as a good reason for doing so this year?

I must tell you that my husband went to Texas just a few weeks ago to give some speaking engagements he made last year when he was still entitled to speak as a resident Southerner. At Austin his subject was Southern Literature, and his paper was so full of you, someone came up afterwards and said, "Why didn't you mention so-and-so! You talked entirely about Ellen Glasgow." I think—and he does, too—that his proportion was just about right!

I seem to be much too effusive in this letter, but I hope you won't mind. One of the nicest things that happened to us in Chapel Hill was seeing you there, and the next-nicest will be seeing you again—here.

Cordially yours— | Bessie Z. Jones

ALS ViU EG Box 16
Address: Miss Ellen Glasgow | 1 West Main Street | Richmond | Virginia. Postmark: Ann Arbor, Mich. | Dec 27 1930

1. The return address and date are written at the end of the letter, following the signature.
2. The Joneses lived in Austin, Texas, and then in Chapel Hill, North Carolina, before moving to Ann Arbor, Michigan, in 1930. Howard Mumford Jones taught at the Universities of Texas, North Carolina, and Michigan.
3. See letter from Zona Gale, April 14, 1927, note 2.

To Irita Van Doren

February 28th, | 1931 | ONE WEST MAIN STREET | RICHMOND, VIRGINIA
Dear Irita;

Can you use a long review of Emily Clark's book or would you rather I gave it to the Virginia Quarterly?[1] I remember telling you I would do a short review; but it seems to grow longer and longer. The book is amusing, and as I lie in bed with influenza, I find it amusing to say things about it. You might be able to boil it down; but I don't see how you could use fifteen hundred words—— and I still have more to say. The Quarterly might use it as an article with a broader title. I had called it "Another Light that Failed"; but it might be "An Experiment in Southern Letters" or, better still, "To Encourage and arouse the South", for that was the avowed purpose of The Reviewer.[2]

Let me know what you think. Of course I am doing it only because I am fond of Emily. It does complicate life to become fond of people. I wish I didn't.

Is there any chance of your coming South in the spring? I should love to take you to the University.[3]

My love to you always, | Ellen

I don't in the least mind your cutting the review; but I am not sure that you can. If you think you'd better have a short one, I must get in touch, for Emily's sake, with the Quarterly.

TLS DLC

1. See EG's letter to IVD, [June 6, 1930?], note 2.
2. Literary magazine (1921–1924) founded in Richmond by Emily Clark, Margaret Freeman (who later married James Branch Cabell), Hunter Stagg, and Mary Dallas Street. At its inception, EG endorsed the magazine, and she was one of its contributors.
3. Initial planning for the Southern Writers Conference, which EG was instrumental in initiating and that was held at the University of Virginia in Charlottesville on October 23–24, 1931, was already under way.

To Bessie Zaban Jones

March 29th | 1931 | ONE WEST MAIN STREET | RICHMOND, VIRGINIA
Dear Bessie,

I was so glad to have your delightful letter, but, alas, a few days afterwards I came down with influenza, (for the second time) and I am only beginning to feel well again. This is just a line to send my thought of you, and to say that I hope you and Howard will really come to Virginia this spring. If you do, and when you do, of course you will make me a visit. I should love to see the house in Ann Arbor "on the edge of town," and to stay in it. It is charming, I know, and I am proud to imagine an "Ellen Glasgow room" or even shelf. Howard's article was very able and I like immensely, too, the essay he had in Scribners "On Leaving the South."[1] The other article furnished me with a splendid quotation. I suppose he received the paper I sent him. (The Herald-Tribune) So few persons have understood the South so thoroughly.

I meant to send only a word or two, and see how I have rambled on—If I had known I should write so much, I should have taken a typewriter.

No, my very next book is somewhat, but not entirely, in the vein of "They Stooped to Folly."[2] After this, I hope to write a companion piece to "Barren Ground." That is the one of my books I like best.

Affectionately yours, | ELLEN GLASGOW

ALS MNS
Publication: *L* 107.

1. Howard Mumford Jones, "On Leaving the South," *Scribner's* 89 (January 1931): 17–27. The other is unidentified.
2. EG's "next book" is *SL*. The "companion piece" she mentions in the next sentence is *VOI*.

To Bessie Zaban Jones

May 16th, 1931 | ONE WEST MAIN STREET | RICHMOND, VIRGINIA

Dear Bessie,

It is always delightful to have one of your charming letters. You and Howard are such real persons that I feel as if I had known you forever.

It was a great disappointment that you could not come to Virginia this year. Never was there a more lovely spring, belated but filled with fragrance and bloom. However, I think you were right to buy that house, I know it is charming and homelike, and I hope to see it some other spring. Only I am sure rural Michigan would break my heart. I was born to worship trees, and I cannot bear to see one destroyed. The roads in Virginia are a tragic sight to one who, like myself, must have been a dryad, not a mermaid, in the age of fable.

I was very grateful to Howard for making that translation, and I am looking eagerly forward to his article in the Virginia Quarterly.[1] I hope it will be in the next number.

What you tell me of your classes[2] is most amusing. Please, for my sake, love *Tom Jones*. I have always considered it the greatest of all English novels. Nowhere else can one find such vividness, such vitality. And *Amelia!* Do you suppose I am the only person left who has read *Amelia* straight through from beginning to end, not once but twice, and adored every word of it? But even then, I like *Tom Jones* best of all English and American novels. The Russians, of course, are in a different world, and supreme. Yet I find the latest Russian novels hard reading.

Do write me again when you are not too busy.

With affectionate greetings to you both,

As always, | ELLEN GLASGOW

TLS MNS
Publication: *L* 108–9.

1. A translation of an article by Frederic Brie, "Ellen Glasgow," *Germanisch-Romanischen Monatsschrift* 19 (1931): 114–24, signed by Howard Mumford Jones, is in EG's papers. Jones's "Mr. Lewis's America" appeared in *The Virginia Quarterly Review* 7 (July 1931): 427–32.

2. Jones was taking classes at the University of Michigan.

To Irita Van Doren

September 22nd, 1931 | ONE WEST MAIN STREET | RICHMOND, VIRGINIA
Confidential
Irita dear,

It was a disappointment not to see you on my way home; but the heat was so intense I stayed only a day in New York. My glimpse of you on the upward trip was delightful. You are always my chief satisfaction on New York; and I look forward every six months to seeing you and Pat and one or two others.

Now I am asking a favor, though not a great one. Mr Gannett's comment[1] upon the Harper prize award made me so indignant that I am enclosing a telegram from Harper on the subject. Instead of selecting Brothers in the West, I used all my influence with the publishers to make them withdraw the prize this year because I felt that none of the books deserved even a minor award. As the enclosed telegram will prove, I refused to accept Brothers in the West, and withdrew my name as one of the judges. Moreover, I resigned my position as judge in any future contest.

Without offending the publishers, I cannot say this in the newspapers; but will you be so kind as to show this telegram to Mr Gannett and tell him I think he owes me an indirect handwritten apology. Then, please, my dear, return the telegram to me. I know I can trust you in this as in everything.

Much love always, | Ellen

I seldom yield to an impulse of this literary nature; but the heat is at boiling point, and I am truly indignant.

TLS DLC

1. Unidentified. *Brothers in the West,* in the next sentence, is a 1931 novel by Robert Raynolds (1902–1965).

From Isa Glenn

The Kennedy-Warren | 3133, Connecticut Avenue | Washington, D. C. |
2 December 1931

Dear Ellen:

It was so splendid, to see you! To be sure, I wasn't able—in spite of my wise precautions—to get rid of my sister. I'm devoted to her; but she drives me crazy. However, nothing could mar the perfection of Ellen Glasgow in her home! It will remain one of the unforgettable scenes—in the secret places of my mind where I store those things that I protect from the wear and tear of life amongst the Intelligentsia. You are right, that I should at once settle myself in some little house in the South: Charlottesville, and now Richmond, have shown me that I was homesick. When I finish the book,[1] I shall go down to Fredericksburg and find out what they are asking for my great-grandmother's house, Federal Hill. If there are to be ghosts near at hand, as I get to be an old lady, I want them to be nice, friendly, kinfolk ghosts.

Thank you for showing me what has been the matter with my spirit!

Affectionately, | Isa Glenn

TLS ViU EG Box 15
Address: Miss Ellen Glasgow | 1, West Main Street | Richmond | Virginia
Postmark: Washington, D.C. Dec 3 1931

1. Probably *Mr. Darlington's Dangerous Age* (1933).

To Page Cooper

ONE WEST MAIN STREET | RICHMOND, VIRGINIA | March 8th, 1932[1]

Dear Miss Cooper:

I am sorry that I have been so long answering your letter.

No, I have not met Mr. Flannagan;[2] but I am glad you are giving him a good start. It always pleases me when a new writer has a fair beginning.

Amber Satyr (the title is misleading and pretentious) shows genuine promise, and I feel that Mr. Flannagan has the making of an able novelist. Only—— only he must avoid obvious temptations to cheapness, refuse to have his head turned by indiscriminate praise, and resolve to be a novelist first and a journalist not at all.

This book has two unusual qualities in modern American fiction:—humanity and sincerity. But it has also every fault of newspaper writing:—lack of precision in the use of words, a certain roughshod movement, and an evident desire to be well within the current fashion of Freudian horrors. No subject could be more repellent and painful (this is not quite true because there are subjects of cruelty that would be more painful); yet I predict that the success of the book will depend less upon its merits, which are many, than upon the deliberate shock it will afford morbid sensibilities. This, is not meant, however, by way of criticism. It is natural that a young writer should wish to arrest attention, and the only, or certainly the easiest way to arrest critical attention in the present age it to shock the mind either into sadism or into horror that such things can be in the world.

The figure of Luther is well thought out and very pathetic. Sarah seems to me rather more of a study from a psychiatrist's case-book. The episode of the letters is entirely too improbable. Such a woman would not have been able to read—or, if she had learned to read, would have known better than to write those letters to a man who could not read. That incident made too loose and easy an end to the story.

The whole book might be vastly improved by revision; but few young writers are capable of careful revision.

It is not often that I write detailed criticism of a first or second book, or indeed of any book. Seldom have I found that such criticism does any good, though I would have given years of life for just that kind of help in the beginning. But I wish Mr. Flannagan all the good in the world, and I hope that his success will not be merely the usual flash in the pan. If he is saved, it will be because he has sufficient character to cultivate the artist's disdain for the easiest way.

Sincerely yours, | (signed) Ellen Glasgow

I am ashamed of this typing, but Miss Bennett is out walking with Billy, who was adopted when he was very young by my beloved Jeremy.

TCC of TLS NNC
Accompanying this copy is a typed cover memo of March 15, 1932, from Dan Longwell to Harry Edward Maule, both of Doubleday: "Here are two letters from Ellen Glasgow. I asked her if we could use a quote from her letter to Cooper. Hence her reply to me. I think these are the two best letters I've read in some time. Ellen is a very great and gallant lady." Maule responds by underlining Longwell's final sentence and adding, "Yes indeed. And all true about Amber Satyr & just what made us hesitate at first. But a lot of critics of a younger school wont have her reservations. H.E.M."

1. The letter is a carbon copy. The typed word "(COPY)" appears, centered, above the typed letterhead.
2. Roy C. Flannagan (1897–1952), *Amber Satyr* (Garden City: Doubleday, Doran, 1932).

From Page Cooper

DOUBLEDAY, DORAN AND COMPANY | INCORPORATED | PUBLISHERS | GARDEN CITY, N.Y. | August, 23, 1932[1]

Dear Miss Glasgow:

The advance copy of next Sunday's Times' has just come in and we are rushing around showing it to each other with joy. This is the first of our novels which has ever had a front page.[2] I can't wait until Sunday for you to see it, so here is a Tear sheet.

You probably know that we are printing the second edition. Altogether we're feeling very happy about publication date tomorrow.

Sincerely, | Page Cooper

TLS ViU EG Box 13

1. Below the letterhead and date, Cooper includes EG's name and address.
2. J. Donald Adams reviewed *SL* for the *New York Times Book Review* on August 28, 1932 ("Ellen Glasgow's Finest Novel: In 'The Sheltered Life' Her Several Qualities Achieve a New Fusion," pp. 1, 13).

To Sara Haardt Mencken

August 29th | 1932 | ONE WEST MAIN STREET | RICHMOND, VIRGINIA

Dear Sara,

It was good of you to review *The Sheltered Life,* and it pleases me very much to know that you like it best of my books.[1] One should grow as long as one lives and writes.

I should love to see you again; for you came close to me on that brief visit. Are you coming this way again?

Will you give my cordial regards to Mr Mencken, and tell him that his *Treatise on the Gods* is still one of my favorite books. Because it is different, I think people failed to realize how profound it is beneath its brilliant surface. I have had many discussions about it. Are you writing anything now. Do not give up.

Affectionately yours, | ELLEN GLASGOW

ALS MdBG Rare 816 G548Js
The original letter is in Sara Haardt Mencken's copy of EG's *SL.*
Publication: *L* 123.

1. Sara Haardt, "The First Reader," *Norfolk Virginian Pilot,* August 29, 1932, sec. 1, p. 4. Haardt wrote, "Miss Glasgow has never written so brave a book; she reaches a superb level of drama and reality which she has never reached before" (*EGCR* 336).

From Amélie Rives Troubetzkoy

CASTLE HILL | COBHAM, ALBEMARLE COUNTY | VIRGINIA |
3ᵈ *September 1932*

Ellen, my dearest,

I have been living with your deep, dear, subtle mind and glowing heart ever since your book, with its lovely dedication[1] came to me. I have finished reading it, and I have the impression of having looked on a portion of life, quivering through your intense imagination and compassion, like a landscape through transparent heat waves. All the pathetic comedy that is ever bound up with human tragedy you create for us in that strange stillness of art that is like the stillness at the centre of a typhoon. In poor Mrs. Birdsong you have given us the most tragic—to me, at least—of all beings—the self-martyr of a trivial cause, a false ideal. And yet, perhaps that isn't quite true, for she did not think it true.

Oh, Ellen, I wonder if you really know how I have missed you all these years?—I long so to talk with you sometimes that it becomes a real pain.

I have wanted many times to write and ask you if you ever received a letter[2] that I sent you nearly a year ago, asking if you could not come for just a few days to Castle Hill, and saying how glad I should be to have Miss Bennett if you would like to bring her.

I haven't asked you before because I felt that if the letter were lost, it would seem so strange to you. But I did write it, dearest Ellen, & addressed it to One West Main Street. I am really sure that you never received it, because I never had any answer for you. Maybe you were away from home & it got lost in being forwarded.

I would not want for you to come in such horrible weather as this, but perhaps later in the Autumn if you feel able to, you will give me this great happiness.

I would give you the panelled room on the first floor with its own bath, & there are two beds in it, so if you preferred Miss Bennett could sleep near you.

I am sending you a sonnet[3] that I wrote a few months ago, for I think it will speak all its meaning to you.

Bless and bless you my dear great-hearted one.

Ever & always | Your same devoted | *Amélie*

ALS ViU EG Box 18

1. ART may be referring to EG's formal dedication of *SL* to her brother Arthur ("For Arthur Graham Glasgow, whose affection is a shelter without walls") or to a personal inscription in ART's copy.

2. This letter (February 26, 1931) is present in EG's papers.

3. ART's poem "Ave ataque Vale" ("hail and farewell") remains with the letter in EG's papers.

September 1932

From Léonie Villard

24 rue Tronchet. | Lyon, Sept. 9th 1932

Dearest Ellen,

Your pretty card from Italy was sent on, by mistake, and I found it yesterday, on my return to Lyon, after a long and pleasant stay in the Basque country—the French Basque country, I mean!—

I hope you have been well and have enjoyed this glorious summer. I am enjoying it very much and have also been working hard at several things I have in hand, one my "Impressions de voyage" and the others on less personal subjects.

Did I tell you that your lovely photo occupies, as it deserves, a place of honour in my room? My delightful stay with you remains the loveliest memory of my recent stay in America; I had never spent such a perfect evening as that of your dinner-party, when you wore a red dress and looked so pretty! I was lately with friends who told me how disappointed they had once been when they met Pierre Loti in the flesh, and they said it was better to know great writers only through their books! I said there were exceptions to that rule and adduced your name as an instance of a great writer whose personal charm is as great as the power of her genius. I admire you for yourself as well as for your books and am very glad to have seen you in your own lovely house. It does make a difference, as Browning says, to have "once seen Shelley plain."[1]

Please remember me to Miss Bennett and Mrs Duke, to whose visit I am looking forward when she comes to Lyons in search of antiques.

My grateful and affectionate thoughts are with you, dearest Ellen, I hope I may soon come back to America and see you,

Affectionately yours, | Léonie Villard

ALS ViU EG Box 19
Address: Miss Ellen Glasgow | 1 West Main Street | *Richmond* | (Va) | U.S.A. | Etats-Unis d'Amérique
Postmark: Lyon, Brotteaux, 9 Sept 1937, 11:30

    1. From Robert Browning's "Memorabilia": "Ah, did you once see Shelley plain, / And did he stop and speak to you . . . ?"

To Martha Saxton

September 17th | 1932 | ONE WEST MAIN STREET | RICHMOND, VIRGINIA
Dear Mrs Saxton, (I always think of you as Martha and Gene calls me Ellen)

It is delightful to have your letter, and to know that *The Sheltered Life* has touched you so deeply. Yes, I meant the characters to be universal, not Southern especially. I have always written, or tried to write, not of Southern characteristics, but of human beings. I am glad you like that part about Jenny Blair's childhood. It seems to me one of the truest things in the book, though General Archbald is the real protagonist.

I hope to be in New York a little later, and I am looking forward to seeing you and Gene.

Sincerely yours, | ELLEN GLASGOW

ALS ViU EG 6865

To Sara Haardt Mencken

October 17th | 1932 | ONE WEST MAIN STREET | RICHMOND, VIRGINIA

Dear Sara,

That was a charming lunch yesterday, and I enjoyed every moment. You were just as I remembered you, and I felt instantly at home with your Henry and very congenial. He is so natural and genuine that I can scarcely believe I have not been friends with him for years. Your marriage seems to me ideal, as my Amanda[1] would say, only I mean far more than she would imply by the word.

Do come to Richmond before the autumn is over.

My love to you and my affectionate regards to "Henry."

As always yours. | ELLEN GLASGOW

ALS MdBG Rare 816 G5486Js
The letter is in Sara Haardt Mencken's copy of EG's *SL*.
Publication: *L* 126.

1. Amanda Lightfoot of EG's *RC*.

From Isabel Paterson

BOOKS | NEW YORK HERALD TRIBUNE | 230 WEST 41ST STREET, NEW YORK
[December 2, 1932?]

Dear Ellen Glasgow—

Though the phrase sounds funny and stilted, as we have no modern equivalent I must say that I feel greatly honored by such praise from you.[1] Not only because it is praise but because it is so beautifully expressed. To have been (like Falstaff) the occasion of wit in others—such a charming bit of writing . . .

If my publishers could use selections from that letter, I know it would be invaluable. But if you would rather revise it after second thoughts, of course I should understand—you mightn't think so highly of the book on second thoughts anyhow. I will not give them the letter for their use until I hear from you, saying that I may. I'd always keep the original for myself anyhow. No matter what anyone else may write now, I am sure I shall value this most.

While I was writing the book, I had a vague idea, a hope or intention, of dealing with a generation that seemed to me to have been missed out in American fiction. It would be more or less my own generation; in actual time, it would be more or less yours too, but the South, to which you belong, had its own chronology, not identical with the West and Middle West; however, it would be the generation in between Eva Birdsong and Jenny Blair.[2] The West was different because it had no fixed social mould. The girls I was thinking of wore pompadours and dip-front blouses at seventeen; and then Empire dresses. And Merry Widow hats! A distinct "period" style, which had very quick transitions. They were out on their own, and went around with their noses in the air—rather funny and yet really a style, I mean in the right sense of the word—it had character. It was very hard to catch. The novels written in that period never dealt with it at all—they were all really dated twenty years earlier, or of no date, just a stale literary convention; with a very few exceptions such as your own, which naturally did not take in the West. There weren't any Western novels. Nothing but cowboy yarns. I remember being perfectly astonished by the outbreak of the flapper in fiction. It sounded like nursery tantrums. Or some high-school child announcing that the Dutch had taken Holland. I suppose that was partly because I didn't know anything about the East, or about women who really did lead sheltered lives; and the flapper novels had no background, so that they were incomprehensible; a good novel creates its world so that whatever happens in it is understood.

So I suppose mine is intrinsically a Western novel. But I didn't want to label it. I hoped it was distinctly American, so that you, for instance, would understand it. I hoped so especially when I read "The Sheltered Life," because that is American—so much larger than any locality. I wouldn't have ventured to hope for such generous enthusiasm—but that is yourself.

I'm so sorry you've been ill. One comes up against the end of the chain in illness: the knowledge of mortal limitations, the jerk of pain and the dead weight.

You will not mind if I thank you again.

Affectionately and gratefully, | Isabel Paterson

TLS ViU EG Box 17

1. EG's review ("Modern in Tempo and American in Spirit") of Paterson's *Never Ask the End* appeared in *NYHTB* (January 8, 1933), p. 3. Paterson's letter suggests that EG had sent at least some of her remarks to Paterson in advance.

2. Characters in EG's *SL*.

From Dorothy Scarborough

COLUMBIA UNIVERSITY | IN THE CITY OF NEW YORK | THE WRITERS CLUB |
50 Morningside Drive | December 22, 1932.

Dear Miss Glasgow:

May I tell you with what pleasure I have read and re-read your latest novel, *The Sheltered Life*? I think it is extraordinary in its combination of humor, irony and tragedy. Every now and then I quote bits from it and use it to illustrate points I wish to make in my course in Technique of the Novel at Columbia.

I hope it receives the Pulitzer Award for this year,—and I wish I were on the committee! I had a novel out this year myself,[1] but that doesn't change my critical opinion,—which is that *The Sheltered Life* stands at the head of the American novels for the year. More power to your pen!

Sincerely yours, | Dorothy Scarborough

TLS ViU EG Box 18

1. *The Stretch-berry Smile* (Indianapolis: Bobbs-Merrill, 1932).

From Isa Glenn

Washington, D. C. | 7 May 1933

Dearest Ellen:

I missed seeing the list of the Pulitzer prize winners in the papers, but Bayard has just told me that Stribling got the novel.[1]

I am very indignant, honey. I hold, and I'm sure all of us hold, that THE SHELTERED LIFE should have got it. It is your best novel which means that it is the best novel of a long list of splendid novels written by you. You should have had the Pulitzer before; but this time I saw no way out of your getting it. I was so stunned. THE STORE was a good study of conditions of which I know nothing. But I hold firmly to my belief that a novel must not only be a story of human beings, but that it must have a style, must be written beautifully. I don't come up to my own ideals; but you do! Well—damn it! That, in short and vulgarly, sums up my emotion on the subject of this ridiculous overlooking of THE SHELTERED LIFE.

I am almost ready to send on to Doubleday the last third of my own new novel.[2] I sent on, by request, the first two thirds, and they have written that they think it "gorgeous". It changed on me; they always do, don't they, when you get them going? First, I had to change the name of the man from Mr. Pratt to Mr. Gallatin. I found that the *word* Pratt froze my sympathy. Then, I had to change him from a Boston banker to a New York banker; because I found I couldn't care what happened to a man from Boston. You see, he is a gentleman; and I still doubt the existence of such in Boston: a narrow prejudice that I thought I'd outgrown. As to how you are going to like it—I don't know. You remember that I told you I want to dedicate the first of my books that you like through and through to you?[3] Well, then when this one gets into proof, I shall ask Harry Maule to send a set on to you and then you must be honest with me, and say what you think. If you don't like this one, we'll wait for the next.

Lots of love. | Isa

TLS ViU EG Box 15
Address: Miss Ellen Glasgow | 1, West Main Street | Richmond | Virginia.
Postmark: Washington DC, May 7 1933

1. T. S. Stribling's (1881–1965) *The Store,* the second novel in a southern trilogy (the first was *The Forge,* 1931), won the Pulitzer Prize for 1932.
2. *Mr. Darlington's Dangerous Age* (1933).
3. The novel is dedicated "To Ellen Glasgow."

To Irita Van Doren

September 8th, | 1933 | ONE WEST MAIN STREET | RICHMOND, VIRGINIA
All this is just for you, of course. Mere rambling.

Dear Irita,

I should like to help you with your *Fall Book Number;* but where can I possibly find fifteen forthcoming American novels that I should consider worth recommending? Other books I might choose. I am carried away by *Flush* (but Virginia Woolf is a genius and English); I am reading with much interest Henry Hazlitt's Anatomy of Criticism: I am looking eagerly forward to *The Fathers,* by Allen Tate. Yet these three books would be left out of a list of "forthcoming fiction."

The sad truth is that I find most American novels of today hard and bitter reading. I passed my peasant stage early (while other people, who were in the fashion, read Henry James and Oscar Wilde and even Edith Wharton), and the peasant mind, even at its lowest in modern fiction, no longer excites me. I dislike sophistication, especially sophisticated barbarism; but I am sufficiently out of the mode to prefer a civilized style.

I suppose the fashion will pass sooner or later. Meanwhile, I am not sure that it is wise for me to choose fifteen or twenty titles when these titles are confined to American fiction that has not yet appeared. It is true that I might like *The Farm* which I have not read; I respected the New England backbone in *As the Earth Turns;* but the Southern peasants in *South Moon Under* and even the

Florida swamps, all seemed to me to be made of wool.[1] Also, I may confess, Faulkner's school of Raw-Head-and-Bloody-Bones sends me back, not to realism anywhere on earth, but to the *Weird Tales* of Hoffmann. Gothic tales have their place; but, after all, why do all mushrooms have to be toadstools?

Affectionately always, | *Ellen Glasgow*

I am far from an expert typist, and Miss Bennett is exercising Billy. It is true that I am looking forward to Isa Glenn's book.

TLS DLC
Publication: *L* 143.

1. *The Farm* (New York: Harper, 1933) by Louis Bromfield; *As the Earth Turns* (New York: Macmillan, 1933) by Gladys Hasty Carroll; *South Moon Under* (New York: Scribners, 1933) by Marjorie Kinnan Rawlings.

To Irita Van Doren

Friday | ONE WEST MAIN STREET | RICHMOND, VIRGINIA
[early September 1933?]

Irita dear,

Partly for love of you and partly for love of Flush, and the fear that he may fall into the wrong hands, I will try my pen in a review.[1] But I cannot attempt to do justice. I am at the hardest turn of my book,[2] and I cannot take much time away from it. Then I feel that I write better when my pen is barbed with satire, and I cannot be satirical about Virginia Woolf. Now, if only it were Mr Ernest Hemingway and his school of sophisticated barbarians——

I have written Alfred Harcourt a letter which he intends to quote. Do you think it would be better for him to wait for the review? If you do think this, will you telephone him.

Always affectionately, *Ellen*

I hope you will let me mention five books in the Christmas number instead of three.

How I wish you could drop down this autumn!

TLS DLC
Publication: *L* 144.

1. EG's review of Woolf's *Flush*, "Portrait of a Famous and Much Loved Dog," was published in the *NYHTB*, October 8, 1933, sec. 3, p. 21.
2. *VOI*.

To Irita Van Doren

November 2nd, | 1933 | ONE WEST MAIN STREET | RICHMOND, VIRGINIA
Irita dear,

It was delightful to see you in New York and to hear all your plans for making the world safe for books.

When Stark Young's Civil War book comes out, I'll do the article for the front page, if you wish, and I shall pay my respects to the whole Raw-Head-and-Bloody-Bones school.[1] The truth is I am sick of Sadism, and I cannot be comforted with rotten apples.

As always affectionately, | *Ellen*
Can you make a title out of that? By no means.

TLS DLC

1. EG reviewed Young's *So Red the Rose:* "A Memorable Novel of the Old South," *NYHTB,* July 22, 1934, pp. 1–2.

To Dorothy Canfield Fisher

November 19th, | *1933* | ONE WEST MAIN STREET | RICHMOND, VIRGINIA
My Dear Dorothy Canfield,

It was charming of you to send me *Bonfire.*[1] I was delighted when I opened the package, and immediately I put aside my work for the rest of the day.

Now, after living with this book, I feel that I have spent some other life in a Vermont village and that I have known intimately all the characters in your novel. How real they are and how utterly natural and individual!

Many, many thanks for the pleasure you have given me. So much American fiction, like so much American life, seems to me to be all surface; but your sympathy and understanding give substance to these people—even to the least of them.

With friendly regards, | Sincerely yours. | ELLEN GLASGOW

ALS VtU

1. Fisher's 1933 novel (New York: Harcourt, Brace).

To Irita Van Doren

November 21st, 1933 | ONE WEST MAIN STREET | RICHMOND, VIRGINIA
Dear Irita,

I enjoyed Virginia Woolf's letter, which I am now returning.[1] It is pleasant to know that she did not hold me responsible for that misprint.

Isn't it delightful to find a really modest author—a writer of whom it can be said with truth, "he builded better than he knew"?[2] While *Flush* was running in the Atlantic Monthly, she wrote me just what she said to you in her letter. That was why I remarked casually in my review "It is probable that Mrs Woolf herself does not realize the accuracy," etc., and in my first copy I added "as Louis Carroll did not realize the perfection of Alice." But I wished to make a different approach and to show that Virginia Woolf simple is more vital than Virginia Woolf complicated, and that the book, as someone said of *Moby Dick* was successful only because "it transcended its purpose."

It may be true that I over praised *Flush;* but it is so easy to write a disparaging review (anybody with a typewriter and a touch of smartness can do that!) and so very difficult to write an enthusiastic one that is not flat when it settles.

With love always, | Ellen

TLS DLC

1. Woolf wrote Irita Van Doren, who had sent Woolf a copy of EG's review of *Flush* with apologies for a mistake in the opening paragraphs. In her gracious letter, Woolf absolves EG from the "obvious" error and appreciates EG's generous review, which, according to Woolf, overpraises *Flush*. The letter is in IVD's papers.

The mistake is not as obvious as everyone involved suggests. A few possibilities are: the final reference in the fourth paragraph to *To the Lighthouse* perhaps should be to *The Waves;* Woolf's essay on the new biography is not included in *The Common Reader,* as EG's discussion in the third paragraph might suggest; and there are two slight misquotations, one from Woolf's "The New Biography" (third paragraph), and one from *Flush* (in the long quotation in the third column of EG's review).

2. From Ralph Waldo Emerson's 1839 poem "The Problem": "He builded better than he knew;— / The conscious stone to beauty grew."

To Bessie Zaban Jones

December 29th | 1933 | ONE WEST MAIN STREET | RICHMOND, VIRGINIA
Will you send me your *permanent* address. There are three different ones in my address book.
Dear Bessie,

You are, I maintain, one of the very few genuine Eighteenth-century letter writers now left alive. I feel that you deserve a place, and an honorable one, among the choice spirits who could make a letter as human as a talk before an open fire.

How I wish I could have been with you and Howard in London! Like you, I love London and dislike Paris. London is, for me, the city of imagination, but Paris is merely the city of the senses. Only the rich should visit it—only the rich who are not troubled by imagined distress—and the heartbroken, of all sensation-seekers. The wrecks of humanity under the bridges and the most wretched looking horses on earth!

Yes, I am always at work on a novel. I have been writing one for a year and it will probably take two years longer.[1] A very full, long novel covering the last twenty years. I have taken a new (for me) background—the Scotch-Irish of the upper Valley of Virginia. My father was born there, the old Glasgow plantation, Green Forest (Glasgow means green forest in Gaelic) is still there, though cut up into lots. The original plantation (1766 included five thousand acres) and now the land has been made into ugly little towns.

But I come of a divided heritage, for my mother's people were all from the Tidewater, and English. Love to you and Howard, and every blessing.

Ellen

ALS MNS

1. *VOI.*

To Bessie Zaban Jones

February 7th, | 1934 | ONE WEST MAIN STREET | RICHMOND, VIRGINIA
Dear Bessie,

Another good talk with you before the fire in your living-room. This is the way I felt when I read your delightful letter. And how proud I am to know anyone who has read even a single of book of the *Old Testament* in Hebrew! Not that I should prefer it in Hebrew. As I like it best, it has "had the advantage," so Lytton Strachey observes, "of being translated by a board of Elizabethan bishops."[1] But it is my favorite book, I believe, taken as literature and discarded as prophecy, especially the Old Testament. Yet even the *New Testament* seems to me finer as literature than as religion. I cannot accept a creed that divides man from the rest of creation. Evolution was in my blood and bone long before I had ever read Darwin.[2]***** But the literature of the Old Testament is superb, and even Christianity might not have failed if it had ever been tried.

******Yes, I enjoyed *Peter Abelard*.[3] It is a fine re-creation, which is quite as difficult, I suppose, as a creation. **** I agree with you that the Gothic horrors of William Faulkner are legitimate material for grotesque tales, like the Weird Tales of Hoffmann, but not considered as realism or even as naturalism. He says in his introduction to *Sanctuary,* "To me this is a cheap idea because it was deliberately conceived to make money."[4] That covers a good deal of that kind of writing nowadays in the South. If anything is too vile and too degenerate to exist anywhere else it is assigned to the "honest" school of Southern fiction, and swallowed whole, bait and all, by Northern readers, who have never been below Washington, but have a strong appetite.

Do you, by the way, really feel that people, especially "poor white" people talk and think as they do in the books of Elizabeth Madox Roberts?[5] Are they convincing to you? To me they are a strange breed and I find them singularly repulsive, except in *The Great Meadow.* This book is impressive; but, as Dorothy Van Doren remarked of it, "the characters are lost in a fog of language." Strangely enough, since it moved so many other readers, *The Time of Man* left me cold and even sceptical. Her writing seems to me over-strained and unrelated to the life she portrays.

And now *Marcus Aurelius*! It has been twenty years or more since I looked at him; but he carried me over one of the worst times in my life. I have a little volume, heavily underscored, which I used as a girl, and bore with me over Europe, as Byron bore "the pageant of his bleeding heart."[6] I had marked it in Egypt, in Greece, in Constantinople, in Italy and in the hands of God generally. As an ever-present help in time of trouble, I have found stoicism a greater comfort than any religion that one cannot believe in. But, in the end, nothing outside myself has ever really helped me very much.

This brings me to your question;—"Have you liked your life?" And I answer, not one day, not one hour, not one moment——or perhaps, *only one* hour and one day. When I read of D. H. Lawrence and all the other strutting sad-eyed martyrs of literature, I tell myself that they do not know the first thing about suffering. So long as one is able to pose one still has much to learn about suffering.——
**** No, I haven't read Horace Walpole for years, and I have almost forgotten about Byron. I read constantly the letters of Keats—my poet among poets. Recently, I read the letters of Mrs. Carlyle over again, and I liked her and loved her. Another favorite of mine is Dorothy Wordsworth. I love the way she wrote of beggars and of picking up sticks with Wordsworth to make a fire in Dove Cottage. I shall never forget those damp stone floors in Dove Cottage. They needed a fire——but they were happy! There are few things more heartening to read than Dorothy's Journal.

I wish I could write on, but I must stop for lunch. My love to Howard. When—when—*when* shall I see you both again?

Affectionately yours as always, | *Ellen*
Please forgive this inexpert typing.⁷

TLS MNS
Publication: *L* 150–52.

1. The quotation is unidentified.
2. EG acquired Darwin's *The Descent of Man* and *Origin of Species* in 1894 (*CLEG* 15.245). Her copy of *The Thoughts of the Emperor Marcus Aurelius Antoninus,* trans. George Long (Philadelphia: Altemus, n.d.), mentioned later in this letter, is heavily marked (*CLEG* 1.16). The typed asterisks here and elsewhere in the letter are EG's.
3. Novel (New York: Holt, 1933) by Helen J. Waddell.
4. Faulkner's 1932 introduction to *Sanctuary* (1931) begins, "This book was written three years ago. To me it is a cheap idea, because it was deliberately conceived to make money."
5. Kentucky poet and novelist (1881–1941); the books EG mentions were published by Viking in 1930 and 1926, respectively.
6. From Matthew Arnold's "Stanzas from the Grand Chartreuse" (1855): "What helps it now, that Byron bore / . . . The pageant of his bleeding heart?"
7. The postscript is handwritten.

To Irita Van Doren

May 23rd, 1934 | ONE WEST MAIN STREET | RICHMOND, VIRGINIA

Dear Irita,

On Sunday I am leaving for Philadelphia, and by the end of next week I hope to be at the Hotel Weylin in New York (Madison and Fifty-Fourth) I am looking forward eagerly to a nice quiet talk with you, world without end. Will you keep an evening, or lunch if you prefer, and let me know by June the first. I shall be in town only a few days, and it will seem like getting back to sophisticated barbarism after the more civilized provinces. A visit from Emily Clark yesterday gave me the impression that, unless one enjoys burglars, New York and Philadelphia had best be avoided. I hope to see Pat, and I shall write to her soon. Also to Lewis Gannett, if he is in town. Do you, by the way, know where the Hazlitts are now, and what he is doing?

I have just finished advanced proofs of Stark Young's new book.¹ It is by far the best thing he has ever done, and it is, in my opinion, the finest novel of the deep South in the Civil War that has ever been written by anybody. Where Du Bose Heyward failed, Stark has succeeded. Of course it gives the point of view of the far Southern planters; but, after all, they had a point of view and they paid a great price for the privilege. Certainly, they have as much right to a fair presentation as have the sodden futilitarians and the corncob cavaliers of Mr. Faulkner.

I assume that you still wish me to write this review. If you have any one else in mind that you would prefer, please send me a telegram. I am trying to write it before I go away, and so clear the ground for my own book when I return.[2] After two years of hard work and complete immersion, I have just finished the first draft. That is why I am taking a short rest. I think this novel will be a triumph. It is different and yet not different from my others, and I am tremendously interested in writing of a fresh background and a different stock. Yet I know both quite as well I know as the Tidewater.

Much love always, | *Ellen*
I hope I may have at least a glimpse of Carl.

TLS DLC
Publication: *L* 154.

1. *So Red the Rose* (New York: Scribners, 1934). For EG's review, mentioned in her final paragraph, see her letter to IVD dated November 2, 1933, note 1.
2. *VOI*.

To Irita Van Doren

June 9th. | 1934 | ONE WEST MAIN STREET | RICHMOND, VIRGINIA

Dear Irita,

You have heard, of course, that Dan has left Doubleday, Doran.[1] This means that I shall go with this novel (my best or one of my *very* best) and not wait for the autobiography.

Whenever an opportunity occurs, will you take up the question with Harcourt or Houghton, Mifflin. Everything will depend upon the terms offered and upon what I feel to be a proper enthusiasm for my books. It was dear of you to say that you would represent me in my absence.

I was so sorry that you couldn't come to see me again and bring Mr. Davis to tea.

With much love always, | *Ellen*

ALS DLC
Publication: *L* 156.

1. Dan Longwell left Doubleday for a journalism position; EG changed publishers (to Harcourt) beginning with *VOI* (1935). Longwell wrote to IVD: "Ellen ... took the news calmly—said right off, 'That's fine—now you can get me good reviews in Time. I never have got good reviews there'" (June 7, 1934; IVD papers, DLC).

To Irita Van Doren

June 18th, | 1934 | ONE WEST MAIN STREET | RICHMOND, VIRGINIA

Dear Irita,

What a treasure you are, and (unlike some other treasures I have known) how unerringly wise and intelligent![1]

I agree with every word you write, and I can prove this in no better way than by taking your advice from beginning to end. Certainly, if I go to Alfred Harcourt, I shall do so because I believe in him and have faith in his word and his ability as a publisher. The mere idea of my consulting any one else after I have chosen A. H. for my publisher, is simply ridiculous and, as you say, would be ruinous. No, I shall not make trouble of that kind for him or any one else.

I have had the most beautiful letter from Ferris Greenslet. While I read it, I thought, "Oh, he must publish my books!" But I trust greatly to your judgment, and you think that A. H. is best for me. What really wins me, I think, is the passage in your letter "quoting A. H. "He would make you the leading author on his list, and would consider you and your novels as the outstanding, etc."

Of course, I shall have to have very good terms. Since so much that I put away has been lost,[2] I am obliged to make up what I can in a diminished income. I shall talk over any contract with you, and there are many small details to be considered. But for the major points in the contract do you think an advance of twenty thousand on a straight twenty per cent royalty, and a guarantee of fifteen thousand to be spent in advertising the next novel would be right? I have just written to Raymond Everitt that I could not have an agent act for me. It pained me to write the letter; but I think A. H. is right, and I must not, at this time, when I need to act with wisdom, let anything stand in the way of my professional interest.

I have just reached home. Everything is in confusion, and I am rushing this off to you without reading it over.

Much love and many, many thanks, dear Irita.

Ever yours, | *Ellen*

TLS DLC
Publication: *L* 159–60.

1. IVD's letter of June 15, 1934, details her business conversations with Dan Longwell and Alfred Harcourt about publishing EG's future work.
2. From the stock market crash in 1929 and the ensuing Depression, presumably.

To Irita Van Doren

July 11th, | 1934 | ONE WEST MAIN STREET | RICHMOND, VIRGINIA
Dear Irita,

You have been so very good about taking an interest in my affairs. I do not wish to come to any decision without consulting you; but it will be difficult to put off matters indefinitely. Ferris Greenslet and Alfred Harcourt are both coming down next week, I think. I tried to put Mr Greenslet off by saying I had made a decision in my own mind, though I did not wish to sign a contract.

When do you think it would be wise to commit myself? Would you go over the contract and might I tell Mr. Harcourt to send it to you? If he agrees to my terms, I doubt if I could do better even in the event of inflation, which every one dreads.

I hope you will have a beautiful vacation. It was lovely to have that nice talk with you in New York. You are a darling, and one of the very few absolutely satisfactory persons I have ever known.

Much love, | Ellen
Miss Bennett is *not* responsible for this typing![1]

1. The postscript is handwritten.

TLS DLC

To Irita Van Doren

July 26th, | 1934 | ONE WEST MAIN STREET | RICHMOND, VIRGINIA
Irita dear,

I have so much to tell you that I do not know where to begin. Rather unexpectedly, I had a telegram from Ferris Greenslet, and he came to see me several days ago. This morning he sent me an offer, which I suppose is as good as I shall have from any one. He agrees to my main points, including an advance of twenty thousand dollars, of which five thousand would not be deducted from my royalties, but would be a kind of bonus. In his conversation he had said the "bonus" would be ten thousand, but I notice that in the written offer, it has been reduced to five thousand. He gave me many reasons why I should come to them instead of going to Harcourt. I quote from his letter today:
"The fact that we have only been restrained from approaching you earlier because of our relations with our common friend F.N.D. fairly offsets Harcourt's alleged priority of proposal, and the grave and protracted illness of Miss Sedgwick makes it possible for us to give you the same pre-eminence on our list that Harcourt could give you on his through the loss of Sinclair Lewis to Garden City."[1] I wish I could show you the whole letter; but I don't like to send it.

Within the next fortnight Mr Harcourt will come down to see me. After I have talked with him, I shall decide definitely, and of course your advice means more to me than that of any one else. Other things being equal, are you still firmly convinced, without fear of change, that Harcourt will be better for me? My own leanings are in his direction, and I have just had a letter from Dan urging me to go to Harcourt if I leave Doubledays. This, I think, is rather fine of Dan. He is a good sport.

On the other hand. Mr Greenslet reminds me that H. M. is an older and more stable firm, and has kept its entire staff during the depression, whereas H. B. has turned away some of its best salesmen.[2] This, of course, is confidential. I don't wish to make trouble by repeating things. Only Mr. Greenslet insists that, for me, there is no choice between the two firms. I ought to have my autobiography with Henry Adams, he remarked, and not with Mabel Dodge Luhan.[3] I told him I had never read Mrs. Luhan's and never expected to. He replied that I ought to read it before deciding. Again this is confidential.

I should love to come to West Cornwall[4] and I hope it may be possible some day. It means a great deal to me whenever I see you, for you are always near to my heart.

After I have seen Alfred Harcourt I shall write you again.

With much love, | Ellen

TLS DLC

1. F. N. D. is Frank N. Doubleday. Anne Douglas Sedgwick (1873–1935) was a popular leading author at Houghton Mifflin. Sinclair Lewis had changed publishers to Doubleday, located in Garden City, New York.

2. H. M. is Houghton, Mifflin; H. B. is Harcourt Brace.

3. Henry Adams is the well-known author of *The Education of Henry Adams* (1907), which EG admired. Luhan (1879–1962) published her four-volume *Intimate Memories* beginning in 1924. She is known for her New York salon at 23 Fifth Avenue and her move (in 1923) to Taos, New Mexico, where she encouraged artists and authors such as Georgia O'Keeffe, Willa Cather, and D. H. Lawrence.

4. The location of Irita Van Doren's weekend home in Connecticut.

To Irita Van Doren

August 2nd, 1934 | ONE WEST MAIN STREET | RICHMOND, VIRGINIA

Irita dear,

Your letter came at the right moment and has finally decided me.[1] I cannot tell you how much I appreciate your interest and sympathy and all the trouble you have taken with my problem.

Alfred Harcourt came down on Tuesday, and we had a perfectly satisfactory talk. He told me I might write my own contract, but I did not wish to do that.

I asked him to tell me what he would feel justified in offering me, and then to let me take his offer or leave it. In the end, though he said he had never given any one a straight twenty per cent, he would do it for me if I asked for it. Instead, I suggested fifteen per cent up to thirty thousand, and he made it twenty-five. So these are his terms. An advance of twenty thousand on a basis of fifteen percent to twenty-five thousand and twenty per cent afterwards. A guarantee of fifteen thousand to be spent on advertising this novel. All the other points I could think of were decided agreeably, and I was impressed by the man's conviction and integrity. He would handle all my marginal rights on a ten per cent basis, as any other agent would do. I liked him very much.[2]

I suppose he will talk to you, and I told him I wished you to see the contract before he sent it to me. But I have not said positively yet I shall go to him. I am waiting until I hear from him because if his enthusiasm has waned since he returned to New York, I could be perfectly satisfied to change to Houghton, Mifflin. I like Mr. Greenslet, too, and he seems quite as appreciative. The terms are almost the same, though A. H's may be a little better. The Houghton Mifflin guarantee is for the least that they are to spend and only on newspaper publicity, not on promotion. Then they offer a bonus, which brings the royalty advance to very nearly the same figure.

But I have decided for Harcourt, and on the understanding that I cannot promise to deliver the manuscript at any specified date. If I did that, I should never be able to write the book at all.

I have worked harder than I have done for years, and I am staying here all summer for that reason. Never has any of my novels taken so strong a hold on me as this one.[3] It is a big book, not a slight one, and it has a great many characters. The whole idea and handling will be a new departure for me. I have a sense of mastery which I trust will not mislead me.

Much love, dearest Irita. How I wish I could see you. I know the country did you good. That is just the kind of summer I like best.

Ellen

I am waiting to write to Ferris Greenslet until I hear again from A. H. If he shows the slightest sign of regretting his offer, please let know. As it is, I hate to write to Mr. Greenslet.

TLS DLC
Publication: *L* 159–61.

    1. In her letter of July 30, 1934, IVD had written that as an editor she could not recommend one publisher over another; as a friend, she felt that Harcourt was the better choice (ViU EG Box 19).
    2. This sentence is handwritten.
    3. *VOI*.

August 1934

To Irita Van Doren

August 12th, | 1934 | ONE WEST MAIN STREET | RICHMOND, VIRGINIA
Irita dear,

A book like "Lee" will receive so much technical revieweing that I think it would be well to have it interpretated by a poet who is familiar with the subject.[1] There was so much pure poetry in Lee's nature.

A letter accepting Mr. Harcourt's offer lay for a week on my desk while I was having a correspondence with Garden City. At last the letter has gone, but the whole thing has been difficult and rather painful. Nelson, so far, has been really lovely, and shown a side that is human and appealing. But they could not understand in the firm that I had reached a decision. Last evening Dan came down and talked for two hours trying to persuade me not to leave. He brought two contracts, one blank but signed for me to fill in. It had never occurred to me that they would take my going as "a personal blow." I do not like to write of this, but I know I am safe with you. And it is just as well that Harcourt, Brace should realize that, good as their terms are, I am able to command them elsewhere.

Will you go over the contract before Mr. Harcourt sends it down to me. Two matters I should like cleared up. First, what can be done to save my definitive edition[2] from being "remaindered". Secondly can H. B. handle the foreign rights as well as a London agency might handle them? Personally, I should rather have Alfred Harcourt take care of them if has had such experience.

How I wish I could see you, dearest Irita, and I am looking forward to being with you in the country next summer, if only for a day.

Much love always, | *Ellen*

I do not expect Harcourt to spend money on my old books. Last night I heard again that they would not be sold. But I am anxious.

TLS DLC
Publication: *L* 161–62.

1. IVD had asked EG's advice about "Steve Benet versus a professional historian" as a reviewer for Douglas Southall Freeman's biography of Robert E. Lee (From IVD, [August 1934?], ViU EG Box 19).

2. E.G.'s *Old Dominion Edition*.

To Irita Van Doren

August 17th, 1934 | ONE WEST MAIN STREET | RICHMOND, VIRGINIA

Irita dear,

I intended to write to you yesterday, but I spent the better part of the day with Nelson, and in the afternoon I had a headache.

It was dear of you to call me (by the way, you must charge that call to me) and I was worried from what Anne Virginia told me because I was afraid you might not have had an entirely pleasant time. I sent the telegram as you suggested, saying positively that I had signed the agreement and it was useless for him to come down. That is settled, I thought, and put the matter out of my mind. But the next morning a nine o'clock James came up to say that "a gentleman was downstairs and he had offered him breakfast." I was dreading a storm and as I went down I reminded myself that an old friend used to tell me my greatest gift was the ability to take the sting out of people. But, believe it or not, and even attribute it if you please to my sting-extracting gift, he was perfectly angelic. It's a nuisance to be forever putting yourself in some one else's place; but I came to understand him so well in those few hours that I felt as if I had been born in his skin in some other life.

Well, he asked first of all if I would authorize him to "go to Alfred and buy that contract." And he would really have done it. He would have spent any amount of money, thrown it away, in ordr to gain his point. If he had come to upbraid, he stayed to lunch instead, and at the critical moment Anne Virginia brought in large and fragrant mint juleps in my finest Georgian goblets. It was the first time I had ever seen him alone, and I liked him better than I had ever done in my life. He talked to me of his difficulties and said "I know I do a lot of things than seem to you cheap; but I don't do them from choice, I have to make that plant pay its expenses, My father invested nine million dollars in it in all, and it employs eleven hundred people." I could feel sympathy in all that; but of course it did not change my feeling that he was not the right publisher for my books. I do not want to make my living out of the mass mind.

I was glad, though, that things ended pleasantly. He reassured me entirely about my edition. Nothing would induce him to remainder them, and he would do anything I wished and protect my interests in every way. He even offered me an advance on my old books, and was eager to give me enough money to go over to my niece's wedding in October.[1] It is useless to deny that he has very generous impulses, and is as mild as a May morning if you know how to take him, which is rather as one would take an over-grown child.

I told him that you had nothing whatever to do with my changing publishers, that I had decided to go before I talked with you. You will be amused to hear that you made a deep impression upon him. He said, "She is fine. I wish

I knew her better. She is worth a dozen of Carl". Needless to say, he did not draw an argument from me by that statement.

The agreement has gone to Harcourt, and I cannot tell you how grateful I am to you for all your trouble. You have been perfect as always.

Much love, dearest Irita, | *Ellen*

My review of *So Red the Rose* has brought me endless bother.[2] Every publisher (to say nothing of the writers) in the country appears to be animated by a desire to have me review a book. And I hate doing it above all things.

TLS DLC
Publication: *L* 163–65.

1. Marjorie Glasgow (later Congreve).
2. See EG to IVD, November 2, 1933, note 1.

To Bessie Zaban Jones

January 8th, | 1935 | ONE WEST MAIN STREET | RICHMOND, VIRGINIA

Dear Bessie:

I was so glad to have your letter, for I think often of you and Howard, and always with interest and affection and the wish that it were possible to see more of you.

For the past two years I have been completely absorbed in my novel,[1] and the actual world has receded. There is another year's work ahead, and yet I dread the time when I shall finish this book and send it out into the world that "knows not Joseph." No novel has ever meant quite so much to me. It is, I feel sure, my best book, completely realized and created before I put pen to paper. After my three comedies of manners,[2] I have returned to my earlier kind of novel. This book is like, and yet utterly unlike, *Barren Ground*—if you know what that means. It is long, thoughtful, tragic, but not melancholy (though I like melancholy novels when they are genuine), and saturated through and through with reality. Modern but not sprawling.

Do tell me more of yourself and your life. Your personality interests me more and more, and whenever I have a letter from you, I seem to catch a fresh slant of light on your mind. I wish I could see you, though I really have no life except in my work. There, and there alone, have I found peace. But it took years and years of anguish and of seeking to find peace even within. The agony of the world has always pressed in upon me, even when I was a child, and the curious part is that my power of suffering, both personal and vicarious, has not diminished as I have grown older. I still blaze with rage at the injustice and cruelty of life. Only I realize now that it is all wasted, like Heaven's rage at the sight of a robin redbreast in a cage. Do you love Blake as I do? Especially that poem, "A robin redbreast in a cage, Puts all Heaven in rage." and the "Milton?"[3]

Do write me again and tell me of yourself. No, my book has not been delayed. I have lingered over it because I shall be sorry to reach and end and find only a blind alley ahead of me. Sometimes it is hard for me to write; but this novel has not been difficult, except of course that the effort to find the exact right word and phrase is always difficult. I wrote the first draft very quickly, for me, though it sounds long because it took me almost two years. That was the vital and living whole. Then I went back, and I have been on the rewriting ever since last spring. Did you, I wonder, see my essay in Dr. Canby's series in the *Saturday Review*?[4] It appeared in the Christmas number, December the 8th? So many teachers of English have told me that it was an article they needed. You might be interested if you would look it up in the library. And I think Howard would be too.

Love to Howard, and every good wish in the world.

Affectionately yours, | Ellen

TLS MNS
Publication: *L* 171–72.

1. *VOI* (1935). In the following sentence, EG quotes from Exodus: "Now there arose up a new king over Egypt, which knew not Joseph" (Exod. 1:8).
2. *RC* (1926), *TSTF* (1929), *SL* (1932).
3. William Blake's "Auguries of Innocence" ("A Robin Red breast in a Cage / Puts all Heaven in a Rage") and "Milton: A Poem in 2 Books."
4. EG, "One Way to Write Novels," *Saturday Review of Literature,* December 8, 1934, 335, 344, 350.

To Gertrude Stein

ONE WEST MAIN STREET | RICHMOND, VIRGINIA | *Thursday* [February 1935?]
Dear Miss Stein,

I am so glad to have the book with the charming inscription and the portrait of Basket.[1] How we wish he could have been here with you!

Yes, it was a pleasure to have you and Miss Toklas under my roof with our friend Carlo. I hope it is a pleasure that will go on longer and longer.

Sincerely yours, | *Ellen Glasgow*

ALS CtY

1. To thank EG for a party on February 5 given in Stein's honor at EG's home, Stein sent EG a copy of *The Autobiography of Alice B. Toklas* (New York: Harcourt, 1933) and, apparently, a photograph of Basket, Stein's dog. The book's inscription reads: "For Ellen Glasgow

whom I have liked from the beginning and meeting now we feel the same about dogs living and woolen, which is a pleasure and a great pleasure to be continuing. Gtde. Stein" (*CLEG* 17.277–78). The photo of Basket (identified only as a photo of a "dog"), taken by Carl Van Vechten, is in EG's papers.

To Gertrude Stein

April 30th, | 1935 | ONE WEST MAIN STREET | RICHMOND, VIRGINIA

Dear Gertrude Stein,

It was charming to send me your book of lectures, which I found awaiting me when I reached home yesterday. I am delighted to have the book from your own hand, with the most kind inscription.[1]

That glimpse of you in New York was a great pleasure, and I hope that the three of us may meet again soon. My love to Miss Toklas, and to you——

Ellen Glasgow

ALS CtY

1. *Lectures in America* (New York: Random House, 1934). The book's inscription reads, "For Ellen Glasgow in memory of such a charming time in Richmond we did so enjoy being with you. Always, Gtde. Stein" (*CLEG* 17.275).

To Irita Van Doren

June 18th, 1935 | ONE WEST MAIN STREET | RICHMOND, VIRGINIA

Dear Irita,

I am sorry to say (how sorry only a reader who has suffered from the same misfortune can understand) that I have read every book I ever meant to read. It has always been a regret to me that more books—I mean good books—were not written. Some books I have deliberately avoided, and some other books I have left unfinished. But when your telegram came I was trying to decide whether to read over *The Martyrdom of Man* or (for the fourth time) *The Chronicles of Barsetshire*.[1]

(For You)

At last—at last—at last my book[2] is finished, and I feel that I must thank you again for your great help in selecting a publisher. There is no doubt in my mind that this is my best and truest book. For many years (so many that I couldn't count them) I have had it in my mind to write of the Valley of Virginia, which I know quite as well as I know the Tidewater. I feel sure that you will like it. My father's earliest American ancestor of the Glasgow family settled in the Valley before the Revolution.

I hope Pat will not fail me, for I like the reviews she writes, and I would rather have her than any one else.[3] If, for any reason she is unable to review *Vein of Iron,* could you ask Henry Commager. Though I have never met him I have a feeling that he will understand this book, and I hope he is going to review Stark's short stories. I do not think it matters in the least whether a reviewer has ever before reviewed fiction or not. Insight is the one thing needed, and insight is given by God alone.

I hope to see you in July if you will still be in town.

Much love always, dear Irita, | *Ellen*

TLS DLC
Publication: *L* 185–86.

1. Novels by the English writers William Reade Winwood (1838–1875) and Anthony Trollope (1815–1882), respectively, the former published in 1872 and the latter, in six titled volumes, in 1855–1867.

2. *VOI.*

3. It was not Isabel Paterson (Pat) but Dorothy Canfield (later Fisher) who wrote the review of *VOI* for *NYHTB* ("Ellen Glasgow's Fine Tribute to Courage," September 1, 1935, pp. 1–2).

To Bessie Zaban Jones

August 10th, 1935 | ONE WEST MAIN STREET | RICHMOND, VIRGINIA

Dear Bessie,

It was so nice to have a word from you after this long silence. Yes (to me at least) this is the most satisfying novel,[1] both from a human and an artistic point of view, that I have ever written. As a comedy of manners, I feel (why should I pretend to false modesty?) that The Romantic Comedians has never been surpassed in the novel form. But this book strikes its root far down in the soil. It is, of course, far deeper than a study of the pioneer spirit in Virginian civilization. I have used as my theme:—what is the motive that enables human beings to endure life on the earth? One by one, I have tried to interpret these various motives;—religion, philosophy, love, simple human relationships, and the strain of fortitude that has held families and races and nations together. After all human life has endured, when to a civilized mind, general self-destruction would have appeared at times the only logical choice. I have tried, too, to interpret the age in which we are living and our own special form of disintegration.

In a theme like this, placed in the Virginia Valley, that glancing wit would have sounded a false note. But I have never given more care to a style which I have deliberately subordinated to fidelity and characterization. For the first time, in what I feel to be my last novel), I have depended upon a mature art and dared to do what I wished. I have tried to make every sentence fit perfectly, without an extraneous edge, into the whole pattern. You will notice, when you read the book over very slowly, the various uses of rhythms in the thoughts of my five persons seated about the fire in the manse. There are the different cadences, caught from life and carefully sustained, from the long slow rhythms of age to the aimless staccato recollections of a child. Of all these things, I am justly proud. Then, too, I have never lived so completely in any of my other characters. For three years (I began this book before The Sheltered Life was published) I have lived night and day with these people. In John Fincastle (my favorite) I have written of the loneliness of the scholar in America, of the thinker among the dynamos.

But if I ever write another book, I think now that it will be my autobiography.

Affectionately yours, | *Ellen*
I am ashamed of this dreadful typing, but it is this or nothing, and so I send it.

TLS MNS
Publication: *L* 193–94.

1. *VOI*.

To Anne Virginia Bennett

Sunday | ONE WEST MAIN STREET | RICHMOND, VIRGINIA
[September 28, 1935]

The Sunday Times & Herald are very encouraging,[1] but of course luck doesn't last. I hope you saw them.
Dearest A.V.

It is a perfectly gorgeous day, cool, bright, & bracing. I wish you were here if you ever like the sea.

Yesterday late, after resting on the bed all day, we went out up the boardwalk, & I feel better this morning.

There were more people even in Ventnor on Saturday & quite a few dogs—most of them accompanied, but one or two alone. All appeared friendly.

Cordelia is excellent so far. I hope she will last, but so few good things do. We had her husband Frank, very efficient & nice-looking, to serve last night because I had asked Mary & the two others she was with to dinner. They have done so much for us in little ways, but I am not equal to sociability. That is the last. Two unexpected men arrived & we had seven! But left at 9.30 for a service. Now, I am going into seclusion. Frank was so useful. He charged only 1.50.

Please tell Miss Trigg I shall be more interested in her young nephew than in anyone else, to review at the Club. I can't think of a reviewer, but I am sure Hunter S. would be too smart & superficial.

I am to be here (D.V.) the full month. Mary says she meant a month. You must come on whenever you feel like it—either the 22 or the 24. The only addition will be Nathaniel hanging about. But there must be drivers. If the Cabells & Crutchfields don't come, I may ask Berta for two days. I had a sad letter from her, yearning for the sea.

Ever E

ALS ViU EG 5083 Box 28
Address: Miss A. V. Bennett, | 1 West Main Street, | Richmond, | Virginia.
Postmark: Atlantic City N.J. | Sep 28 1935 | 10 P.M.

1. Presumably EG refers to reviews of *VOI* in the New York papers: J. Donald Adams, "A New Novel by Ellen Glasgow: *Vein of Iron* Is a Story of Striking Depth and Power," *New York Times Book Review,* September 1, 1935, sec. 6, pp. 1, 15; and Dorothy Canfield's in *NYHTB* (see previous letter).

To Anne Virginia Bennett

Ventnor. Saturday. | ONE WEST MAIN STREET | RICHMOND, VIRGINIA
[September 30, 1935]

Dearest A.V.

It has been beautiful here, but very hot. Last night it poured all night & we haven't been out today. The air seems cooler, but it is damp for the first time.

We are quite comfortable. The place is very simple, & a cottage furnished simply but everything is so clean by the sea. We have all conveniences & Cordelia is a good cook & does all the work. One of the neighbors lent her to us. She is her maid & she will go back to her when we leave. They are all so kind, but there is one great drawback, as you may surmise.

I am not eager for visitors, though I want to ask them. We have four small bedrooms & two baths. You must certainly come for a week. It is very quiet & there is scarcely anybody on the board walk.

The sea is beautiful in the evening. I need some summer clothes. They say it is often hot in October. Will you send that purple flowered dress with purple coat & the brown shoes in my closet. I bought for $22. that pretty hennacoloured velvet. Will you hang up whatever I send. But for too much sociability, the place is just what I needed—quiet & restful. I walked too much the first day & my feet have been swollen & aching. Then my head ached, & today my back is very painful.

I hated to accept that offer from the moving picture producer, but I did not feel I could refuse that extra money in these hard times.[1]

Love to Billy & Pal.

As always Ellen

ALS ViU EG 5083 Box 28
Address: Miss A. V. Bennett, | 1 West Main Street, | Richmond, | Virginia.
Postmark: Atlantic City NJ | Sep 30 1935 | 8 P.M.

1. EG sold the movie rights to *VOI* for an undisclosed sum. See "Miss Glasgow Sells Book to Hollywood," *Richmond News Leader,* October 15, 1935, sec. I, p. 1.

To Anne Virginia Bennett

Monday | ONE WEST MAIN STREET | RICHMOND, VIRGINIA
[September 30, 1935]

Dearest A.V.

I can find no writing paper I am not ashamed to use. Will you send me immediately the paper in the long box behind my sofa. Also a few typewriters' sheets. You might order more before I return.

I have notes to write and *no paper.*

As ever | E

ANS ViU EG 5083 Box 28
This note was mailed from Ventnor, New Jersey, in the same envelope with the letter of September 30, 1935, above.

To Irita Van Doren

November 21st, 1935 | ONE WEST MAIN STREET | RICHMOND, VIRGINIA

Dearest Irita,

It was a joy to see you, but I was so rushed those last two days that I did not have time to send you this list of books. Now I have just stepped off the train and flown to my typewriter.

I cannot take your advice and leave out SMITH.[1] Though we are friends, we still admire each other's work, J. B. C. and I; and the book, needless to say, is beautifully written. As for the hint of apparent boosting—we have before us the famous precedent of the Brothers Van Doren, Carl and Mark; and they appear to have made a success of that method. I know you won't mind my saying this in a chaffing tone.

I was greatly taken with Margaret. She has so much unspoiled freshness, and so little of that terrible sophistication of modern youth. Do bring her with you to Richmond next spring.

Dearest love, but simply dropping from fatigue, | *Ellen.*
I have so many—oh, so many amusing things to tell you!

TLS DLC

1. Novel (New York: McBride, 1935) by James Branch Cabell.

To Irita Van Doren

November 23rd, 1935 | ONE WEST MAIN STREET | RICHMOND, VIRGINIA
Irita, dear,

After I posted my hasty note to you, I was worried it might seem abrupt instead of merely amusing. The truth is that I was too tired to write (and did not read it over) but I knew it would not reach you in time unless I mailed it that night. However, I can trust you to understand that I appreciate everything you said about B. C.,[1] and agreed with your point. Only, as it happens, I could not, at this time especially,[2] appear to be unfriendly.

I had a beautiful time in New York. It was my best visit because I was feeling the tonic of my weeks by the sea. Then I met so many interesting people, and began one or two real freindships.

Every time I see you I enjoy you more. There are few persons in the world for whom I feel so deep an affection; and there are even fewer persons whom I admire so sincerely. I always have so many things I wish to discuss, and then, when we begin to talk, they slip out of my mind. I wished so much to talk to you of my plans (whether to give another three years to a novel before beginning my autobiography), but by the time you left I had said nothing of this. Never since my first book, and perhaps The Romantic Comedians, which bubbled over of itself, have I enjoyed writing a book so intensely, in spite of the physical ache, as I enjoyed the three years I gave to *Vein of Iron.* Yet my next work, because of that complete saturation, will be utterly different. Both the novel and the reminiscences are drumming through my creative faculty; and the novel as pure creation is becoming imperative. But my memories, which are as real as experience, are urgent and vital.

I don't know why I am running on like this when I meant to write only a note. Do let me know when Margaret's book of drawings[3] will be published. I hope it will come before Christmas.

My brother liked his few words with you——which reminds me that I had an adorable telegram from Joe Alsop. A nice boy with a winning personality—if he did say I have a shrewd face!

All my love to you. | *Ellen*

I know you would rather have this scrawl than a letter neatly copied by any one else.[4]

TLS DLC

    1. [James] Branch Cabell.

    2. Probably because of Cabell's favorable essay on EG in *The Book-of-the-Month Club News* a few months earlier: "Ellen Glasgow: A Southern Grande Dame and a Genius" (August 1935).

    3. *The Black Pup* (New York: Viking, 1938) by Anne Brooks, illustrated by Margaret Van Doren (later Bevans).

    4. The postscript is handwritten.

To Miss Forbes

December 3rd, 1935 | ONE WEST MAIN STREET | RICHMOND, VIRGINIA

My dear Miss Forbes:

I regret that I have nothing in the form of notes to contribute to your lecture on "Vein of Iron."

This book did not require notes. Indeed, I cannot remember that I have ever referred to notes in writing a novel. "Vein of Iron" was torn up by the roots from the experience and observation and reflection of a lifetime. The background had sunk into my subconscious mind as a child, at the age when impressions are most vivid and lasting. Moreover, my memories were inherited as well as acquired, for my father's ancestors and family connections had helped to conquer and settle the Valley of Virginia. The novel had always existed below the surface of thought; and for the three years while I was actually writing it, I lived in a state of total immersion.

You may understand my amusement when a friend in New York told me that some reviewer had complained that it would be impossible to find a metaphysician in the Virginia mountains. Never having been there, except perhaps as a tourist (and I doubt even this) I suppose he imagined that the Valley of the James River was settled by an unlettered band of Scottish adventurers. As a matter of fact, these first settlers, called Scotch-Irish, were religious pioneers, and in some cases brought over their Presbyterian congregations. The history of the first John Fincastle was not unusual. And the truth is, of course, that the Scottish mind is incurably metaphysical. The doctrine of predestination, for example, is an excursion into pure metaphysics. All my life I have been familiar, though far from sympathetic, with my father's faith, which was that of the Presbyterian church in Virginia. In order to refresh my mind, I read over again not only the Confession of Faith, but the Larger and the Shorter Catechisms.

But John Fincastle was far more than a sceptical philosopher. For twenty years, in my early youth, my chief interest was the study of philosophy; and all that I read and thought was embodied in my favorite character in "Vein of Iron." I had read widely, and I might easily have filled pages with appropriate quotations. However, if there is one failing I dislike in a novel, it is the handing on of second-hand opinions and passages in the form of quotations. In more than thirty years of novel writing, I doubt if I have used as many as a dozen quotations. Knowledge, like experience, is valid in fiction only after it has dissolved and filtered down through the imagination into reality.

I wish I had time to write a longer letter. It seems to me that I have only begun, and should like to correct several obvious misconceptions on the part of reviewers or readers. For instance, the very last thing I had in mind was the thought of writing an economic treatise or a defense of any social order, old or new or uninvented. I am more interested in human nature and in the springs of character than I am in any social system or theory of government. But it appears that economics has become the Banquo's ghost at every modern literary feast. What I tried to do in this novel was neither to defend nor condemn any social order, but to look through human behavior and discover the vein of iron that has enabled human beings to endure and survive in the struggle for life.

Now I must stop. I have written hastily but I hope clearly.

Sincerely yours, | *Ellen Glasgow*

TLS ViU EG Box 14
Publication: *L* 202–3.

To Miss Patterson

March 4th, 1936 | ONE WEST MAIN STREET | RICHMOND, VIRGINIA
My dear Miss Patterson:

Without second thought, I can tell you the names of six books you should select for your study.

The Novel of Character.

Vein of Iron, 1935
Barren Ground, 1925
Virginia, 1913

These three novels are concerned with the place and tragedy of the individual in the universal scheme. They treat of the perpetual conflict of character with fate, of the will with the world, of the dream with reality.

★★

The Tragicomedy of Manners.
> *The Romantic Comedians,* 1926
> *They Stooped to Folly,* 1929
> *The Sheltered Life,* 1932

These depict the place and tragicomedy of the individual in an established society. They illustrate the struggle of personality against tradition and the social background.

Important Note. *The Romantic Comedians, Barren Ground,* and *Virginia* should be read only in the Old Dominion of the Works of Ellen Glasgow, published by Doubleday, Doran & Company. *Barren Ground,* in this definitive edition, is included in the Modern Library.

Required reading. All the prefaces included in the Old Dominion Edition, especially the long preface to *The Miller of Old Church.*

One Way to Write Novels. The Saturday Review of Literature, December 8th, 1934 (Christmas Number)

What I Believe, The Nation, April 12th, 1933. This essay is reprinted in Mary R. Beard's *America Through Women's Eyes.* Macmillan, 1933.

With best wishes, | Sincerely yours,

TLU ViU EG Box 14
Publication: *L* 206–7.

To Mary Johnston

April 17th | 1936 | ONE WEST MAIN STREET | RICHMOND, VIRGINIA

Dear Mary,

I did not know until a few days ago that you were still in the hospital. It seems so long, and I thought you had gone back to Three Hills.

I should love to come to see you when you feel able to talk, and meanwhile I am sending you some sherry for your dinner this evening. I hope it will give you an appetite.

With love always, | Ellen

ALS ViU MJ Box 2
Address: Miss Mary Johnston, | Stuart Circle Hospital.
Hand-delivered. A note pencilled on the envelope by MJ's sister Elizabeth Johnston, reads: "Last letter Ellen Glasgow wrote to M.J. who died a month later / E.J."

To Bessie Zaban Jones

West Cornwall, Connecticut. | July 18th | 1936

Dear Bessie,

It is delightful to see your handwriting again, and I am keenly eager to hear of the change to Cambridge. All Howard told me was that he would be "translated to Harvard." But I am pleased that you will be in the East again, and I think you will like living in Cambridge.

This summer has been quite an adventure. I had never been inside a New England farmhouse, and I did not know that the first thing one did to you was to sprain your ankle. Nothing I ever imagined as a dwelling-place was more uncomfortable than this house. I am afraid that it is too far from Cambridge and there isn't a scrap of a guest-room—but I expect to be here until the middle of September, and I do wish you could find it nearer than it appears on the map.

But I know Richmond will be on your way everywhere, and Richmond will be a perfect place for a reunion. Confederates have given it that habit.

Howard tells me that you are both coming to the Modern Language Association[1] in Christmas week, and I shall expect you to stay with me. I don't know anything about the conference, but if Howard has to be speaking languages all day, you and I can have fun together. Henry Canby will attend, and Dr. Few, and a host of others.

Always affectionately, Ellen

ALS MNS

1. The December 1936 meeting of the Modern Language Association (MLA) was held in Richmond.

To Bessie Zaban Jones

September 9th, | 1936 | WEST CORNWALL, CONNECTICUT

Dear Bessie:

If only I were nearer, I should love to see Howard receive his degree. I have always wanted to know just how one should behave on such important occasions. But, unfortunately, I must go back to Richmond at the end of this week. My old house there is in the hands of painters, and I must hurry home before they begin to mix the wrong colors.

I am so glad you have sold your house and are not tied to the West any longer. And I am simply delighted that you have a Springer spaniel. That is the perfect final touch to our friendship. Do you know there is always a barrier between me and any man or woman who does not like dogs. We have two up here, both inherited, and one sixteen years old. But my one and only treasure[1] died just seven years ago.

The summer has passed almost before I felt that it was beginning. We have motored all through the Berkshires and they are beautiful beyond words, especially the Housatonic Valley, where we are staying. I spent a night and a day up at Bread Loaf,[2] where I had the audacity to take over two classes in English and talk all the time. Though I had gone on the understanding that I should not be asked to speak, I was shocked to find that I enjoyed the sound of my own voice saying unorthodox things.

Please don't judge me by this typing. I do really know better. You wouldn't believe that I had worked on this machine every morning of my vacation.

Give my love and congratulations to Howard. Why is he so much more alive that most other professors? Are you to be thanked, or to be blamed, for that?

It will be lovely to have you in Richmond. Do you know the date of the Conference?[3] Write to me and let me hear all about Cambridge and how Howard looks in the fine new cap and gown. I wish I could see him and you.

Love always, | *Ellen*

TLS MNS
Publication: *L* 214–15.

1. Jeremy.
2. Bread Loaf Writers' School and Conference in Bread Loaf, Vermont, sponsored by nearby Middlebury College, was founded in 1920 (the school) and 1925 (the annual conference). Glasgow was there on July 30, 1936.
3. The Modern Language Association; see previous letter, note 1.

To Clare Leighton

One West Main Street, Richmond, Virginia | September | 9th | 1936 |
WEST CORNWALL, CONNECTICUT

Dear Clare Leighton,

What an adorable person you are! All summer, I have kept your letter on my writing table, and every now and then, when the world looked grey, I have read it over again. If only there were more Clare Leightons in the scheme of life, I am inclined to think we shouldn't need any wild plans for Utopia.

No, I did not go to England. I longed to go, but I couldn't arrange it. My old house at last is in the hands of the painters, and I have spent the summer up here in the Berkshires. These hills are enchantingly lovely, and the emerald valleys remind me of England.

Yes, I loved *The Last Puritan,* and I am glad that you saw my review of it.[1] Are you coming to America next winter? Oh, I hope so.

Affectionately, | Ellen Glasgow

ALS ViU EG 9318

1. "George Santayana Writes a 'Novel,'" *NYHTB,* February 2, 1936, pp. 1–2.

To Bessie Zaban Jones

December 10th, 1936 | ONE WEST MAIN STREET | RICHMOND, VIRGINIA

Dear Bessie:

Please forgive this typing, but I am just recovering from laryngitis and my hand is too tremulous for a pen.

I have never had a program.[1] Everybody thinks I have received one, and everybody thinks wrong. However that doesn't really matter. The good thing is that you and Howard are coming to see me at last. Tell him my only regret is that he won't wear his cap and gown.

Christmas is given over to my family and I am expecting my brother from England.[2] On Monday morning (the 28th) it will all be over, and I hope you can come in time for dinner that evening. Henry Canby is coming a night ahead because he has to go back on Wednesday, and he will dine with us. I took him to Williamsburg one spring when the gardens were in bloom, so he has decided not to go back in winter. But you and Howard ought to go, though it will not look its best.

My garden is simply obliterated. All the old shrubs were killed in the terrible freeze of last year, and the ground is now covered with ice. In winter I turn it into a bird sanctuary—but it is deplorable in appearance. The house is all right, freshly painted, and awaiting you with wide open doors and tightly closed windows. I am looking forward with such joy to having you both under my roof.

You will not mind my being more or less of a invalid. The doctor is very strict with me, and has absolutely forbidden my making a speech or going to parties. But that doesn't matter, for I am going to do both unless I fall ill again.

On Tuesday afternoon, the 29th, I am having an eggnog party for you and Howard (I hope he won't have to go to a meeting) and a number of my friends in the M. L. A. I am asking Richmond people, too, because I think you will like them. We shall have a good time anyway, and I hope Howard will skip some meetings. Love to you both.

As always affectionately, | *Ellen*

TLS MNS

1. For the Modern Language Association meeting; see EG to BZJ, July 18, 1936, and September 9, 1936.
2. AGG.

To Bessie Zaban Jones

March 30th, 1937 | ONE WEST MAIN STREET | RICHMOND, VIRGINIA

Bessie dear,

I was so glad to have your delightful letter the other day. You and Howard have been much in my thoughts but I felt unable to write anything—either novels or letters. The winter has been extremely trying, and that wretched laryngitis has held on inspite of all the doctors could do.

Yes, I liked Howard's poems,[1] and I liked especially the sonnet sequence that sounds so mysterious. Some confiding hour you must tell me about it, for I know he never will. But the whole book has a delightful modern eighteenth-century manner that I found very attractive—too candid to be of the eighteenth century and too delicate to be modern.

I wonder how you like Cambridge, and I hope you are happy. But so often I think of your Tommy and I feel that I miss him in my picture of you.

Yes, the coffee was excellent. I meant to write you about it, but everything has been postponed until that blissful day I shall feel really well and the grasshopper is no longer a burden.[2]

Love to Howard, and to you always, | Ellen

TLS MNS

1. *They Say the Forties* (New York: Holt, 1937).
2. "Remember now thy Creator in the days of thy youth ... Also when ... the grasshopper shall be a burden, and desire shall fail" (Eccles. 12:1).

From Malvina Hoffman

MALVINA HOFFMAN | 157 EAST 35 STREET | NEW YORK | March 31, 1937.

My dear Miss Glasgow:

I shall treasure your letter which you were good enough to write me about "Elemental Man"[1] for my regard for your critical opinion is very high and you were good enough to study this piece of sculpture seriously, for which I am very grateful.

I have received from the English Book Shop a group of your books, which Louise tells me you asked her to send to me, and it will be with extreme interest that I will read these. It was good of you to think of sending them to me and I will spend many evenings in your company in this manner, by reading your thoughts.

We saw our friends, Mr. and Mrs. Weddell, on their arrival from the Argentine and they both seemed very enthusiastic about the Pavlova Frieze[2] remaining in Richmond. Louise expects to go down again next week end to attend to the closing of the exhibition, and she will make a last heroic effort to organize some sort of plan by which funds could be raised for this purpose, connected with the new auditorium to be built on to the Museum. I think you can readily understand how happy it would make me to feel that my visit to Richmond would have a permanent reminder in the hearts of my Virginia friends.

With my affectionate greetings, I am

Very sincerely yours, | Malvina Hoffman

TLS ViU EG Box 15
Address: Miss Ellen Glasgow, | One West Main Street, | Richmond, Va.
Postmark: Grand Cent Annex NY Mar 31 1937

1. A series of 110 bronze sculptures representing the living races of humankind, usually referred to as "The Races of Man" or "The Living Races of Man," which was commissioned in 1930 by the Field Museum of Natural History in Chicago. The series was exhibited at the Chicago World's Fair in 1933.

2. The Pavlova Frieze (officially *Bacchanale Frieze,* 1915–1924), consisted of twenty-six bas relief panels with scenes from the ballet *Bacchanale.* The work was created to honor Hoffman's friend the Russian ballerina Anna Pavlova. The details of its apparent exhibition in Richmond are unidentified.

To Anne Virginia Bennett

CONTI DI SAVOIA | May 14 [1937]

Dearest A.V.

This is the only approach to a letter I shall write. To my surprise we have had a rather rough sea most of the time. I was not at all sick, but my cough has been very troublesome and today I am frozen. Carrie was very sick at first, & Mrs Henry Cabell was so ill they summoned the doctor at three o'clock in the night & he stayed for nearly an hour before he thought it safe to give her a hypodermic. The cabin, sitting-room & veranda are all commodious—the nicest I ever had—but if I ever cross again (which Heaven forbid!) I shall choose a German boat. After all I had heard about this food, I find it very ordinary. The truth is I have not felt glad I came for a single minute so far.

If I had been well New York would have been pleasant. But I had to spend two hours in the office of the American Express signing back all but 9,000 lira in wire cheques. We could not cashed[1] them, they said, & so does this purser. Lily Walker came to see me off and was suitably impressed by our veranda suite. We got lots of mail & telegrams & some lovely flowers—but most of them have stayed in the ice-box the whole way. Stark sent me some champagne, but we have never received it yet. He was nicer than ever. I lunched with him by myself, & he looks ten years younger after getting thin. Donald seems dreadfully depressed and Alya looks blooming. You cannot imagine what Dr. C. is like—life seems positively *sodden* with drink—more than ever, Mrs C says. Louise is in a state of unnatural elation—talks like a Christian scientist & appears a wreck, as people who talk like that usually do. I shall be glad to land, but our time once there is too brief to justify a sea voyage.

Don't expect any letters, but I'll try to send cards. Hallie Belle G sent me gardenias—very sweet of her, but it means a note. They are in the ice-box still.

I hope James is improving.[2] Remember me to him & to Frances & Mattie. I wish I could see Billy starting out to walk.

Try to rest some if you can.

We expect to land between 12. & 1. on Saturday.

Love | E—

ALS ViU EG 5083 Box 28
Address: Miss A. V. Bennett, | 1 West Main Street | Richmond, Virginia | U.S.A.
Postmark: "Conti Savoia" 15 VI 37, 11–12

1. EG's error.
2. James Anderson had been seriously ill and hospitalized in April.

To Anne Virginia Bennett

June 1ˢᵗ [1937] | VILLA MARSILIO FICINO | 9, VIA DEL SALVIATINO | FIESOLE

Dearest A.V.

I keep wishing that you could see and smell this place of flowers. I had never imagined the villa was so lovely and tranquil. The weather is perfect, warm and dry, and we go into Florence once or twice every day. Beulah is angelic to me, and seems to take a genuine pleasure in seeing my appreciation of beauty. The shops are fascinating. There are so many things one wants to buy.

I hope all is well, but I can't write. I have sent dozens & dozens of postcards.

Love— E—

We expect to land July 1st, which is Thursday, and to come to Richmond Friday night, July 2nd.

I shall hate to leave all this. It has been years since I had so restful a break.

It is as if I had stepped out of life, but I know I shall step back again into all the morass of living. Beulah is going to sail back with us.

ALS ViU EG 5083 Box 28
Address: Miss A.V. Bennett, | 1 West Main Street | Richmond, Virginia | U.S.A.
Postmark: Firenze Ferruvia, 1 VI (1 Jne), 37, 17–18

To Amélie Rives Troubetzkoy

July 14— [1937?] | ONE WEST MAIN STREET | RICHMOND, VIRGINIA
Darling Amélie,

Do you remember those lovely nightgowns you had made for me in Italy so long ago? I have just found six that I have never worn and I am sending them to you because you might be able to use them during these hot nights and days. I no longer wear any sleeves, but Berta says that you do, lying down in the day. It will be beautiful if you can make some use of them, and I shall love to think of you with my monogram on your dear, loyal heart.

You were a darling to write to me. I have wanted to answer your letter, for I understand so well how the vacancy seems to widen month after month and the pang of loss goes deeper into the memory and heart. But the very day I reached home this terrible tragedy occurred at Reveille.[1] There are times when the hideous *Chinese* cruelty of life is beyond belief. Poor Lizzie has lost everything, for they were completely happy together and she had no other life.

My blessings on you, precious Amélie. I feel what this summer means to you[2] and I am with you and Pierre in my thoughts.

Devotedly. Ellen

ALS ViU EG Box 14

1. The murder of Elizabeth Patterson Crutchfield's husband in the driveway at their home, Reveille, by their chauffeur.
2. Pierre Troubetzkoy died in August 1936 around the time of ART's birthday.

To Amélie Rives Troubetzkoy

August 23rd, 1937 | ONE WEST MAIN STREET | RICHMOND, VIRGINIA
Darling Amélie,

I am sending this word of love to greet you on your birthday tomorrow. It will be a day of sorrow, I know, and I am thinking of you with a heart filled to overflowing with tenderness. Though we never see each other, I have always the feeling that time has been scarcely more than an illusion between us. Only yesterday (or so it seems to me) I was with you in that dear room of yours, and we were reading your manuscript of "The Golden Rose,"[1]

"Always the painted apple,
never the golden rose."

How many years ago that was, yet I can see your deep eyes when I look up from the page, and beyond the nimbus of your hair, I can see the lacy green of the trees and the flashing wings of the cardinals in the sunshine. Dear, dear Amélie, does that moment still exist somewhere beyond time? Which is more real for you, the lost happiness with Pierre or the present anguish of separation?

I know how you miss Pierre with every move, every heartbeat. Yet you had so much, and when one has had perfection, it is there forever, while the heart is alive and remembers.

And so I am with you in spirit on your birthday. Are you well enough to see me if I were to drive up some afternoon? If you would not, I shall understand perfectly.

Blessings on you, my darling. How I wish I could comfort you.
Ellen

ALS ViU EG Box 14
Publication: *L* 224–25.

1. Novel (New York: Harper and Brothers, 1908) by ART.

From Agnes B. Reese

706 N. 6th St. | Richmond, Va. 11/1/37

My Dear Miss Ellen:—

I hope that this bright sun shine makes you feel better. I am still painful but getting better slowly. When I saw your sweet profile in the Times Dispatch[1] this A. M. and read that you had won high rating among the most charming women in America, I felt very proud and happy. Your rank has always been highest with me.

I know that I thanked you for your kindness when you came to look on Birdie[2] and sent a card of thanks also, but I feel that I must say more than that to you, because your kindness has exceeded any one else's for you have been extraordinary kind.

From the depths of my heart, I want to especially thank you for the $10.00 you sent me by Miss Bennett, the most beautiful spray to cover Birdie's casket, the food James brought, the use of your lovely car and chauffeur, the presence of dear Miss Bennett who represented you and last but not least, the gift of your wonderful book—"Vein of Iron" which I am reading with a great deal of pleasure.

I have tried to be brave and hold up, but find myself lying in bed at night thinking of the many good things done by you to make Birdie comfortable and happy, and with tears running down my cheeks thanking God for such a friend as you. May God bless you and crown all of your efforts with success, and when you reach the sun set of life and all of your good deeds and work is over, may your name be found written high among those to whom the Master will say—"In as much as you did it unto the least of my little ones, you have done it unto me."[3]

Sincerely and Devotedly | Your Friend | Agnes.

ALS ViU EG Box 17

1. Richmond newspaper.
2. Roberta ("Birdie") Richardson, died on October 21, 1937.
3. Matt. 25:40.

To Rebe Glasgow Tutwiler

Friday November 5 1937 | ONE WEST MAIN STREET | RICHMOND, VIRGINIA
Dearest Rebe:

I have tried to write to you every day since you left; but I have been over my head and ears in work. Some proofs came, and that very day I was giving a luncheon for Beulah.

I wish you could have been here, but as far as possible we had it like the other—only there were twelve this time.

I enjoyed your visit so much, and I wish you could have stayed longer. It has turned very cold, and this dreadful hunting season has begun. It makes me sick to think of the hordes of savages roaming the woods and killing all the little wild things that I love. I hope you make your place[1] a refuge for them and feed them. Even here I try to do it, but the wild birds do not come with the pigeons. Isn't it funny. Every year the pigeons go away in the summer and come back to my window on the first bitter day. I have just looked out and seen the first arrivals. Usually, they wait for snow, but this year they have come because it is raw and cloudy.

I am glad you enjoyed the books, and most of them you can keep and read over—except the stories for the sanatorium.

If you want to come down for any shopping before Christmas, just let me know. I don't expect to have any more parties, but one can never tell. I hope your wave has been admired. The next time you must have it done by someone else. I do not think that girl cut it quite right.

I wish I lived in the country.
Devotedly, | Ellen.

TC of TLS FU
Address: Mrs. C. C. Tutwiler, | Brushwood, | Lexington, Virginia

1. Rebe had recently moved to Lexington, Virginia.

To Marion Canby

November 6*th* 1937 | ONE WEST MAIN STREET | RICHMOND, VIRGINIA
Dearest Marian,

It was like seeing you again to open your book of poems.[1] These verses tell me so many things that I feel about you, but had never been able to put into words. They are eloquent not only of feeling but of thought, and that is rare in poetry written by women. It is a joy to me that you should have formed your gift and your own right expression. When I see you again, and that, I hope, will be soon, we will talk of these poems.

I had planned to come to New York this month; but now I find that I must postpone my visit. Do stop when you go South in the spring.

Will you give my love to Henry—I hope he is well and happy after the summer.

Devotedly. | *Ellen Glasgow*

ALS ViU EG Box 26
Publication: *L* 228–29.

1. Probably *On My Way* (New York: Houghton Mifflin, 1937). EG consistently misspells Canby's first name (see also letter dated February 24, 1944).

To Clare Leighton

Christmas Eve | 1937 | ONE WEST MAIN STREET | RICHMOND, VIRGINIA
Dear Clare Leighton,

I cannot wait to tell you what joy your enchanting print[1] has given me. Did I tell you—or was it an intuitive sympathy that told you,—of my feeling for English hayricks? We have nothing like them in America. And the swallows—the lightness, the balance, the flying grace! I shall have the woodcut put in a tiny border and keep it on my desk. What a darling you are! I loved you from the moment you drifted in out of the snow on last New Year's Day.[2] That will always be a blessed memory in my heart.

No, I did not get to England last spring. Italy was a dream of loveliness, for I stayed in an exquisite flower garden. The villa had belonged to Marsilio Ficino and is still named after him. All my time, except for a visit to Ravello, was spent at Fiesole. Next summer I may come to England—or perhaps you will return to America. I have ordered "Country Matters,"[3] but it has not yet come.

Affectionately. | Ellen Glasgow

ALS ViU EG 9318

    1. CL often enclosed original pen and ink drawings or prints of her woodcuts in letters to EG.
    2. EG means January 1, 1936, not 1937.
    3. By CL (Macmillan, 1937).

From Amélie Rives Troubetzkoy

Christmas 1937

For my darling Ellen this old bronze figure of the great Buddha. It is not to our ideas beautiful but it is rare and very ancient. It was given to me by a dear friend who is now dead.[1] With it go all my wishes for all things good and beautiful, not only for this Christmas of 1937, but for the New Year and all New Years to come forever.

Her loving, | *Amélie* | Castle Hill, Virginia

ANS TxU-Hu

    1. Helen Martin. This note accompanied the small Buddha figure that EG later bequeathed to Signe Toksvig.

To Bessie Zaban Jones

December 27 [1937?] | ONE WEST MAIN STREET | RICHMOND, VIRGINIA
Tell me how you like or dislike New England.
Dear Bessie,

    This is only a word to tell you how pleased I was to have one of your delightful letters, and to find myself in touch with you again. Only last evening, while we sipped eggnog in my study, we spoke of you and Howard, and our minds flew back to your visit a year ago. I wish I could have another chat with you by the fireside.

Affectionately, and with every good wish for the New Year, | Ellen
Oh, will you please send me the name of that two volume history of the United States![1] I had not heard of it—and I never see things about myself.

    I forgot to tell you that Scribner's will bring out a very fine edition of my works early next year.[2] It will be a limited subscription edition; like the Santayana set they published recently, and it is to be so costly ($10.00 a volume for 12 volumes) that nobody but the publishers are likely to see it. I am doing 12 long critical prefaces—good studies, I think, of my novels, and I have had to hunt for illustrations that will not disgrace hand-made papers and Caslon Old Face type.

ALS MNS

1. In her letter of December 29, Jones replied: "The history is *Growth of the American Republic* by Samuel Morison and Henry Commager, published by the Oxford Press. You probably would like it except for its Massachusetts moral tone about the secessional South."
2. E.G.'s *Virginia Edition*.

To Rebe Glasgow Tutwiler

ONE WEST MAIN STREET | RICHMOND, VIRGINIA | January 28th, 1938

Dearest Rebe:

I want to send you a note for your birthday; but I have never worked harder[1] except over proofsheets for a book, perhaps, in all my life. This is the first time I ever promised to do a work by a definite agreement. Heretofore, there has always been an "if and when" clause in my contracts.

A few books are off to you, nothing very good, but all I had that was new. The mystery story is above average, which is not saying much. I am glad all the others came in so well.

It is splendid that Lexington suits you so well. I wish I could see the birds feeding, for I enjoy things like that more than anything else, I believe. My tiny back garden is crowded this morning with pigeons and sparrows. But the two cardinals that came for years have not returned. I am afraid they have been killed. Boys are so terrible about destroying birds with air rifles.

I am glad you like the secretary, and I shall be interested in seeing it in place. Carrie has no other that I think so distinguished looking. Most of the good ones have solid doors that I should never choose.

I have had the first three volumes in the Virginia Edition, and the frontispieces are all very good. You will be surprised to see how attractive Green Forest appears, in spite of the added railing to the porch. I wish I had had the picture of the house that was added.

I have just had two very sad letters from Margaret, and I am really anxious about Arthur. He has been ill in bed for a month at Monte Carlo, which she says is "a poisonous" place. The day she wrote he had been out for the first time, and he insisted he was returning to London because he had to get to work again. All the men who helped him have gone, and he has to do more than double work now. Some died and one inherited a large property. It does seem dreadful. He caught influenza as soon as he went back in November or December. They sent him to Monte Carlo in Europe; but it had been bitterly cold there, and he had to stay in bed all the time. This makes [*something omitted, between pages*] miserable about his eyes. I think he has tremendous fortitude. Margaret's letter this morning was to invite me to come over and bring Josephine and spend the month of March! Of all the months of the year, it is the worst, and even here, I am always kept indoors by the winds. In England, just imagine it. Anyway, I am only half through, or two thirds through my prefaces. Of course I could not think of going. Carrie and I talk of going in the summer and renting a Ford car for her to drive; but I have no idea that we can really manage it.

Today it appears to be a lovely winter day. If it isn't too cold, I shall have my hair waved at the Jefferson tomorrow. The other kind of wave came straight out.

I hope you will have a nice birthday and that you will be able to feed the birds out of doors.

Now I must go back to work.

With much love, | Your devoted sister, | Ellen

I have to dash this off. I never read anything more thrilling than the [*word omitted*] of the rescue of the poodle in Phila. The clippings for A.V. have just come.

TC of TLS FU

1. EG was finishing the prefaces for the *Virginia Edition* volumes. The "if and when" clause she mentions at the end of this paragraph refers to a publishing agreement that does not hold EG to a specific deadline or even commit her to completing a piece of writing. For more on Green Forest, mentioned later in this letter, see EG to BZJ, December 29, 1933.

To Rebe Glasgow Tutwiler

February 15th, 1938 | ONE WEST MAIN STREET | RICHMOND, VIRGINIA

Dearest Rebe;

I have just returned from Dr. Wellford's, and his treatment makes me feel too tremulous for work. That is the only time I am free to do anything else, so whatever it happens to be, will be badly done. I have still four prefaces to write, and I weaken at the thought.

Thank you so much for sending the book; but that is not a first edition.[1] The first was in plain tan buckram, no illustrations, with a design of oak leaves and acorn on the cover. It is strange how few of my own books I have in first edition with the original bindings, and they are the only copies in demand. This book of yours was published two years after the first edition, for Christmas, 1902.

Wasn't it odd that I found a first where I never have expected one to be—at Carrie's. It is copy[2] I had given Mrs. Coleman, and Lucy had kept it.

I wonder, if, by any chance, you could help me with "The Descendant?" There is a collector in Chicago who is very much interested, and he writes me that my "firsts" are in growing demand. I should not have suspected it—or, perhaps, I should. Have you a copy of the real first edition on The Descendant. If you know it is a first, will you look at the back pages and tell me in what order the advertisements are placed. Does George Du Maurier's "The Martian" top the page? Or does his "English Society"? I have two copies, one of the first, and one of another edition, and I am not positive which is the first. I think the one with "The Martian" leading, but it is just as possible that I am mistaken. It all hinges on the advertising pages. Otherwise, they are exactly alike. If you can help, will you let me know immediately, so I can set this man's mind at rest.

Lizzie came in to supper with me the [*word omitted, between pages— "other"?*] night, and I am so desperately sorry for her. She seems to be, if possible, in a worse state of mind. I cannot see anything ahead of her, because she says she will never go into the garden or put her foot on the place,[3] except to get in and out of the car.

Edmund Preston came to lunch with me a day or two ago. I am really devoted to him.

Carrie has been in bed with a cold. She usually comes to Sunday dinner, but had to stay in last Sunday.

Yes, I dread receiving degrees, but it would have been ungracious not to accept this one,[4] and they will have a private Convocation. Within the last eighteen months, I have had to decline four, two from very large universities, and two from old colleges of fine standing. But accepting them would have meant taking long trips, in two instances, and all that bother of having a cap and gown. I hope I shan't have to have a gown for this, but I don't know. Anyhow, I look forward to it with dread.

I was so much interesting to hear about the birds in your feeding places. I have a House of Lords (pigeons) and a House of Commons (Sparrows) but the cardinals never come back. I think they are afraid of the pigeons.

If you ever feel like driving down, let me know. I shall be delighted to have you and Cabell come at any time.

Devotedly, | Your sister | *Ellen*

TC of TLS FU
Address: Mrs. C. C. Tutwiler | Brushwood, | Lexington, Va.
Postmark: "Envelope was addressed Brushwood, Virginia—without 'Lexington'—and stamped 'No Such Post Office in State Named'" (MKR).

1. EG's *The Voice of the People* (1900).

2. MKR inserts "(sic)" after "copy."
3. See note 1, EG to ART, July 14, [1937?].

4. An honorary doctorate from the University of Richmond. Although in the next sentence EG mentions receiving four offers, only three are known: Rollins College (Florida), 1935; University of Wisconsin (Madison), 1937; Goucher College (Baltimore), 1938. She accepted a degree from William and Mary the following year, 1939.

To Bessie Zaban Jones

April 11th, 1938 | ONE WEST MAIN STREET | RICHMOND, VIRGINIA

Dear Bessie,

Not for a long time have I enjoyed a letter so much. I wish I could arrange for a weekly column, but I shall never have that luck when I can send only scraps in reply.

Of course, as usual, you put your finger on the spot. It is perfectly true that the portrait is in slim profile, and shows only one angle; but that happens to be the view that J. B. C seems to like best.[1]

It will be lovely to see you and Howard in New York. I hope to be there by the fourteenth. Do let me know when I may keep the time free from engagements. It seems an age since I saw you and Howard.

Of course I should like to have him do something about me, and I am very eager for you both to read these prefaces.[2] I have put so much of myself into them. Just now, I am in the middle of the last one. I had not expected the edition to be reviewed, but Maxwell Perkins, of Scribners, has written me that he expects excellent articles when the set is finished, I hope to Heaven he will not be disappointed.

What do you think of this suggestion. Don't pass it on to Howard unless you approve of it. I feel sure that George Stevens, the new editor of the Saturday Review, would be glad to have Howard write a review of this edition. In that way, George might get a set from Mr. Perkins, and then Howard and you would have it for your own. Does Howard ever suggest the books he would like to review? Any way, George is a good friend of mine, and has a strong liking for my work.

No, the autobiography has been put aside, in the first rough draft. I have a chapter written on my novel,[3] and I am very enthusiastic about it. I hope it will be one of my very best; but it is a big theme, and will take time. For the last six months I have been working on these prefaces. Love to Howard, and love to you.

Ellen

There were so many things I did not say that I have had to tear open this envelope. I simply adore Vermont. It is, in my opinion, the most satisfactory State in the Union, and the most beautiful in the way I like. If only I had a place there!

What you write of Cambridge seems almost incredible. I imagined that it was the one spot in this Republic where standards survived. But I haven't been there for twenty-five years, and then only for a few weeks. I should run over to see you if only I had time. But I am always pressed for time, and so is Carrie Duke, who will be with me. Certainly I agree with all that you say of most of the books Howard has to review. I can read very few modern novels. They are all unspeakably dull to me, and most of them badly written. Speaking of Standards!!

As always, E.

TLS MNS
Publication: *L* 235–37.

1. The portrait is probably *Of Ellen Glasgow: An Inscribed Portrait* by Ellen Glasgow and Branch Cabell (New York: Maverick Press, 1938); J. B. C. is James Branch Cabell.
2. For the twelve volumes of EG's *Virginia Edition*.
3. *ITOL*.

To Bessie Zaban Jones

April 18th, 1938 | ONE WEST MAIN STREET | RICHMOND, VIRGINIA

Dear Bessie:

What a friend you are! The 16th of May will be perfect. That afternoon, I will ask some friends to a little party, among them my very special friends on the *Saturday Review,* and later we can have dinner together, and a good long talk. Carrie Duke will be with me. You remember her? I shall probably stay at the Weylin, but I have not decided.

I think that article may be arranged, and of course I should be delighted. Especially, I wish Howard to have this definitive edition because I have revised all my earlier books—or rather those we include in this set. Then he simply *must* read the prefaces. I think he will find them revealing. You can't imagine how amused I was to find that he had discovered the autobiographical basis of my New York novel, *The Wheel of Life*. Most people have thought I was writing of strange ground, but this was, in fact, the only one of my books that was taken directly from experience. That may be why it was so much less convincing than the Virginia books. I was too close; for the mystic phase, and even the incident of the little blue flower, really occurred. But that book was not a good novel, and I have long since disinherited it. All the work I wish to be judged by is in my Virginia Edition. And, in particular, the style I wish to be judged by is in that edition.

I have dashed this off in a rush of work.

Love to you, | *Ellen*

TLS MNS
Publication: *L* 238.

From Agnes B. Reese

706 N. 6th St. | Richmond Va. 5/14/38

Dr. Ellen G. Glasgow,
My Dear Miss Ellen:—

Miss Bennett told me that you would receive the degree of Dr of Law[1] in a few days, and after a few days I read with great delight of your successful achievement.

Accept our sincere congratulations and hearty good wishes.

Independent of your great talent and learning, I love you because of your affability, kindness and goodness, and I honor your heart even more than your talents.

One of my neighbors took me out to the cemetary the other day and you had sent a man out there and had Birdie's grave shaped and turfed and I want to thank you a thousand times for the same. You are an angel of mercy and love.

The plants you sent Jim are growing and blooming beautifully and one of my rose bushes has two buds on it.

Every morning when we go out to look the garden over, we can not fail to think of you with love for having made us so happy with these beautiful plants. With love and best wishes for your health, honor and happiness

Sincerely Yours | Agnes B. Reese

ALS ViU EG Box 18

1. Duke University offered an honorary Doctor of Letters degree to Glasgow, but she preferred a Doctor of Laws. In May, 1938, Duke mistakenly conferred the Doctor of Letters. Late in the summer, EG received from Duke the Doctor of Laws in a small special ceremony.

To Bessie Zaban Jones

July 19th, 1938 | ONE WEST MAIN STREET | RICHMOND, VIRGINIA

Dear Bessie,

In weather like this how I love to think of you and Howard against the enerald landscape of Vermont. If I were not so hard at work (and my work goes well) I think I should motor up for a breath of New England. I am inclined to think that Vermont is my favorite State.

You did not send me your address, so this hurried word must go to Cambridge. I was so glad to have you letter and to know that the article has gone to the Tribune.[1] I wonder when it will appear? And I am more than glad to hear that Howard will do an essay for the Atlantic.[2] Please keep him reminded of that.

Do try to see me when I come on in the early autumn. Carrie Duke, my main dependence, is sailing tomorrow, with some other friend, for the "cure" at Baden-Baden. I hope it will do her good, for she has not been well, and when she returns, I hope to break away for a brief vacation. But when I can work, that always comes first.

Just now, I am getting off an article to go into a book called "Living Philosophies".[3] The title sounds overpowering, but the essay is not uninteresting to do. Clifton Fadiman is to edit the book, and he persuaded me, rather against my inclination, for I hate to promise any extra work, to go into the series. But speculation—anything in the nature of metaphysics—always interests me enormously.

Do send me a line, just to keep in touch.

Love to you both, | As always, | *Ellen*

TLS MNS

1. Howard Mumford Jones's review of EG's *Virginia Edition:* "Ellen Glasgow, Witty, Wise, and Civilized," *NYHTB,* July 24, 1938, sec. 9, pp. 1, 2.
2. "Relief from Murder," *Atlantic Monthly,* July 1938.
3. EG's "I Believe" appeared in Clifton Fadiman, ed., *I Believe: The Personal Philosophies of Certain Eminent Men and Women of Our Time* (New York: Simon and Schuster, 1938).

To Bessie Zaban Jones

July 28th, 1938 | ONE WEST MAIN STREET | RICHMOND, VIRGINIA

Dear Bessie:

As soon as I had read the splendid article, I wrote to Howard;[1] but I had to send my letter to Cambridge because you had never given me your address in Vermont. I am glad that at last I have run you to earth and know where you are.

I did not say half what I wanted to say about the review. The whole thing pleased me enormously, especially the tone and manner of distinction. It is always a pleasure, and a rare one indeed, to be written of with beauty of style. When we meet in the autumn, as I hope we shall, I will tell you in detail just what I feel about it, and how grateful I am to Howard for taking the trouble to write this penetrating and appreciative essay on my work. As I told him in my note, I liked so much what he said of my prefaces and the part about style and the flow of time, and that fine paragraph making a distinction between psychoanalysis and spiritual strength. Please tell him that the article has had a great success in Richmond, and I have had a number of letters about it.

How I envy you the blue and greed hills of Vermont. When do you leave? I wish Carrie and I could arrange a little trip through New England when she comes back from Baden-Baden and her "cure".

Meanwhile, I am in a working mood, and the book goes well.² The essay, thank Heaven, is finished. It will appear in a book called "Living Philosophies," edidted by Clifton Fadiman, and published by Simon and Schuster. There are eighteen men included, I believe, and only two women, one American and one Englishwoman. Mine is the kind of thing that will shock many of my conservative friends, but at least it is honest, and few people ever tell the truth about what they believe or do not believe.

Love to you both, | As always, | *Ellen*
I am so much interested in the Cather article, and in the one on my work for the Atlantic.

TLS MNS

    1. EG to Howard Mumford Jones, July 22, 1938 (*L* 242–43).
    2. *ITOL;* the essay in the following sentence is "I Believe" (see previous letter, note 3).

To Rebe Glasgow Tutwiler

Monday | ONE WEST MAIN STREET | RICHMOND, VIRGINIA
[September 20th, 1938?]

Dearest Rebe,

This has been a very trying summer, but it has gone very quickly. It is over before I have finished half the work I expected to do.

Now, we are all worried over the European situation, and it looks as if the folly of nations would plunge us into another war. I take off my hat to Mr. Chamberlain. It seems to me that England would be mad to get entangled with any other Continental quarrel, or to defend any borders except her own. There could be but one end if she were to ally herself with Russia and France, and that would be the end of her government and of English democracy. Of course the Communists, who have a strong following in England, are trying to bring on war, and so of course are the Fascists.

Carrie and I expect to go on to New York on the night of October 2nd, and we expect to be at the Weylin (Madison Avenue and 54th Street, until October 15th. I hope the change will help me, but I am very tired and depressed after this hard summer.

When we come back, I hope you will drive down. Yes, I should like to come up for a little while when the leaves are at their best. I suppose this would be the end of October.

I must stop and go back to work.
Devotedly, | Ellen

I hear that Arthur is coming over in November. They must be anxious about the war prospect.

TC of TLS FU
MKR note: "dated by RGT."

To Bessie Zaban Jones

September 27th, 1938 | ONE WEST MAIN STREET | RICHMOND, VIRGINIA
Bessie dear,

Your letter has just come, and I am torn by the wish to visit Cambridge (and stay with you), and the fear that I might fall ill on your hands. If only I were well, I should love to spend several days with you and Howard. Carrie and I always stay together when we go away, and I also have only one guest room. But this will have to be some other time, I think, possibly in the spring.

Now, I am going to New York for two reasons—to see my doctor and to give a ranbling talk before Dr. Lyons' class at Columbia. For years he has tried to make me come to one of his meetings, and six months ago, in a moment of weakness, when I was feeling unusually well, I promised him to speak on October 12th. But I have not been able to write a speech (I simply *cannot* do it) and I do not know what to talk about. Will you ask Howard whether students are more interested in literature in general or in a personal experience. Please send me his advice.

And please, please, please, come over to New York. October 15th comes on a Saturday, and I will stay over that Sunday if you will come. There are a thousand things I wish to discuss with you both, and I have had a genuine friendship and affection for you and Howard (my friendships run deep) ever since we first knew one another at the N. C. University, where you so gallantly came to my rescue.[1]

Do let me know positively, and tell me how long you can stay, and exactly when I may expect you. I shall want to arrange some plans for you. Is there any one especially Howard would like to meet? I wonder whether he is entirely satisfied with his publishers? In his position, I think I would rather have Scribners than any other, and Maxwell Perkins is, in my opinion, the perfect publisher.

The reviews of the Virginia Edition start with Howard's. I like his much the best, and I think it showed the most penetrating insight. But we shall discuss this when I see you.

Only yesterday I was thinking of that sad visit you had in Richmond, when Howard, poor fellow, was down with influenza. Some day you must come again, in a good season, not in Winter, and I will take you to Williamsburg and

Jamestown and the other places. Spring is the best time, but autumn is usually beautiful until the end of November.

Isn't the state of the world simply fearful? I feel as if the universe had turned into a vast lunatic asylum, and the riot of emotionalism bears out my belief that human beings are driven to war by some blind destructive instinct, that the cause of war is deeper than any geographical boundary, and is rooted in the facts of biology, and in primitive impulse.

Well, I am ashamed to send this badly typed letter, but I am not able to write at my desk.

Love to you both, | As always yours devotedly, | *Ellen*

TLS MNS
Publication: *L* 245.

1. EG received an honorary doctorate from the University of North Carolina in Chapel Hill in June 1930, when Howard Mumford Jones was on the faculty there. See Jones's account in *Howard Mumford Jones: An Autobiography* (Madison: University of Wisconsin Press, 1979), 144–45.

To Irita Van Doren

September 30th, 1938 | ONE WEST MAIN STREET | RICHMOND, VIRGINIA

Irita dear,

If I am not in by half past five on Tuesday, just wait for me. I have to go to several places that afternoon, but I am longing to see you and the children.

No, I had never heard a word of this latest act by our Mr. Meade.[1] Carrie had never heard me mention him, and I had never discussed his first offense with her. You know I never talked about it, for it was Anne Virginia Bennett who talked of it to Emily Clark over the telephone. I did not see Emily Clark for a whole year, and I was bored to death by the affair when I did see her.

Well, two days ago, Julian Meade went to see Carrie, after calling up twice from Danville, and he told her such a moving story of the way he might be ruined by this new book that she signed a paper saying she did not know him, and was sure he had not had her in mind.[2] She had not seen or heard of the book, nor had I, and Anne Virginia thinks she should not have written the paper until she had read it.

Anyway, we thought that was the end. But today he appeared again with his publisher and, still feeling sorry for him, Carrie signed the paper again. I suppose this was to protect them from a libel suit.

Then an hour ago, I received a long very ugly letter from him implying that I had tried tried to injure him. I who never had the slightest impulse to injure any mortal thing! "Does it help you in any way," he asks, "for people to go out of their way to make trouble for me?" Then he speaks of my "attitude" to him, as if I'd ever had any attitude—or even any gesture, except the objection to being bored. Of course I shan't reply, and I should not have mentioned it to you if you had not written me.

But I have been deeply touched and heartily pleased at the way my friends have risen to Carrie's and my defense. Nothing in a long time has made me so happy as this. Won't you please tell Hershel and Donald this.

Whether he had ever heard of Carrie or not, I cannot say. Of course he knew me much less well than his book implied. But Anne Virginia is convinced that it was an act of deliberate malice. I hope it wasn't, but Carrie is so well known both here and in Danville that it seems strange. None of us, not even Carrie ever heard of the book.

Much love, | *Ellen*

Please destroy this letter. It seems such a sordid business. And do not believe anything Julian Meade quotes as coming from Carrie. He is trying to make trouble, I fear, with my friends in New York. I had begun to feel sorry for him, but his letter convinces me that he is a dangerous person and will stir up unpleasantness.

TLS DLC

1. Meade's "latest act" is unidentified, although undoubtedly related to his "first offense" (mentioned in the next sentence), which was to publish an unflattering portrait of EG after she had granted him an interview.

2. A copy of a statement by Carrie Duke is included with this letter in IVD's papers: "This is to say that I never saw Mr. Julian Meade until this morning. I don't know anything about him or his work and he knows nothing about me, so I am sure he was not making a character sketch of me when he named one of his religious hypocrites Carrie Duke. All I can say is he chose an ugly name, and as far as he or his books are concerned, I will say in the language of my mammy, It is like the gnat that lit on the ox's horn, 'I don't know when he lit and cared less when he left.'"

To Bessie Zaban Jones

November 21st, 1938 | ONE WEST MAIN STREET | RICHMOND, VIRGINIA

Dear Bessie,

It was the greatest pleasure to see Howard in New York, and I appreciated his coming so far to the hospital.[1] If only you could have come with him!

I had a rather bad time, for they kept me in the hospital for three weeks, and after I came home I suffered from what doctors agree to call "a nervous reaction," which made me feel as if I had fought through a war on the wrong side. The worst part is that my book[2] has been broken up in my mind, and at times I feel that it has evaporated, in company with my intelligence. I even began to look back on my stay in the hospital as the only rest for the nerves that I had had in my whole life: you see it was my first experience with being nursed since my infancy.

But I am out again now, though I have to go very slowly. I cannot write either books or letters, but how I should love to see you both! Why cannot you come in the spring?

Affectionately always, dear Bessie, | *Ellen*

ALS MNS

1. EG required hospitalization for a back injury.
2. *ITOL.*

To Ellen Matthews Bagby

December 5th | 1938 | ONE WEST MAIN STREET | RICHMOND, VIRGINIA
My dear Miss Bagby,

I welcome for my library this very attractive memorial edition of your father's essays.[1] These sketches have always been a part of my Virginian heritage, long before I was old enough to understand or appreciate them. I heard my own father read them aloud to his elder children in the winter evenings by the fireside. The vital warmth and humanity of the writing will give this book a permanent place in the life and literature of Virginia. Some books do not grow old with the years, and these essays seem as fresh to me nowadays as they seemed when I first read them.

Your mother,[2] I knew and loved in our summers together at the White Sulphur. Although I was a girl at the time, she was more interesting to me than the youth of my own generation. I have known few women to compare with her in charm and beauty, as well as in that ageless serenity of heart which comes with years to those men and women who never grow old. I shall always feel that it was a privilege to know her well and to win her friendship.

With many thanks, | Sincerely yours, | *Ellen Glasgow*

ALS ViHi

1. George William Bagby, *The Old Virginia Gentleman and Other Sketches* (1884), ed. with an introduction by Thomas Nelson Page (New York: Scribners, 1911).
2. Lucy Parke Chamberlayne Bagby.

V
1939–1945

> I am still on the edge of my long illness, and there is little to offer you except my joy in your friendship.
> —To Irita Van Doren, August 2, 1945

The last six years of Glasgow's life were characterized primarily by ill health, including three heart attacks. In her letters during this time Glasgow repeatedly expresses regret that the physical weakness caused by her heart disease keeps her even from writing letters comfortably.

In spite of her declining health, however, during these years Glasgow added fresh interests, made new acquaintances, and remained active professionally. She rented her first house in Castine, Maine, for the summer of 1939, and she insisted on spending all but her final summer there, even in the face of the inconveniences caused by her decreased mobility and the hardships of wartime rations. She confided in a letter (August 14, 1943) her belief that Castine had saved her life.

Two of the new friends whose lives touched Glasgow's deeply began corresponding with Glasgow during these years: Marjorie Kinnan Rawlings, who later collected invaluable materials for her planned biography of Glasgow; and Signe Toksvig, to whom Glasgow wrote some of her most thoughtful and intellectually engaged letters beginning in 1943. The first extant letter in the Glasgow-Rawlings correspondence is from Glasgow in 1939. They met for the first time sometime between March and July 1941, when Rawlings felt comfortable enough in their friendship to write Glasgow of a remarkable dream, in which she protected Glasgow from harm. Motivated by professional admiration and sincere personal attraction, Glasgow and Rawlings corresponded until Glasgow's death. By the time Rawlings died in 1953 she had collected extensive notes for a biography of Glasgow. A similar sense of instantly strong friendship is particularly intriguing in the case of Toksvig, whom Glasgow never managed to meet, although they did become quite close, as indicated by the more than thirty extant letters they exchanged over the last two years of Glasgow's life. They shared a dedication to their careers; Toksvig worked as a journalist and editor and was the biographer of Hans Christian Andersen and the philosopher Emanuel Swedenborg, receiving a Guggenheim Fellowship for the latter project. Glasgow and Toksvig's epistolary conversations often discussed seriously their attitudes about literature, philosophy (including mysticism, a topic that fascinated both), travel, and life in general. Most important, perhaps, Toksvig provided a dependable friendship that could be conducted by mail at a time when Glasgow's health kept her homebound. Even though an exasperated Glasgow wrote to Toksvig at one point, "Why couldn't we have known each other when I was well and abounding in vitality?" (March 23, 1945), she seems to have been grateful for the friendship they were able to share by mail.

Although writing became physically difficult for Glasgow—nearly impossible, finally—she continued to work, expressing on several occasions her desire only for the strength to allow her to complete her last (and Pulitzer Prize–winning) novel, *In This Our Life* (1941). Even after doing so she did not stop, however. Besides almost immediately beginning a "sequel" (*Beyond Defeat*) to her final novel, never finished as far as Glasgow was concerned but published posthumously, she also continued to refine her autobiography and published *A Certain Measure* (1943), a collection of her prefaces to the *Virginia Edition* volumes with a new essay on *In This Our Life*. Glasgow's advice in a letter written just four days before she died describes aptly her own lifelong determination when it came to her work: "Go on with your book. Do not give up."

To Clare Leighton

February 16th | 1939 | ONE WEST MAIN STREET | RICHMOND, VIRGINIA
Dear, dear Clare Leighton,

Though I have not been able to write, you have been very much in my mind. Ever since you came in for the first time, on that snowy New Year's morning, you have stood in my thoughts as a symbol of happiness. I cannot bear to think that any cruelty of life (life can be so hideously cruel) has dimmed that clear shining spirit. "She is made for joy," I thought while I looked at you. And this joy you must keep for my sake as well as your own. I must be able to think of one human being who is not living, as Thoreau said, "a life of quiet desperation.[1]

No, I am afraid I shall not come to Baltimore soon. Perhaps, when the spring comes, you might run down for a week-end in Virginia.

I hope the books is going well. Just now, I am in a state of total immersion. A new novel[2] means for me years of retreat. But I know, my dear, I know—[3]

My love to you always, | *Ellen Glasgow*

ALS ViU EG 9138

1. "The mass of men lead lives of quiet desperation," from the first chapter of Henry David Thoreau's *Walden* (1854).

2. *ITOL* (1941).

3. EG may be responding to CL's observation in her letter of February 1 to EG—her first after moving to the United States in early January 1939—that it was difficult to remain isolated enough to get work done and at the same time remain sensitive to others.

To Clare Leighton

March 14th, | 1939 | ONE WEST MAIN STREET | RICHMOND, VIRGINIA

Dear Clare,

It makes me happy to have this word from you, for you have been much in my thoughts.[1] I have felt always that you would be stronger than the suffering through which you have passed. To this end, you will conquer because you have the will and the heart of a conqueror.

This is a hasty note to ask you to stop for at least one night on your way up from South Carolina. I have not been at all well, but I am trying to take a week by the sea, from the 20th to the 27th. Any time after this will find me here, and if you and Miss Musselman are motoring, it would mean a good break on the way back to Baltimore. If you see Henry Mencken, will you give him my love. I am very fond of him; and I adored his wife.

Much love to you, *Ellen Glasgow*

ALS ViU EG 9318

1. Leighton's sad letter of March 13, 1939, describes her depression, perhaps caused in part by a miscarriage during the previous summer and by her turbulent relationship with her estranged husband, of whom Leighton expresses fear. Leighton also writes that she is beginning to emerge from her difficulties, partly through hard work. The letter is in EG's papers at the University of Virginia.

To Marjorie Kinnan Rawlings

April 16th, 1939 | ONE WEST MAIN STREET | RICHMOND, VIRGINIA

Dear Mrs. Rawlings:

If you should go by Richmond on your way North, I hope you will let me know. I should love to talk with you, for I am watching your work with great interest. "The Yearling" seems to me to be a perfect thing of its kind. And this can be said of few modern works of fiction.

Sincerely yours, | *Ellen Glasgow*

TLS ViU EG 8352

To Rebe Glasgow Tutwiler

Saturday | ONE WEST MAIN STREET | RICHMOND, VIRGINIA [June 17, 1939]
Darling Rebe:

I have wanted to write to you; but there has been so much to do and I have felt let down from the intense heat. Any effort has seemed simply too much.

The long day in Williamsburg was very trying, but not so bad as I thought it would be.[1] We sat out of doors, on a platform put out under the beautiful old elms, and A. V. said the birds, many mocking-birds and other kinds, did so much better than the human beings that she couldn't listen to the speeches, or the prayers or the hymn, "Awake, my Soul." It went on for hours. The day was intensely hot, and I sat in the sunshine part of the time. After it was over, Stewart Bryan had a delightful luncheon, and I came home very early in the afternoon. The hood is pretty,—purple, with gold and silver and green, the colours given by the College of Heralds, I think, to the College of W. & M.
[*One half of following sheet cut out of letter.*]

Carrie has returned, beaming with health and happiness. She is going up to Maine with us.[2] I wish you were, too. We have to take Mattie and Nathaniel, and we must motor 850 miles,—or it may be 825. But it is far enough.

Yes, Bonnibel, the little dog is here now. She is very sweet and a beautiful little thing, or will be after a little care. I think we may give her to a friend of Mrs. Maynard. She lives at Fort Myer, near Washington.

Yes, we have our servant troubles, too. And I sympathize with yours. Catherine took exception to something Anne Virginia said to her (I think she told her not to call a message upstairs) and she left in twenty minutes without doing her morning's work. It will save me having to pay her half wages for three months while she stayed at home; but it is exasperating that as you train them how to wait at the table, they pick up and leave. She had been with us[3] for six months, and seemed to be delighted with her place. But she has a husband and he is able to support her. James says there is trouble because she likes to run about so much at night and her husband, a nice colored man, is ten years older. However, I will not let me[4] mind worry over the servant problem. Let them come or go, as they will.

I must stop now. It is a sweltering day, but I have had a long walk at Maymont.

Devotedly, | Ellen

TC of TLS FU
Address: Mrs. C. C. Tutwiler, Brushwood, Lexington, Va.
Postmark: Richmond June 17, 1939

1. EG received an honorary doctorate from the College of William and Mary.

2. EG had rented a house ("Littleplace") in Castine, Maine, for the first of many summers.

3. MKR encloses "us" in brackets, suggesting that the pronoun was omitted in the original.

4. MKR inserts "(sic)" after "me," perhaps missing what might be EG's less than tasteful joke about "the servant problem" by imitating an Irish accent.

To Rebe Glasgow Tutwiler

August 5th, 1939

Darling Rebe,

I am terribly distressed that you have been ill all this time. It is dreadful being shut in like that, and I am sending you some books to help you distract your mind. If you haven't read, Busman's Honeymoon," it may divert it.[1] It is far better than the usual mystery murder.

I have had a trying time with what seems to be neuralgia. I had it for ten days, and I was just on the point of going down to New York, when it got somewhat better. But it is back again now, though not so intense as it was.

This is a beautiful place, so green, so fresh, so clean, with no billboards and not a waste paper anywhere. But the dampness and the fogs have been too much for me. We sat for a solid week in a dense cloud. Then we had two perfect days, with heaven's own light and air. But the fog came back yesterday, and with it my pain. It has not rained so much, not enough for the flowers, but the fog makes everything feel soaked.

I have missed Carrie. She and I walked four or five miles every day, and the trails through the woods are simply magical. Now Anne Virginia goes when she can, but I think Carrie enjoyed the walks more. What A.V. does appreciate is the coolness. I hope to heaven it will do her some permanent good.

How I wish I could send you some blueberries. They are so delicious, and the raspberries too. The marketing here is excellent, and I have delighted in the Maine potatoes. Lobster is abundant, but after the first week we have ceased to want it.

If Mrs. Tucker doesn't take this other dog, I can find her one when I go home. Did you ever see Shetland terriers? I saw two in a car the other day, perfect darlings, and the girl who had them said they were Shetlands.

I must stop now and get ready for walk.[2] When I come in I'm afraid I'll have to return to my aily companion, aspirin and phenacetine. But there is a glimmer of sunshine after two days of heavy cloud.

Do drop me a line in a deeper pencil if you have one. My eyes have been hurting me too. I hope to hear that you are better.

As always devotedly, Ellen

TC of TLS FU

1. MKR omits the opening quotation marks preceding "Busman's," and inserts "(sic)" after the end of the sentence. The inverted order of "mystery murder" is in the copytext. *Busman's Honeymoon* (1939) is a well-known murder mystery by Dorothy L. Sayers.

2. MKR inserts "(sic)" following "walk," and "[daily]" following "aily." The mistaken "aily" may be an error on MKR's part, or it may be intended by EG as a pun.

To Rebe Glasgow Tutwiler

LITTLEPLACE | CASTINE | MAINE | September 5th, 1939

Darling Rebe:

I imagined that I came here for complete isolation; but for ten days or two weeks I had an incessant stream of visitors, most of them eager to pour out their emotional disturbances. The blessed state of "all passion spent" certainly invites confidences.

I had Claire Leighton, Eleanor Musselman, the Nelson Doubledays, and four or five others. Now I have a letter saying the Saxtons may be on their way. I hope so, for I should like to see them.

The weather is so damp and raw today that I cannot go out to walk. It has been foggy for several days. After the fog autumn ought to be here to stay, and I hope to stay with it until the end of the first week in October. After surviving the fog, I want the benefits of the fine weather. But, really, there has been less fog than I expected, and after that first bad week of it, I have had much less neuralgia.

I was glad to have your letter, and so relieved to hear that you are better. Take the best care of yourself, and do not work in the garden. Anne Virginia has more delphinium seeds to send you, and I have just given her a box of books to address to you, and tie up. Gene Saxton sent me a box of their new books, but I doubt whether I shall be able to read a single one of them. I already had bought (worse luck) a copy of "Children of God",[1] so I am giving you my extra copy. I think the subject ought to be interesting, but I found the book rather tiresome in parts, or in most parts. However, it is readable and long, and he ought to know the truth about the Mormons, being one of them. They were certainly a most repulsive people, and remind one of that repulsive and primitive race, the Boers. The new book by Cloete, by the way (you remember The Turning Wheels)[2] might have been written by Rider Haggard, except for the superior style. I am sending it now. And I am interested in it.

Some one gave me a lunch the other day, two extremely nice and intelligent women, Miss Trumbull and Mrs. Gause. The same afternoon Mrs Thomas Scott had a tea at the Manor, a really delightful inn kept by three nice young woman, on the top of a hill. They are (or one is) related to Mrs. Bowie. Blythe Branch and his English nurse are there, and he is giving a supper on Wednesday evening. I shall have to go, and it won't be trying, as most of the people have gone, and the food is excellent. He has a private dining-room, but all the Manor people will be there. There is a darling little chipmunk living outside my window, behind some big stones in the garden. I feed him all the time, and he plays about.

The war has overwhelmed me, and I try to forget it, since there is nothing to be done about it. I have no sympathy with either side. Hitler is a psychological tornado, and the other countries should have stood aside and left him to spend himself in Eastern Europe. Instead, they have gone out of their way to be destroyed, for, if one thing is certain, it is that what we know as civilization and democracy will be destroyed in this war, and that there will be no victors. I must stop now.

Devotedly, Ellen

You have not told me the names of the new man and his wife. I hope they will be satisfactory.

TC of TLS FU
Address: Mrs. C. C. Tutwiler, Brushwood, Lexington, Va.

1. *Children of God: An American Epic* (New York: Harper & Brothers, 1939), by Vardis Fisher (1895–1968), won the Harper Prize Novel Award.
2. The new book by the fiction writer Stuart Cloete (b. 1897; *The Turning Wheels* [New York: Penguin, 1937]) was *Watch for the Dawn* (Boston: Houghton Mifflin, 1939).

To Clare Leighton

Littleplace, Castine, Maine. September 20th, 1939 | ONE WEST MAIN STREET | RICHMOND, VIRGINIA

Clare dear:

I take out my brightest paper[1] (so bright that I seldom use it) to send you a doleful letter. It is a relief to have your letter in typewriting, because, bad as my typing may be, my penmanship is far worse ...

I am distressed to hear of your troubles, especially of your physical illness. You had seemed so well that I had regarded you as a kind of goddess of perpetual youth and beauty. Do take care of yourself until you are quite strong again, and do not, I implore you, go back to England. You would only makes things worse over there for the people who love you. In your present state of mind, and of body, it is infinitely wiser to stay on in this country and try to build yourself back to health. You are right to keep out of any and every "mess."[2] After the terrible strain you have been though, your first and foremost duty is to yourself and your own life. I cannot bear to think of you as "derelict." With your enormous capacity to give and to receive happiness, with your extraordnarily vital personality, you are too valuable to the world of the living. Do your Hardy book[3] through memory and imagination. I am thoroughly convinced that a return to England will mean for you only endless confusion and disaster. Oh, my dear, do not let your sympathy persuade you to begin again the old round of unhappiness, the old conflict of hope with thwarted desires . . .

I know exactly what you are suffering now from the horrors in Europe and the general misery of war. All through the last war I was scarcely more than a shell of agonized vibrations. That hypersensitivity is mine also, and it is one of the most real things on earth, not an imaginary affliction.

For me, dear Clare, life has always been a series of conflicts. I smile when you and Don speak of my "calmness", for that calmness is nothing more than the quiet in the heart of a storm—or, more accurately, the peace that comes when one has escaped at last from an inferno. Some day I will tell you more, but not now. My greatest fear at present is that even now, at sixty-odd, I may be drawn back into the blind chaos, that I may find my hardwon fortitude to be merely a false front to life, and that the outer walls of the spirit may topple over again. The peace I have found is the kind that you would scorn to accept, that I myself rejected until I had reached middle age. Resignation has no part in it, nor has acceptance of fate. The contentment I seem to have attained (even yet I do not know that it is permanent) is founded upon a complete disillusionment with experience. My strength, and I hope my security, lies in the feeling that I have suffered all things, and that all things do not matter overmuch in the end. In the past few years I have been able to rise above merely personal disappointments, and *except in the case of my work,* not to care greatly what happens. Yet I am still subject to the anguish that comes from vicarious pain and torment. Even a paragraph in a newspaper telling of the suffering of an individual human being or a helpless animal will cause me days and nights of sympathetic misery . . .

I have written this in haste because I did not want your letter to remain an hour unanswered. My love goes to you, and to your splendid friend, Eleanor. Do let me hear from you. I carry you in my mind and heart, and I long to know that all is well with you.

I, too, had a letter from Don telling me of his decision. What, I wonder, will come of it in the future?

Devotedly, | *Ellen*

TLS ViU EG 9318

1. The paper is a bright, deep cornflower blue. EG's comment in the next sentence acknowledges CL's apology, in her letter to EG of September 17, [1939?], for typing rather than handwriting her letter.

2. As CL's letter of September 17 makes clear, EG refers to the domestic troubles in

the Don and Alya Adams family, which are a subject in other letters between EG and CL. EG seems to be warning CL not to become romantically involved with Don Adams, an implication that recurs in letters between CL and EG.

3. CL illustrated editions of Thomas Hardy's *Under the Greenwood Tree* and *The Woodlanders* (both 1940).

To Bessie Zaban Jones

Littleplace, Castine, Maine | October 2nd, 1939 | ONE WEST MAIN STREET | RICHMOND, VIRGINIA

Dear Bessie:

I was delighted to have your letter (even though it was not one of your major efforts!) for I do not like to slip out of touch with you and Howard. I think of you often, and always with great affection.

The summer has gone South, and in a few days we shall follow. I have played longingly with the idea of stopping to see you, but it is really impossible at this time. There are so many uninteresting complications (what else is life?) that I am obliged to hurry home. Even New York has had to be given up, or put out of mind until later. But it is dear of you to want me, and I hope to come to you at some other season.

Do write to me. It has been long since I had one of your very own letters.

Love to Howard and to you.

As always, Ellen

I have never worked so well, except in Richmond, as I have this summer. The first draft of my novel[1] was finished yesterday. But this is merely a beginning.

TLS MNS

1. *ITOL*.

To Catherine Turney

November 14th, 1939 | ONE WEST MAIN STREET | RICHMOND, VIRGINIA

My dear Miss Turney:

I am sorry, but it is true that I am able to answer few letters. Yes, I have refused a good many offers to dramatize *The Sheltered Life* but so far none of them has seemed to contain the right possibilities. The book would require delicate handling and the kind of subtle acting that is not popular in this age of the literary broadsword and tomahawk.

Frankly, I do not know what to say to you. I know so little about the modern theatre—or any theatre, indeed—that I shall have to put the matter in the hands of my publisher.[1]

As for the pictures——no, no, no, not for *The Sheltered Life*. After seeing Hugh Walpole's presentation of David Copperfield,[2] I decided that I would never go to see another novel made into a movie. Last week, after several years of abstinence, I went to Drums Along the Mohawk. Another fine novel ruined.

Thank you for your pleasant letter, which reached me in the most direct way. One of my publishers is coming next Thursday, and I will turn your suggestions over to him.

Sincerely yours, | Ellen Glasgow

TLS Private

1. Although letters dated later in the same month from Alfred Harcourt to Turney indicate that EG did enlist Harcourt in handling Turney's request to dramatize *SL,* EG also continued her own correspondence with Turney for over a year. "Modern" is typed above the line, with a typed caret below it, before "theatre."

2. George Cukor directed *The Personal History, Adventures, Experience, & Observation of David Copperfield the Younger* (*David Copperfield* in the United States) for MGM in 1935. EG's friend Hugh Walpole adapted the screenplay from Dickens's novel. The director John Ford's *Drums Along the Mohawk* (20th-Century Fox, 1939), which EG mentions in the next sentence, was an adaptation of Walter D. Edmonds's 1936 novel of the same name.

To Clare Leighton

December 3rd, | 1939 | ONE WEST MAIN STREET | RICHMOND, VIRGINIA

Clare dear,

Through a week of great stress your book[1] has been my heartening companion. It is so intensely alive that it sheds a kind of physical warmth, and I seem to feel the heat of its pulse. You have done fine and beautiful work, a perfect thing in its own rare field. Though I cannot now share the book's ecstasy, I can remember moments in the past when I have lived with that positive flame, beyond time and repose.

Much love to you, | Ellen

I was disappointed that "Sometime—Never" reached me too late to be included in my *Herald-Tribune* list.[2] When it did not come, I tried to get the book in Richmond, but it had to be ordered, and that took a week. However, I am richer by two copies.

ALS ViU EG 9318

1. CL's fantasy novel, *Sometime—Never* (New York: Macmillan, 1939).

2. In the December 3 issue of *NYHTB,* EG (along with many other authors) listed recent "Books I Have Liked."

To Rebe Glasgow Tutwiler

December 30th, 1939 | ONE WEST MAIN STREET | RICHMOND, VIRGINIA

Darling Rebe,

I am not yet equal to letters,[1] but I want to tell you how much I enjoyed and appreciated your lovely presents. The fan is exquisite, and the lovely tray set will be very useful. Thank you so much.

I am glad the tray suits your room and that you have a place for it.

The weather has been dreadful, frozen and sleety. There has been some snow, and the birds in my garden are flocking after the grain. But they are almost all pigeons and sparrows. I shall wait until Cabell comes to put up the new house, which will be an ornament all the year round.

Heaven knows when I shall be able to go out, but I stay up now all day, except for an hour in the afternoon. People have sent me the most beautiful flowers. It would be a good time to die, surrounded by roses. Much love and a prosperous and cheerful year.

Devotedly, | Ellen

TC of TLS FU
Address: Mrs. C. C. Tutwiler, Lexington, Va.

1. EG had her first heart attack the first week in December 1939.

To Bessie Zaban Jones

April 24th, 1940 | ONE WEST MAIN STREET | RICHMOND, VIRGINIA

Bessie, dear,

You will never know how much good it did me to see you and Howard, and your letter meant more to me than anything I have had in a long time. All this dreary shut-in winter, when I have been in pain or weakness most of the time, I have felt as if I were, in some queer way, standing outside the world. It has given me a lost and friendless feeling, and this is why your letter helped me trememdously. Your affection means more to me than I can ever tell you.

After all, I am not to be in New York in May. The doctor thinks it would not be wise, and I do not wish to go on and merely "lounge aroun' an' suffer," Like Brer Terrapin.[1] But I have taken a house at Castine,[2] and I am saving my strength for that trip. It is a little bigger than the house I had last year, and I might be able to make you and Howard comfortable if you could drive up for a weekend. I will tell you more after I have been over the place. Outside, it is very attractive, but I cannot say so much for the interior.

Anyway, I shall probably go on by train, if I feel that it is less exhausting, and you might be in New York at the time, which will be, I think, the last week in June. Or is this your important week at Harvard.

Give my love to Howard. It was a delight to see him again.

With much love always, | Ellen

TLS MNS

    1. See EG to AVB, July 27, [1927?], note 3.
    2. The Horsey Place (see next letter).

To Clare Leighton

June 16th 1940 | ONE WEST MAIN STREET | RICHMOND, VIRGINIA

Dearest Clare,

How I loved your letter—and, oh, how I should enjoy seeing you! Are you coming to Maine this summer, and is there the slightest chance of your being in New York between the 21st and the 28th of June? If you happen to be in town then, call me at the Hotel Weylin in Madison Avenue at 54th Street.

This is just a word of greeting as I start on my flight. As I am unequal to the long motor trip, my friend Carrie Duke and I expect to go by train, leaving Anne Virginia and our small white foundling dog[1] to follow by motor, with the cook on the front seat. I have taken another home at Castine, not nearly so attractive inside, but delightfully situated, with a lovely view of the water. It is called the Horsey Place, and you will know it by the fine old apple trees guarding the front of the cottage. I do hope that you and Eleanor will come north again. Don writes me that Jo has rented a cottage in Connecticut. I am sorry that I shall not see her, and I feel for her deeply, but I feel also that things are ending the best way—and the inevitable way for a man like Don. He is too fine and sensitive to hurt anyone, and Mary will always be first with him.

If you see our Henry, do remember to give him my love. I am relieved that he is not one of your suitors. As for the other loves—well, all passes, and all loves and lovers——

Devotedly, dearest Clare, | Ellen

ALS ViU EG 9318

    1. Bonnie.

To Clare Leighton

Saturday, | June 29th | 1940 | DOCTORS HOSPITAL | EAST END AVE.
AT 87TH ST. | NEW YORK

Clare, dearest,

Here I am, resting from the world, with a failing heart. I got no further on my way to Maine, but I hope to continue my journey on July 24th. The doctor thinks he can bring me back to the right condition after four weeks of complete rest and treatment.

Meanwhile, I was so tired—so unimaginably tired—that I am thankful to lie still and not speak.

Write to me if you have a free moment. I saw dear Don, and thought him very sad. He will never, I think, bring himself to hurt Alya and Mary more deeply.

Devotedly, | Ellen

Give my love to our Henry if you should see him.

ALS ViU EG 9318

To Bessie Zaban Jones

June 30th 1940 | DOCTORS HOSPITAL | EAST END AVE.
AT 87TH ST. | NEW YORK

Dearest Bessie,

After all, I got no further than this on my way to Maine. I had known, of course, that I felt like the Wrath of God, but I had believed that it was only a nervous condition, and anyway I did not much care! Here the doctors insisted on Xrays and cardiograms, and they found that my heart is in a pretty bad way, but may be restored if I lie flat on my back for a month and do not talk to anyone, not even my nurse. Thank Heaven, it is not angina. There is no pain, only enlargement and muscular failure.

What brought me, though was the threat that I might not last long enough (at the present rate of speed) to finish my book.[1] I should hate to leave a piece of fine work unfinished.

But the nurse says "No more!"

Devotedly, | *Ellen*

They think I shall recover and go on into "happy years."

ALS MNS

1. *ITOL.*

To Clare Leighton

July 6th 1940 | DOCTORS HOSPITAL | EAST END AVE. AT 87TH ST. | NEW YORK
Clare, dearest,

How I love the Hardy scenes![1] They do open the hospital doors and released some imprisoned longing for the woods and the English countryside, which I have loved so dearly and shall probably never see again in this troubled world.

I am sure I had your long letter if you wrote only that one. In the haste of my packing for the hospital all my letters were put into a suitcase for Castine, and I did not charge my mind with your changed address. I am so glad you are in that lovely country. So far, the doctor has not allowed me to see anyone, but the very first person will be Don, and I shall try my best to mend matters between you. Of all my friends in New York he comes closest, and after him, Irita Van Doren. But Don has a closed soul, and his reserve must be touched with the most delicate perceptions. Bless his heart, he is fine through and through.

The nurse says I must stop. All my love, dearest Clare,[2] and a thousand thanks for the enchanting and cheering prints. Your woodcuts go down to the very heart of things.

Ellen

ALS ViU EG 9318

1. Two small woodcuts accompanied CL's letter of July 5, 1940. EG's language in this letter echoes CL's in the autographed captions to the woodcuts: "For Ellen with love from Clare Leighton | to open her hospital doors" and "For Ellen in hospital that she may walk in the woods | With love from Clare."

2. EG seems originally to have concluded the letter here, followed by her signature, but then added the next part of the sentence.

To Bessie Zaban Jones

July 9th, 1940 | DOCTORS HOSPITAL | EAST END AVE. AT 87TH ST. | NEW YORK
Dearest Bessie,

I was just thinking of you and your dear letter when the lovely flowers came, and now they are close on the table beside me. It is seven o'clock in the morning and I have been awake ever since five. When the nurse walks in she will say, "Now, you ought not to be doing that!"

But I want to send you just a line with my constant love. What you wrote of Chapel Hill brought it all back to me, the beginning of our friendship. From the first, I recognized some tie or flash of kinship, and I have loved you ever since. You were and are, so valiant and blade-straight, and so small to be so spirited and alive.

The nurse has come. And so, no more——I do want to see Howard.
Devotedly, | Ellen

ALS MNS

From Catherine Turney

410 E. 50 | New York City. | July 16, 1940.

My dear Miss Glasgow,

Your letter of April 18 has remained long unanswered because there were so many things to attend to, and so many meetings and discussions concerning THE SHELTERED LIFE.[1] I will tell you what has taken place. Before doing this, I do want to express my sympathy in your illness, and trust that the brisk air of Maine will make you feel better. I am sure it will.

After receiving your letter, I had a long talk with Miss Gertrude Macy, Miss Cornell's manager, and also an acquaintance of mine. At her suggestion I worked out an outline—in order to show what I thought could be done to put your novel into play form. This I showed to her and to Mr. McClintic. All plays go through him, rather than Miss Cornell, who abides by his decisions. After a few days I had another long talk with Miss Macy and she told me what he had said.

He seemed quite struck with the outline, but felt it was well nigh impossible to recreate in such a bald thing as an outline—the sum and substance of your book. There is a nostalgic quality—and an atmosphere which needs further developement. I agreed with him. He also made a few suggestions as to the developement of Eva's character—bringing out various facets which had not been completely brought out.

At first I was tempted to send the outline to you, but decided against it because I knew that you might feel your beautiful book stripped pretty bare. There is something about an outline which does make an idea look a little bleak. And especially in a book like THE SHELTERED LIFE, which is not a plotty novel, but rather one of mood and character and idea.

At Miss Macy's suggestion, I have gone ahead and written the first Act. That takes care of all that happens in Book One of the novel. The three acts run very much according to the book.[2] The first act ends with the scene in the children's bedroom at the Peyton ball.

She wishes me to send her a copy of this act so that she can look it over—make what suggestions she has—and then I am to go ahead and finish the play. We all feel this is the only way to see how it is going to turn out. Since I have gone this far, I might as well go the whole way.

Frankly, I am quite pleased with this first draft of Act 1. I have let one or two people look it over who have not read the novel in a deliberate effort to see if things get over in the play. So far, they have done so admirably.

I know you will not object to my finishing the play before submitting it to you, since I am gambling anyway, and I would so much rather give myself every opportunity to make good. I know you would rather see the finished product, and I would rather have you see it.

When it is finished, I will send it to you immediately, and you can give me your honest reactions. I will also let the McClintic office have it too. I hope, after you have read it, that I may be able to talk to you in person. I adore writing the play, and begrudge every moment spent away from it. My radio program (which affords me bread and butter) takes up three or four days of each week, and it always seems like a holiday when I can once more sit down with Eva and George and the others.[3] So even if nothing should ever come of it, I have had an interesting experience and one I do not regret at all.

If luck is with me, I ought to be able to have it done within a month. Do you plan on being in Maine all summer? If so, I might be able to drive up there for a day or so since I want to drive into New England anyway. I could spend a few hours with you, and you could tell me what you thought.

If you have a moment, please drop me a line and let me know where in Maine I am to send the manuscript. Once more, my regrets on your illness, and hope for your full recovery.

Most sincerely yours, | Catherine Turney

P.S. After August first my address will be

330 E. 58.

New York City.

TLS ViU EG Box 19

1. EG's letter to Turney is dated April 17, not April 18, 1940. Turney completed her play based on *SL* (two original typescripts exist), although it was never produced. EG most likely did not read the finished play. EG wrote that she reluctantly agreed to Turney's attempt on the condition that the play be submitted only to Katharine Cornell (see EG to Turney, December 2, 1940; and EG to Alfred Harcourt, October 29, 1941, *L* 289).

2. The novel's three sections are "The Age of Make-Believe," "The Deep Past," and "The Illusion."

3. Characters in *SL*.

To Irita Van Doren

CASTINE, MAINE August 1, 1940

Irita, dear,

I was so glad to have your letter last night, but I am not strong enough yet to do more than scribble a line or two. If only we could have had more time together in New York!

Yes (Heaven be praised!) I have escaped from that hospital bed and the quite dreadful heat of New York. The latest X-ray showed no organic impairment, but I am still firmly convinced that only an Act of God can ever kill me. And I ask really so little—just the strength to go to work and finish my book.[1]

I have written the telegram,[2] but we cannot send it until we are able to go to Ellsworth. That will be in a day or two, I hope, for I shall be delighted to send it if you *will prepare the way* for my approach. Otherwise, I should feel as if I were intruding. The telegraph office here is utterly inadequate. If there is any change of address within the next few days, be sure to let me know, and do send me also your address for the summer and the number of your apartment-house. I cannot remember whether it is Seventy-second Street or Seventy-something else.

I am wearing a Wilkie pin, and A.V. says that everyone she has seen in Maine, except the postmaster, is for Wilkie. It was nice that you saw Lily Walker. She is a darling, and I cannot say that of all of my cousins. Do drop me a line.

With much love, | Ellen

My house is not nearly so attractive as it appeared, behind its apple-trees, from a distant view. The place is a very old farm-house which has been spoiled by a taste for modern comfort and Southern porches. Oh, how I hate Southern porches in New England! The landscape calls everywhere for the enchanting New England doorways, just as our Southern background demands white columns. Yet even in Connecticut I was condemned to a Southern porch.

ALS DLC

1. *ITOL.*
2. Unidentified.

To Bessie Zaban Jones

September 25th, 1940 | CASTINE, MAINE

Dearest Bessie:

I have thought often of you and Howard, but it has been impossible for me to write. You have not heard, I know, that I was desperately ill after I left the hospital and came to Castine. On the 9th of August I had a severe heart attack and the doctor did not know whether or not I should come through. To me, the interesting part of it was that I was entirely conscious, except when I fainted for a few minutes, and though I was too weak to do more than flutter my eyelids, I knew and remembered everything that I thought and felt. While the doctor sat for an hour with his stethoscope on my heart and his finger on my pulse, afraid to do anything more, lest, as he said, it would "push me over the ragged edge", I really thought I was dying, and I felt not the faintest fear or reluctance or even a wish to hold back a moment. My philosophy held firm, for that I was thankful, and I knew then that there was nothing to cling to in life and nothing, or less than nothing, to fear in death. Afterwards, I was tremendously interested, and even at the time, Anne Virginia said she believed my only sensation was one of curiosity. Anyway, I remember thinking, while they thought I was dying, "As long as I can't finish my book, I hope I can go quickly."

Well, I came through, and I had an excellent doctor. He kept me in bed, without letting me stir for weeks, and all I saw of Maine was a tall pointed fir outside my window. I have become much attached to this tree, and I feel that it has a kinship with something deep down in myself. Or, maybe, this is vanity. Illness is apt to give one extravagant values.

Even now, I am permitted to go downstairs only once a day. I have been for four short drives, but no walks, which I loved best of all. Ten days ago, the doctor told me I might work fifteen minutes a day, and now I work half an hour every morning. But what a life! What a world! The horrors in Europe hang over me like vultures of darkness. I cannot put them out of my mind, and I can do nothing.

Do let me hear from you. I expect to go home on October 20th, but I shall not be able to motor down.

That was a dear visit from Howard when I was in the hospital. He looked so well and seemed so interested in this sorry world. How I should love to see you both again; but I do not know whether I shall ever be any better than an exasperating invalid. I have just told the doctor that I prefer death to a neurosis. It was refusing to live safely, however, that brought on my unpleasant, yet not unenlightening, match with fate on August the 9th. So I shall have to go either too slowly, or too fast and make a clean end of it.

My love to you both. You have been near me through all this dreary summer, while I lay in my room and watched the fir tree against a blue or gray sky. It is stormy and wild today. This has been an unhappy September, gray and rainy, with only a few glorious days now and then.

I haven't your new address, but I hope this will reach you.

Devotedly, Ellen

I do not like this letter. It has an egotistical tone, and I have been obliged to tap it out hurriedly. But if I tear it up, I may not be able to write another for weeks. So please make excuses for me and my general inadequacy.

But the book[1] marches on!

TLS MNS
Publication: *L* 269.

1. *ITOL*.

From Margaret Mitchell

MARGARET MITCHELL | Atlanta, Georgia | November 11, 1940

Dear Miss Glasgow:

I did not realize until I had left your house that I had stayed over an hour. Then I was filled with remorse and anxiety that I had worn you out. The time went by so swiftly because I had the feeling that I was with someone I had known a great many years. Perhaps I had the feeling because I had read and loved your books and your personality which shone through the books. And perhaps it was because you yourself have that charm of manner which delights the stranger and makes the stranger feel at home.

At any rate, I thank you for your generosity with your time and I apologize if I wearied you.

My husband hopes that if we make another visit to Richmond he may have the pleasure of meeting you. Everything I told him about you tied in so perfectly with the things Herschel Brickell and other mutual friends had told us about you. John has long admired you, not only for your books but for the way you have carried success and public acclaim—not just a brief grass-fire flare of notoriety but solid success that grew from year to year, which was based on true worth of character and back-breaking work. It is no small feat to carry success with dignity that has no stuffiness and with graciousness that has no condescension. He'd like to have the opportunity to tell you these things personally, and I hope some day you will let him do this.

I hope your doctor is kind to you and lets you get on with your book, but I hope he is firm enough to put you back in bed when you need it. We need people like you and books like yours, so please take things easily and don't try to go too fast.

I shall never forget my lovely visit in that pretty room. Thank you for making it possible. My best regards to Miss Bennett.

Cordially, | Margaret Mitchell Marsh

TLS ViU EG Box 17

To Catherine Turney

December 2nd, 1940 | ONE WEST MAIN STREET | RICHMOND, VIRGINIA
Dear Miss Turney;—

I was ill at Castine all summer, or I should have written to you long before this.

You know how I felt in the matter of wasted endeavor; and you know, too, what my stand is, and has always been, on the subject of this particular play.[1]

Even now, I cannot feel that the play has advanced far enough for me to justify calling in my publishers. I am not eager to see the novel put on the stage; but, on the other hand, I should love to have Miss Cornell play the part of Eva Birdsong. This was the condition I made, you will remember. If Miss Cornell takes the play, and in that event alone, I shall agree to the dramatization of "The Sheltered Life". As I understand, you are in complete sympathy with this point of view. I hesitate to give any one the "rights" to the book, because there is always a danger that the work might be offered elsewhere. But, always provided that Miss Cornell acts in the play, I am willing that you should take up the matter with Messrs. Harcourt, Brace and Company. In this case, the rights to the dramatization should most certainly be yours.

I hope this letter does not sound ungracious toward the stage in general; but I have a strange reluctance to turning a novel into a play.

With all good wishes,
Sincerely yours, | *Ellen Glasgow*

EG:AVB
TLS Private

1. Turney's proposed play based on EG's *SL* (see letters dated November 14, 1939, and July 16, 1940).

To Irita Van Doren

December 19th, 1940 | ONE WEST MAIN STREET | RICHMOND, VIRGINIA
Irita, dear:

You have been constantly in my mind since that evening in New York; but this is the first day I have been able to write letters. I had a severe collapse after I reached home. The doctor made me stay in bed, and he has not yet given his consent to my going downstairs. Against his advice, I have kept up a little work each day, and now, at last, my novel[1] is finished. All I had to do, of course, was the second writing of the last chapters. Alfred has been down for the manuscript, and he thinks it is my best work. I cannot tell about that, but Heaven alone knows what it has cost me!

If only I might have a heart to heart talk with you. I want to hear that you are happy and more peaceful, and that, since the election,[2] you have stopped getting thinner. I know it must be easier for you now; yet I am still anxious. I feel that that you should have the best of life, and I cannot bear that you should be denied your rightful inheritance.

They are sendig me back to bed. How utterly weary I am of trying to spare a heart that longs only to stop beating! But I am still gay.

With all my love to you, | Ellen

I should hesitate to ask you to come for a tiresome trip when there is nothing whatever for you to do, except talk to me. If the time ever comes, however, when you would like just to rest for a few days, do let me know. I should love to see you above all things! My blessings for the New Year are with you and the children.

TLS DLC

1. *ITOL.*
2. Presidential election of 1940, in which Franklin D. Roosevelt defeated Wendell Willkie. EG often misspells Wilkie.

From Eleanor Brooks

VAN WYCK BOOKS | Alexandria | Friday [February–March 1941?]
Dearest Ellen,

Tomorrow Van Wyck and I start north, taking many happy memories with us, but the most radiant, and certainly the most precious of all was of the day we spent with you.

We believe there is some magic about your household, so that if one sets foot in it he is immediately and continuously happy, so long as he is there. And we know very well just where that magic flows from!

The one pang in my memory is that—because of my horrid sniffles—I simply didn't dare go into those generous arms and give you the kiss I longed to.

I send it now, sanitarily, by post! to a gallant, gallant lady, and a very dear one.

Won't you please remember me affectionately to Mrs Duke, and to Miss Bennett who gave me the best lunch I ever ate!

Ever with love | Eleanor.

ALS ViU EG Box 12

To Bessie Zaban Jones

March 6th, 1941 | ONE WEST MAIN STREET | RICHMOND, VIRGINIA

Dearest Bessie:

I can send but a word, and this is to tell you, as well as Howard, that the article for the S. R., apart from being a review, is a fine and penetrating piece of literary criticism.[1]

I am glad you like my latest (and last) novel.[2] You will like it better, I think, after a second reading.

My critics and readers are devided between those who prefer Barren Ground and those who think The Sheltered Life is my best book. Sometimes I am on one side, and again I pass over the way, but I am usually faithful to B. G.

My love to you both, | Ellen

TLS MNS

1. Howard Mumford Jones reviewed *ITOL:* "Product of the Tragic Muse," *Saturday Review of Literature,* March 29, 1941, pp. 5–6.
2. *ITOL.*

To Irita Van Doren

March 27th, 1941 | ONE WEST MAIN STREET | RICHMOND, VIRGINIA

Irita, dear:

I liked Mrs. Becker's review[1] very much. All her points are good. Please thank her for me and tell her how much I appreciate it.

It was delightful to have your long letter, and I only wish I were able to answer it as I should like to do. No, I have not yet seen *Time;* but if they quote nothing worse than that, no harm is done.[2] I cannot tell you how they kept after us for an interview; but I was really not well enough and at last an interviewer called up Anne Virginia with a list of question, and, failing of satisfaction called up Carrie! In some way they had heard she was my closest friend in Richmond. I hope what they discovered was worth the trouble.

I am so very much interested in your news of the family. Do try to run down some week end before summer is on us. Barbara's marriage is exciting, and so is Margaret's baby; but, to me, Anne's book is even more exciting.[3] Make her send me a copy.

Why do you suppose so many persons find, or remark, that In This Our Life is tragic? What else, in this world and age, do they expect in a truthful book? Pap for babes in the years of the locust?

But both Don and Mrs Becker struck the right note, I think, and so did

Van Wyck Brooks, who liked the tragic sense undefeated. Heaven knows I have seen and felt tragedy! And little else in this life.

Devotedly, | *Ellen*

I liked the heading of Mrs. B—'s review. Not lost but running away.

TLS DLC

    1. May Lamberton Becker, "A Generation Not Lost But Running Away: Ellen Glasgow's Fine Novel Deals With Our Troubled Life Today," *NYHTB,* March 30, 1941, sec. 9, p. 1. Becker is the "Mrs. B—" in EG's postscript. The review by Don that EG refers to in the last paragraph is J. Donald Adams, "A New Novel by Ellen Glasgow," *New York Times Book Review,* March 30, 1941, sec. 6, p. 1. The reference to Van Wyck Brooks is unclear; he published no review of *ITOL.*

    2. The review in *Time* (March 31, 1941, pp. 72–74), which pronounced EG's *ITOL* "[n]ot her greatest book," opened with a barbed quotation from James Branch Cabell: "'When I consider [EG] as a person . . . she arouses in me a dark suspicion'" (*EGCR* 426).

    3. The book by Anne Van Doren (later Ross) is unidentified.

To Rebe Glasgow Tutwiler

June 14th, 1941 | CASTINE, MAINE

Darling Rebe:

    I reached here more alive than dead. That is all I can say. The doctors in New York, at least those at the hospital, told me over again what my other doctors had said. But I have so little strength that the trip on the train, with every comfort and attention, was entirely too much. Then after two days rest I made the mistake of motoring to Bar Harbor yesterday, and came back more dead than alive this time.

    June is the month for Castine. The country looks as if it had just been created. Such flowers, the lilacs just beginning to be in full bloom. We bought pots and tubs of pink geraniums yesterday, and a tree of heliotrope which is a mass of purple sweetness. I hope they will be in bloom when you come. For the first three days the air was heavenly, the ideal bracing Maine air, but it is raining today, and I am glad because the farmers are so much in need of rain.

    The house looks very attractive.[1] Mr. Wardwell has had fresh paper put on the living-rooms and hall, and everything appears much improved improved. We have just had a man working for a week on the lawn and garden, and today we expect the truckload of flowers. A.V. seems to have bought everything that was not sold, but all the biggest tubs of geraniums had been ordered by somebody else.

    I am glad you are through with your worst trials with the doctor. Do try to rest more.[2]

    I shall expect you on the 15th of July. A. V. and Mrs. Bowi[3] have gone to Ellsworth. Carrie is delighted with the house. She bought four pair of shoes in New

York, and has not one single pair made to walk in. She minces over the country on spiked French heels, just as the women mince along in New York. It is amusing how feet and legs are played up at the expense of the rest of female anatomy. They move exactly as Chinese women did in the old sheltered days of China.

Devotedly, | E.

I simply cannot write!!!

TC of TLS FU
Address: Mrs. C. C. Tutwiler, Brushwood, Lexington

1. The Horsey Place (which EG called Appledoor). In the next sentence, the double "improved" appears in MKR's transcription.
2. MKR inserts a paragraph symbol here, indicating a typist's error.
3. Probably Bowie (Elizabeth, or Lizzie, Branch).

From Elaine J. Dean

1803–4ᵀᴴ St., N.W. | Washington, D.C. | June 26, 1941

My dear Miss Glasgow,

My purpose for writing this note is to express profound appreciation for your novel, "In This Our Life." I read with interest every page of the book, and noted with particular zeal your admirable portrayal of colored people. To me, Minerva and Parry[1] were respectable human beings with dignity, ideas and opinions. As a member of this minority group, I thought as I read, of the many colored people who have ideals, who lead decent lives, who are ambitious, and who, in many instances, do achieve more than an average share of success in life.

Your own personality must be attractive to humanity, your magnanimous spirit and character must be real and beautiful; your fine qualities must be really sterling; everything about you must represent truth and reality, for you see human beings as they are, and feel keenly, human problems and emotions.

I am a teacher of English in the Cardozo High School, Washington, D. C., with an A. B. from Howard University, and an M. A. from Ohio State University. I shall present our library with a copy of this book, so that many young people will have free access to it.

Again, I want to express my heart-felt and sincere gratitude for the kind heart, the deep understanding of human nature, and the liberal conceptions which assisted you in writing such a novel.

With best wishes for far-reaching success, I am

Gratefully yours, | Elaine J. Dean

ALS ViU EG Box 13

1. Characters in *ITOL*.

From Marjorie Kinnan Rawlings

MARJORIE KINNAN RAWLINGS | FLORIDA | Crescent Beach |
RFD St. Augustine | July 19, 1941

My very dear Ellen Glasgow:

I had such a vivid dream about you last night, that I must write you—which I have been meaning to do ever since our delightful brief visit together.[1] The reality of a dream can never be conveyed to another, but you came to live with me. I was away when you came, and on my return, to one of those strange mansions that are part of the substance of dreams, you were outside in the bitter cold, cutting away ice from the roadway and piling it in geometric pattern. I was alarmed, remembering your heart trouble, and led you inside the mansion and brought you a cup of hot coffee. You had on blue silk gloves, and I laid my hand over yours, and was amazed, for my own hand is small, to have yours fit inside mine, much smaller. You chose your room and suggested draperies to supplement a valance. The valance was red chintz and you showed me a sample of a heavy red brocade of the same shade. I told you that from now on I should take care of you, and you must not do strenuous things, such as cutting the ice in the roadway. James Cabell came into the room and asked what the two of us were up to. (As of course he would!)

My memory of my time with you is quite as vivid as the night's dream. I have thought of you oftener than I can tell you. So often a personality is detached from writings, and the two in fact seem to have nothing to do with each other. You as a person have the vitality, the wit and the irony of your work, but I was not prepared to find you so warm and so beautiful, in spite of the devotion of your friends, which would indicate those things in you.

I am at my cottage on the ocean, and have been working very hard on my book,[2] so hard that I put myself in the hospital for a week. It wouldn't seem necessary to tie oneself into knots to get out a few ideas, but while I *feel* at the drop of a hat, thinking is terribly hard work for me! The first draft of the book is nearly done. Much of it is very bad indeed, and after Max Perkins has seen it and given me, I hope, some of his marvelous suggestions, I shall go at it again.

I am wondering if you went to Maine, and if there is any chance of your visiting Florida this winter. I do hope you are strong again and that I shall see you here.

With much affection, | Marjorie

TLS ViU EG Box 17
Publication: *WW* 294; Bigelow and Monti, eds., *Selected Letters of Marjorie Kinnan Rawlings* 206–7.

1. This suggests that MKR visited EG in Richmond earlier in the year, as MKR proposed in her letter of March 30, [1941]. It would have been their first meeting.

2. In 1939 MKR purchased an oceanfront cottage at Crescent Beach, Florida, a few miles south of St. Augustine; her book is *Cross Creek* (1942).

To Marjorie Kinnan Rawlings

July 24th, 1941 | APPLEDOOR | CASTINE, MAINE

My very dear Marjorie:

I cannot tell you how much your letter meant to me—and still means. It came last night after a trying day, and it brought a thrilling sense of friendship and sympathy.

That was an extraordinary dream, and it was the more extraordinary because you have been so frequently in my mind since I have been at Castine. It was singular that the cold, and my cutting ice in geometrical patterns, should have come in. Ever since I finished "In This Our Life" I have felt as if I were drifting in an icy vacuum toward something—or nothing. I wonder whether other writers have this sense of being drained and lost and surrounded by emptiness whenever they have finished a book. Of course, my illness and five years of work that was like pushing against a physical obstacle may have intensified this feeling of being swallowed up in the void.

But the dearest part of your dream was the way you brought me in and told me I must do no more cutting of ice in the roadway. And the warmth of the red curtians and the valance! Even the way James popped in and asked what we were up to had the accent of reality. I am so glad you wrote me about it.

Ever since you came to see me, so strong and warm and vital, I have felt very near to you, and you have had your own chosen place in my life, just as I had in the house of your dream. I am tremendously interested in the new book,[1] and I know it will be good when you let it go away from you. But there is a kind of slow agony, after the first rush of impulse, in bringing a book into the world. I shall send my helpful wishes to you every day, with the hope that you may feel them. You must keep well and not have a return of the hospital.

No, there is not a great chance of my ever seeing Florida. I, too, went into the hospital when I came through New York, and I heard yet once again that I had "absolutely no cardiac reserve strength." Well, no matter. My heart has served me hard and long, and I think a rest has been earned.

My love to you, dear Marjorie, | *Ellen*
Something has happened to the spacing of my typewriter.[2] It is very annoying.

TLS ViU EG 8352
Publication: *L* 286–87.

1. *Cross Creek* (New York: Scribner's, 1942).
2. The spacing throughout the letter is very erratic.

To Rebe Glasgow Tutwiler

August 21st, 1941 | APPLEDOOR | CASTINE, MAINE

My darling Rebe:

I have missed you all the time, and I was so glad to have your letter yesterday. It is too bad that you are feeling so far from well, and I hope the doctors will be able to find out what causes that backache. Try to rest as much as possible.

This is a perfect day, and autumn is already in the air. The fields are covered with golden-rod. We went to Ellsworth, and stopped to walk by the haunted house, where they were cutting all that beautiful silvery grass. A man with two superb horses was cutting it with a reaper.

I never saw it more beautiful there than it was late last evening, when we went out, after having tea with Miss Safford and Berta.

I came home this morning with acute neuralgia and an aching back. Everything tires me so. I shall have to stop now and go to my little sofa.

I am so thankful you could have that visit, because this is probably my last summer in Maine. Even if I live till next summer, and I am hoping to be spared that, I shall not be able to take this house, and, anyway, Ralph Wardwell has just written me he is going to advertise it and put a mortgage on it, but, of course, I do not wish to buy any place anywhere.

Do take care of yourself. You are really all I have, and you are bound up with my childhood and with my memories of Mother, who seems to come nearer to me as I go on.

Devotedly, | Ellen

TC of TLS FU
Address: Mrs. C. C. Tutwiler, Brushwood, Lexington

From Agnes Reese

706 N. 6th St. | Richmond, Va. Dec. 27/41

My Dear Miss Ellen:—

I hope you are feeling better today and that you have enjoyed your Xmas so far and that the New Year holds in store every blessing that will bring happiness to you.

Jim and I thank you so much for our lovely Xmas gift which certainly brought happiness to us.

Jim had another nervous break down and has been in the Veterans hospital at Roanoke since Nov 3rd. I am sending him a box today and will let him know that your gift is included in it. He does not write as he is too nervous to write, but I hear from him thru the Dr. We thank you for and appreciate all of the flowers you have given us and for those which you will give in the spring. Flowers are so sweet and beautiful but there isn't any as sweet as you are with such a *beautiful* soul.

When I read your beautiful card signed—"with love from the 3rd generation," it made me think what a lovely place this world would be today—if nations had a little of that kind of love in their hearts for each other.

Our love for each other teaches me how firm a foundation of love was laid by our first generations for the second and third to build upon. May God bless you and all others who possess that kind of love.

I am sending you an old fashioned pound cake that I made and baked in mother's earthen mould. I hope you and Miss Bennett will enjoy it. I am not expert enough to keep it from cracking on top but will keep on trying. With love for you and Miss Bennett,

I am Your devoted grateful friend | Agnes B. Reese

ALS ViU EG Box 17

To Marjorie Kinnan Rawlings

February 24th, 1942 | ONE WEST MAIN STREET | RICHMOND, VIRGINIA
My very dear Marjorie:

For weeks you have been in my mind, and I have wanted to send you a message. But this has been a very trying winter——though I am not going to begin on the subject of tribulations.

Instead, I shall tell you how happy it makes me to hear of your happiness.[1] It is just right that this marriage should bring you the serenity you had lost in all those years of distress and disappointment and mistaken endeavours. Everything you say of Norton Baskin makes me feel that you have made the one and only decision that could mean happiness for your future life, and security for your growing work. I wish you both every good fortune. I not only wish it; I believe in it.

Carrie Duke has just come back from her delightful visit to St. Augustine; and she is bubbling over with all that she has to tell me of the Cabells and of you. She likes your husband so very much; she says he adores you; she is enthusiastic about Castle Warden. . . .[2] And all this makes me regret that I am not strong enough to come to St. Augustine. The hotel sounds most alluring; but, unhappily, it appears to be written in the stars that I shall never see Florida. I must content myself with remembering the far-off places I have seen and loved before two world wars destroyed them.

James[3] seems to be very well and perfectly satisfied to be in the city he loves. I thought his latest book enchanting—the best thing he has done since he turned, ungratefully, into Branch Cabell. He writes to me occasionally, and he always speaks warmly of his friends at Castle Warden. But Carrie tells me all the little things that bring me so close to you. I heard of the luncheon and of the evening party, of the attractive dresses you wore, and how charming you looked. She thinks you are lovely, and, of course you are.

I am waiting eagerly for your book.[4] I wonder how it happened that I did not ask you to write in my copy of The Yearling". I shall send it to you for the inscription it lacks.

Always affectionately, | Ellen

TLS UVA EG 8352

1. MKR married Norton Baskin on October 27, 1941.
2. Baskin's hotel in St. Augustine.
3. James Branch Cabell and his wife, Priscilla Bradley Cabell ("Percie"), lived in St. Augustine intermittently after 1935. In the next sentence his "latest book" is *Hamlet Had an Uncle* (1940), the last one he published as Branch Cabell before resuming his full name on publications.
4. *Cross Creek* (1942). EG's copy of *The Yearling,* which she mentions in the next sentence, has no inscription, but only MKR's holograph signature (*CLEG* 17.272).

To Marjorie Kinnan Rawlings

April 20th, 1942 | ONE WEST MAIN STREET | RICHMOND, VIRGINIA
My very dear Marjorie:

I have just finished "Cross Creek," and I am overwhelmed by the sheer breath-taking magic of the book. The writing seems less a vehicle of expression than a luminous web, which captures and holds some vital essence of a particular place and moment in time: heat, light, color, scents and sounds. Even the primitive enjoyment of killing, from which my inadequately covered nerves are inclined to flinch, I recognize as an essential part of the truth. Too well I know the cruelty that runs through the beauty of all things Southern—perhaps, though I am less sure of this, through the beauty of all things human.

But, as an interpretation of a special aspect of life, "Cross Creek" appears to me to be flawless... Not that this, or any other book, can ever take, for me, the place of "The Yearling". There is no Jody in "Cross Creek," and no Flag. For the rest, I would add nothing, and take nothing away. You have uprooted a landscape, with its tendrils still living, and you have made it over into a book that would bleed if you tore it apart. How could you keep up the rhythm, page after page, without a pause or a break?

My favorite chapters, I think, are "For This Is An Enchanted Land" and "The Magnolia Tree". I, too, am a tree worshipper, and after that heart failure in Maine, when I was thought to be dying, I lay for weeks gazing at the top of a single tall pointed fir.

I wish I were able to write more—or, better still, to talk with you for a whole long day. But, after all, what could I say but the same thing, over and over. You have written a gorgeous book.

With my love and admiration, | *Ellen Glasgow*

Oh, one incident did hurt me. With your deep sympathy for the human species, even for the utterly undeserving, like Leroy, how could you bring yourself to betray the confidence and the good will of the yellow catch-dog? After reading that passage, I laid the book aside for a few hours, but you write so vividly that, even then, I could not put the story out of my mind. I suppose he is dead now, and it is too late to make amends in his old age. But so much good will to be wasted in a world where other beings have so little!

TLS ViU EG 8352
Publication: *L* 293–94.

To Rebe Glasgow Tutwiler

Wednesday [May 6, 1942?] | ONE WEST MAIN STREET | RICHMOND, VIRGINIA
My darling Rebe:

You are in my thoughts all the time, but I have not felt able to write letters. I shall be so glad when you are up and about, but please be careful or you will have a return. I want you to cash that check and spend the money on yourself. That is what I sent it for, and you must do it now.

It looks as if we should not get to Castine. The expense, apart from being without the convenience of a car, makes to simply too much.[1] I should have to send five persons by train, and the Bonnie is a problem. She would have to be taken in on a "container".

James has just brought me another handful of telegrams.[2] I have had so many that the telegraph boy wanted to know "whether it was a wedding or a coming out party."

Devotedly, | Ellen

Margaret is in the Doctors' Hospital for an operation for gallstone trouble. She wrote me Arthur insisted on moving to the hospital to spend a month while she was there.

Can you tell me when little Samuel Creed was born? I mean whether he came just between you and me. I want to know before I put my manuscript[3] in the bank. Don't trouble to look it up, but he must have been born a year and nine months before you, and two years after me.

Do you recall the name of the Colonel or captain who spent the night on Mother's porch, after General Hunter tore up her note asking for a guard? Was it Milroy? I think it began with an "M", and I remember her telling us several times of that incident. You know, General Hunter sent word to her "Make your damned Rebel husband come home to protect you."

. . . .

I felt like telegraphing the Columbia Trustees "Too little and too late," and I almost did it.

TC of TLS FU
Address: Mrs. C. C. Tutwiler, Brushwood, Lexington

1. MKR inserts "(sic)" before the period.
2. Congratulatory messages on EG's Pulitzer Prize.
3. EG's autobiography, *WW.* See *WW* for accounts of Samuel Creed (88) and the incident mentioned in the next paragraph (39–40).

To Bessie Zaban Jones

June 26th, 1942 | SPRUCE KNOLL | CASTINE, MAINE

Dearest Bessie:

Your letter came just as I was leaving Richmond, and how delighted I was to have news of you and Howard! My winter had been very painful, and the intolerable heat of summer in Richmond is something one must feel in order to understand what it means. That about finished me, and I put myself in the place of all the other ill persons who ought to escape, and cannot.

How strong you are to look so small and childlike—yes, and innocent of the world. After your service with the strange and lost on our shores,[1] I cannot help feeling that anything else is too much to ask of you. I am not in the least reconciled to your being a nurse's aid. That sounds even worse than being a nurse; and the nursing profession, however noble in act, has never appealed to me. Even if, as you say, the bed pan has not changed its shape, it has remained for me an abomination. In the hospital, it was the one thing I successfully rebelled against; for it seemed to me to put the ultimate degradation upon human dignity, if there exists such a state. But, then, I wasn't born noble. I can only stand and gasp, and admire and envy nobility in others. And you, lovely and prim-looking and eager-hearted little creature, why can't you stop doing good for a season, and sit back and let the mad world be damned if it wants to be damned?

How I wish I could see you. An eternity of change has come and gone since the Christmas week with the long talks and the egg-nog in Richmond. Life goes it own way in spite of us.

No, I did not see the movie of I.T.O.L.[2] The advertisements were enough to make me understand that Hollywood had filmed a different book, not mine at all, and had entirely missed the point of my novel. I hated the whole thing, but there were practical reasons why I had to let it be done. The sister conflict was, of course, a minor theme, and the character of Stanley a minor figure, who was treated objectively, from the first page to the last. The major theme, as I meant it, and you must have understood, was the conflict of human beings with human nature. In Asa and in Roy, I probed into this, but how brutally obvious one has to be in print to be comprehended. And how I dislike the obvious in any and in every form! Yet was the question too subtle? What is the essence, what is the spiritual quality, that will hold a man together after he has lost everything else?

Dearest love to you and to Howard when you write to him. If only you were both here in this sparkling blue air of Castine! After the intense heat, we entered the Arctic Circle, and the first night, with the stove on and a log fire in my bedroom, I slept undr two two blankets and two quilts. We came a day ahead and the house[3] was just opened.

Do write again.

Devotedly, | Ellen

Forgive this wholly inadequate typing, but the machine is easier on my hand[4] than the pen.

TLS MNS
Publication: *L* 301–2.

    1. Glasgow presumably refers to the "refugee project" Jones mentions in her letter of December 29, 1940.

    2. The film version of EG's *ITOL* (Warner Brothers, 1942), was directed by John Huston and starred Bette Davis and Olivia de Havilland. EG received $40,000.00 for the film rights. Stanley, Asa, and Roy Timberlake, mentioned in this paragraph, are characters in the novel and film.

    3. Spruce Knoll.

    4. A window had fallen on and injured Glasgow's left hand. Although there were no broken bones, the injury meant wearing a sling and typing "with one finger" (*L* 305).

July 1942

To Bessie Zaban Jones

July 20th, 1942 | CASTINE, MAINE[1]

Dear Bessie:

Your letter was delightful, and I cannot tell you how much I enjoyed it. As it happened, your comments on that maternity ward helped me to round out a paragraph I was writing.[2] It was all so amusing, and your insight was so perversely acute.

What you tell me of Howard's study of my work makes me feel immensely proud and pleased and gratified all together. I only wish it were possible for me to go to Columbia and listen to his lecture. Do you think he might send me a copy?

All my life, or so it seems, something, usually frail health, has kept me from doing anything I really wanted to do. My one eager desire, as far back as I remember, has been to start out, quite alone, and go round round the world by myself. Yet, though I have travelled a great deal, I have always been shielded and looked after, and advised and warned and retarded. For years, I was so sensitive about my deafness that I would not go into a shop unless someone was with me, and in earlier years I would not even see a caller alone. . . . I suffered from a morbid sensitiveness that was a kind of tepid Hell, and even now, I have not entirely got over it. My whole life has been a struggle not to be helped.

I don't know why I am writing you this. Your letter, which I have just reread, started a train of reflection; and I felt an impulse to assure you that there are more serious impediments to happiness than an enlarged conscience. I doubt, moreover, whether your analysis has not left out the chief element. You are, I think, singularly unselfish, and your sense of responsibility for the universe is probably an inherited misfortune. Didn't you have a righteous father or an overrighteous mother somewhere in the background? I had a father who believed that to disbelieve in Hell was the Great Refusal; but his orthodoxy merely sent me off on a new departure of heresy. Even as a child, I suspected that he might be to blame for my being one of ten children, but I certainly wasn't. Eight children before me had drained the vitality of my adorable mother, and in the years before I came the Reconstruction Acts combined with the struggle to rebuild a devastated region had worn her to a beautiful shadow. So, whatever I brought into the world with me, it wasn't a conscience, and it wasn't enlarged.

Your letters invariably start an idea scampering out of its hole. Do write again, and tell me more of your hospital days. I hope with all my heart that I may see you and Howard before I turn back to Richmond. Everything is so upset nowadays that I cannot look ahead or make a sensible plan.

My love to you both, Ellen

I forgot to tell you that I am trying my hand a short sequel to "In This Our Life." So many readers missed the point of that book that I should like to do a less subtle approach. The broad pattern was meant to include the whole group consciousness of a community, using the ebb and flow, in a somewhat rambling stream, through different minds. My coloured people were very nearly, if not quite actual portraits of a family that had belonged to my mothers ancestors for over a hundred and fifty years. I particularly liked Minerva, who was a collective portrait of several sisters. But, of course, the theme holding the various elements together was the perpetual conflict of human beings with human nature. In Asa, I was depicting, not a failure in life, but a man in whom character, not success, was an end in itself.

But I am not sure that this sequel will ever be published.

TLS MNS
Publication: *L* 302–4.

1. "Spruce Knoll," imprinted on the letterhead, has a line drawn through it, probably by EG.
2. EG may refer to a paragraph—perhaps one she omitted in revision, since there is no passage that fits her description here—in the "sequel" mentioned in her postscript. The short novel was not completed to EG's satisfaction, but was published posthumously as *Beyond Defeat: An Epilogue to an Era*, ed. Luther Y. Gore (Charlottesville: University Press of Virginia, 1966).

To Bessie Zaban Jones

October 19th, 1942 | ONE WEST MAIN STREET | RICHMOND, VIRGINIA

Dear Bessie:

I am so sorry to hear of your brother's death, and I wish I had known you were in Richmond. About ten days ago I came home in a state of utter exhaustion, and I have been trying ever since to recover at least a degree of my Maine spirit.

This is just a hurried line to send you my sympathy, and I must write on the typewriter, because my hand still troubles me after that accident. But I understand how it is when a large family begins to break up. We were ten children, there were seven when I grew out of childhood, and now only three of us are still living.[1]

Tell Howard I share his anxiety over the defeat of the humanities. I suppose war and culture are eternally hostile; yet Jane Austen could write her quiet novels in the Napoleonic era and never so much as mention "the Corsican Monster". The world, it appears, has become too small. We feel the nations closing in on us. What is the use? Must we wait in the hope of a joyful resurrection which may never come?

Thank you for telling me of the Kazin book.[2] Henry Canby is enthusiastic about it.

Always affectionately yours, | Ellen

TLS MNS
Publication: *L* 308.

    1. AGG, EG, and RGT.
    2. Alfred Kazin's *On Native Grounds* (New York: Harcourt Brace and Co., 1942) discusses EG's work (247–64).

From Radclyffe Hall

The Wayside. Lynton | N. Devon. | March 22nd 1943.
My dear, my very dear Ellen.

What a joy to get your long letter this morning; and if there is such a thing as an Angel Guardian of letters written from the hearts of friends, then undoubtedly that good spirit was watching over yours, for it had been rescued from the sea as the official stamp on the envelope testifies—in other words saved from 'Enemy Action.' But not much, if any, damage to the letter itself though the envelope has been badly damaged of course.

In spite of the happiness I feel at being once more in touch with you, I am worried and anxious about your health, for I now know that you have been very seriously ill, and still have to take the greatest care of yourself—and then the pain, I can't bear to think of your suffering pain—was it, is it because of your heart? Please tell me when next you write, Ellen. But I cannot help feeling that it must be worthwhile to go through almost anything for the sake of having the wonderful experience of which you speak.[1] Was it, perhaps, "The peace that passeth all understanding"? I think it was. You see I have always felt that there was a great goodness in you, a great and generous & pitiful kindness of heart and spirit—I felt this when I first met you and I have felt it ever since, and what you tell me now makes me certain that I was and am right. Such experiences as yours are only given to the worthy. And now you know what death, so called, can mean, a lovely fulfillment, a happiness beyond anything that is given to the poor, anxious flesh—in a word a union with the source of all true and indestructible happiness, with God. But words are such poor and inadequate things, and I feel that I am putting all this very badly.

As for me, I have never been afraid of death any more than you. I have always had an unshakable belief in an after life. People say what? what proof have you? I can only answer that the proof lies within myself, in my own instinctive conviction. I just *know* and there it ends. During my serious illness I had moments when I vaguely realized that I might die. I was not at all afraid, but for a minute, and I felt peaceful and willing to just drift, as it were, but it was not given to me to have what I may almost call: "The Beatific Vision" I expect I was unworthy, yes, I expect it was that. I am much consoled and strengthened by your experience, and so thankful that your letter telling me of it was saved. I shall always keep your letter by me. It has a very special value in as much as it is written by a woman whose brain I respect and who, or so I think, had no preconceptions regarding the next life—yes, indeed, I am lucky to have received that letter. Also it has given me courage—if you could write your book[2] despite such physical disabilities, surely I can and *will* write mine, though when it will be finished I do not know, for it is not only a difficult and complicated study of two characters, but it is insisting on being long, and at times I am still much troubled by my eyes and a great tiredness, so that I am forced to put down my pen. But as I have said, if Ellen can John can—I have just got: "In This Our Life," but yes, the print is not good, moreover I cannot resist the chance you have given me of having a copy dedicated and sent to me by you. And I want a copy of: "Vein of Iron" as well. I have not read that either, for in 1935 my eyes were not all that they should have been. Yes, yes, *please*—send me the books as soon as possible, and may they reach me safely.

The War. There are times when people like you and I just dare not think if we are to remain sane. Even in this quiet and lovely place war is all around one, one cannot escape it. As for London, well no more about that. The old Germany of sentiment and romance, of Christmas time & little children's toys, of great thinkers and even of great Saints—where is it? Perhaps, after all, it is still there, ready to blossom forth again when this hideous weight of madly wrong-thinking has been lifted off it so that it can breathe once more—I like to think so. I finished my education in Dresden, and have often been to Germany since then. As a country rich in history and art, beautiful in its scenery too, I had an affection for it. The kind of affection that one has, as life goes on, for things and places connected with one's youth. But for very many years an ugly, aggressive and selfish pride has been growing up in the Germans, and a ridiculous desire to assert their own superiority, hence the "Herren Volk."[3] Pray God that when this unspeakable horror comes to an end, all the peoples of the earth will realize that the fundamental emotions of the human heart are the same in all countries, and can thus be forged into a link that should be unbreakable. A dream? Well, perhaps, but a kind, good dream that helps to drive away this nightmare, at all events for a little while, so let us go on dreaming when we can, even if only for moments. Dear Ellen, we two might very well have met on the other side of this earthly existence—what a charming & happy meeting too. At this moment we might have been discussing our books, for of course we should not have been drifting on clouds or anything like that, we should just have been ourselves: Radclyffe Hall and Ellen Glasgow. But I have Una to think of these days, and for her sake I am glad that I did not die, this is not the time to leave a loved one alone. And you must live too so that we may meet again. I am longing to come out to Richmond to see you.

>Meanwhile take care of yourself, & God bless you and keep you safe for
>Your affectionate friend | John.

Una sends you much love & many thoughts—she will probably be writing to you herself.

PS Have you got a photograph of yourself? If so do please dedicate it & send me this also—I don't care whether it is a good or a bad one, *I want it.*

ALS ViU EG Box 15

1. EG's mystical experience after her heart attack in August 1940 (see EG to BZJ, September 25, 1940; and *WW* 288–90).
2. *ITOL*. Hall's book in progress, which she never finished, is *The Merano Shoemaker*, destroyed in manuscript by Una Troubridge after Hall's death.
3. Hitler's "master race."

To Signe Toksvig

March 26, 1943 | ONE WEST MAIN STREET | RICHMOND, VIRGINIA

Dear Miss Toksvig:

It was kind of you to write to me, and I heartily enjoyed your letter. I feel as you do about the "dreadful callousness" and the cheapness of most contemporary standards, and I may confess that I resent the lack of a subtle sense of quality in current fiction.

This is modern, I suppose, but it is not, really, so new as one might imagine. I have done the work I wanted to do for the sake of that work alone; but always I have felt that I was pushing against the stream, and against immovable obstacles. If I had cared more for popularity than for craftsmanship and simple truth telling, I should have given up long ago. But I held on, and I smile to think that it has taken me more than forty years to win my place in American letters. . . .

I do not often write about myself, and I am telling you this because your letter is unusual, and, I think, extraordinarily sympathetic to my point of view.

No, I feel sure your friend is mistaken in what he says of the older residents in Newtown.[1] I know Virginia better than I know Connecticut, but I am positive that not one American of an older generation, or, for that matter, of any generation, would rather have Hitler than Roosevelt. I believe all Americans are determined to win this war, but some of them dislike the effort to introduce national politics into a world conflict.

I am slowly recovering from a long illness, and I may have to give up my usual summer in Maine and miss, also, my brief spring visit to New York, but if you should come to Virginia, I hope you will let me know.

Sincerely yours, | Ellen Glasgow

TLS TxU-Hu
Publication: *L* 315–16.

    1. ST's town of residence in Connecticut.

To Rebe Glasgow Tutwiler

Monday [May 4, 1943?] | ONE WEST MAIN STREET | RICHMOND, VIRGINIA
Darling Rebe:

First of all, before it slips out of my mind:—Those are the only really good canned peaches I ever ate. They have so much flavour. I think it must be the special kind of peach, and I like them because they are soft and ripe and easily mashed, not pale and tasteless like the others. Can you get that peach in Lexington? I wish you could buy some for me, and Addie could put them up, if you could find glass jars in the store for me.

Your diary[1] came this morning. It is a wonderful diary, and reading it brings back all that winter and spring in Egypt. Some of my recollections were of other things; but your description of our afternoon and night with the Pyramids and the Sphinx revives the whole experience so vividly. I wish I could read the rest of the diary. Do you remember the lattice windows of the house next to the Hotel du Nil, and the garden with a fountain and cypresses? I have never forgotten the grey and black ravens, or rooks, that were always flying back and forth. And I have never forgotten the near minaret, of a greenish colour, where a crier would come out and call the muezzin.

For one so young, you certainly looked deeply into the eyes of the Sphinx. I shall always be thankful that we saw the world, and especially Egypt, when it was most beautiful and unspoiled.

I enjoyed your visit so much, and I do wish you could come again. Since these strikes have begun, I can make no definite plans; but the doctors insist I must leave Richmond for the summer. Still, I should not wish to be held in Maine for the winter. Thank you for copying all those pages. It was so good of you when your eyes are not well. We have had a near panic about coal. For the first time in my life, waiting to put in a stoker, I have not laid up my coal for the next year. And now I may not be able to get it. Ellison and Hawes say they can not sell more than a ton at a time. I do not know how we shall manage.

Please be careful not to work too hard in the garden, and keep away from any burning leaves or brush, which might have twigs of poisonous ivy or oak.

Yes, I would not take anything for that visit to our section in Hollywood. Poor Mother, I think of her more and more.

Irene is sick at home this week, and we are under a dreadful strain.

Devotedly, | Ellen

TC of TLS FU
Address: Mrs. C. C. Tutwiler, Brushwood, Lexington
Postmark: May 4 1943? (MKR note)

1. For published excerpts from this diary, kept by RGT during the 1899 trip taken by the Glasgow sisters (CGMcC, EG, and RGT), see *EGN* 35 (Fall 1995), 36 (Spring 1996), and 37 (Fall 1996).

To Signe Toksvig

May 21st, 1943 | ONE WEST MAIN STREET | RICHMOND, VIRGINIA

Dear Signe Toksvig:

Your letter gave me much pleasure, and you have been in my thoughts, though this wretched illness has prevented my writing. It is a sharp disappointment that you were not able to come to Richmond. I admire Francis Hackett; I know his work very well; and it would be a delight to welcome you both to Virginia.

But the summer here is intolerable, and if I am sufficiently well, the doctors will make me leave for Maine before the middle of June. I spend my summers at Castine, Maine, a most lovely place, with crystal blue hills and a blue rippling bay.

How I should enjoy reading your biography of Hans Andersen![1] I adored his fairyland as far back as I can remember, and I still love his stories, long after the fairy element has vanished from life. No, I am utterly ignorant of Swedenborg, but I shall look forward to your book with great interest. Though I am not in the least "psychic", I have had always a deep interest in mysticism. For many years, I studied transcendental philosophies, and, oddly enough, in spite of a firm foundation of realism in my attitude toward life, I still turn to Plotinus when I seek wisdom and need consolation. . . . . Just here, I break off to remind you that material for bindings will return after the war, and I shall expect, when peace, or what we call peace, has come, a copy of your life of Hans Andersen.

If the world holds together, my publishers are planning to bring out a new book of mine in the autumn.[2] It seems to me a bad time, but one of the Harcourt, Brace firm came down yesterday, and almost persuaded me that all times are equally bad, mad, and sad for books, especially for a book that is not fiction, and has nothing to do with fighting. This is a work of literary criticism, personal and impersonal, and I shall hope to send you one of the early copies. I hope, too, that you will not find it unsympathetic.

Do let me know your address on Martha's Vineyard.[3] If I am strong enough to make the trip——and of this I cannot be sure——my post office until October will be Castine, Maine.

I have said—and this is true—that I am not in the least psychic; yet I have had in my life, very occasionally, the sense of a beginning friendship so strong that it seemed to hold the quality of recognition. Your first letter brought this to me, and I feel that we shall grow to understand each other, as if we had always been friends.

Sincerely yours, | *Ellen Glasgow*

TLS TxU-Hu
Publication: *L* 319–20.

1. ST's *Life of Hans Christian Andersen* (London: Macmillan, 1933; New York: Harcourt, Brace and Co., 1934). The book EG anticipates two sentences later is ST's *Emmanuel Swedenborg, Scientist and Mystic* (New Haven: Yale University Press, 1948).
2. The war had delayed the publication of *CM* until October 1943.
3. Chilmark, Massachusetts, where ST summered.

To Signe Toksvig

June 8th, 1943 | ONE WEST MAIN STREET | RICHMOND, VIRGINIA

Dear Signe Toksvig:

Your Hans Christian Andersen has meant a great deal to me. Not only has it brought both you and Hans Christian near to me, but it has given me a vivid impression of the world when it appeared (whether or not this could be true) younger and more vital and hopeful. Even when people were unhappy, they seemed still to keep faith in life, and in dreams too. Much in your little lonely Hans Christian reminded me of the time when I dreamed dreams, and was little and lonely.

Are you like me, I wonder, about books. When you take a book in your hands and open the covers and read the first paragraph, does something tell you whether the book will come alive in your grasp or remain merely inanimate matter? Well, your Hans Christian came to life in the very beginning, and he stayed alive until ——no, he did not die, really, for he stays on, with the breath of life in your beautiful work. For the art with which he is presented is all that it should be; it is sympathetic, sincere, candid, and singularly revealing in character. That your words should be so naturally the *right* words came rather as a surprise to me. One would assume that English is your native speech, but, I suppose, it is not. . . .

I wish I could go on and on. There is so much I should like to say to you. The memory of certain pages or paragraphs in your work flow in my mind as a stream of impressions. One of these, I think, is the beginning of, I think, Chapter IX, when Hans Christian looks out of the dormer window in his attic and sees the bright view of Copenhagen, with the red-tiled roofs slanting in all directions. This is only one picture, and there are many others, and underneath, of course, is the deeper subjective current of being. . . . But I must stop.

An intolerable wave of heat prostrated me, and the doctors are trying to send me away on the fifteenth. For the past two years my daily living has been at the mercy of a wholly inadequate heart. If nothing prevents, however, I hope to leave for Maine next Tuesday, and we ought to reach Castine on Thursday, the 17th. Usually, I spend a week in New York, for the pleasure of seeing my friends there, but this year I am not strong enough. . . . Yes, Castine is enchanting, and so cool and bracing. Do write to me there.

I must tell you how much I like the illustrations of Hans Christain, especially those charming little scenes inside the bindings. If I have to send back this copy (and I am leaving it wrapped and addressed to Chilmark), I hope I shall find my exchange copy exactly like it. Macmillan did very well by you. So often the outside of a book is inappropriate.

It is disagreeable having to sue for plagiarism. I know just how you feel. This happened to me once, years ago. An Englishman boldly plagiarized my book, The Battle-Ground,[1] but he disappeared and could not be traced. It was all done under an assumed name.

I hope you will have a satisfactory summer———one dares not wish happiness in a war-torn world. Oh, yes, I have, or had, Mckenna's translation of Plotinus. That had a beauty of its own, but my worn-out copy, heavily marked, after a bad habit of mine, is one of the old Thomas Taylor's translations.[2] His were the earliest translations, were they not?

Since I know you better, there is an essay of mine I should be glad to have you read, and I regret that I haven't a copy to send you.[3] You could find it in a large library, but perhaps not in a small place. This is in a collection of essays, entitled *I Believe*. It is published by Simon and Schuster, and edited, oddly enough, by Clifton Fadiman, who, probably, did not suspect what he was doing. Some other time, when you are in New York and have an idle hour, you might drop into the library and look up this volume. I put a good deal of myself into this confession of faith.

Now that I really know you, as always, | *Ellen Glasgow*
On a damp day like this the typewriter ribbon smuts dreadfully, but I find hold-

ing a pen too exhausting since my illness. I send this because I am unable to write it over, and I shrink from dictating a letter to you.

TLS TxU-Hu
Publication: *L* 321–23.

    1. H. Grahame Richards (pseudonym), *Shadows* (New York: Dodd, Mead and Co., 1917); see *EGN* 13 (October 1980): 6.
    2. EG owned *Select Works of Plotinus, with an Introduction Containing the Substance of Porphyry's Life of Plotinus,* trans. Thomas Taylor (London: Bell, 1895). She also owned a similar edition (1817), with uncut pages.
    3. "I Believe," in *I Believe: The Personal Philosophies of Certain Eminent Men and Women of Our Time,* ed. Clifton Fadiman (New York: Simon & Schuster, 1938); rpt. *EGRD,* 228–45.

From Signe Toksvig

Chilmark, Mass. | July 5, 1943

Dear Ellen Glasgow,

    It seems black ingratitude to wait nearly a month to thank you for your letter to me about my Andersen biography, but it is due to my having wanted first to read your Credo in "I Believe", a book which it took our librarian in Edgartown[1] some time to get for me. Now I have read it, but first let me try to tell you how much your letter meant to me. My Andersen sold less than a thousand copies here, being treated as a "Juvenile", by Harcourt. (He told me airily himself that he gave it to the juvenile editor. I was living in Ireland at the time.) Well, it was a complete failure from any practical point of view, and I wonder how it is that one should be affected by that, except financially, but one is. I suppose one does want one's book read! Especially if you love the subject, as I do Andersen. BUT, when I hear from someone like you (that is, from you, as there isn't someone like you!) that the book had meaning for you, then all is well. More particularly now when I have to fight this really rather loathsome plagiarism of the book (by Mrs Burnett, widow of little Lord Fauntleroy);[2] it makes the fight seem worth while. I so much want the right version of Andersen to prevail, and some day I'll get a publisher to republish it. Do please keep the copy I sent to you, I find I don't need it.
    I am so happy you think I write English; it has become my first language, really, though I dearly love Danish and can do intimate things with it that seem to me possible in no other medium; since I was sixteen I've tried to write English; though I suppose I didn't really speak it till I was eighteen or so. I was born and brought up in Denmark.
    Yes, I'm like you in this that a book comes alive for me or does not in the first paragraph, though I often just open a book and try for the sign of life

on any page I open at. That was how I discovered "Vein of Iron". Life leaped out of it.

There is really so much I want to talk about that it is hard to begin. In the first place, fancy my only finding you at this late date! I must explain that my first fifteen years in the U.S. were one long fight for education and existence, during which I scarcely read any fiction, then soon after my marriage[3] we went to live in Europe for twenty years, and have only returned here at the beginning of 1940. It is like getting acquainted with a new country. But now I have found you and you are the very best guide (among other things that you are) to this strange new country. I am reading "In This Our Life", having just finished "The Battle-ground", I took them as far apart as that on purpose, and there is much I want to say about that later, if you'll let me. It is the treat I save for myself at the end of the day when I'm in bed early because of the black-out. We live on the sea, here.

Virginia and Betty versus Stanley and Roy![4] But I must wait.

Your credo comes to me at a time when I am more than ever busy trying to find one of my own, and I must say that in reading yours I kept nodding my head and saying, yes, yes, just so! Except for my early background, which was strictly rationalist and agnostic, because my beloved father was, I've gone questing in the same directions that you have. But in a different order. No, perhaps not. I was going to say that I read the Hindu mystics before I read the Christian. At any rate, my interest began with the study of Comparative Religions, which I took up largely to gain weapons against Christian dogmatism. As my father, a radical editor, had been persecuted by orthodox clergymen I had an antipathy to Christianity which it took me long to get over, so that I loved Buddha long before St Francis or Jesus. (What a marvellous story the one you tell about the Franciscans!) And I loved the respect for intelligence which original Buddhism shows. The eightfold Path is clear.[5]

"Grief and illness" are perhaps the father and mother not of mysticism but of an interest in it, but what a rewarding interest! In your Credo, I feel that you let us see less of what it has meant to you than you do in "Vein of Iron". There the light which shone for you that August afternoon in the Alps is shared more fully with us. And that is just as well, for most of the company you are in, in the "I Believe", would have been the Darkness that seeth not. (I quite agree with you that Clifton Fadiman didn't know what he was doing when he let you in! I regard him as one of those who have tried to rot the America I have loved.)

Boehme is too obscure for me, the little I've read, but I wonder if you know Eckhart?[6] I wish I had a translation I've made of some of his talks. But it's in England.

Yes, I can see that Darwin's bible of evolution might indeed be a cornerstone and a whole foundation if "implications and inferences" are carried out. That's personal, perhaps. "Not by one road alone is so great a goal reached".

The last two pages I most sincerely subscribe to. I am so glad you dare to be for "good taste". If you and E. M. Forster were the arbiters we might go far with that. I'm glad he's in the pew next to you, I like him, knowing him a little personally.

"The only sin is inhumanity", & cruelty. Yes, absolutely. If by human you mean humane.

I talked with a Danish sailor who had been on a raft up under Greenland for nineteen days. He had saved the lives of his fellow cast-aways, so they told, by his ingenuity, and their icy feet from gangrene by tucking them into his own armpits. It was terribly hard to drag any information from him, but I said "Why were you the only one to play the stove?" He said, "Well, it was to my interest to keep them alive." —"Why?" I said, looking him straight in the eye, pinning him down. He didn't answer a word, but his cool, shy glance changed into a steady, warm, luminous look that I shall never forget. It was the "Good" that you speak of. It does exist. But it is not omnipotent, it has to be helped, by sailors, and even I suppose by soldiers. But I fancy sailors.

Francis and I nearly settled in Virginia when we returned here; but accident sent us to Connecticut and Martha's Vineyard. Yet the South is where we feel most at home somehow, although the discussion of ideas is not quite "good taste"!

I hope you are well. I can't tell you how I appreciate your having written to me on that hot day, with the smudgy ribbon, and with your heart which you so incorrectly describe as inadequate!

Yours | Signe Toksvig

I know that physically your heart leaves something to be desired; and I worry about that. I shouldn't like you to feel you have to write to me. I know you're there.[7]

TLS ViU EG Box 18

 1. See previous letter, note 3, for EG's "credo." Edgartown is on the eastern coast of Martha's Vineyard.
 2. The plagiarism case is unclear. Burnett died in 1924, nearly a decade before ST's biography of Andersen appeared.
 3. To Francis Hackett.
 4. Virginia and Betty Ambler (*B-G*) and Roy and Stanley Timberlake (*ITOL*) are sisters in EG's novels.
 5. The way to Nirvana (ultimate bliss) in Buddhism: right faith, right judgment, right language, right purpose, right practice, right obedience, right memory, and right meditation.
 6. Jakob Boehme (1575–1624) and Johannes Eckehart (ca. 1260–ca. 1327) were German mystic philosophers.
 7. The postscript is handwritten.

To Signe Toksvig

BATTLE AVENUE | CASTINE, MAINE | August 14th, 1943

Dear Signe (that is how I think of you):

Your letter meant, and still means, so much to me, for it is a rare pleasure indeed to find a writer or a friend who speaks my own language and who, stranger even than that, has approached life by the road I travelled long ago, when I was very young. Yes. Oh, yes, like you, I was, in youth, brought up against the ugly side of Christian dogmatism, against its cruelty, its narrowness, its blindness. My father, who sprang from that stalwart breed, the Scotch-Irish, so-called, was an elder in the Presbyterian church, and, in my childhood, I revolted from the creed, as well as from the severe conscience, of Calvinism. Like you, also, I had an early antipathy to Christianity, and I loved the broad humanity and the respect for the intellect I found in original Buddhism. But the teaching was too lofty for the human mind, and the metaphysical doctrine too profound for the human heart which craves a future of unbroken identity.

I had the misfortune, for I regard it, in my special case, as a misfortune, to inherit a long conflict of types, for my father was a descendant of Scottish Calvinists and my mother was a perfect flower of the Tidewater, in Virginia. Her ancestors had been broad Church of England and later agnostics. This conflict began in my soul as far back as I can remember. I adored my mother, and, even today, I cannot read Browning's "My Last Duchess" without seeing her luminous image.

But I think (and I am speaking now of my earliest youth) that the quality I disliked most in orthodox Christianity was its arrogant self-righteousness, that state of mind or soul which a great student of the animal world has called, "the anthropomorphic delusion of grandeur." In my childhood, animals were very close to me. They were among my best friends, and after my mother, I loved best my dog. It was the Christian attitude toward animals that estranged me then, and turned me, in later years, toward more humane religions. My father was a sterling character and a zealous Calvinist; but he was without feeling for any creatures other than human beings, and among human beings, he firmly believed that the vast majority would be condemned to eternal torments. It appears incredible, now, and appalling, but that was the creed my elders tried to teach me in my impressionable infancy. Because my mother believed none of this, I found a way of escape. (This is a cold day, not like the hot day in Richmond, but there is a heavy fog, and I see the smudges beginning) But, of course, I hasten to explain, I soon discovered that only original Buddhism was really merciful. We see, in later years, an almost fanatical Catholic, such as the wife of Richard Burton, carrying the gospel of humanity to India, the home of Gautama.[1] Life, as I have lived it and observed it, has taught me that a man's humanity, as well as a man's goodness, bears no very close connection with a man's abstract belief. I have known gentle human beings who believed that, if one died without the sacrament of baptism or even without extreme unction, one would spend an eternity in physical of spiritual torment, and I have known, too, or known of, simple monsters of cruelty, who accepted the rule of reason and every theory of science. Is there a spirit above and beyond any belief, any conviction? "O Thou Who dost take the shapes imagined by Thy worshippers!"

No, I have not read Eckhart. I wish I could read your translation. Yes, by inhumanity, I mean cruelty. Cruelty, I truly believe, is the one and only sin. It is the sin against the Holy Ghost. There is another Hindu invocation that I treasure. I found it in Schopenhauer, who was bitter because he was too humane to enjoy life as he found it. This, he says, was the prayer with which the ancient Hindu closed his athletic games, and Schopenhauer calls it the noblest of all invocations: "May all that have life be delivered from suffering."

Well, I must stop now for lunch, and I am only beginning. Castine has, I think, saved my life. When I came, on June 17th, after frightful heat in Virginia, this place appeared an earthly paradise, with air sparkling like wine, and the lilacs in bloom by the door. I am even writing a little, a brief sequel to "In This Our Life." This will bring my work from 1850 up to the autumn of 1942... Tell me more of yourself. I am tremendously interested in all that concerns you... And forgive the smudges. I am a most wretched typist. My typewriter has its own special, and very odd, system of spelling.

Yours, | *Ellen Glasgow*

TLS TxU-Hu
Publication: *L* 329–32.

1. Isabel Arundell Burton (1831–1896), was from an upper-class British Catholic family. Living in India with her husband, the adventurer, linguist, and translator Richard Francis Burton, she championed animal rights and agitated for an Indian branch of the SPCA. EG's source may have been Jean Burton's *Sir Richard Burton's Wife* (New York: Knopf, 1941), although it is not among the books she owned.

To Signe Toksvig

Sunday, August 15th, 1943 | BATTLE AVENUE | CASTINE, MAINE

Is it true, as I said, yesterday, in my letter, that a man's abstract belief has no close relation to a man's humanity? You recall Voltaire's illuminating comment on his age: Men will commit atrocities as long as they believe absurdities. Surely, that is an admonitory truism. Yet it is true, also, that I have known kindly and gentle natures, as I said before, human beings with goodness of soul, who clung to the most terrible doctrines in morality and religion. Well, as my colored mammy used to say, Well, well, the Lord made us all, and He must bear with us!

Some other Sunday morning, when I have time and freedom, I shall tell you more of that golden August afternoon in the Alps, and more, too, of a wonderful adventure I began, and did not finish, three years ago, in Castine. It was in my severest heart attack. The doctor thought I was dying, and I came as near death as one may come and return. Yet I was completely conscious until the last glorious moment, when I felt that I was lifted up, on the crest of a wave, and swept out into some perfect fulfilment. I am not, as I told you before, in the least psychic, nor am I a believer in supernatural manifestations. Most of these occurrences, as they are reported to me, appear insincere, and simple examples, deliberate or otherwise, of morbid self-consciousness.

But I have known these two moments of vision, though I do not write of them, or even speak of them except in circumstances that are remote from the ordinary surface of living...

Another interruption... Here is my morning cup of hot milk. Then, after a little, a very little work, I shall go out for a short walk, and, on this walk, I take bird-seed and honey and water to the empty cottage of a friend who could not come back this summer. The birds near her porch are quite tame, and they return every year from the South. The humming-birds (we have only one species, the ruby-throated) come back, from their long and far migration, to the same spot in the woods. At our first whistle, they darted out of the fir-trees, and circled about us, waiting until we put out the small bottles of honey-and-water. Few forms of life are so engaging as birds.

Yours, | E. G.

TLS TxU-Hu
Publication: *L* 331–32.

To Signe Toksvig

September 4th, 1943 | BATTLE AVENUE | CASTINE, MAINE

Dear Signe:

As soon as I had finished "Port of Refuge",[1] I felt that I must write to you. But my heart had been giving a little trouble, and I was obliged to sink back and rest idly for a few days. Not to be strong is an unbearable nuisance—yet one can only bear it ... and pretend not to mind it.

The book—a young book, it seems to me—is singularly living. The factory part, all of it, has a pulse of its own. I felt and heard those machines, and that terrible noise, roaring on into space. And then that amazing, that miraculous vision of a world beyond sense and beyond matter. I was interested and thrilled and excited to know that it was true, and that you had actually lived through it, and that the visitation had saved you. Otherwise, how could you have survived that particular horror? And yet the meaning ... What was the inner truth of it all? Ever since I read of that miracle, I have been haunted, and I have tried to find the cause and the reason. Was it merely a revolt of exhausted nerves that turned, for sanctuary, to the secret province of imagination? Or was a reality deeper than other realities? What puzzles me is the power you found to invoke and sustain the vision. That golden afternoon in the Alps came to me in the light and the air, and it passed on into the wind and the moving grass. But I could never recall, for so much as an instant, a glimmer of that ineffable sense beyond sense. Only when I seemed to be dying did I have the faintest return of the ecstasy, and this was so different, though, in some way, a part of it... But I never write of this, except to you, and I cannot speak of that moment. The nature of it has always been, and is still, indescribable. I have almost persuaded my mind that it was an escape for tormented nerves, after "a dark night of the soul."

But your profound release for the spirit has seemed to cast light on that obscure border of dreams.

I wish I were able to write on and on. There are so many subjects I should like to discuss with you. But this is the poorest excuse for a letter. The warning tremor begins, and I must give way to it.

I shall send the book to you, for you may have no other copy. But shall I return it to your Connecticut address? The whole story has a moving quality, so vital and ardent with youth, and with delight in the entire range of experience. Your personality shines through the pages.

As ever yours, | *Ellen Glasgow*
When do you leave Chilmark? I hope to stay here until October 18th, and I shall expect some advance copies of my book[2] early in October.

And you love the Bhagavad-Gita ... Some other day, when I feel no warning, I shall tell you how much that has meant in my life. Not now. but when I was young, and when I was searching for a truth that I could not find. Like you, I doubt if higher ethical spheres have ever been reached ... than in that revelation.

TLS TxU-Hu
Publication: *L* 332–34.

1. Novel by Toksvig (London: Faber & Faber, 1938).
2. *CM*.

To Rebe Glasgow Tutwiler

ONE WEST MAIN STREET | RICHMOND, VIRGINIA | January 31st, 1944

Darling Rebe:

This is your birthday, and I have not been well enough even to write you in time. Irene is off this week. A. V. has had to bring up most of my meals, as I have not been downstairs for two weeks, and the house is wholly upset. The doctor has been every day, but he said I was much better this morning.

I have had you in mind, and I go back so often to our childhood, and poor Mother, whose life was so tragic. Few families, I imagine, have known more tragedies.

A pile of books has steadily collected for you, but A. V. has not had time to wrap them until today. None is worth reading, but two of the mysteries are above the average, and one is a good and interesting picture of wartime England, with rather able characterization. This has not gone off yet, because A. V. is keeping it to read. It is "To What Dread End."[1] D. D. sent me two copies, and at least it held my interest when I was sick and terribly nervous. One story by the Mrs. Campbell you spoke of is not bad. "Ringed with Fire," another war story.[2] I found "Signed with Their Honor" which I had seen praised very mushy and second rate. All the others are trash mostly, sent to me by the publishers; but I thought you might need them for some sleepless night.

This is the first day I have been able to tap on the typewriter, and I find a pen more painful. Please burn my scrappy letters.

Charley Towne is here today. I had asked him to dine with me tonight, but of course I had to break the engagement. I am sorry, because I am very fond of him, and he is lovely to me when I am in New York . . . a place I shall probably never see again. . . .

Cabell sent me the most wonderful present at Christmas. It was a great surprise that Carrie and A. V. were able to find it. Both gave me their rations, and C. gave me the fine Scotch. The only two bottles to be found in Richmond.

Did I tell you how much I enjoyed Dr. Murray's address on the flight of the birds to the South? He is an able man, and this article has a fine and unusual quality. Most articles on birds are apt to be dry, but this was so different. It was alive and interesting, and I could feel the movement overhead.

I must stop now. Best love, and many, many happy returns. I have the dimmest memory—or I may have imagined it—of spending in old Mrs. Does doll-shop the morning that you were born.[3]

Devotedly, | Ellen

TC of TLS FU
Address: Mrs. C. C. Tutwiler, Brushwood, Lexington

1. Murder mystery by M[ary] V[iolet] Heberden (1906–1965). In the next sentence, "D. D." is Doubleday, Doran.

2. Alice Campbell (b. 1887), *Ringed with Fire* (New York: Random House, 1942). *Signed with Their Honor,* in the next sentence, is unidentified.

3. MKR: "last sentence sic."

To Signe Toksvig

February 4th, 1944 | ONE WEST MAIN STREET | RICHMOND, VIRGINIA
Dearest Signe:

Your letter has just gladdened my heart, and I feel I must send you a very small word of grateful appreciation. Some weeks ago (that time is no longer divided) a "mild" attack of influenza proved almost too strong an antagonist, and I have not yet recovered sufficiently to tap out a whole letter. When my fingers touch the wrong key, I lack the energy to do more than make a worse smudge with the eraser.

How serene you appear in these little pictures, and how victorious over fate—or over circumstances! I love them, and I thank you for sending them to me. I am enclosing a passport picture[1] taken before my long illness, in 1937, when I was sailing for my last—my very last—trip to Italy. I looked younger than my years then; but since those years of physical suffering, I am more broken and I appear frail, instead of vital....

All you write of *Barren Ground* touches me deeply. That book was torn out of myself, and it was written in one of those blessed pauses that fall between the "dark wood" of the soul and the light on the horizon. Yes, it is true, as you understand, the land and the sky, time and space, are the great harmonies. The moment of madness in which Dorinda had the impulse to kill Jason is true, psychologically, I feel, of her nature. The dark wood was there as well as the light on the hills.

There is so much I wish to say to you, but, even after so brief a note, my touch has begun to grow more uncertain. The reason, I suppose, that your husband missed *Barren Ground* is not far to seek. It came out in 1925, and, in the decade of the lost generation, most American novels (all the popular fiction, in fact) were rooted, not in the American soil, but in the boulevards of Paris. Francis Hackett and you had both left America before my book was published, and in some way you must have missed reading it in Denmark....

The two books of mine I like best are *Barren Ground* and *The Sheltered Life*. They are very different, but equally true to experience. For sheer craftsmanship and for more than craftsmanship—for swiftness of vision, and for penetration into the hidden truth of life—I value the second section of The Sheltered Life, the part of it called The Deep Past. But that whole book interprets a dying age and a slowly disintegrating world of tradition....

I rejoice, with you, to hear that your two dear brothers in Denmark are unharmed. That has been in my mind constantly. Whenever I see the name Denmark, I remember you and your anxiety. But I am thankful for your refuge of work, and I look eagerly forward to the biography you are writing.

Now, my fingers have refused to go on. No, I could not send you a dictated note. I have a secretary,[2] but she copies, she does not write any but business letters. Since my illness, she has been overworked, and she is not well. How I wish I had known you in other and happier days, when this old house was gay, at times, with visitors. War has made living conditions very hard in Richmond. It is true that I have a Fluvanna, but "she" is a man, who has been in our family for nearly thirty-five years.[3] He used to be a remarkable cook, but now he is old and decrepit, though still faithful. There are few of his generation left anywhere, and least of all, I believe, among the coloured younger servants in the South.

We are living without adjustments, in a broken world. The pattern has changed so utterly that we have almost forgotten it. But what I regret most will always be the lost harmonies of the spirit, as one regrets the great music in a period of jazz or swing. Will the people who set the tone and dictate the manners of today ever prefer the greater harmonies, or ever ... ever like all the little lost graces that made life so much easier? ... Then I ask myself whether more good may not come to the many? After all, I suppose, the little graces, as well as the great harmonies, had their part in a smaller world. Has the world of the spirit, or of the inner life, ever held many seekers of truth?

Devotedly, | Ellen

There are mistakes and smudges that I cannot erase. So I give them up. I am still hoping that you may come to Richmond when I am stronger.[4]

TLS TxU-Hu
Publication: *L* 341–43.

1. A passport photograph and one of EG's bookplates still are enclosed with this letter.
2. AVB.
3. James Anderson.
4. The postscript is handwritten.

To Marion Canby

February 24th, 1944 | ONE WEST MAIN STREET | RICHMOND, VIRGINIA
Dearest Marian,

Even when we do not write, I have a happy sense of companionship. It takes more that space really to separate us.

Your dear and lovely visit has been the one bright recollection of a winter. A few weeks after you went away, I came down with this wretched influenza, and my wholly inadequate strength has suffered from my heart, which was weak before, to my head, which has felt weak ever since. I have not yet been out of the house, and I have been downstairs only once in the past four or five weeks. When your card reached me, I was feeling that I should never need a street dress again. But it was dear of you to attend to it, and if I am well, or fairly well again, I know I shall regret not ordering it. But can you, in your glowing health, imagine a state of mind when so simple an exertion as taking one's measure seems entirely too much?

And now no more about illness. Your letter from Washington lifted my spirit. How—oh, how I wish I might have been with you in the Mellon Gallery![1] There are times when I am hungry for pictures, yet I have never been strong enough, when I was in Washington, to go to a gallery. Always, I am in the hands of a doctor, and that leaves nothing over. I saw my last "real pictures" in Florence in the spring and early summer of 1937. Then I would steal away, with Mrs. Duke, from the villa at Fiesole, where we were visiting, and we would spend the morning in a church or a gallery. Sometimes I would see only one picture, but that picture would be a Botticelli, and usually my choice would be the Birth of Venus. But there were many that I loved. Do you recall what Heine said of Mary Magdalen? "She was a catholic soul, and loved not only much but many."[2] That was a happy June. I stayed in a villa that had once belonged to Marsilio Ficino, and it was still called by his name. The garden was a paradise of all the flowers God ever made. We spent, too, a whole day, far up in the Apennines, at La Verna, among the singing birds of St. Francis....

I have read your letter over again, and I feel as if we had talked together as we talked for hours on those two days in Richmond. Yes, we started life in the same way, only my sadder childhood was different. But I feel very near to you, and I felt this at our first meeting. You are right in thinking we met first in my sitting-room in some New York hotel, long before I began to stay at the Weylin. It was the Chatham, I believe, and we met that first time with a strong sense of friendship. That is the kind of recognition one never forgets, and, strangely enough, because it is so sudden, it rarely betrays one. The feeling does not come often, but when it comes, it has a kind of inevitability, as if one discovered a kinship of personality. I suppose this gives an extraordinary value to your insight into my prefaces. Certainly, I treasure that, and your complete understanding of motives beneath my life and my work. You have so much to give, and of all blessings I have missed most, and needed most, the intellectual sympathy that overflows from your mind, and the warmth and tolerance of your perceptions. Your visit gave me happiness, and you must come again, when I am over this relapse and this dark mood that appears to wait upon influenza. The "peace at last" seems now to have receded ... or, perhaps, it has only declined for the moment.

My friendship with you and Henry has been a great joy in my life. Will you give him my love and, will you keep my heart's share for yourself. After all, you did not send me the book of first poems, and you did not write in the volume I have, On My Way."[3] I feel in your verse the quality that I found in you, and that is a rare kind of nobility, detached and yet strangely human.

Devotedly, dear Marian, Ellen

I must stop or the pain may come back. Forgive me for my long silence, and for this typing. A pen is beyond me just now.

TLS ViU EG Box 26
Publication: *L* 343–45.

1. The Mellon Gallery, or the West building of the National Gallery of Art in Washington, D.C., opened in 1941.
2. Probably from Heinrich Heine's poem *Atta Troll* (1847).
3. Canby's first book of poetry was *High Mowing* (1932), and *On My Way* (1937) the second.

To Irita Van Doren

March 25th, 1944 | ONE WEST MAIN STREET | RICHMOND, VIRGINIA

Irita, dear,

You will never know how much good your visit meant to me—and how much happiness. I cannot begin to tell you how deeply I appreciate your coming. If only you could have stayed longer!

My spirit, which had drooped all winter is feeling the April you and Frank[1] brought with you out of that wintry weather. I enjoyed every moment of seeing you, and my mind is relieved of anxiety for the future of my autobiography, which is very near to my mind and heart.

This is just a word that could never tell you all I should like to say. What it means is that I value your friendship more than any words can express. But you know that without my trying to put it in cold typing. And you know, too, that for many years I have loved you dearly.

Devotedly always, Ellen

TLS DLC

1. Frank Morley.

To Marion Canby

April 12th, 1944 | ONE WEST MAIN STREET | RICHMOND, VIRGINIA

Dearest Marian:

Your poems were late in reaching me. The book[1] came only two days ago, but I have had it beside my bed, and I have turned back to it in the dark hours.

These verses bring you closer to me, and I think they express your natural inner self, and your heart in the flush of youth. Even if they were written later, they are poems of youth. The first two make a deep appeal to me, because I might have written them when I was young and defiant. I am still defiant, but I am no longer young, though I have not yielded an inch in my rebellion against the cruelties of the world. In *Delivered of My Life,* you have uttered my secret, as well as your own the "Lift of air upon the topmost sky." That is asking of life more than life can ever give.

What more can I say? I love the poems, and I love you.

Your visit is still a bright gleam in a dark winter. How I should love to see you again this spring, but it looks as if you would have to wait till autumn to come. Do you recall the alcove in my guest-room? Well, a few days ago the whole ceiling fell, and the place has been a mess of plaster and wood. We are trying to have the ceiling put up (a new one, of course), but it will not be possible to have it painted until later in the summer.

This is a very old house, but nothing like that had happened before, and, most fortunately, no one was staying in that room at the time. I am so thankful that Irita and you had come earlier, and my sister had put off her visit.

But I shall look for you in the autumn. This has been the most wretched spring, rain and wind, and only one or two days of fair weather.

I am hoping to go away for the summer, but this is only a hope. I shall not know for week or two.

All my love, dearest Marian, and my love, too, to Henry.

Yours ever . . . and ever, | *Ellen*

TLS ViU EG Box 26
Publication: *L* 345–46.

1. Canby's *High Mowing.* The inscription in EG's copy reads, "Belatedly, with always increasing love and sympathy, To Ellen from Marion Canby. April 1st, 1944" (see *CLEG* 17.256).

To Signe Toksvig

October 8th, 1944 | BATTLE AVENUE | CASTINE, MAINE

Dear Signe:

Thank you for the translation. The poem has a moving quality and I am glad to have it.

You have been in my thoughts, but this has been a most trying summer, and I have waited to write, in the hope that I might be equal to a long letter. I have suffered physical pain, and for the first time, this summer, I have felt no wish ever to return to Castine. Not that I wish to go anywhere else. Castine is still lovely, and so peaceful, so bathed in the air of tranquillity. Yet there are moments when surrounding tranquillity stabs into the mind as if it were violence. Autumn, the most beautiful of our seasons is coming on in a flame of colour, and there are moments, too, when colour may hurt one. We are planning to leave on October 22nd, and we must spend four nights on the road, because my heart compels me to go slowly . . . I, who have always hated to go slowly and softly!

All you think and write of "The Sheltered Life" interests me deeply. It is, to me, the second favourite among my books. I mean, after "Barren Ground" I like it best of my novels, and I think the middle section called "The Deep Past" contains the writing I should wish to be remembered by in the future. This reflective vision pierces more deeply, I have always felt, than most visions. General Archbald was profoundly real to me, and I seemed to discover in him level after level of downward seeking and upward springing, which I thought of as the inner poetry (or rhythm) of life. While I was writing this, I used to wonder whether others would see what I meant and was trying to do. It was a surprise to me that so many readers appreciated so quiet and subtle an analysis of the mind and the heart of age. Even when I was very young, I liked to write of old people, because the old had attained a kind of finality. . . . You are right about John Welch. Of all the characters in that book, he interested me least. He had the stiffness he would have had in the actuality, and indeed he was suggested, more or less, by an actual person. Yet he had his place, and there are many of his sort still in the town I call Queenborough. . . . Compared to the General, he is inanimate, for I feel, with you, that General Archbald lives and walks and is rounded out in his own special shape. Jenny Blair is true in every fluttering heartbeat, and so is Eva Birdsong, and George I have known, and known well in reality. . . .

To turn to the Germans. Yes, as A Dane, you know them far better than I ever have, or ever can know them. At this moment, they fill me with horror, yet I cannot see any end either to them or to the horror they will continue to make in the world and in the pages of history. What can be done to make them safe, or at least harmless, neighbours. My own belief is that nothing will be done, just as nothing was done after the First World War. We had the opportunity then, and we did nothing, because we were mad for sensation, avid for the taste of pleasure and the delight of whirling back into the life we had remembered. Have you read Henry J, Taylor's "Time Runs Out"?[1] It is a good book, and I recall the shock he felt, when he came to England from a newly liberated Europe, and found that people in London were thinking only of how or where or when they might enjoy themselves. I hope everything will be different after this war, but... but...

No, I have not read your husband's book on Denmark.[2] That nice Terence Holliday, of the Holliday Bookshop (do you know it?) has advertised for it, without success as yet, and he told me earlier in the summer that Doubleday had no copies in stock. I am resentful of the way publishers let good books drop out of print; and yet they never seem to lack the pulp for the printing of trash. And it angers me, too, to think of all the beautiful trees that have been sacrificed to make our many horrible and hideously cheap magazines....

My love to you, dear Signe. How I hope we may meet this coming autumn, and I shall expect to be in Richmond by the first of November.

Write to me there when you have a free moment. I was interested to see that Francis Hackett will take John Chamberlain's place on the Times.[3] Though I subscribe to the Times, it stopped immediately after that announcement, and I do not know whether the change has occurred. Something must have happened to the circulation department, for I have received my paper at rare intervals, and the post here is uncertain, as Mr. Pickwick[4] observed of the morals of coachmen.

As always, | Ellen

Forgive this scrambled letter. It is the best I am able to do. I have written it in bits, and it sounds stilted.

TLS TxU-Hu
Publication: *L* 354–56.

    1. EG's copy of Taylor's book (Garden City, NY: Doubleday, 1942) is inscribed, "For my friend Miss Glasgow—who spoke to me about Finland—in the hope that she may find some part of this book interesting—this is inscribed in esteem—Sincerely—Henry J. Taylor, Virginia House—October 10, 1942, Miss Ellen Glasgow, Richmond, Virginia" (*CLEG* 17.276–77).

    2. Francis Hackett, *I Chose Denmark* (Doubleday, 1940).

    3. As an editor with the *New York Times*.

    4. From Charles Dickens's *The Posthumous Papers of the Pickwick Club,* better known as *Pickwick Papers* (1836–1837).

To Irita Van Doren

October 9*th*, 1944 | BATTLE AVENUE | CASTINE, MAINE

Dearest Irita,

I am shocked and grieved by the sudden irreparable loss of Wendell Willkie,[1] not only to the world but to us, his friends.

This age needed his brave spirit, and I can see no one who is able to take his place. He was so strong, so vital, so complete in courage, in humanity, in magnanimity.

I know that the absence of his perfect friendship, which never failed you, will make a vast emptiness in your life. How I wish I might see you and talk with you! Is there a possibility of your coming to Richmond this autumn or winter?

My summer has not been easy. For once, Castine has failed in its old magic, for, when one is in pain, beauty may hurt more than it heals. We are planning to leave on October 22nd, and I am compelled to go slowly—I, who always hated to go slowly and softly.

All my love to you Irita, dear.

Devotedly, | *Ellen*

ALS DLC

1. Willkie died October 8 after a heart attack.

To Signe Toksvig

October 19th, 1944 | BATTLE AVENUE | CASTINE, MAINE

Dear Signe,

I was grieved to hear that you had suffered this summer (I have a horror of hospitals), but I rejoice with you that the malady was "benign". Yes, it is a curious word, but what tremendous significance it contains!

Your article[1] is especially sympathetic to my mood, for I lived in a world of Nature spirits when I was a child, and sometimes I still feel or see their genial forms, or formless happiness, in my memories. As a small being, I used to think that all the trees around our country house were separate and distinct personalities. I had names for them, every one, human names, and How I loved them! But that was in the long ago, and as I grew out of my child's world, I lost my friendly unseen spirits, with other lovely, and never entirely forgotten, things . . .

I should like, by the way, to subscribe to that magazine. I have never seen a copy, but I liked particularly a very penetrating review of my latest book in *Tomorrow*.[2] That seems to me an excellent reason. . . .

I am so glad that you sent me Francis Hackett's reviews. How has he kept, after all you must have seen and felt of two world wars, that remarkable freshness of mind and of writing? Distinction is so rare a quality today that I prize it, I believe, above every other merit in both poetry and prose. I wish you could send me the other reviews from the Times. That paper has the most careless circulation department. By the same post, on the same day, with the same amount of money, I ordered, before I left Richmond, the *Times* and the *Herald-Tribune*. The Times came infrequently, and finally stopped entirely a month ago, while the Herald has reached me every day since I came to Castine.

But I was pleased when Francis Hackett met in print and remarked upon vulgarity, which has a curious kind of renown— . . . I had almost said, an evil prestige in contemporary fiction. And I use "vulgarity" in the American sense, not in the English, which seems to imply merely commonness. We have no exact word for that trait—nor, I imagine, had the Greeks such a word. "Obscenity" will not do, for that suggests a mature lewdness of behaviour, and the modern taste for vulgarity (I am obliged to fall back upon the word) resembles rather the snigger of a nasty-minded small boy when he writes bad words on back fences. . . . When we grow up, I suppose, these giggles with no longer amuse us. . . .

And how I enjoyed the comment on Boston Adventure.[3] The publishers sent me that endless exercise, but I could only gasp, "How terrible! and "Why Boston?" Any other town, east or west, on the map might have done quite as well. To anyone who has known Boston and Back Bay, the setting of that adventure is more ludicrous than amusing. . . .

Yes, I should be delighted to have you lend me the book on Denmark. Post it to Richmond, for we are leaving on Sunday, and we are now packing and house-cleaning, though I can do very little to help. The man is waiting for my typewriter, and even if I had the strength, which I have not, I should not be able to copy this untidy letter. . . . It is so beautiful here, and I have just come in from one of my last walks in the birch-woods. Beyond golden leaves, I look out, when I lift my eyes, on the rippling bay in a high wind, and on the deep blue shadows blowing over the Camden Hills. How I wish you could come to this charming village. Though I am Southern in every drop of my blood, I find a strong kinship with the people and the background of New England. I like the cold, pure outlines of these autumn and winter landscapes. . . .

How dear of you to send me this new translation of the Bhagavad Gita.[4] I have loved that song of songs, the noblest expression, I think, of man's spiritual groping after the Highest Good. I placed a verse from the Bhagavad Gita on the tomb of my dearly beloved sister,[5] who died thirty-three years ago. "The unreal has no being. The real never ceases to be. . . ."

No, I have seen no review of Dunsany's novel.[6] Could you send me that and any others of which you may have extra copies . . . though, for that matter, I shall return them. I did so heartily enjoy the two you sent me. . . . Well, goodbye for a little while. . . . My typewriter is going before me to Richmond. I am looking eagerly forward to seeing you . . . really seeing you, dear Signe, before the year is over. That will help me to keep well, or at least not to fall ill again.

Devotedly, | *Ellen*

I am heartily ashamed of this typing, but I would rather be ashamed than try to copy it in longhand.[7]

TLS TxU-Hu
Publication: *L* 356–59.

   1. "Nature Spirits of North America" was published in 1944 in the magazine *Tomorrow*..
   2. Katherine Woods, "*A Certain Measure,*" *Tomorrow* 3 (December 1943): 50–51.
   3. First novel (1944) by the novelist and short story writer Jean Stafford (1915–1979).
   4. EG owned a heavily marked copy of Annie Besant's 1896 translation (*CLEG* 1.3).
   5. CGMcC, who is buried in the Glasgow family plot at Hollywood Cemetery.
   6. *While the Sirens Slept* (1944) by Lord Edward John Moreton Drax Plunkett Dunsany (1878–1957), playwright and figure in the Irish Renaissance.
   7. The postscript is handwritten.

To Signe Toksvig

November 1st, 1944 | ONE WEST MAIN STREET | RICHMOND, VIRGINIA

Dear Signe,

The post here is entirely too slow. I had no sooner mailed the postcard to you than your copy of "I Chose Denmark" was brought to me. I am reading my copy now, and yours will go back to you today or tomorrow. The book has an enchantment. I, too, who once lived in Arcadia,[1] would choose Denmark if it is all that F. H. observed or imagined. The bare cleanliness! The fresh purity of the earth and the sky! So far, because I must go slowly, I have read only half of the book; but I have lingered over the charming impressions, alive and brilliant in color, of the Signe I know in my mind and heart. That first glimpse of you at the New Republic was wholly delightful. I could wish, much as I enjoy the other part, that there were more of you in each page. There aren't many women one would like, if one were a man, to be married to; but even when you are absent from this book, you leave the impression of perfect companionship.

Yes, I like the reviews you sent me, most of all, I think, I like the distinction of mind, the feeling that manner is not a thing detached from life, but that it is a part of morality. By manner, I mean what we used to call, and still should call (for God knows we need it!) "good taste." For good taste expresses and involves the knowledge of right and wrong, of good and evil....

Oh, there is so much to say, if only I were able to write!

Thank you, Signe dear, for the new version of my old friend, the Bhagavad-Gita. I am reading it over with much interest and satisfaction, and I am glad that this volume contains the magnificent legend of Yudhisthira,[2] for Yudhisthira has always been, for me, the King among kings. I have a very beautiful translation, in poetry, of that legend.

Though I am overjoyed to have this modern translation of the Gita, it does not (perhaps because of a certain scientific bareness) come so close to me, with its more poetic phrasing. For example, a single word may come in one's way, and I find myself unmoved by the word Atman, while the phrase "the self within the self" stirs some far-off memory or association of ideas. But poetry will defy translation; and for me, poetry (I mean English poetry) has taken the place in life that other persons may give to music. This may be only because I am a lover of words. All modern versions of the Bible provoke me, while I love, as literature, the King James's version. Do you recall Lytton remark: "And, in any case, who remembers prophets? Isaiah and Jeremiah, no doubt, have gained a certain reputation; but then Isaiah and Jeremiah have had the extraordinary good fortune to be translated into English by a committee of Elizabethan bishops." The pity is that the the many scholars who have known Sanskrit have had so little feeling for English. . . . Yes, I agree with you, Aldous Huxley "somehow alienates me whatever he writes."

And I have a very small opinion of the Theosophists,[3] especially of their lunatic fringe. Yet I am grateful to that Society for one thing, and for one thing alone: when no one else would publish the Vedanta[4] works, they brought out some really beautiful translations from the Sanskrit. . . . What a curioos mixture I am! A lover of the Vedanta, of Plotinus, and of the later Mystics, and yet, inherently, a skeptic regarding the evidence of things seen or unseen, a believer or an unbeliever whose only creed holds that it is better to fight on the side of the Eternal . . for the Eternal, whether we recognize its likeness or not, must be the Good....

Now, the warning comes to me, and I must break off. How I wish I might go on. No, I have never written of my feeling for what we call nature. Castine was satisfying, but I am thankful that you chose Connecticut for your home. The war has done its best to ruin Virginia. Connecticut, as I drove through, appeared lovely, but I have never imagined such dust or such dirty streets as I found here, in Richmond.

As always devotedly, | Ellen

I liked the end of Hypothesis and Belief[5] better than the beginning, which had, I thought, the flavour or lack of flavour I feel in Huxley. I do not believe that science and faith can be reconciled. For who knows what is "true science" or what is "true faith"? The diving bomb, the tank, the poisonous gas? Or the praying hands and the incense of goodness?

TLS TxU-Hu
Publication: *L* 359–61.

    1. EG alludes to the Latin phrase *Et in Arcadia ego* (I, too, in Arcadia), shorthand for simplicity and goodness in a natural world.
    2. One of the five Pandavas (brothers); a hero of the Hindu epic the Mahabharata.
    3. Members of the Theosophical Society (founded 1875) believed in direct apprehension of God through intuition, illumination, or communion.
    4. The sacred books, collectively, of the Brahmins, or members of the highest caste in Hinduism.
    5. Christopher Isherwood's essay, published in *Vedanta for the Western World* (1946).

To Signe Toksvig

December 4th, 1944 | ONE WEST MAIN STREET | RICHMOND, VIRGINIA
Dear Signe,

I loved your letters, and I should have written long before this; but I have had a sad time since I came home from Maine.... The sudden drop has been almost too much for me....

How unerringly you interpret my books! Your insight penetrates and finds the hidden meaning that so few readers ever discover, or even suspect. What you write of "The Miller" and "They Stooped to Folly" means more to me that you will ever know. Yes, I have always felt that the chapter bearing Mrs. Burden's stream of memory[1] was a part of my best work.... If only I had sprung up in New England or, better still, in the Middle West, or even the Far West, I suppose it might not have taken me forty years to achieve recognition.... But the North has its own peculiar delusions regarding the South, and the South has no delusions about books, because it never reads them. Occasionally, perhaps, after it has heard a Northern critic discourse before serried rows of complacent ladies in pursuit of culture in programmes....

And, now, what about your visit to Richmond? I am trying to find several addresses for you, but the town is flooded with an overflow from Washington, and the war, as I think I wrote you, has destroyed all the native charm of Virginia. How I wish it were possible for me to ask you both to come straight to me. In happier days this would have been my first thought; but my long illness and the many war problems have changed my whole way of living. I can no longer have guests, and I never know, from day to day, how well or how ill I shall be. What distresses me is that I shall be able to do so little to make your stay pleasant. I was talking this over with a close friend only yesterday, and we both regretted the excursions we used to make to the places on James River. In the spring, these old places are lovely, with a singular and very special poetry of the past. But all such visits are now over, at least for "the duration", detestable phrase! I hope in my heart that you will come. I shall love to see you both, and my only fear is that Richmond will bore you, and you will find life here uninteresting. As for me, I feel, too, that I am merely the shadow of myself, and that you will meet only a part of what I have been in the past. A few of my friends still think the hard trip is justified; but, for the most part, the war has cut me off from New York, and from my friends there who speak my own language.... I am trying to write frankly, because I should not like to feel that you and Francis were disappointed.... I hope ... I cannot keep from hoping that you will come and that I shall be much, much better....

And now for possible places, none good, I fear, but places are no longer good even in New York. These persons might, or might not be able, to take paying guests for a few days. Most of them, I believe take in guests for months or even for a year.

Miss Munford, 307 West Franklin Street, Richmond 20. This house has a romantic history, but you would find only old or elderly guests, all in the greater Victorian tradition. For years, the house was run by four sisters, who were girls in the Civil War, and have never lived far beyond the battles around Richmond, when their adored young brother was brought, dead, to them, up this same tree-shaded Franklin Street. Theirs was one of the great Virginia families, but after the Civil War, the four women, still young girls, were completely impoverished. Like other women in South who had neither an aptitude nor an income, nor any special strain of intelligence, they turned, instinctively to teaching as a means of livelihood. I have described this in my "Virginia". Some day you must read that book.

But, as a small child, I went to school in this house, and was taught by a Miss Munford, who was still a great lady.

Other addresses will come, I hope. One of the advantages of going to this house is that it stands in a secluded block only a little way from my corner. Then there is always the old Jefferson Hotel, with a distinguished past but a wholly inadequate present. Many persons I know live there, but I could not honestly recommend any hotel in Richmond. I know the food must be uninteresting, but the Van Wyck Brookses preferred it to the commercial John Marshall, and so does Frank Morley, who stays there when he come down to see me. That, also, is very near my corner, only too blocks away. I think you know Frank, and you might ask him about the hotel.

Dear Signe, I am finding an almost forgotten thrill in this search for a place. I must thank you, too, for the pleasant and very apologetic letter I received from *The Times*. They wished to send me the paper for two months, but I have a satisfactory arrangement with the Jefferson, and I send every morning for the day's paper. I am enjoying F. H.'s reviews, but I looked in vain for your article. It will come later, I suppose. Yes, I wish I might read that book.

My typewriter is deranged this morning....

I forgot to tell you that only one of the four Munford sisters is now living. She is or was the youngest, "Miss Etta", and was born, I imagine, some years after the War Between the States. I have not been to the house since, as a little child, I climbed up four steep winding stairs to the schoolroom at the top. The three elder sisters have all died, I think, of old age; for I thought of them as old when I was a child. I am sure the house must be very depressing; but it has its tragic history.

Much love to you, | *Ellen*

Tuesday.

Last night, before going to bed, Miss Bennett, my secretary, who lives with me, talked over the telephone with Miss Munford and with Mrs. Marshall Milton, who has a house just across the street from the Jefferson. Miss Munford thanked us for thinking of her, but said she had every room taken until summer. Mrs. Milton said she might have a room at Christmas. She was not sure. The room was on the third floor at the front, had no private bath, but was near the bathroom. She said some people preferred to take a room with bath at the Hotel Jefferson (Franklin Street) and to come to her for their meals. I have an idea that she has better food than you would find at the hotel. Her address is: Mrs. Marshall Milton, 20 West Franklin Street, Richmond 20, Virginia.

Of course, the advantage of these places is that they at so near to me, and I should want to see as much of you both as I can. Christmas might be pleasant, but people are simply begging for places to stay. There are so many soldiers here or in camps near by. But it would be lovely to have you come if you are not bored. Anyway, I always have Virginia eggnog at Christmas.

I am dashing this off, without reading it over.

TLS TxU-Hu
Publication: *L* 362–65.

1. In the second section of *TSTF.*

To Rebe Glasgow Tutwiler

December 27th, 1944 | ONE WEST MAIN STREET | RICHMOND, VIRGINIA
My darling Rebe:

I began a letter to you yesterday, but I could get only as far as the envelope. Your gift was wonderful. There is nothing I should rather have, though you gave me entirely too much. I know how expensive that rare perfume is now, and a single bottle would have been an abundance. Already, I have used some, and enjoyed it.

Cindy's present, too, was much appreciated and her card was so enchanting that I put it away in Grimms' Fairy Tales. The black spaniel was exactly like her. Bless her little heart, it is sad to think she is so feeble. She has been so good all her life, a saint in ebony....

I am horrified by what you write of that dreadful garbage disposal plant in the midst of the lovely valley. What a Council for any town! Can you imagine such an outrage to beauty happening in Connecticut?

I hope Cabell will be able to buy that piece of land. Otherwise, I think similar desecrations will crop up as long as you live there. But it makes me so indignant when I think how much your coming to Lexington has meant. You are not strong enough to have these nervous recoils. And they all seem, and are, so needless.

I must stop now. Writing is simply too much for me. I am having a rather wretched time, and it does me no good whatever to reflect on a world in tragedy. The war news has been disheartening; but when victory comes, as it must and will, I suppose the world will forget all the sorrow and suffering and the loss of young lives....

Thank you again for your splendid gift.
Devotedly, | *Ellen*

TC of TLS FU
Address: Mrs. C. Cabell Tutwiler, Brushwood, Lexington

To Signe Toksvig

February 5th, 1945 | ONE WEST MAIN STREET | RICHMOND, VIRGINIA
Dear Signe,

Your letter lifted my spirit. You have been much in my mind, but I suffered a sharp setback at the new year, or just before, and I have not recovered my strength. I hope the spring will revive me. You cannot know how I look forward to seeing you and F. H. A few years ago, what gorgeous times we might have had on James River!

Your note enclosing the clipping by F. H. has just come. I love those notes. They have a rare quality. I taste the salt in the mist. It is easy, I think, for a Virginian to understand the Irish mood of that coast. We were brought up on dreams, so many of us, because, after the Civil War and the Reconstructions Acts, we had so little else. Though I came in the next generation, I still heard and felt the loss of satisfying realities.

I must stop now, but I must tell you to look up Norma and Herschel Brickell if you ever find yourself near them. When they came by Richmond a week ago, I had no hope of being able to see them. However, that was one of my better days, and I had a glimpse of them when they stopped to speak to Miss Bennett. I made her bring them up stairs, and I found that Norma was overflowing with her recent discovery of the Isherwood translation of The Bhagavad-Gita. She had found it, quite by accident, when she was in a hospital in South America. I should like her to tell you what it meant to her. So far, I can follow her, but I take wings and fly away at the faintest shadow of Theosophy or Christian Science. I have a painful suspicion that most of these modern direct intuitions are cheap emotional transports.

But none of this is about Norma. We talked only of The Gita, and I shared her enthusiasm. She is interesting and very attractive. They are both dear friends of mine, and I should like you to know them.

Yes, F. H. must write his memoirs. The book would make a companion volume to "I Chose Denmark."

Devotedly, | Ellen

I loved your Chinese rose at Christmas.

TLS TxU-Hu

To Rebe Glasgow Tutwiler

Sunday Feb 5 1945 | ONE WEST MAIN STREET | RICHMOND, VIRGINIA

Darling Rebe,

I am worried about your cold and your having to go out every night in this bitter weather. Let me know how you are.

It is impossible for me to write. I cannot remember that I ever felt weaker. The doctor is increasing my digitalis, and this keeps me unable to eat. Of course, it is good for shortness of breath, and that has troubled me a great deal, that and being shut in the house all these dark freezing days.

I have reached the state when I seem to have read everything that is worth reading. No good books are left, for the sloppy modern way of writing makes me understand why Henry James stopped reading novels, by other authors, because he felt obliged to write over every sentence.

I have read over most of Anthony Trollope (how pefectly he knew human nature under its mask of gentility!), and now I am going through Jane Austen. The trouble is that I remember all the characters too vividly. My Jane Austen has splendid print, and that is a great comfort after trying to read war-time printing.

To return to Trollope, do you remember that the delightful affair between

Mr. Palliser and Lady Dumbello occurs in The Small House at Allington? I had thought it was in a later novel. But isn't the subtle humor delicious of those two earls? There is no doubt about it—the Victorian novelists created and finished the English novel. All contemporary novelists (except Virginia Woolf, who was more poet than novelist) appear thin and vulgar and oddly scurrilous beside the greatest Victorians. Among these, of course, Hardy is ageless and timeless.

Do let me hear how you are.

Devotedly, | Ellen

I do wish you could hear definitely about that nuisance.

TC of TLS FU
Address: Mrs. C. Cabell Tutwiler, Brushwood, Lexington

To Signe Toksvig

March 23rd, 1945 | ONE WEST MAIN STREET | RICHMOND, VIRGINIA

Signe, dear:

Miss Bennett is writing this for me, because I have been very ill for weeks, and I am not strong enough to write a letter or to see my friends. But the bitterest disappointment is that I must be denied the joy of your visit.

The one thing I had hoped for was that I might see you both in April. But it would not be fair to let you come.

I send my devoted love and my blessing. Why couldn't we have known each other when I was well and abounding in vitality?

The way now is very hard and steep, and I seem to be slipping back, though my doctors say otherwise.

As always yours, | *Ellen*

Dear Miss Toksvig:

Ellen has been seriously ill, and she is deeply disappointed. We hope that she will improve, and that some day in the future you may be able to come to Richmond.

Sincerely yours, | Anne Virginia Bennett

TLS with TNS (AVB to ST) TxU-Hu

To Irita Van Doren

August 2nd, 1945 | BATTLE AVENUE | CASTINE, MAINE

Irita dear,

How I should love to see you! Is there any chance that you might come to Castine? It would be dull for you. I am still on the edge of my long illness, and there is little to offer you except my joy in your friendship.

This is my first attempt at the typewriter since I came home from the hospital.

With all my love, | Ellen

We have few of the comforts of civilized life.

TLS DLC

To Rebe Glasgow Tutwiler

August 16th, 1945 | BATTLE AVENUE | CASTINE, MAINE

My darling Rebe:

Could Cindy stand the long trip if you make frequent stops? Now that gasoline rationing is over, how I wish you could have this change.

I cannot write, but I think of you all the time.

Devotedly, | Ellen

I have just come in from the woods. They are filled with crowds of Indian Pipes, so ghostly and lovely.

TC of TLS FU

To Rebe Glasgow Tutwiler

August 25th, 1945 | BATTLE AVENUE | CASTINE, MAINE

My darling Rebe,

I have been worried about those hornet stings on your leg. They may be so easily infected, and there were so many. Let me know if you are over them.

It is cold and rainy today, but we have had some perfect summer weather. How I wish you could come. A. V. thinks Cindy could stand the motor trip, but I am not sure. Poor little saint in ebony. Life is too terrible.

I especially wish you could have the change, because I hope, in my heart, I shall never have to come back to Castine. The village is charming, and to escape the heat of Virginia means everything, but I am unutterably bored by the life here. Not that it is any worse than what I endured before I came.

There will be no sale for the blind this year.

Dearest love, but I cannot write letters. Josephine is a great help.

Devotedly, | Ellen

TC of TLS FU
Address: Mrs. C. Cabell Tutwiler, Brushwood, Lexington

To Marjorie Kinnan Rawlings

November 17th, 1945 | ONE WEST MAIN STREET | RICHMOND, VIRGINIA

Dearest Marjorie:

What a precious letter! If only I were strong enough, I should love to spend the winter in St. Augustine. But I am not equal to anything, at present, in the way of an effort. I came from the Maine bracing air to a long spell of October heat in Virginia; and this has been almost too much for me.

It was dear of you to write to me. Your place must be adorable. How I should love to see that and you! Many thanks for the lovely fruit. I was away when the mangoes came, but my friends enjoyed them.[1]

Go on with your book.[2] Do not give up. You have great gifts.

My love to you always. | *Ellen*

Yes, I read "Colcorton",[3] and admired it. It held much promise and was work of a high order.

TLS ViU EG 8352

1. The last two sentences in this paragraph are handwritten.
2. *The Sojourner* (1953).
3. Novel by Edith Pope (New York: Scribner's, 1944).

Calendar

Below, listed chronologically by year, is all known correspondence between Ellen Glasgow and other women. Letters included in the present volume are italicized. Letters with partial or uncertain dates are dated as accurately as an educated guess makes possible; these are listed at the beginning of their probable month, season, and/or year of composition and posting when any more precise date is not known or ascertainable. Undated letters that have been impossible to date are listed separately at the end. Square brackets encompass three categories of letters. Those dated by postmark rather than a date written on the letter itself are enclosed in square brackets only; those undated letters whose dates are likely are enclosed in square brackets with a terminal question mark; letters dated "Christmas" or "Christmas Eve" are identified as such, without the presumed dates (i.e., December 25 or 24). When only the year is probable, letters are noted with [n.d.]. A question mark within square brackets marks letters whose dates are speculative. A question mark within square brackets following a month and day indicates that no year can be confirmed by the letter writer or postmarks, even when conjecture makes the year probable.

All listings are letters unless identified otherwise (as postcards or telegrams, for example). In a few instances, when a letter is known only from previous publication, the published source is provided parenthetically (i.e., *EGN* or *L*). When a letter no longer exists but is referred to by date elsewhere by a correspondent, parentheses following the correspondent's name contain a question mark. Letters from private collections are designated as "Private." For most letters, the provenance is provided parenthetically for all locations other than the Albert and Shirley Small Special Collections Library at the University of Virginia (ViU); all letters with no designated provenance are housed at the University of Virginia.

1884
January 7   *To Rebecca Anderson Glasgow* (ViLxW)
1885
March 17   *To Rebecca Anderson Glasgow* (ViLxW)
1895
August 29   To Mrs. Francis Smith (*L*)
1896
[April 28?]   To Cary Glasgow McCormack
July 23   To Cary Glasgow McCormack
[early August]   To Cary Glasgow McCormack
August 2   To Cary Glasgow McCormack

September 9	*To Cary Glasgow McCormack*
1897	
September 22[?]	*To Mrs. [Rush?] Huidekoper*
1898	
October 26	*To Elizabeth Whiting* (NjMoHP)
1902	
January 2	*To Elizabeth Patterson*
March 22 [?]	*To Elizabeth Patterson*
[late March–April?]	*To Ann Seddon Roy Rutherfoord* (NcD)
1903	
July 2	*To Lucy Bramlette Patterson* (NcD)
1904	
[n.d.]	To Mary Johnston
March 22	To Mary Johnston
1905	
[n.d.]	To Mary Johnston
January 15	To Eleanor Robson (NNC)
February 3	To Mary Johnston
[early March?]	To Mary Johnston
[March 24?]	To Isabelle Holmes Perkinson (NcD)
[April 2?]	To Eleanor Robson (NNC)
May 29 [?]	To Eleanor Robson (NNC)
[June–early July?]	To Mary Johnston
[early October?]	To Louise Chandler Moulton (DLC)
October 5	To Louise Chandler Moulton (DLC)
November 10	To Louise Chandler Moulton (DLC)
December 10	To Louise Chandler Moulton (DLC)
[late autumn?]	To Mary Johnston
[late 1905?]	To Mary Johnston
1906	
January 28	To Louise Chandler Moulton (DLC)
March 18	*To Louise Chandler Moulton* (DLC)
April 18	*To Louise Chandler Moulton* (DLC)
[spring?]	*To Rebe Glasgow Tutwiler* (FU)
[spring–summer?]	To Rebe Glasgow Tutwiler (FU)
[spring–summer?]	To Rebe Glasgow Tutwiler (FU)
[summer]	To Mary Johnston
August 15	*To Mary Johnston*
September 15	*To Mary Johnston*
[December 7]	*To Rebe Glasgow Tutwiler* (FU)
December 13	*To Louise Chandler Moulton* (DLC)

[December 14]	To Rebe Glasgow Tutwiler (FU)
[December 16]	To Rebe Glasgow Tutwiler (FU)
[December 20]	To Rebe Glasgow Tutwiler (FU)
[December 23]	To Rebe Glasgow Tutwiler (FU)
December 26	To Rebe Glasgow Tutwiler (FU)
December 30	To Rebe Glasgow Tutwiler (FU)
1907	
January 3	To Rebe Glasgow Tutwiler (FU)
[January 18]	To Rebe Glasgow Tutwiler (FU)
January 26	To Rebe Glasgow Tutwiler (FU)
January 30	To Rebe Glasgow Tutwiler (FU)
February 17	To Rebe Glasgow Tutwiler (FU)
[May 22]	To Rebe Glasgow Tutwiler (FU)
[May 23]	To Rebe Glasgow Tutwiler (FU)
[May 24]	To Rebe Glasgow Tutwiler (FU)
[May 28]	To Rebe Glasgow Tutwiler (FU)
[May 30]	To Rebe Glasgow Tutwiler (FU)
[June 4]	To Rebe Glasgow Tutwiler (FU)
[June 13]	To Rebe Glasgow Tutwiler (FU)
[June 29]	To Rebe Glasgow Tutwiler (FU)
[July 2]	To Rebe Glasgow Tutwiler (FU)
July 20	To Mary Johnston
[October ?]	To Rebe Glasgow Tutwiler (FU)
[early autumn]	To Rebe Glasgow Tutwiler (NcD)
December 15	To Elizabeth Patterson
December 23	To Rebe Glasgow Tutwiler (FU)
1908	
[April?]	To Lucy Parke Chamberlayne Bagby (ViHi)
April 28	To Elizabeth Patterson (APS)
April 29	To Elizabeth Patterson (APS)
July 4	To Mary Johnston
July 14	To Elizabeth Patterson
August 1	To Elizabeth Patterson (APS)
August 5	To Rebe Glasgow Tutwiler (FU)
August 13	To Elizabeth Patterson
1909	
April 28	To Cary Glasgow McCormack
August 13	To Elizabeth Patterson
August 14	To Rebe Glasgow Tutwiler (FU)
August 17	To Elizabeth Patterson
September 2 [?]	To Elizabeth Patterson

September 3	*To Cary Glasgow McCormack*
December 21	From Lucy (Mrs. Arthur Page) Brown
December 29	To Elizabeth Patterson
1910	
December 8	*From Ruth McEnery Stuart*
December 24	To Elizabeth Patterson
1911	
November 30	*To Lila Hardaway Meade Valentine (ViHi)*
1912	
February 20	To Annie Glasgow Clark (ViW)
[March 29]	*To Elizabeth Patterson*
[early July?]	To Mary Johnston
July 1	*To Lila Hardaway Meade Valentine (ViHi)*
[July 3]	*To Elizabeth Patterson (FU)*
[October 12?]	To Elizabeth Patterson
1913	
July 23	To Gertrude Foster Brown (NN-B)
October 27	From Amélie Rives Troubetzkoy
[November 23?]	*To Julia Sully*
1914	
January 1	To Elizabeth Patterson
[May 31]	*To Rebe Glasgow Tutwiler (FU)*
June 6	*To Rebe Glasgow Tutwiler (FU)*
June 17	From Ada Galsworthy
July 2	To Elizabeth Patterson (ViRCU)
November 1	*To Mary Johnston*
1915	
[n.d.]	To Mary Johnston
January 17	To A[lice] Kauser (TxU-Hu)
January 26	*To Lady Kentore*
April 8	To Elizabeth Garver Jordan (NN-B)
May 3	*To Katharine Baird Hopper (MdBG)*
July 5 [?]	From Gertrude Atherton
July 27	*To Rebe Glasgow Tutwiler (FU)*
August 12	To Elizabeth Patterson (APS)
October 15 [?]	From Rebe Glasgow Tutwiler
[December 27]	*To Elizabeth Patterson*
[December 27]	*To Rebe Glasgow Tutwiler (FU)*
1916	
[February 18]	To Rebe Glasgow Tutwiler (FU)
[March 11]	To Elizabeth Patterson

[March 28]	To Rebe Glasgow Tutwiler (FU)
[April 26]	To Rebe Glasgow Tutwiler (FU)
June 26	From Lillie Hamilton French
August 12	To Elizabeth Patterson (APS)
[autumn?]	To Mary Johnston
[November 4]	*To Rebe Glasgow Tutwiler* (FU)
November 13 [?]	From Rebe Glasgow Tutwiler
1917	
[May 30]	To Rebe Glasgow Tutwiler (FU)
1918	
September 3	From Rebe Glasgow Tutwiler
November 19	From Laura E. Anderson
1919	
[November ?]	To Adele Clark (ViRCU)
1920	
September 17	*To Lila Hardaway Meade Valentine* (ViHi)
1921	
June 28 [?]	From Rebe Glasgow Tutwiler
[October 8?][?]	From Rebe Glasgow Tutwiler
October 17	From M. Jeannette Mitchell
December 15	From Rebe Glasgow Tutwiler
Christmas Day	From Rebe Glasgow Tutwiler
1922	
February 26	*To Irita Van Doren* (DLC)
June 16	From Amélie Rives Troubetzkoy
August 22	To Anne Virginia Bennett (APS)
1923	
March 20	*To Rebe Glasgow Tutwiler* (FU)
November 4	To Irita Van Doren (DLC)
December 17	From Jessie Conrad
1924	
January 6	From Agnes Repplier
January 22 [?]	From Agnes Repplier
February 14	From Jessie Conrad
[February 18]	To Rebe Glasgow Tutwiler (FU)
March 2	From Louise Collier Willcox
March 30	*From Agnes Repplier*
May 22	From May Sinclair
August 17	From Louise Collier Willcox
September 5	*To Agnes Repplier* (PU-Sp)
September 15	*To Irita Van Doren* (DLC)

November 24   To Lucy Parke Chamberlayne Bagby (ViHi)
1925
January 7   To Irita Van Doren (DLC)
January 21   From Amélie Rives Troubetzkoy
January 22   From Amélie Rives Troubetzkoy
March 8   To Irita Van Doren (DLC)
March 10   *From Irita Van Doren*
March 11   *To Irita Van Doren* (DLC)
April 8   From Mary Johnston
April 12   *From Louise Collier Willcox*
April 21   *To Irita Van Doren* (DLC)
April 30 [?]   To Irita Van Doren (DLC)
May 10   *From Agnes Repplier*
June 10   To Irita Van Doren (DLC)
June 17   *To Agnes Repplier* (PU-Sp)
August 14   To Mrs. Copeland
August 25   To Irita Van Doren (DLC)
August 29   To Irita Van Doren (DLC)
October 24   *To Blanche Knopf* (TxU-Hu)
October 38 [28?]   *To Blanche Knopf* (TxU-Hu)
November 5   To Blanche Knopf (TxU-Hu)
December 20   To Irita Van Doren (DLC)
December 27 [?]   *To Rebe Glasgow Tutwiler* (FU)
December 28   To Miss Bagley (Private)
December 28 [?]   From Fannie Hurst
1926
"Sunday" [n.d.]   To Rebe Glasgow Tutwiler (FU)
"Monday" [n.d.]   To Rebe Glasgow Tutwiler (FU)
January 3 [?]   To Rebe Glasgow Tutwiler (FU)
January 4   From Amélie Rives Troubetzkoy
January 20   From Amélie Rives Troubetzkoy
February 16   To Irita Van Doren (DLC)
February 27   To Irita Van Doren (DLC)
March 27   To Mrs. Colman (MHi)
March 31   To Irita Van Doren (DLC)
August 23   To Irita Van Doren (DLC)
September 17   To Irita Van Doren (DLC)
September 26   *To Irita Van Doren* (DLC)
October 21   *To Irita Van Doren* (DLC)
November 26   From Margaret Deland
December 14 [?]   From Rebe Glasgow Tutwiler

Christmas Day 1927	*To Rebe Glasgow Tutwiler* (FU)
[n.d.]	To Helen McAfee (CtY)
April 14	*From Zona Gale*
[April 24]	To Rebe Glasgow Tutwiler (FU)
April 26	From Margaret Branch Glasgow
June 1	To Rebe Glasgow Tutwiler (FU)
June 3	To Margaret Dashiell (APS NcU)
June 7	To Irita Van Doren (DLC)
June 15	From Mary Johnston
June 26	*To Rebe Glasgow Tutwiler*
July 3	To Anne Virginia Bennett (APS)
July 13	To Anne Virginia Bennett (APS)
July 14	From Margaret Branch Glasgow
July 18	To Anne Virginia Bennett (APS)
July 23	*To Rebe Glasgow Tutwiler*
July 25	To Anne Virginia Bennett (APS)
July 26	*To Anne Virginia Bennett*
July 27 [?]	*To Anne Virginia Bennett*
July 30	To Anne Virginia Bennett (APS)
July 30	*To Rebe Glasgow Tutwiler*
August 2	To Anne Virginia Bennett (APS)
August 3	To Anne Virginia Bennett (APS)
August 3	To Margaret Dashiell (APS NcU)
August 6	To Anne Virginia Bennett (APS)
August 6	To Margaret Dashiell (APS NcU)
August 7 [?]	*To Anne Virginia Bennett*
August 7	*To Rebe Glasgow Tutwiler*
August 7	From Virginia Woolf
August 9	From May Sinclair
August 11	*To Rebe Glasgow Tutwiler*
August 12	To Anne Virginia Bennett (APS)
August 14 [?]	*To Anne Virginia Bennett*
August 17	From F. E. Hardy
August 19	*To Anne Virginia Bennett*
August 21	To Anne Virginia Bennett (APS)
August 22	To Anne Virginia Bennett (APS)
August 24	*From Radclyffe Hall*
August 24	*To Rebe Glasgow Tutwiler*
August 25	*To Anne Virginia Bennett*
August 25	To Anne Virginia Bennett (APS)

August 25	To Amélie Rives Troubetzkoy (APS)
August 26	To Anne Virginia Bennett (APS)
August 26	*To Rebe Glasgow Tutwiler*
[August 27]	To Anne Virginia Bennett
August 31	To Anne Virginia Bennett (APS)
August 31	To Anne Virginia Bennett (APS)
August 31	To Anne Virginia Bennett (APS)
August 31	*To Rebe Glasgow Tutwiler*
September 1	*To Anne Virginia Bennett*
September 4	*From Radclyffe Hall*
September 6	*To Rebe Glasgow Tutwiler*
[September 14]	To Anne Virginia Bennett
December 13	From Nina Hamilton
[late?] December	To Sophie Kerr (ANS NNC)

1928

"Friday" [?]	To Irita Van Doren (DLC)
January 31	*To Helen McAfee* (CtY)
February 8	To Irita Van Doren (DLC)
April 4 [?]	*From Frances Newman*
April 27	To Irita Van Doren (DLC)
June 5	From Irita Van Doren
[July 8]	From Zona Gale
October 30 [?]	To Irita Van Doren (DLC)
[December 22]	From Zona Gale
December 25	From Amélie Rives Troubetzkoy

1929

January 25	To Irita Van Doren (DLC)
April 12	To Irita Van Doren (DLC)
[July–August?]	*To Irita Van Doren* (DLC)
August 19	From Elizabeth Lucas
[September 14]	From Radclyffe Hall
September 27	*From Mary Johnston*
September 29	*From Radclyffe Hall*
[autumn?]	To Josephine Clark
October 8	To Irita Van Doren (DLC)
[October 16]	*To Anne Virginia Bennett*
November 19	From Elizabeth Shepley Sergeant

1930

[January 20?]	*To Irita Van Doren* (DLC)
February 7	To Irita Van Doren (DLC)
February 19	From Amélie Rives Troubetzkoy

Calendar

May 11	To Irita Van Doren (DLC)
[May 20]	To Irita Van Doren (DLC)
May 30	To Rebe Glasgow Tutwiler (FU)
[June 6?]	*To Irita Van Doren (DLC)*
[June 12?]	To Rebe Glasgow Tutwiler (FU)
[June] 16	*To Anne Virginia Bennett*
June 18	*To Rebe Glasgow Tutwiler* (FU)
June 21	*To Anne Virginia Bennett*
July 24	From Radclyffe Hall
August 21	To Anne Virginia Bennett (APS)
August 23	From Radclyffe Hall
August 24	*To Anne Virginia Bennett*
September [?]	To Anne Virginia Bennett (APS)
September 3	To Anne Virginia Bennett (APS)
September 14	*To Sara Haardt Mencken (MdBG)*
November 12	*From Radclyffe Hall*
November 17	From Isa Glenn
December 27	From Bessie Zaban Jones (MNS)
December 29	To Bessie Zaban Jones (MNS)
1931	
February 19	From Amélie Rives Troubetzkoy
February 26	From Amélie Rives Troubetzkoy
February 28	*To Irita Van Doren (DLC)*
March 29	*To Bessie Zaban Jones (MNS)*
May 16	*To Bessie Zaban Jones (MNS)*
[June 25]	To Anne Virginia Bennett
[July–August]	To Anne Virginia Bennett (APS)
[July–August]	To Anne Virginia Bennett (APS)
[July–August]	To Anne Virginia Bennett (APS)
September 22	*To Irita Van Doren (DLC)*
December 2	*From Isa Glenn*
[December 5?]	To Rebe Glasgow Tutwiler (FU)
December 17	From Irita Van Doren
1932	
[January?]	To Winnie [Bryan?]
January 4 [?]	To Rebe Glasgow Tutwiler (FU)
[February 9?]	From Bessie Zaban Jones (MNS)
March 8	*To Page Cooper (NNC)*
June 11	From Radclyffe Hall
[August 9?]	From Marie Howland
August 14	From Radclyffe Hall

August 16	From Page Cooper
August 23	*From Page Cooper*
August 29	From Blanche T. King
August 29	*To Sara Haardt Mencken (MdBG)*
September 3	*From Amélie Rives Troubetzkoy*
September 6	From Mary Johnston
September 9	*From Léonie Villard*
September 15 [?]	From Martha Saxton
September 17	*To Martha Saxton*
September 29	From Radclyffe Hall
October 12	To Sara Haardt Mencken (MdBG)
October 12	From Dorothy Van Doren
October 13	To Sara Haardt Mencken (telegram MdBG)
October 17	*To Sara Haardt Mencken (MdBG)*
October 26 [?]	From Rebe Glasgow Tutwiler
[December 2?]	*From Isabel Paterson*
December 7	From Eleanor Hubbard Garst (IaU)
December [8?]	To Eleanor Hubbard Garst (telegram IaU)
December 19	From Amélie Rives Troubetzkoy
December 22	*From Dorothy Scarborough*
1933	
January 6	From Dorothy Canfield Fisher
January 16	To Bessie Zaban Jones (MNS)
January 26	To Bessie Zaban Jones (MNS)
April 7	To Helen McAfee (CtY)
May 6	From Mary R. Beard
May 7	*From Isa Glenn*
May 8	From Amy Loveman
May 8	From Jean Kenyon Mackenzie
May 15	From Mary R. Beard
May 26	From Radclyffe Hall
August 4	From Isa Glenn
September 6	From Léonie Villard
September 8	*To Irita Van Doren (DLC)*
[early September?]	*To Irita Van Doren (DLC)*
September 27	To Irita Van Doren (DLC)
October 17	From Irita Van Doren
October 30	To Sara Haardt Mencken (MdBG)
October 31	From Sara Haardt Mencken
[early November?]	To Sara Haardt Mencken (MdBG)
November 2	*To Irita Van Doren (DLC)*

November 19	*To Dorothy Canfield Fisher* (VtU)
November 21	*To Irita Van Doren* (DLC)
December 18	From Elizabeth C. Morrow
December 23	Mrs. Vernon Monroe
December 29	*To Bessie Zaban Jones* (MNS)
1934	
February 7	*To Bessie Zaban Jones* (MNS)
February 20	From Jeanne Dauban
May 21	From Sara Haardt Mencken
May 23	*To Irita Van Doren* (DLC)
May 24	To Dorothy Canfield Fisher (VtU)
[June 5]	From Dorothy Canfield Fisher
June 9	*To Irita Van Doren* (DLC)
June 15	From Irita Van Doren
June 18	*To Irita Van Doren* (DLC)
June 20	From May Lamberton Becker
June 28	From Irita Van Doren
July 11	*To Irita Van Doren* (DLC)
July 14	From Irita Van Doren
July 26	*To Irita Van Doren* (DLC)
July 30	From Irita Van Doren
[August?]	From Irita Van Doren
August 2	*To Irita Van Doren* (DLC)
[August 5]	From Marjorie Glasgow Congreve
August 12	*To Irita Van Doren* (DLC)
August 17	*To Irita Van Doren* (DLC)
September 15	To Antoinette (Mrs. Alan Lindsay) Hart (ViRCU)
1935	
January 2	From Nina Hamilton
January 6	To Clare Leighton
January 8	*To Bessie Zaban Jones* (MNS)
[February?]	To Gertrude Stein (CtY)
April 30	To Gertrude Stein (CtY)
[June 1?]	To Anne Virginia Bennett
June 18	*To Irita Van Doren* (DLC)
July 16	From Frances Leigh Williams
August 10	*To Bessie Zaban Jones* (MNS)
August 29	From Amélie Rives Troubetzkoy
[September 28]	*To Anne Virginia Bennett*
[September 30]	*To Anne Virginia Bennett*
[September 30]	*To Anne Virginia Bennett*

October 2	To Mary Johnston
November 11	From Clara Claasen
November 21	*To Irita Van Doren* (DLC)
November 23	*To Irita Van Doren* (DLC)
December 3	*To Miss Forbes*
December 30	To Kathleen (Mrs. Albert) Bourland (Provenance unknown)

1936

January 4	From Clare Leighton
January 17	From Olive Glasgow Titus
February 25	To Mrs. [Howard S.] Gordon (ANS Private)
March 4	*To Miss Patterson*
March 15	From Radclyffe Hall
April 8	From Radclyffe Hall
April 16	To Agnes Johnson Holden (TxU-Hu)
April 17	*To Mary Johnston*
April 22	From Marion Canby
May 29	To Anne Virginia Bennett (APS)
June 2	From Clare Leighton
July 12	From Emily [Clark]
July 18	*To Bessie Zaban Jones* (MNS)
September 9	*To Bessie Zaban Jones* (MNS)
September 9	*To Clare Leighton*
October 23	To Bessie Zaban Jones (MNS)
December 4	To Bessie Zaban Jones (MNS)
December 10	*To Bessie Zaban Jones* (MNS)
December 15	From Amélie Rives Troubetzkoy
December 16	From Thalia Newton Brown

1937

January 3	From Amélie Rives Troubetzkoy
January 6	To Bessie Zaban Jones (MNS)
January 26	To Antoinette (Mrs. Alan Lindsay) Hart (ViRCU)
[January–February?]	To Marion Canby
[January–February?]	To Marion Canby
March 2	From Lillian A. Comstock
March 16	From Léonie Villard
March 30	*To Bessie Zaban Jones* (MNS)
March 31	*From Malvina Hoffman*
May 9	To Bessie Zaban Jones (MNS)
May 14	*To Anne Virginia Bennett*
May 24	To Anne Virginia Bennett (APS)

May 27	To Anne Virginia Bennett (APS)
May 28	To Anne Virginia Bennett (APS)
May 30	To Margaret Dashiell (APS NcU)
June 1	*To Anne Virginia Bennett*
June 2	To Anne Virginia Bennett (APS)
June 20 [?]	From Clare Leighton
June 30	From Amélie Rives Troubetzkoy
July 13	From Amélie Rives Troubetzkoy
July 14 [?]	*To Amélie Rives Troubetzkoy*
July 18	From Amélie Rives Troubetzkoy
August 23	*To Amélie Rives Troubetzkoy*
August 25	From Amélie Rives Troubetzkoy
September 9	From Amélie Rives Troubetzkoy
September 10	From Amélie Rives Troubetzkoy
September 13	From Millie H. Sanford
September 26	From Amélie Rives Troubetzkoy
[September 28]	To Amélie Rives Troubetzkoy
October 6	From Amélie Rives Troubetzkoy
October 22	To Rebe Glasgow Tutwiler (FU)
November 1	*From Agnes B. Reese*
November 5	*To Rebe Glasgow Tutwiler* (FU)
November 6	*To Marion Canby*
November 24	To Irita Van Doren (DLC)
December 14 [?]	From Clare Leighton
[December 24]	*To Clare Leighton*
[December 25]	To Bessie Zaban Jones (MNS)
[December 25]	*From Amélie Rives Troubetzkoy* (TxU-Hu)
December 26	From Amélie Rives Troubetzkoy
December 27 [?]	*To Bessie Zaban Jones* (MNS)
December 29	From Bessie Zaban Jones
1938	
January 28	*To Rebe Glasgow Tutwiler* (FU)
February 15	*To Rebe Glasgow Tutwiler* (FU)
April 11	*To Bessie Zaban Jones* (MNS)
April 18	*To Bessie Zaban Jones* (MNS)
May 5	To Bessie Zaban Jones (MNS)
May 14	*From Agnes B. Reese*
May 16	To Bessie Zaban Jones (MNS)
May 21	To Bessie Zaban Jones (MNS)
June 8	From Amélie Rives Troubetzkoy
[June 23]	To Rebe Glasgow Tutwiler (FU)

June 24	To Bessie Zaban Jones (MNS)
July 19	*To Bessie Zaban Jones* (MNS)
July 28	*To Bessie Zaban Jones* (MNS)
[September 20?]	*To Rebe Glasgow Tutwiler* (FU)
September 21	To Bessie Zaban Jones (MNS)
September 27	*To Bessie Zaban Jones* (MNS)
September 30	*To Irita Van Doren* (DLC)
[November 19]	To Rebe Glasgow Tutwiler (FU)
November 21	*To Bessie Zaban Jones* (MNS)
December 5	*To Ellen Matthews Bagby* (ViHi)
[mid-December?]	To Ellen Matthews Bagby (ViHi)
[late December?]	To Ellen Matthews Bagby (ViHi)
December 16	From Grace D. Vanamee (telegram)
December 22 [?]	To Bessie Zaban Jones (MNS)
1939	
February 1	From Clare Leighton
February 10	From Grace D. Vanamee
February 16	*To Clare Leighton*
February 17	From Grace D. Vanamee
[February 21]	From Rebe Glasgow Tutwiler
[Spring?]	To Rebe Glasgow Tutwiler (FU)
[March–April?]	To Rebe Glasgow Tutwiler (FU)
March 13	From Clare Leighton
March 14	*To Clare Leighton*
March 22	To Bessie Zaban Jones (MNS)
March 22	To Rebe Glasgow Tutwiler
April 16	*To Marjorie Kinnan Rawlings*
April 25	From Marjorie Kinnan Rawlings
April 26	From Eleanor Brooks
May 12	To Bessie Zaban Jones (MNS)
[May 26?]	To Rebe Glasgow Tutwiler (FU)
[*June 17*]	*To Rebe Glasgow Tutwiler* (FU)
August 5	*To Rebe Glasgow Tutwiler* (FU)
August 25	To Margaret Dashiell (APS NcU)
August 31	From Clare Leighton
[September 1]	From Caroline Coleman Duke
September 2	To Rebe Glasgow Tutwiler (APS FU)
September 5	*To Rebe Glasgow Tutwiler* (FU)
[September 10]	From Virginia Watson
September 17 [?]	From Clare Leighton
September 20	*To Clare Leighton*

September 20 [?]	From Betsy Burke Mayo
September 21	To Margaret Dashiell (APS NcU)
October 2	*To Bessie Zaban Jones (MNS)*
November 13	To Clare Leighton
November 14	*To Catherine Turney (Private)*
November 18	From Clare Leighton
December 3	*To Clare Leighton*
December 12	To Clare Leighton
December 27	From Clare Leighton
December 30	*To Rebe Glasgow Tutwiler (FU)*
December 30	From Léonie Villard
1940	
January 4	To Bessie Zaban Jones (MNS)
[January 6]	To Kathleen (Mrs. Albert) Bourland (Provenance unknown)
January 7	From Eleanor Brooks
[February 20]	From Clare Leighton
March 29	To Bessie Zaban Jones (MNS)
April 17	To Catherine Turney (Private)
April 22	To Rebe Glasgow Tutwiler
April 24	*To Bessie Zaban Jones (MNS)*
May 2	From Grace D. Vanamee
May 3 [?]	From Clare Leighton
May 30	From Marjorie Kinnan Rawlings
June 12	To Marion Canby
June 12	To Bessie Zaban Jones (MNS)
June 16	*To Clare Leighton*
June 17	To Amy Loveman (NNC)
June 23	From Clare Leighton
June 29	*To Clare Leighton*
June 30	*To Bessie Zaban Jones (MNS)*
July 5	From Clare Leighton
July 6	*To Clare Leighton*
July 9	*To Bessie Zaban Jones (MNS)*
July 16	*From Catherine Turney*
August 1	*To Irita Van Doren (DLC)*
August 5	From Marjorie Glasgow Congreve
August 7	To Catherine Turney (Private)
[late summer]	From Alice (Mrs. George James) Farnsworth
September 3	From Irita Van Doren
September 11	From Ellen Knowles Harcourt

September 25	*To Bessie Zaban Jones* (MNS)
September 28	From Bessie Zaban Jones
October 16	To Bessie Zaban Jones (MNS)
October 22	From Grace D. Vanamee
November 11	*From Margaret Mitchell*
November 26	From Clare Leighton
December 2	*To Catherine Turney* (Private)
December 6	From Grace D. Vanamee
December 19	*To Irita Van Doren* (DLC)
December 20	From Helen Taylor
December 23	To Bessie Zaban Jones (MNS)
December 23	To Clare Leighton
December 29	From Bessie Zaban Jones
1941	
January 18	From Mary Monty
February 25	To Bessie Zaban Jones (MNS)
[February–March?]	*From Eleanor Brooks*
March 6	*To Bessie Zaban Jones* (MNS)
March 18	To Rebe Glasgow Tutwiler (FU)
March 19	From Irita Van Doren
March 27	*To Irita Van Doren* (DLC)
March 30	From Marjorie Kinnan Rawlings
April 1	To Marjorie Kinnan Rawlings
April 2	To Mrs. Copeland
April 24	To Sally Anderson & Kathleen (Mrs. Albert) Bourland (Provenance unknown)
[April 25]	To Rebe Glasgow Tutwiler (FU)
[April 25]	To Rebe Glasgow Tutwiler (FU)
[early June?]	From Eleanor Brooks
June 13	From Malvina Hoffman
June 14	*To Rebe Glasgow Tutwiler* (FU)
June 26	From Elaine J. Dean
July 19	*From Marjorie Kinnan Rawlings* (FU)
July 24	*To Marjorie Kinnan Rawlings*
August 3	From Gabriella Page
August 21	*To Rebe Glasgow Tutwiler* (FU)
October 6	To Amélie Rives Troubetzkoy (APS)
October 31	To Clare Leighton
[November 27]	To Rebe Glasgow Tutwiler (FU)
December 17	To Margaret Dashiell (NcU)
December 23	To Rebe Glasgow Tutwiler (FU)

Calendar 271

December 27   *From Agnes B. Reese*
December 31   To Rebe Glasgow Tutwiler (FU)
1942
January 3   From Nina Hamilton
January 4   From Amélie Rives Troubetzkoy
January 5   From Amélie Rives Troubetzkoy
January 17   From Marjorie Kinnan Rawlings
February 11   From Ellen Knowles Harcourt
February 24   *To Marjorie Kinnan Rawlings*
April 14   From Marjorie Kinnan Rawlings
April 16   From Elena Mitcoff
April 20   *To Marjorie Kinnan Rawlings*
May 5   From Edith & Katherine (telegram)
May 5   To Irita Van Doren (DLC)
May 6   From Jubillant Mai Clark (telegram)
[May 6?]   *To Rebe Glasgow Tutwiler* (FU)
May 8   From Amy Loveman
May 11   From Marjorie Kinnan Rawlings
June 9   From Leonora Speyer
June 26   *To Bessie Zaban Jones* (MNS)
July 20   *To Bessie Zaban Jones* (MNS)
August 24   From Margaret Branch Glasgow
September 20   From Ella Howard Bryan
October 19   *To Bessie Zaban Jones* (MNS)
December 9   From Rebe Glasgow Tutwiler
[December 12?]   To Rebe Glasgow Tutwiler (FU)
December 19   To Josephine Clark
Christmas Eve   From Amélie Rives Troubetzkoy
December 25   To Margaret Dashiell (APS NcU)
1943
Friday   To Ann Page (Mrs. Frank) Johns (ViRCU)
January 7   From Radclyffe Hall
February 26   From Rebe Glasgow Tutwiler
March 15 [?]   From Leonora Speyer
March 22   *From Radclyffe Hall*
March 26   *To Signe Toksvig* (TxU-Hu)
April 28   From Rebe Glasgow Tutwiler
[May 4?]   *To Rebe Glasgow Tutwiler* (FU)
May 21   *To Signe Toksvig* (TxU-Hu)
June 1   From Signe Toksvig
June 8   *To Signe Toksvig* (TxU-Hu)

July 5	*From Signe Toksvig*
August 14	*To Signe Toksvig* (TxU-Hu)
August 15	*To Signe Toksvig* (TxU-Hu)
August 23	From Signe Toksvig
August 24	From Signe Toksvig (APS)
September 4	*To Signe Toksvig* (TxU-Hu)
September 9	From Signe Toksvig
September 10	From Signe Toksvig
October 7	From Marjorie Kinnan Rawlings
October 12	To Signe Toksvig (TxU-Hu)
October 19	From Signe Toksvig
October 29	From Margaret Dashiell
November 21	To Marion Canby
December 13	From Signe Toksvig
December 20	To Signe Toksvig (TxU-Hu)
December 28	To Rebe Glasgow Tutwiler (FU)
1944	
January 9	From Signe Toksvig
January 31	*To Rebe Glasgow Tutwiler* (FU)
February 1	From Signe Toksvig
February 4	*To Signe Toksvig* (TxU-Hu)
February 7	From Signe Toksvig
February 23	From Annette I. Clark
February 24	*To Marion Canby*
March 7	From Katherine Woods
March 10	From Mary Carter Anderson (Mrs. Charles S.) Gardner
March 21	From Irita Van Doren
March 25	*To Irita Van Doren* (DLC)
April 12	*To Marion Canby*
April 21	From Irita Van Doren
April 22	To Irita Van Doren (DLC)
May 22	To Marjorie Kinnan Rawlings
May 24	From Marjorie Kinnan Rawlings
June 26	To Signe Toksvig (TxU-Hu)
September 20	To Helen McAfee (CtY)
October 8	*To Signe Toksvig* (TxU-Hu)
October 9	*To Irita Van Doren* (DLC)
October 11	To Margaret Dashiell (APS NcU)
October 19	*To Signe Toksvig* (TxU-Hu)
November 1	*To Signe Toksvig* (TxU-Hu)

November 6	From Signe Toksvig
November 15	To Irita Van Doren (DLC)
November 26	From Priscilla Cabell
December 4	*To Signe Toksvig* (TxU-Hu)
December 9	From Signe Toksvig
December 17	To Rebe Glasgow Tutwiler
December 18	To Signe Toksvig (TxU-Hu)
December 22	To Rebe Glasgow Tutwiler
December 27	*To Rebe Glasgow Tutwiler* (FU)
1945	
January 29	From Signe Toksvig
[February–March?]	To Rebe Glasgow Tutwiler (FU)
February 3	From Signe Toksvig
February 5	*To Signe Toksvig* (TxU-Hu)
February 5	*To Rebe Glasgow Tutwiler* (FU)
February 14	From Rebe Glasgow Tutwiler
February 27	From Bessie Zaban Jones
March 1	To Bessie Zaban Jones (MNS)
March 8	To Irita Van Doren (DLC)
March 23	*To Signe Toksvig* (TxU-Hu)
March 25	From Signe Toksvig
[March 30]	From Rebe Glasgow Tutwiler
April 4	To Rebe Glasgow Tutwiler
May 15	From Marjorie Kinnan Rawlings
May 15	From Signe Toksvig
[June 7]	To Rebe Glasgow Tutwiler (FU)
July 14	From Eleanor Brooks
July 14	To Signe Toksvig (TxU-Hu)
August 2	*To Irita Van Doren* (DLC)
August 16	*To Rebe Glasgow Tutwiler* (FU)
August 25	*To Rebe Glasgow Tutwiler* (FU)
September 8	To Rebe Glasgow Tutwiler (FU)
September 30	From Signe Toksvig
October 7	From Eleanor Brooks
October 14	To Signe Toksvig (TxU-Hu)
October 18	To Rebe Glasgow Tutwiler (APS FU)
November 9	From Marjorie Kinnan Rawlings
November 17	*To Marjorie Kinnan Rawlings*
Undated (alphabetical)	
Tuesday	To Sally Anderson & Kathleen (Mrs. Albert) Bourland (Provenance unknown)

Tuesday	To Sally Anderson & Kathleen (Mrs. Albert) Bourland (Provenance unknown)
n.d. [before 1927]	To Lucy Parke Chamberlayne Bagby (ViHi)
Tuesday	To Kathleen (Mrs. Albert) Bourland (Provenance unknown)
[early 1930s?]	To Josephine Clark
Saturday	From Katharine Cornell
Christmas Day	To Mary Johnson
n.d.	To Elizabeth Garver Jordan (APS NG–B)
Saturday	To Blanche Knopf (TxU–Hu)
Saturday [before 1915]	To Elizabeth Patterson
n.d.	To Emma Gray Trigg
Sunday	To Irita Van Doran (DLC)
n.d.	To Lily (Mrs. John Y. G.) Walker

Biographical and Geographical Register

All of EG's correspondents and any persons mentioned in the letters and known to EG, whether identified or unidentified, are included here. As elsewhere, the names of persons frequently mentioned are abbreviated. Multiple entries under the same name (Frank, for example) assume that the context in the letters identifies them; when this is not the case, they are briefly identified in a note following the relevant letter. For individuals to whom EG or her correspondents refer sometimes by full name and sometimes by a title (such as Miss), the title is listed in parentheses with the full name entry; entries are alphabetized according to full name rather than title. Individuals referred to only by title are listed accordingly. Descriptions for well-known public figures whom EG knew (writers, for example) are limited to highlights of their relationship to EG. Allusions in the letters to authors, historical figures, or living famous persons (such as political figures) whom EG did not know personally are identified in notes following the relevant letters. Geographical identifications are limited to those places EG visited or mentioned in letters but that are not easily identified with a standard atlas, guidebook, or other reference. Typically these are long- or short-term residences or places she frequented on her travels. A few place-names are identified in notes following the letters in which they are mentioned. The names of authors or recipients of correspondence included in this volume appear in italics.

Adams, J[ames] Donald ("Don") (1891–1968), editor, author, and literary critic best known for his column "Speaking of Books," which appeared in the *New York Times Book Review* beginning in 1943.
Addie, probably a domestic worker in RGT's household in Lexington, Virginia.
Agglesby, Mrs., unidentified correspondent of AGG.
A. H. See Harcourt, Alfred.
Akermann, unidentified Englishman living alone in a log cabin near Woodland Park, Colorado.
Alderman, Edwin Anderson, president of the University of Virginia after his installation on April 13, 1905. EG probably did not attend the ceremony, to which she was invited, because of her sister CGMcC's health.
Alfred. See Harcourt, Alfred.
Alsop, Joseph Wright, Jr. (1910–1989), reporter and later columnist for the *New York Herald Tribune*.
Alston, Mr., unidentified resident or visitor in Denver, Colorado.
Alya, Alya Adams, wife of J. Donald Adams.
Amélie. See Troubetzkoy, Amélie Rives.

Anderson, (Colonel) Archer, son of Joseph Reid Anderson, EG's paternal great-uncle. Joseph Reid Anderson was president of Richmond's Tredegar Iron Works, where EG's father and brother Frank also worked.

Anderson, Henry (1870–1954), partner in the Richmond law firm of Munford and Anderson and unsuccessful Republican candidate for governor of Virginia in 1921. Met EG in spring 1916; they became engaged on July 19, 1917. Commissioned as a colonel in charge of Red Cross operations in the Balkans during World War I; reputedly had an affair with Queen Marie of Romania. He and EG remained friends for the rest of her life, although her unflattering portrait of Anderson as "Harold S—" in *WW* suggests lingering bitterness on her part.

Anderson, James, EG's cook for more than thirty years and a legatee in her will.

Anderson, Laura E., Henry Anderson's mother.

Anderson, Mary, probably EG's cousin, perhaps related to Joseph Reid Anderson, EG's paternal great-uncle.

Anderson, Sally Archer (1863–1954), Richmond resident and cousin of EG.

Anne, Anne Van Doren (later Ross), daughter (born ca. 1915) of IVD and husband, Carl; author of unidentified book, published ca. 1941.

Anne (Little Anne), dog EG encountered on her 1927 trip to England.

Anne Virginia. See Bennett, (Miss) Anne Virginia.

Annie. See Clark, Annie Gholson Glasgow.

Anthony, Katharine Susan (1877–1965), American biographer; author of *Catherine the Great* (Knopf, 1925).

Appledoor, house rented by EG in Castine, Maine, in the summers of 1940 and 1941; located at the corner of Perkins and Madockawando and known as the Horsey Place, the house was owned by Ralph S. Wardwell. EG called it Appledoor for the apple trees framing the front entrance.

Archer, Cousin. See Anderson, (Colonel) Archer.

Arthur. See Glasgow, Arthur Graham.

Atherton, Gertrude Horn (1857–1948), prolific San Francisco writer.

A. V. See Bennett, (Miss) Anne Virginia.

B., Beulah. See Branch, Beulah (Mrs. John Kerr Branch).

Bagby, Ellen Matthews (1874–1960), daughter of George William Bagby and Lucy Parke Chamberlayne Bagby of Richmond.

Bagby, Lucy Parke Chamberlayne (1842–1927), Richmond resident, wife of George W. Bagby and mother of the prominent Richmond preservationist Ellen Matthews Bagby.

Bagley, Miss, unidentified Richmond resident and correspondent of EG.

Balch, (Mrs.) Emily Clark. See Clark, Emily.

Barbara, Barbara Van Doren (later Klaw) (1920–2002), daughter of IVD and husband Carl; author (under the pseudonym Martin Gale) of *A Pony Named*

Biographical and Geographical Register 277

Nubbin: A Story (New York: Viking, 1939), which her sister Margaret illustrated. Later became an editor of the monthly magazine *American Heritage*.

Barrows, EG's butler in London.

Baskin, Norton, hotelier in St. Augustine, Florida; husband of Marjorie Kinnan Rawlings (m. October 27, 1941).

Battle Avenue, house rented by EG in Castine, Maine, in the summers of 1943–1945.

Bayard, unidentified friend of Isa Glenn.

Beard, Mary R[itter] (1876–1958), historian and feminist activist. Her *America through Women's Eyes* (1933) included an essay by EG.

Becker, (Mrs.) May Lamberton (1873–1958), New York author and editor at the *New York Herald Tribune* and the *Saturday Review of Literature*.

Bell, Mr., unidentified acquaintance or relative of MJ, whose great-grandfather's surname was Bell.

Belmont, Eleanor Robson. See Robson, Eleanor.

Ben, husband of Lila Meade Valentine.

Bennett, (Miss) Anne Virginia (1884–1956), EG's live-in companion and secretary, first hired in 1910 as nurse for EG's ailing sister CGMcC; stayed to care for sister Emily and then father, Francis T. Glasgow. Served in France as Red Cross nurse 1918–1919; organized EG's household, took care of EG's affairs, and protected EG's work times. EG's will stipulated that AVB be allowed to remain in the house at One West Main Street as long as she wished. The income from EG's trust fund (less fifty dollars per month for James Anderson) went to AVB.

Bennett, Arnold (1867–1931), English novelist whom EG met during her 1914 trip to England. In *WW* she notes the "scintillating audacity of his wit" (204).

Berta. See Wellford, Roberta.

Betty, Miss, Elizabeth Patterson's mother, Elizabeth Anne Duval Patterson.

Beulah. See Branch, Beulah (Mrs. John Kerr Branch).

Billy, EG's white poodle, who died at age 16 in November 1938.

Birdie. See Richardson, Roberta.

Blair. See Niles, (Mary) Blair Rice.

Bob, EG's stage driver in Colorado in 1909.

Bonnibel. See Bonnie.

Bonnie, dog rescued in 1939 by EG and AVB for the SPCA.

Bourland, Kathleen (Mrs. Albert), Richmond acquaintance of EG.

Bowie, (Mrs.) Elizabeth (Lizzie) Branch (1861–1954), member of prominent Richmond Branch family; cousin to Effie Kerr Branch, who owned a villa in Castine, Maine, where EG summered, and to Margaret Branch, AGG's wife.

Branch, Beulah (Mrs. John Kerr Branch), sister-in-law of Margaret Branch

Glasgow, who was married to EG's brother AGG. Branch, an heiress, and her husband owned Villa Marsilio Ficino in Fiesole, Italy, where Glasgow and Carrie Duke stayed in summer 1937.

Branch, Blythe, brother to Effie Kerr Branch, John Kerr Branch, and Margaret Branch.

Branch, Effie Kerr, sister of Margaret Branch Glasgow, wife of AGG. She owned a villa, "The Play-House," in Castine, Maine, where EG later would spend her summers.

Branch, John Kerr, banker, brother of Margaret Branch Glasgow (AGG's wife), and husband of Beulah Branch.

Brickell, [Henry] Herschel (1889–1952), writer; he and his wife, Norma, were friends of EG.

Brooks, Eleanor (d. 1946), first wife of Van Wyck Brooks (m. 1911); EG's friend and correspondent beginning in 1939.

Brooks, Van Wyck (1886–1963), husband of EG's correspondent Eleanor Brooks; professor of American literature; author of *The Flowering of New England: 1815–1865* (1936) and other works. In *The Confident Years: 1885–1915* Brooks praises EG as a hopeful writer with faith in human goodness.

Brown, Gertrude Foster (1867–1956), concert pianist and suffragist; probably met EG in about 1913 while the latter was living in New York City.

Brown, Lucy (Mrs. Arthur Page), resident of San Francisco; perhaps met EG in Colorado in 1909.

Brown, Thalia Newton, secretary of the American Woman's Association in New York.

Bryan, Ella Howard, relative of John Stewart Bryan and fan of EG's writings.

Bryan, (John) Stewart, president of the College of William and Mary and chair of the board of trustees of the Richmond Public Library. At his invitation, EG received an honorary Doctor of Laws degree from the College of William and Mary in spring 1939.

Bryan, Winnie, Richmond acquaintance of EG; perhaps related to John Stewart Bryan.

Bryce, Carroll, unidentified butler admired by EG.

Budrau, dog EG encountered on her 1927 trip to England.

Burgess, [Frank] Gelett (1866–1951), editor of *The Lark,* a magazine that published his famous quatrain beginning "I never saw a purple cow" in the first issue (May 1895). Known for his word play, Burgess coined the word "blurb" (dust jacket description). He introduced EG and Zona Gale.

Burnett, (Mrs.) Frances Hodgson (1849–1924), English-born American writer best known for her children's books, including *Little Lord Fauntleroy* (1886) and *The Secret Garden* (1910); perhaps involved in unidentified plagiarism case with Signe Toksvig.

Butcher, Fanny, writer for the *Chicago Tribune.*

Biographical and Geographical Register 279

C., Dr., unidentified visitor (with Mrs. Clark) to EG or AGG in London in 1927; perhaps, although spelled differently, Dr. Clarke (see Clarke, Dr.) or a relative of EG's friends Adele or Emily Clark; perhaps a relative by marriage of EG's sister Annie Glasgow Clark; perhaps Dr. Collier, Louise Collier Willcox's father.

C, Mrs., unidentified; traveled on the *Conti di Savoia* with EG to Italy in 1937.

Cabell. See Tutwiler, Carrington Cabell.

Cabell, James Branch (1879–1958), prolific Virginia author whose works include the series of novels collectively known as the *Biography of Manuel*. He and EG were sometimes friends, sometimes rivals, and sometimes coworkers. With irony as well as respect, perhaps, they dedicated novels to each other: Cabell's *Something about Eve* (1927) and EG's *TSTF* (1929). Cabell in later years felt that EG failed to credit him for help he provided with her work.

Cabell, Mr. See Cabell, James Branch.

Cabell, Mrs. Henry, unidentified traveler with EG on the *Conti di Savoia* to Italy in 1937.

Cabell, Priscilla ("Percie"), James Branch Cabell's first wife.

Canby, Henry Seidel (1878–1961), chair of the editorial board and cofounder of the *Saturday Review of Literature,* chair of the editorial board of the Book of the Month Club, and husband of Marion Canby.

Canby, Marion Ponsonby Gause, poet, author of *High Mowing* (1932) and *On My Way* (1937), EG's friend and correspondent beginning in 1936. Wife (m. 1907) of Henry Seidel Canby. EG consistently misspells Canby's first name as "Marian."

Canfield, Dorothy. See Fisher, Dorothy [Dorothea Frances] Canfield.

Carl. See Van Doren, Carl Clinton.

Carlo. See Van Vechten, Carl.

Caroline, household servant of EG.

Carrie. See Duke, (Mrs.) Caroline Coleman.

Carrington. See Tutwiler, Carrington Cabell, Jr.

Carrol, presumably EG's alternative spelling for Lafayette Carroll.

Carroll, Lafayette, unidentified friend or business associate of AGG in London.

Cary. See McCormack, Sally Cary Glasgow.

Castine, Maine, village overlooking Penobscot Bay where EG spent summers from 1939 to 1945. See Appledoor, Battle Avenue, Littleplace, and Spruce Knoll, the houses EG rented in Castine.

Castle Hill, seat of the Rives family of Virginia, and home to EG's friend Amélie Rives Troubetzkoy.

Catherine, EG's household servant in 1939.

Chamberlain, John [Rensselaer] (1903–1995), assistant editor of the *New York Times Book Review* and editor of a daily book column for the *New York Times;* his successor was Francis Hackett.

Chanler, John Armstrong, New York attorney and first husband (m. 1888) of ART.
Chestnut Hill, residential area of Philadelphia where RGT lived (ca. 1914–1937), first at 430 W. Chestnut Street and then at 9000 Crefeld Street.
Christine. See Willcox, Christine.
Chummy, dog EG encountered on her 1927 trip to England.
Cindy, RGT's dog Cinders.
Claasen, Clara, staff member at Doubleday, Doran.
Claridge's, fashionable London department store frequented by EG.
Clark, Adele, EG's friend and member of the Equal Suffrage League (later the Virginia League of Women Voters) in Richmond.
Clark, Annette I., secretary of the board of trustees for Smith College, which offered EG an honorary doctorate in 1944.
Clark, Annie Gholson Glasgow (1857–1917), EG's older sister; married Frank Tarleton Clark, with whom she had a son, Francis Glasgow ("Glasgow"), and a daughter, Josephine.
Clark, Emily (1893–1953), EG's friend, reviewer, author, and founding editor of the Richmond-based literary journal *The Reviewer* (1921–1924); married wealthy adventurer Edwin Swift Balch.
Clark, Francis Glasgow (Glasgow) (1899–1984), EG's nephew, son of Annie Glasgow Clark.
Clark, Josephine (1891–1984), EG's niece, daughter of Annie Glasgow Clark. Josephine, who was born at One West Main Street, was close to her aunt, whom she called "Aunt Lellie."
Clark, Jubillant Mai, unidentified resident of New York.
Clark, Mrs., unidentified visitor (with Dr. C.) to EG or AGG in London in 1927; perhaps married to a misspelled Dr. Clarke; perhaps a relative of EG's friends Adele or Emily Clark (or Adele herself; EG on at least one occasion addressed a letter to her as Mrs. Clark); or perhaps a relative by marriage of EG's sister Annie Glasgow Clark.
Clark, Mrs. Meade, unidentified person who sent EG flowers as she embarked for her 1930 trip to England and Scotland; perhaps related to Emily Clark Balch.
Clarke, unidentified.
Clarke, Dr., unidentified friend or acquaintance of RGT; perhaps a misspelling of Clark.
Clephan, Annie, daughter of the wealthy English art collector Edwin Clephan.
Clifford, Mrs., popular English novelist and dramatist Lucy (Mrs. W. K.) Clifford (ca. 1853–1829), whom EG knew in England; EG describes her as the "ever kind Mrs. Clifford" (*WW* 206).
Coleman, Carrie. See Duke, (Mrs.) Caroline Coleman.
Coleman, Lucy Singleton (1869–1936), sister of Carrie Coleman Duke; suffrage supporter; principal of Richmond Training School for Kindergartners.

Coleman, Mattie, domestic worker in EG's household.

Coleman, Mrs., resident of Richmond; probably the mother of Carrie Coleman Duke and Lucy Singleton Coleman.

Colman, Mrs., unidentified resident of Washington, D.C. EG declined her invitation, perhaps to speak, in April 1926.

Comstock, Lillian A., correspondent of EG, probably a secretary or personal assistant to Samuel A. Everitt of Doubleday, Doran.

Congreve, Marjorie Glasgow, EG's niece, daughter of AGG and Margaret Glasgow; married Scotsman Cochrane Congreve in London in October 1934.

Conrad, Jessie George, wife of Joseph Conrad and occasional correspondent of EG. During her 1927 trip to England, EG visited Jessie Conrad at "The Old Farmhouse," the house at Oswalds, Bishopsbourne (near Godalming), where the Conrads had moved in October 1919.

Conrad, Joseph (1857–1924), Polish-born English novelist (born Teodor Jósef Konrad Korzeniowski) whom EG met in England in 1914 at his home, Capel House, in Kent. During his first visit to the United States, in 1923, Conrad declined EG's invitation to Richmond.

Conrad, Mrs. See Conrad, Jessie George.

Cooper, Page, staff member at Doubleday, Doran and Company publishers.

Copeland, Mrs., unidentified wife of a Mr. Copeland who knew EG's father, perhaps through Tredeger Iron Works, where EG's father worked, or through one of Mr. Glasgow's Richmond causes (such as prison reform).

Coralie, MJ's cousin.

Cordelia, cook and housekeeper for EG during an early fall visit to Ventnor, New Jersey, in 1935; married to Frank, also a servant for EG at the same time.

Cornell, Katharine (1893–1974), actress in major plays in the United States and Europe, including *Romeo and Juliet* in 1934, *Saint Joan* in 1936, and *Antigone* in 1946.

Creed, Samuel. See Glasgow, Samuel Creed.

Cross, Mr., unidentified resident of Richmond.

Crutchfield, Elizabeth Patterson. See Patterson, Elizabeth.

Curtis, Mrs., unidentified resident of English almshouse at Glastonbury Abbey, where EG visited in 1927.

Dahl, Mrs., unidentified; perhaps a domestic employee of EG.

Dan. See Longwell, Dan.

Dashiell, Margaret (Mrs. J. P.?), artist and supporter of the Richmond SPCA; EG's occasional correspondent.

Dauban, Jeanne, French agent of the Prix Femina and organizer of the Prix Femina Americain (est. 1931).

Davis, EG's table steward on the SS *Olympic* for her voyage to England in June 1927.

Davis, Mr., acquaintance of IVD; perhaps Howard Davis, business manager for the *New York Herald Tribune* (ca. 1930 and after).

Dean, Elaine J., African American English teacher at Cardozo High School, Washington, D.C. (A.B. Howard University; M.A. Ohio State University), who wrote EG in admiration of *ITOL*.

Deland, Margaret (1857–1945), born Margaretta Wade Campbell in Allegheny, Pennsylvania; prolific author of essays, fiction, and poetry.

Dimple, perhaps a nickname for EG's dog Jeremy.

Doctors Hospital, EG sometimes was hospitalized here; located at East End Avenue and 87th Street, New York City.

Don. See Adams, J[ames] Donald.

Donald. See Adams, J[ames] Donald.

Doubleday, Frank N., founder of Doubleday, Page and Company in 1906.

Doubleday, Nelson, son of Frank Nelson Doubleday; joined the firm (which became Doubleday, Doran in 1927) in 1922.

Duke, (Mrs.) Caroline Coleman ("Carrie"), EG's close friend from childhood; her family owned the property adjacent to Jerdone Castle, the EG's family's summer country retreat. An antique dealer (her store was located across from the Jefferson Hotel in Richmond), Carrie traveled with EG, stayed with her when AVB served in France as a Red Cross nurse, was married in 1919 at One West Main, was a frequent visitor during EG's final serious illness, and, with AVB, signed the telegram announcing EG's death.

Duke, Jane Taylor (1883–1965), sister-in-law of Carrie Coleman Duke; author of magazine articles on Virginia homes and gardens; golf partner of EG (see Duke, "Golfing with Genius").

Dwyer, Ada (1863–1952), later Ada Dwyer Russell; actress and friend of Eleanor Robson. After 1912 the companion and, later, editor of poet Amy Lowell.

Edith, unidentified cousin of EG and resident of Virginia Beach.

Eleanor. See Musselman, Eleanor; see also Brooks, Eleanor, and Robson, Eleanor.

Elizabeth. See Patterson, Elizabeth (Crutchfield).

Ella, household servant of EG.

Ellsworth, a town about twenty miles from Castine, Maine, which EG sometimes visited.

Ellwanger, Mrs., unidentified resident or visitor in Colorado Springs, Colorado.

Eloise, MJ's sister.

Emily. See Houston, Emily Taylor Glasgow; also Clark, Emily.

Eva. See H., Mrs.

Evans, Mr., employee (perhaps editor or publisher) of Heinemann, the prestigious London publishing firm (est. 1890).

Evans, Mrs., host of 1927 London luncheon honoring EG; wife of Mr. Evans (above).

Everitt, Raymond, unidentified; perhaps a literary agent who approached EG in 1934 about representing her.

Farnsworth, Alice (Mrs. George James), EG's summer neighbor in Castine, Maine.

Farrar, John Chipman (1896–1974), author, editor (of *Bookman*), and publisher; co-founder (1929) of Farrar & Rinehart; founder (1946) of Farrar, Straus & Co.

Few, (Dr.) William P., president of Duke University at the time EG received her honorary doctorate in 1938.

F. H. See Hackett, Francis.

Fiesole, Italy, location of the Villa Marsilio Ficino, given (according to EG, *WW* 264) by Lorenzo Medici to Marsilio Ficino after the latter's translation of Plato. Owner Beulah Branch (widow of John Kerr Branch) hosted EG and Carrie Duke at the villa in 1937.

Fisher, Dorothy [Dorothea Frances] Canfield (1879–1958), well-known novelist (*The Bent Twig*, 1915; *The Brimming Cup*, 1921) and prolific translator who lived in Arlington, Vermont (about fifteen miles north of Bennington). It is not clear when EG and Fisher met.

Forbes, Miss, unidentified correspondent who requested EG's notes for a lecture on *VOI*.

Frances, domestic worker in EG's household.

Frank. See Glasgow, Francis Thomas (brother); also see Morley, Frank Vigor; Paradise, (Mr.) Frank; and Swinnerton, Frank. The domestic worker Cordelia's husband also was named Frank.

Freeman, domestic worker of EG.

French, Lillie Hamilton (b. 1854), writer; secretary and editor of the journal of the National Institute of Social Sciences, which awarded EG a medal in 1916 (presented 1917).

Frothingham, Cornelia, civic activist in Philadelphia; friend of Agnes Repplier.

G, Hallie Belle, unidentified; sent flowers to EG when the latter embarked for her 1937 trip to Italy.

Gale, Zona (1874–1938), Wisconsin fiction writer and advocate for social reform, best known for stories set in the fictional Friendship Village, based on Gale's home town of Portage; her dramatization of her 1920 novel, *Miss Lulu Bett*, won a Pulitzer Prize in 1921.

Galsworthy, Ada, wife of John Galsworthy (m. 1902); EG met her at her home in England in 1914.

Galsworthy, John (1867–1933), English writer of novels and short stories, especially known for the works that make up *The Forsyte Saga* (1922); met EG at his home in England in 1914.

Gannett, (Mr.) Lewis (1891–1966), author of a popular column, "Books and Things," for the *New York Herald Tribune*.

Gardner, Mary Carter Anderson (Mrs. Charles S.), Richmond resident and reader of EG's writings. As Miss Mary Carter Anderson, the only teacher at the Buttermilk Institute, a school in Hanover County, Virginia.

Garst, Eleanor Hubbard, book editor at *Better Homes and Gardens* magazine; EG declined her invitation to contribute garden photographs of One West Main and a short statement about "How I Happened to Write."

Gause, Mrs., unidentified resident of or visitor to Castine, Maine; gave a luncheon for EG in Castine in 1939.

Geroni, P. G., Franciscan monk who acted as EG's interpreter in Assisi, Italy; EG misspells his name "Jeroni."

Gian-Luca, fictional character in Radclyffe Hall's novel *Adam's Breed* (1926), to whom EG frequently refers. Gian-Luca's forest is the New Forest.

Glasgow, EG's nephew (son of her sister Annie Glasgow Clark).

Glasgow, Anne Jane Gholson (1831–1893), EG's mother, whose nervous disposition EG ascribes to sensitivity and the strain of bearing eleven children (the first stillborn and two others dead within one year of their birth).

Glasgow, Annie Gholson. See Clark, Annie Gholson Glasgow.

Glasgow, Arthur Graham (1865–1955), EG's older brother; successful engineer, founding partner in Humphreys and Glasgow of London (est. 1892), a fuel plant. AGG provided financial support to EG for trips, house remodeling, and medical expenses.

Glasgow, Betty, unidentified relative (perhaps by marriage) of EG.

Glasgow, Emily Taylor. See Houston, Emily Taylor Glasgow.

Glasgow, Francis Thomas (1829–1916), EG's father, whom EG characterizes as sternly Protestant and emotionally distant. Worked for Tredeger Iron Works for most of his adult life, first in Virginia counties away from Richmond and then, as manager, in the main factory in Richmond.

Glasgow, Francis Thomas (Frank) (1870–1909), EG's brother; committed suicide in his office at Tredegar Iron Works, where he worked with his father, on April 7, 1909, a few days after EG reached London.

Glasgow, John McNutt, EG's paternal uncle.

Glasgow, Joseph Reid, EG's paternal uncle; also EG's brother (1860–1876), who died of diphtheria at age sixteen, when EG was three.

Glasgow, Margaret Branch, EG's sister-in-law. A celebrated beauty, she married AGG in Richmond in 1902.

Glasgow, Margaretta Gordon (Aunt Maggie), EG's paternal aunt.

Glasgow, Marjorie. See Congreve, Marjorie Glasgow.

Glasgow, Mary Jane, EG's paternal aunt.

Glasgow, Rebe Gordon. See Tutwiler, Rebe Gordon Glasgow.

Glasgow, Rebecca Anderson (Aunt Bec), EG's paternal aunt, who encouraged EG in her reading and writing; according to EG, "the perfect storyteller" (*WW* 24).

Glasgow, Sally Cary. See McCormack, Sally Cary Glasgow.

Glasgow, Samuel Creed (1875), EG's infant brother, born October 14, 1875; died of diptheria at two weeks.

Glenn, Isa (1888–1951), novelist, author of *Heat* (1926), *Southern Charm* (1928), and *Mr. Darlington's Dangerous Age* (1933), among others. Her brother, a Richmond attorney, defended James Branch Cabell during an obscenity trial for his novel *Jürgen*.

Gordon, Mrs., unidentified Richmond tailor.

Gordon, Mrs. [Howard S.], unidentified fan of EG's *VOI*.

Green Forest, EG's father's ancestral home in Rockbridge County, Virginia.

Greenslet, Ferris (1875–1959), editor in chief at Houghton Mifflin who tried in 1934 to sign EG to his firm.

H., Mrs., Eva (Mrs. Alexander Crombie) Humphreys, wife of AGG's business partner Alexander Crombie Humphreys.

H—, Mr. See Humphreys, Alexander Crombie.

Haardt, Sara. See Mencken, Sara Powell Haardt.

Hackett, Francis (1883–1962), Irish-born critic, journalist, and husband of Signe Toksvig. Hackett wrote for *The New Republic* and the *New York Times*, as well as writing history and fiction.

Haddon, Judge, unidentified.

Hadfield, Lady, the former Frances Wickersham, sister of U.S. attorney general George W. Wickersham and Red Cross volunteer in France during World War I. According to some, she groomed Henry Anderson in social skills.

Hall, [Marguerite] Radclyffe (1883–1943), or "John" to her closest friends; English author (with an American mother) of novels including *Adam's Breed* (1926) and *The Well of Loneliness* (1928), which was censored in England and the United States for its representation of lesbianism. First met EG in London in June or July 1930 after corresponding for three years.

Hamilton, Nina (Duchess of Hamilton), humanitarian activist (founder of Ferne Humanitarian Institute for Children and Animals) whose English country home, Ferne, EG visited in 1927. Another home was a castle in Dungavel, Scotland.

Hansen, Harry, writer for the *Chicago Daily News*.

Harcourt, Alfred (1881–1954), publisher, cofounder in 1919 of the publishing firm that became Harcourt Brace Jovanovich. Harcourt was president of the firm until 1941.

Harcourt, Ellen Knowles (1889–1984), assistant to Alfred Harcourt at the newly formed Harcourt, Brace & Co., in 1919. By 1920 she had been elected to the board of directors, the first woman in publishing to hold such a position. She later married Alfred Harcourt.

Hardy, F. E., Thomas Hardy's wife, whom EG met in 1914 and 1927 and corresponded with occasionally.

Hardy, Thomas (1840–1928), English novelist and poet, author of *Tess of the D'Urbervilles* (1891) and *Jude the Obscure* (1896), among others. EG especially admired Hardy, met him on two trips to England (1914 and 1927), and visited him and his wife at their home, Max Gate, in Dorchester.

Hart, Antoinette (Mrs. Alan Lindsay), Richmond resident, probably a distant cousin of EG.

Hartley, Mr., unidentified friend of Hugh Walpole; perhaps writer L. P. Hartley (1895–1972).

Harvie, Lu, unidentified cousin of EG.

Hasley, chauffeur employed by AGG; drove for EG and Carrie Duke during their 1927 tour of the English countryside.

Hazlitt, Henry (1894–1993), American editor, critic, and author best known for his financial writings. His connection to EG is not known; it is possible they met through H. L. Mencken, for whom Hazlitt worked for a time, or through IVD and New York publishing circles.

Hemming, Mrs., perhaps the proprietor of a beauty salon in London to which EG and Carrie Duke went in 1927.

Henry. See Anderson, Henry; Mencken, (Mr.) H[enry] L[ouis] ("our Henry" to CL; "your Henry" to Sara Powell Haardt Mencken); Canby, Henry Seidel.

Hergesheimer, Joseph (1880–1954), popular American novelist and short story writer.

Herschel. See Brickell, [Henry] Herschel.

Heth, Miss, unidentified assistant or acquaintance during EG's 1915 trip to San Francisco.

Hoffman, Malvina (1887–1966), American sculptor whose works are on permanent display in New York (Metropolitan Museum and the American Museum of Natural History), Chicago (Field Museum of Natural History), and Washington, D.C. (National Museum of Women in the Arts). EG may have met Hoffman through their mutual friends the Alexander Weddells.

Holden, Agnes Johnson, sister of poet, editor, and public figure Robert Underwood Johnson (1853–1937); probably met EG through Robert Johnson's connections to the American Academy of Arts and Letters.

Holliday, Terence (ca. 1885–1969), with his wife, Elsa Detmold Holliday (1891–1991), owned Holliday Bookshop, which EG patronized. Located after 1925 at 49 West Forty-ninth Street in New York City, the well-known shop sold rare and unusual editions.

Hollywood, cemetery (dedicated in 1849) in Richmond where many of Glasgow's family members were buried, and where EG is buried. Its interred include presidents, Confederate heroes, and members of Richmond society.

Hopper, Katharine Baird, unidentified resident of Baltimore and correspondent of EG.

Horsey Place. See Appledoor.

Houston, Emily Taylor Glasgow (1855–1913), EG's eldest sister; married Herbert Tedd Houston.

Howard. See Jones, Howard Mumford.

Howe, Mr., unidentified wealthy visitor in Woodland Park, Colorado, in 1909; perhaps related to the U.S. inventor Elias Howe (1819–1867), who, at his death, had amassed a fortune from his sewing machine patent.

Howland, Marie, unidentified fan of *ITOL*.

Hugh. See Walpole, Sir Hugh Seymour.

Huidekoper, Mrs. [Rush?], probably the wife of the writer Rush Huidekoper, author of *The Cat* (1895).

Humphreys, Alexander Crombie, AGG's business partner in Humphreys and Glasgow of London. He and his wife, Eva, hosted EG on her first trip abroad in 1896.

Hurricane, the lodge in Hurricane, Essex County, New York, where EG and her sister RGT stayed in 1906.

Hurst, Fannie (1887?–1968), prolific Ohio-born author of novels, short stories, radio scripts, and other writings, including *Imitation of Life* (1933), which was filmed in 1934 and 1959.

Irene, domestic worker in EG's household.

Irita. See Van Doren, Irita.

J. See Sully, Julia.

James. See Anderson, James; also Cabell, James Branch.

James, Henry (1843–1916), highly regarded American novelist who became a naturalized British citizen in 1915. EG first met James, whom she described as "imposing" and "urbane," during her 1914 trip to England, and encountered him occasionally at social events during her other visits to England (*WW* 206).

Jay. See Jay's Mourning Warehouse.

Jay's Mourning Warehouse, a fashionable and modern shop in London's Regent Street in the West End district, where EG shopped when in London.

Jays. See Jay's Mourning Warehouse.

Jean, unidentified friend or relative of EG.

Jefferson Hotel, hotel at 101 West Franklin Street in Richmond where EG's guests sometimes stayed and EG conducted personal business (such as hairdressing); now a national historic landmark.

Jeffery, Mrs. Richard, unidentified Richmond resident; perhaps a neighbor of EG's family.

Jerdone Castle, the summer country retreat near Richmond owned by the Glasgows from 1879 to 1887. There, EG says, she began writing, and developed her love of nature.

Jeremy, EG's beloved Sealyham terrier, given to her by Henry Anderson for Christmas 1921; died September 5, 1929.

Jeroni, Padre. See Geroni, P. G.

Jim, the husband or other male relative of Agnes B. Reese.

Jo, unidentified friend (perhaps romantic) of J[ames] Donald Adams.

Jock, one of RGT's pets.

John. See Hall, [Marguerite] Radclyffe; also see Branch, John Kerr; Marsh, John.

John, Uncle. See Glasgow, John McNutt.

Johns, Ann Page (Mrs. Frank), writer, niece of Thomas Nelson Page; requested EG's permission to name some of her verses the "Queenborough Poems" for EG's fictional town.

Johnston, Jas., unidentified; perhaps MKR's mistranscription of Jos., or Joseph (Joe).

Johnston, Joseph Eggleston (1807–1891), Confederate general and relative of MJ and her cousin Coralie.

Johnston, Mary (1870–1936), Virginia writer of popular fiction including *To Have and to Hold* (1900). Johnston moved with her family to Richmond in 1902, at which time she may have met EG. Became EG's close friend, especially in the first decade of the twentieth century, when the two shared an interest in women's suffrage.

Johnston, Mrs., unidentified; perhaps a relative of MJ.

Johnston, Walter, MJ's brother.

Jones, Bessie Zaban (1898–1997), wife (m. June 1927) of professor Howard Mumford Jones; first met EG in June 1930 in Chapel Hill, North Carolina, where EG received an honorary Doctor of Letters. Worked as copy editor and advertising manager at the University of North Carolina Press before moving to Ann Arbor, Michigan, and then to Cambridge, Massachusetts. The Joneses visited Richmond and stayed at Glasgow's home in late December 1936, when they attended the Modern Language Association meeting there.

Jones, Howard Mumford (1892–1950), professor at the University of Texas, University of Michigan, and Harvard University who helped encourage the development of American literature as a scholarly field. He wrote intelligently (and favorably) about EG's place in American letters.

Jones, Lizzie, EG's childhood caregiver (whom she called her mammy), who encouraged EG's story-telling imagination. Jones subsequently worked for Elizabeth Patterson's family in about 1880, when EG was seven.

Jones, Llewellyn, unidentified journalist or editor in the Chicago area.

Jordan, Elizabeth Garver (1865–1947), journalist and suffragist named editor of *Harper's Bazar* in 1900. EG probably met Jordan around 1915 in New York.

Joseph, Uncle. See Glasgow, Joseph Reid.

Josephine. See Clark, Josephine.

Joy, EG's pet Irish terrier, acquired around 1901.

Julia. See Sully, Julia.

Katherine, unidentified cousin of EG and resident of Virginia Beach.

Kauser, Alice (1872–1945), well-established literary agent (especially representing dramatists) in New York.

Kentore, Lady, English women's suffrage sympathizer; perhaps an acquaintance EG made through her brother AGG and his wife.

Kerr, Sophie (1880–1965), novelist and short story writer.

Kibble, Rhoda, EG's mother's childhood "mammy."

Killman, Mr., unidentified publisher of Kate Douglas Wiggin.

King, Blanche T. (Mrs. George T.), treasurer of Sheltering Arms Hospital (charity) in Richmond.

King, Mr., unidentified friend or business associate of AGG in London.

Knopf, Blanche (née Wolf), business partner and wife (m. 1916) of publisher Alfred Knopf, with whom she cofounded Alfred A. Knopf, Inc., in 1915.

Knopf, (Mr.) Alfred (1892–1984), prominent publisher; in 1915 he and Blanche Wolf (later Knopf) cofounded the publishing firm Alfred A. Knopf, Inc., which became synonymous with good taste and quality in publishing.

Krock, Arthur (1886–1974), Pulitzer Prize–winning journalist who worked in Louisville and Washington, D.C., before joining the *New York Times* in 1927.

Lambs, EG's nickname for Billy and Jeremy, her dogs.

Lankes, Mr., Julius J. Lankes (1884–1960), artist best known for his woodcuts, including those used as illustrations for EG's novels. EG used a woodcut of her Richmond home at One West Main Street first as a Christmas card in 1927 and later as the frontispiece for the *Virginia Edition* volume of *Life and Gabriella*.

Leighton, Clare Veronica Hope (1899–1989), artist who emigrated from England to the United States in 1939; naturalized in 1945. Although also a writer, CL is best known for her wood engravings; her illustrations appeared in the *New Left Review* and in many books, including reissues of Thomas Hardy's novels.

Lelia, unidentified friend of EG; her granddaughter Lelia Ann Munce Rowe (College of William and Mary, class of 1940) signed the back of the photograph of EG reproduced in this volume.

Liberty's, fashionable clothing and furniture shop in London's West End, where EG sometimes shopped.

Lind-af-Hageby, (Miss) E[melia] A[ugusta] L[ouise] (1878–1963), Swedish-born anti-vivisectionist, humanitarian worker, and friend of Lady Nina Hamilton, both of whom EG met in 1927 in England.

Littleplace, house in Castine, Maine, owned by Mrs. Alan Tucker (who spelled it Little Place) and rented by EG during the summer of 1939.

Lizbeth. See Patterson, Elizabeth (Lizzie).

Lizzie. See Patterson, Elizabeth; Jones, Lizzie; Bowie, (Mrs.) Elizabeth Branch.

Longwell, Dan, editor with Doubleday, Doran and Company.

Louise. See Willcox, Louise Collier.

Loveman, Amy, editor for the *Saturday Review of Literature.*

290   *Biographical and Geographical Register*

Lucas, Elizabeth, antique dealer in London from whom EG purchased china dogs for her collection.

Lucy. See Coleman, Lucy Singleton; also a domestic worker of EG.

Lutie, unidentified; probably MKR's mistranscription.

Lyon, (Dr.) John Henry Hobart, professor at Columbia University whose class EG visited as a speaker in October 1938.

Mabie, Hamilton (1845–1916), American editor, critic, and writer who, with his wife, was a friend of EG's correspondent Ruth McEnery Stuart.

Mackenzie, Jean Kenyon (1874–1936), author known especially for her books about Africa.

Macy, (Miss) Gertrude, manager of the actress Katharine Cornell.

Maggie, Aunt. See Glasgow, Margaretta Gordon.

Mahony, Mrs., according to EG, aunt of the unidentified Richmond resident Mrs. Richard Jeffery.

Malcolm, Miss, unidentified acquaintance of MJ.

Mansfield, Mrs. Damon, unidentified host during EG's 1915 trip to San Francisco.

Margaret. See Glasgow, Margaret Branch; also Margaret Van Doren (later Bevans), IVD's daughter (b. 1917), who, at age fourteen, illustrated a children's book, *The Black Pup* by Anne Brooks (New York: Viking, 1938).

Maria, domestic worker for EG.

Marjorie. See Congreve, Marjorie Glasgow.

Marsh, John, husband of Margaret Mitchell.

Martin, Nathaniel, EG's chauffeur.

Mary. See Johnston, Mary; also the name of more than one of EG's temporary domestic workers, including "the Bishop's Mary," who worked for an unidentified Richmond family. An unidentified Mary was EG's dinner guest in Ventnor, New Jersey, in 1935; also Don and Alya Adams's daughter.

Mary, Aunt. See Glasgow, Mary Jane.

Mary Ellen, unidentified; adopted daughter of Jane Williams.

Mattie. See Coleman, Mattie.

Maule, Harry Edward, editor with Doubleday.

Maymont, one hundred–acre estate and landscaped grounds on the James River, completed in 1893 by the wealthy Richmonders James Henry Dooley and his wife, Sallie Dooley; bequeathed to the city of Richmond. EG walked there on at least one occasion, in 1939.

Maynard, Mrs., unidentified Richmond resident sympathetic to the SPCA.

Maynell, W. B. See Meynell, W[ilfred].

Mayo, Betsy Burke, graduate student at Southern Methodist University (Dallas, Texas). Under Professor E. E. Leisy, with whom EG corresponded briefly in 1939, wrote a master's thesis entitled "The Virginian Woman of the New South" in EG's novels.

McAfee, Helen, editor at *Yale Review.*

McClintic, Guthrie (1893–1961), stage director, producer, and husband of the actress Katharine Cornell.

McCormack, George Walter (1868–1894), Charleston attorney who married EG's sister CGMcC in 1892. Encouraged the younger EG's intellectual development. He committed suicide on June 17, 1894.

McCormack, Mrs., unidentified resident of Norfolk, Virginia; perhaps related to CGMcC's deceased husband.

McCormack, Sally Cary Glasgow (1863–1911), EG's older sister Cary; married George Walter McCormack in 1892. Encouraged EG's writing and served as an intellectual guide before her own death, after a long illness with cancer, in August 1911.

McKee, Mr., Benjamin Harrison ("Baby") McKee (b. 1887), grandson of President Benjamin Harrison; he received much public exposure as a child living in the White House. EG met him on board the SS *Homeric* en route to England in 1930.

Meade, Julian R[utherfoord], author of *I Live in Virginia* (New York: Longmans, Green and Company, 1935), which contained an unflattering (and unfair, she felt) portrait of EG.

Mencken, (Mr.) H[enry] L[ouis] (1880–1956), editor, journalist, and writer from Baltimore, most closely associated with *The American Mercury* (which he cofounded) and *The Smart Set*. Married the writer Sara Haardt in 1930.

Mencken, Sara Powell Haardt (1898–1935), writer and critic; probably met EG in October 1928 when she interviewed her for an article in *The Bookman*. Married H. L. Mencken in 1930; contracted tuberculosis in 1925, and died in 1935 of meningitis.

Mercer, Mrs., wealthy Philadelphia woman, according to EG, whom CGMcC visited in 1884.

Merrill, Mr. (George F.), teacher at John H. Powell's Richmond Female Seminary, 3 East Grace Street, where EG briefly attended school as a child.

Meynell, W[ilfred] B. (1852–1948), author, editor, and husband of the poet and essayist Alice Meynell.

Milton, Mrs. Marshall, owner of boardinghouse in Richmond at 20 West Franklin Street, near the Jefferson Hotel.

Minnie, unidentified; perhaps a domestic worker for RGT.

Mitchell, Margaret (1900–1949), author of *Gone with the Wind* (1936), Pulitzer Prize winner and successful motion picture in 1939; probably met EG around November 1940.

Mitchell, M. Jeannette, English resident of Nottingham who wrote EG of her admiration for *The Builders*.

Mitcoff, Elena, resident of Newark, Delaware, who wrote EG of her admiration for *ITOL*.

Molly. See Johnston, Mary.

Montague, Andrew Jackson, governor of Virginia.

Monty, Mary, reader and EG fan from Lehighton, Pennsylvania.

Moore, Anne Carsall, unidentified; sent flowers to EG for the latter's 1930 voyage to England and Scotland.

Morley, Frank Vigor (1899–1980), author and publisher; chosen by EG in about 1935 as one of her literary executors (with IVD).

Morris, Miss, unidentified Richmond tailor.

Morrow, Elizabeth C., chair of the Prix Femina Americaine.

Moulton, (Mrs.) Louise Chandler (1835–1908), American author and host (with her husband, the publisher William U. Moulton) in Boston and New York literary salons. EG met Moulton in Paris in 1905, introduced by letter from their mutual friend Amélie Rives Troubetzkoy.

Munce, Mr., unidentified member of Men's League in Richmond, associated with the women's suffrage movement there.

Munford, [Robert] Beverley, attorney and member of old Richmond family; partner in law firm Munford, Hunton, Williams, and Anderson; married to Mary Cooke Branch.

Munford, Miss, probably Mary Branch Munford, sister of Elizabeth (Lizzie) Branch; after the Civil War the sisters ran both boardinghouses and schools, one of which EG attended as a child, in Richmond.

Munroe, Mrs. Vernon, acting chair and representative of the American committee for the Prix Femina, an annual French literary award.

Murray, (Dr.) Joseph J. (b. 1890), author of books on the birds of Virginia, including *The Land Birds of Rockbridge County, Virginia* (Albion, New York: np, 1936).

Musselman, Eleanor, friend with whom CL stayed in Baltimore when the latter first arrived to live in the United States in January 1939.

Nathaniel. See Martin, Nathaniel.

Needham, family home of EG's mother, Anne Jane Gholson, in Cumberland County, Virginia.

Nelson. See Doubleday, Nelson.

Newman, Frances (1883–1928), witty and daring author of *The Hard-Boiled Virgin* (1926), which she described as the first fiction in which a woman told the truth about herself. Her short story "Rachel and Her Children" (1924), published in *The American Mercury,* won an O. Henry Award.

Nicholls, Miss, unidentified.

Nicholson, Mrs. See Sackville-West, Vita.

Niles, (Mary) Blair Rice (1880–1959), successful Virginia writer of novels and travel books. She inscribed a copy of *The James,* her 1939 book on the James River, to EG (*CLEG* 17.271).

Norcross, Mr., unidentified business associate of AGG.

Norwood, a suburb of London where the Humphreys family had a second residence, which EG may have visited in 1896.

One West Eighty-fifth Street, the address of EG's apartment on Central Park West in Manhattan; the building no longer exists.

One West Main Street, the address of EG's family home in Richmond, Virginia. The gray stucco Greek Revival house was built in 1841 by the wealthy tobacconist David M. Branch, who sold it in 1846 to the Davenport family. EG's father purchased the house in 1887, and EG lived there for the rest of her life, with the exception of a short residence in New York City from 1911 to 1915.

Paddon, Mr., unidentified friend or business associate of AGG in London.

Page, Gabriella, unidentified; perhaps a resident of Castine.

Page, W[alter] H[ines] (1855–1918), journalist, editor, founding partner in Doubleday, Page and Company, and early literary advisor to EG; appointed in 1913 as U.S. ambassador to Great Britain. With his wife, Willa Alice Page, entertained EG both in the United States and in London.

Pal, pet dog of EG's.

Paradise, (Mr.) Frank, minister (Episcopalian) whom EG and RGT met in Hurricane, New York, in 1906. He officiated at RGT's wedding in 1906 and was engaged to EG ("experimentally," she says in *WW*) for about three years after that time.

Pat. See Paterson, (Miss) Isabel Bowler; also the name of one of EG's childhood pet dogs.

Paterson, (Miss) Isabel Bowler (1885–1961), author of several novels, including *The Fourth Queen* (1926) and *The Golden Vanity* (1934). Paterson was best known for her literary column "Turns with a Bookworm" (1926–1949), which appeared in the *New York Herald Tribune*.

Paterson, Mrs. See Paterson, (Miss) Isabel Bowler.

Patsy, domestic worker for EG.

Patterson, Elizabeth (Lizzie), one of Glasgow's closest Richmond friends. The Pattersons' home, Reveille, was near the Glasgows' farm and summer home, Jerdone Castle. At about age seven EG met Patterson when Lizzie Jones, Glasgow's mammy, went to Reveille to work. The Patterson family owned Lucky Strikes, which later became the American Tobacco Company. In July 1937 Patterson's husband (E. M. Crutchfield) was murdered by their chauffeur at Reveille.

Patterson, Lucy Bramlette (1865–1942), organizational leader, literary figure, public speaker. First president of North Carolina Federation of Women's Clubs.

Patterson, Miss, unidentified correspondent who requested EG's advice about how to study the latter's novels.

Patterson, Mrs., unidentified correspondent of EG.

Patterson, Nita, unidentified; perhaps a relative of Elizabeth Patterson Crutchfield.

Patton, Mr., editor with University Publishing Company, a textbook publishing firm; read EG's first novel, *The Descendant,* and convinced Harper's to publish it (see *WW* 111–12, 121).

Paxton, Gordon, unidentified guest of EG.

Perkins, (Mr.) Maxwell E. (1884–1947), well-known chief editor at Scribner's whose authors included Fitzgerald, Hemingway, and EG's friend MKR.

Perkinson, Isabelle Holmes, correspondent of EG; owned boardinghouse in Charlottesville, Virginia.

Peterkin, Julia Mood (1880–1961), South Carolina writer whose work focused on the Gullah. She won a Pulitzer Prize in 1928 for the novel *Scarlet Sister Mary.*

Phelan, James Duval (1861–1930), U.S. Senator (1913–1919) from California and previous mayor of San Francisco, where EG met him in 1915.

Phillips, Mr. George, prior of the Sherborne Almshouse, which EG visited in England in 1927. She later sent him Virginia tobacco (see *WW* 252–253).

Pierre. See Troubetzkoy, Prince Pierre.

Powell, John (1882–1963), accomplished classical pianist from Richmond whose outspoken racism damaged his career.

Poynter, Mr., unidentified person EG associated with the revolution in Turkey in 1907–1908.

Pratt, Mrs., unidentified contributor to Afro-American Old Folks Home in Richmond; also gave EG flowers in 1930 as EG left for England and Scotland.

Preston, Edmund Myers (d. 1945), Richmond attorney.

Rascoe, Burton (1892–1957), journalist and reviewer who was early to recognize James Branch Cabell's talent; literary editor of the *Chicago Tribune* and later editor of *The Bookman.*

Rawlings, Marjorie Kinnan (1896–1953), author of *The Yearling* (1938), for which she won a Pulitzer Prize, and *Cross Creek* (1942), her account of her life in central Florida where she settled in 1928. At the time of her death from cerebral hemorrhage in 1953, MKR was working on a biography of EG.

Rawlings, Virginia, companion to EG's mother (Anne Jane Gholson Glasgow) and governess for EG's three oldest siblings (see *WW* 38–40).

Rebe. See Tutwiler, Rebe Gordon Glasgow.

Reese, Agnes B., granddaughter of Rhoda Kibble, EG's mother's childhood mammy. EG modeled Minerva Clay of *ITOL* on Agnes Reese and her sister, Roberta ("Birdie") Richardson.

Reid, Mary, unidentified friend of LCW. Perhaps a relative of EG, since Reid was a common Glasgow family name.

Repplier, Agnes (1855–1950), Philadelphia writer of articles (her first appeared in the *Atlantic* in 1886), biography (*The Life of Père Marquette,* 1929), and a study of humor (*In Pursuit of Laughter,* 1936).

Reveille, Elizabeth Patterson's family's country home, outside Richmond and near Jerdone Castle.

Richardson, Roberta ("Birdie") (d. 1937), sister of Agnes Reese and granddaughter of Rhoda Kibble, EG's mother's childhood mammy.

Richmond Society for the Prevention of Cruelty to Animals (SPCA), founded 1892. EG became a member in 1893 and president in 1924, a position she held for twenty years. The animal shelter at the SPCA, for which Glasgow provided substantial financial support, was located in an old grocery store at 203 South Jefferson Street.

Riggs, Mrs. (George). See Wiggin, Kate Douglas.

Rives, Mrs., unidentified; probably a relative (perhaps mother) of ART.

Robert, probably Robert Arthur Glasgow, EG's paternal uncle.

Robson, Eleanor (1878–1979), popular English-born American actress; married the wealthy New York financier August Belmont. Robson played in the dramatic adaptation of *Audrey* by MJ, through whom EG met Robson.

Rutherfoord, Ann Seddon (Roy) (1832–1906?), wife of John Coles Rutherfoord, resident of Rock Castle in the Valley of Virginia, where EG traveled in preparation for writing her 1902 novel, *B-G*. EG thanks Rutherfoord for helping in her research.

S., Hunter. See Stagg, Hunter.

Sackville-West, Vita [Lady Victoria Mary Sackville-West] (1892–1962), later Mrs. Harold Nicolson, British author of biographies, essays, novels, and poems. She was born at her family's estate, Knole, near Sevenoaks in Kent, England, which she was prevented from inheriting because she was female, a story dramatized by Virginia Woolf in *Orlando.* EG visited Sackville-West and Knole in 1927.

Safford, Miss, unidentified resident of Ellsworth, Maine, with whom EG had tea in August 1941.

Sally, dog EG encountered on her 1927 trip to England.

Sanford, Millie H., resident of Mamaroneck, New York, who wrote EG of her admiration for *VOI*.

Saxton, Eugene (Gene) P., editor in chief at Harper & Brothers; married to Martha Saxton.

Saxton, Martha, wife of Eugene P. Saxton and correspondent of EG.

Scarborough, Dorothy (1878–1935), novelist, folklorist, and scholar; taught at Columbia (Ph.D., 1917). Her novel *The Wind* (1925) was successfully filmed in 1928. Scarborough's sister lived in Richmond, where she may have met EG.

Scott, Mrs. Thomas, unidentified resident of or visitor to Castine, Maine; gave a tea attended by EG at the Manor, an inn in Castine, in 1939.

Selfridge's, a large, modern department store that opened in 1909 on Oxford Street in London's fashionable West End. EG shopped there while in London.

Sergeant, Elizabeth Shepley (1881–1965), author, especially of books about American literature. She thanks EG for her admiring letter about Sergeant's *Short as Any Dream* (1929).

Shepstone, Miss, unidentified domestic employee of AGG.

Sherman, (Dr.) Stuart Pratt (1881–1926), critic, editor, teacher at Northwestern University and the University of Illinois; became editor of the *New York Herald Tribune Books* in 1924.

Simon, dog EG encountered on her 1927 trip to England.

Simpson's, restaurant in London's Strand; EG ate there in 1927.

Sinclair, May (1863–1946), English novelist and critic who first used the term "stream of consciousness" in print; influential in developing the psychological novel. EG for a time shared Sinclair's commitment to women's suffrage in the early twentieth century, and she admired Sinclair's writing. Sinclair held a tea in London in EG's honor in 1909.

Smith, Mrs. Francis, acquaintance of CGMcC and wife of a professor at the University of Virginia. Early in her writing career EG appealed to Smith for publishing advice.

Speyer, Leonora (1872–1956), Pulitzer Prize–winning (1926) poet.

Spruce Knoll, house in Castine, Maine, where EG lived during the summer of 1942.

Stagg, Hunter, Richmond reviewer and EG's correspondent; an editor of *The Reviewer* (1921–1924), the Richmond literary magazine.

Stallings, Mr., friend or acquaintance of Alfred and Blanche Knopf, who introduced him to EG; perhaps playwright, screenwriter, and novelist Laurence Stallings (1894–1968), whose 1924 play, *What Price Glory?* (coauthored with Maxwell Anderson), had been a hit on Broadway.

Stark. See Young, Stark.

Stein, Gertrude (1874–1946), expatriate American author of *The Autobiography of Alice B. Toklas* (1934). EG hosted a party at her home for Stein during the latter's 1934–1935 U.S. tour, arranged by their mutual friend Carl Van Vechten.

Stephie, patient at the sanitarium in Clifton Springs, New York, where Elizabeth Patterson's mother also was a patient.

Stevens, George, editor of *The Saturday Review of Literature*.

Stuart, Ruth McEnery (1849–1917), Louisiana author of novels and short fiction, including *A Golden Wedding and Other Tales* (1893) and *Aunt Amity's Silver Wedding and Other Stories* (1909).

Sully, Julia, Richmond friend who accompanied EG to Colorado in 1909 and to Petersburg, Virginia, in autumn 1911, where EG prepared for writing her novel *Virginia*.

Sully, Miss. See Sully, Julia.

Swinnerton, Frank (1884–1982), English critic and author of *George Gissing* (1912) and *The Two Wives* (1939). EG met Swinnerton and his wife during her 1927 trip to England, where she visited them at their cottage, "Cranleigh," in Surrey.

Taylor, Helen, advertising and publicity director for Harcourt, Brace.

Thompson, Dr., EG's eye doctor in New York.

Three Hills, MJ's large home in Bath County, Virginia, near Warm Springs, which she built for her and her siblings in 1912. Currently it is a bed and breakfast.

Thurman, Mr., unidentified friend or business associate of AGG in London.

Tina, probably Katherine McNutt Glasgow, EG's paternal aunt.

Titus, Olive Glasgow, relative (probably a distant cousin) of EG.

Toklas, (Miss) Alice B[abette] (1877–1967), longtime companion of Gertrude Stein; author of *The Alice B. Cookbook* (1954) and *What is Remembered* (1963) celebrating her years with Stein and their circle in Paris.

Toksvig, Signe (1891–1983), Danish-born author of *The Life of Hans Christian Andersen* (1934) and *Emmanuel Swedenborg, Scientist and Mystic* (1948) and an editor at *The New Republic;* married to the journalist Francis Hackett. Toksvig and EG never met, although they corresponded steadily from 1943 to 1945 after ST wrote to EG.

Tommy, Tom Moore, the springer spaniel owned by Bessie Zaban Jones and Howard Mumford Jones. The dog, named for Byron's friend and biographer, on whom Howard Mumford Jones had published a book, died around New Year's Day in 1937.

Towne, Charley, Charles Hanson Towne (1877–1949), New York–based journalist and acquaintance of EG; also played the role of the clergyman in the film *Life with Father* (1940).

Tricobys, unidentified friends of AGG.

Trigg, (Miss) Emma Gray, Richmond poet and longtime friend of EG; founding member of Ellen Glasgow Society. Trigg's nephew, to whom EG refers, is unidentified.

Troubetzkoy, Amélie Rives (1863–1945), Richmond-born novelist (*The Quick or the Dead?* [1888]), playwright, and poet who lived at her family's estate, Castle Hill, in Albemarle County, Virginia. It is not certain when ART and EG first met; they were close enough friends by March 1905 for Troubetzkoy to inscribe a book to EG and for ART to write a letter of introduction for EG to Louise Chandler Moulton at about that time.

Troubetzkoy, Prince Pierre (1866–1936), portrait painter and descendant of Russian royalty who married Amélie Rives in 1896; painted EG's portrait in 1912–1913.

Troubridge, Una (1887–1963), Una (Taylor), Lady Troubridge, artist and translator who was Radclyffe Hall's live-in partner for twenty-eight years.

Trumbull, Miss, unidentified resident of or visitor to Castine, Maine; gave a luncheon for EG in Castine in 1939.

Tucker, Mrs. Alan, owner of Littleplace (or Little Place) in Castine, Maine.

Turney, Catherine (1905–1998), writer of fiction, nonfiction, plays, radio shows, and, most notably, screenplays; wrote unproduced play and film treatment based on EG's *SL*.

Tutwiler, Carrington Cabell ("Cabell"), husband of EG's sister RGT.

Tutwiler, Carrington Cabell, Jr. ("Carrington"), EG's nephew, son of RGT; professor of English at Virginia Military Institute and editor of *CLEG*.

Tutwiler, Rebe Gordon Glasgow (1877–1967), EG's youngest sister and the youngest Glasgow child; married to Carrington Cabell Tutwiler (son Carrington Cabell Tutwiler Jr.). RGT was one of EG's constant childhood playmates, and the two maintained a close adult sibling relationship, particularly late in EG's life.

Tweedie, Mr., employee on the SS *Olympic* during EG's 1927 voyage to England.

Una. See Troubridge, Una.

Valentine, Lila Hardaway Meade [Mrs. B. B.] (1865–1921), prominent Richmond supporter of education and women's suffrage; first president of the Virginia League for Woman Suffrage (known later as the Equal Suffrage League of Virginia), formally organized on November 20, 1909.

Vanamee, Grace D., assistant to the president of the American Academy of Arts and Letters.

Van der Hooy, Dr., unidentified guest at One West Main Street.

Van Doren, Anne. See Anne.

Van Doren, Carl Clinton (1885–1950), literary critic (literary editor of *The Nation*, 1919–1922); his *Benjamin Franklin* (1938) won the Pulitzer Prize for biography in 1939. Married to IVD until 1936.

Van Doren, Dorothy Graffe (b. 1896), editor and writer; wife of Mark Van Doren.

Van Doren, Irita (1889–1966), literary editor of the *New York Herald Tribune* (1926–1963) and one of EG's two literary executors; they first corresponded in 1922. After graduate study at Columbia University (1909–1912), IVD worked for *The Nation* and then the *New York Herald Tribune*. Married to Carl Van Doren (divorced 1936); their daughters were Anne, Barbara, and Margaret. IVD had a long-term romantic relationship with Wendell Willkie.

Van Doren, Mark (1894–1972), editor, literary critic, poet, and teacher; Carl Van Doren's brother. His *Collected Poems* (1939) won a Pulitzer Prize in 1940.

Van Doren, Mr. See Van Doren, Carl Clinton.

Van Vechten, Carl (1880–1964), American critic, novelist, and later photographer; sponsor of Gertrude Stein's lecture tour in the United States.

Van Wyck. See Brooks, Van Wyck.

Villard, Léonie, writer and critic, first woman in France to hold a chair of literature at a French university (Lyon); received honorary D.Litt., from Mount Holyoke College in 1937.

Virginia, Miss. See Rawlings, Virginia.

Walker, Lily (Mrs. John Y. G.), EG's cousin.

Walker, Mrs., unidentified; perhaps Lily Walker.

Walpole, Sir Hugh Seymour (1884–1941), New Zealand-born best-selling English novelist; friend of EG; visited her in Richmond before their later falling-out.

Walter. See McCormack, George Walter.

Wardwell, (Mr.) Ralph S., owner of Appledoor (Horsey Place).

Warm Springs, Virginia ("the Warm"), resort in Bath County where EG's family sometimes vacationed.

Warner, Sylvia Townsend (1893–1978), English author of *The True Heart* (novel, 1929), a biography of T. H. White (1967), and short stories, many of which were published in the *New Yorker.* Although EG suggests that they met, there is no record of their connection.

Watson, Virginia, New York writer whom EG saw in Castine, Maine, in 1939.

Webster, Mrs., owner of curiosity shop in London where EG shopped in 1927.

Weddell, (Mr. and Mrs.) Alexander, residents of Richmond and friends of EG; Alexander Weddell was U.S. ambassador to Argentina.

Wellford, Dr., a physician of EG in Richmond; perhaps a relative of Roberta Wellford.

Wellford, Judge, unidentified; perhaps a relative of Roberta Wellford.

Wellford, Roberta ("Berta"), Richmond friend who had been, according to EG, CGMcC's closest friend. EG and Wellford were brought nearer by CGMcC's illness and death; EG in her autobiography remembers Berta as particularly supportive while her sister was dying.

Wessex, Thomas Hardy's dog, a wirehaired terrier.

West, [Tanner?], unidentified; sent EG flowers aboard the SS *Homeric* in June 1930.

West. See Willcox, Westmore, Jr.

Westmore. See Willcox, Westmore III.

White Sulphur Springs, West Virginia ("the White"), a resort in Greenbrier County, West Virginia, where EG's family sometimes vacationed.

Whiting, Elizabeth, unidentified correspondent of EG; perhaps related to May B. Whiting, who published a 1927 review of EG's *Barren Ground* in the *Dearborn Independent.*

Wickersham, Miss (Frances). See Hadfield, Lady.

Wiggin, Kate Douglas (1856–1923), American author of *Rebecca of Sunnybrook Farm* (1903).

Wilcox, Mrs. See Willcox, Louise Collier.

Willcox, Christine, LCW's daughter; opera singer in Europe and the United States.

Willcox, Louise Collier (1865–1929), writer, book reviewer, editor, and friend of EG. Helped EG place her first novel, *The Descendant* (1897), by providing EG a letter of introduction to her brother Price Collier, who worked for Macmillan. Wrote several reviews of EG's novels, and occasionally accompanied Glasgow on her travels ("the White" in 1907, England in 1914).

Willcox, Westmore, III, LCW's son, a businessman; killed in action in World War II.

Willcox, Westmore, Jr., LCW's husband.

Williams, Frances Leigh, cousin of EG, reporter for *Richmond News Leader*, research assistant to the historian Douglas Southall Freeman, biographer.

Williams, Jane, the imposing Aunt Jane, "granddaughter of [EG's mother's] Mammy Rhoda," of EG's autobiography (*WW* 28). As an elderly woman, she was a resident of the Afro-American Old Folks Home in Richmond, where EG helped pay for her care.

Willis, Dr., unidentified guest at One West Main Street.

Willkie, Wendell (1892–1944), presidential candidate in 1940 who had a long-term romantic relationship with IVD.

Wilmer, Dr., unidentified friend or physician of AGG.

Winter, Mr., unidentified admirer of RGT and acquaintance of EG.

Woodall, Corbet (1841–1916), business associate and friend of AGG in London; governor of Gas Light and Coke Company and president of the Institute of Gas Engineers; knighted in 1913.

Woodall, Miss, eldest of five daughters (there were also six sons) of Corbet Woodall and his wife.

Woods, Katherine (b. 1886), Philadelphia-born author, editor, and journalist in New York and Paris.

Woolf, Virginia Stephen (1882–1941), well-known and influential English essayist and novelist, whom EG admired and regretted never meeting.

Young, Stark (1881–1963), journalist, novelist, professor, and critic; writer for the *New Republic;* one of twelve authors included in the Southern Agrarian manifesto *I'll Take My Stand* (1930).

Word Division

The following list identifies words hyphenated at the ends of lines by the letter writer in the original letters. The first group (I) lists compound words that EG or her correspondents could write either as hyphenated or not. The second group (II) lists two categories of words: those that are consistently spelled with a hyphen by EG or her correspondents, as verified by internal textual evidence in the letters, and those words for which there is no reason to question a non-hyphenated, standard spelling. Words are listed by page number. In the two instances where words have more than one hyphen, the writer's word division is indicated by a vertical line (for example, whither- | so-ever).

I			
		19	ex-ceedingly
16	whither- | so-ever	20	suc-cumbed
29	thirty-two		con-crete
33	to-night		remem-ber
42	ball-room		dis-tinctly
76	tea-drinkings		communica-tion
100	Stow- | on-the-Wold		de-lighted
102	seventy-four		any-thing
106	dining-room	21	opera-tion
109	multi-millionaires		*Pro-fundis*
142	living-room		develop-ment
149	twenty-five		en-ters
151	sting-extracting	22	gratifica-tion
163	dwelling-place	24	ab-sence
202	apartment-house		some-day
209	far-reaching		libera-tion
			to-gether
II		25	Februa-ry
9	con-sider		eager-ness
	cathe-dral	26	tele-phoned
	chimpan-zees		disagreea-ble
16	quo-tation	27	beauti-ful
18	Mort-imer	29	re-cuperation
	re-sistless		be-fore
	a-weary		philos-ophy
	dare-say		metaphy-sics

30	moun-tain	84	en-chanting
	possi-ble	86	some-thing
	in-creasing	87	some-thing
31	disman-tled	94	propor-tion
	be-cause	95	when-ever
	rap-ture	96	any-thing
	a-gain	97	sur-roundings
	sympa-thy	98	Shore-ditch
33	delight-ful	99	our-selves
42	saunter-ing	100	mono-gram
	comforta-ble	101	intelli-gent
	partic-ularly	102	heart-broken
	D'artag-nan	105	every-one
44	sup-pose	106	fire-place
	un-happy		com-placent
47	Every-thing	111	com-fortable
	Sin-clair's		com-mercialized
48	Sin-clair		reminis-cent
	every-body		our-selves
51	al-ways	113	any-thing
53	rest-ing		inconve-nient
59	Canter-bury	122	Mackin-toshes
60	Eliza-bethan	126	prom-inently
	dream-ing	147	indefinite-ly
	charac-ters	148	auto-biography
	al-ways	151	morn-ing
	disap-pointment	155	relation-ships
63	thought-fulness	160	predestina-tion
67	was-ted	161	imagina-tion
69	have-n't	166	grate-ful
70	indomi-table	170	beau-tiful
71	achieve-ment	171	thank-ing
	domin-ating	177	engage-ments
	happi-ness	179	affabil-ity
72	evan-escent	203	egotisti-cal
	wonder-ful	204	inadequa-cy
73	under-standing	211	type-writer
	pro-foundly	212	hap-piness
74	Rich-mond		

Works Cited and Consulted

Works by Ellen Glasgow (in chronological order)

Fiction

The Descendant. New York: Harper, 1897.
Phases of an Inferior Planet. New York: Harper, 1898.
The Voice of the People. New York: Doubleday, Page, 1900.
The Battle-Ground. New York: Doubleday, Page, 1902, Rpt. Tuscaloosa: University of Alabama Press, 2000.
The Deliverance. New York: Doubleday, Page, 1904.
The Wheel of Life. New York: Doubleday, Page, 1906.
The Ancient Law. New York: Doubleday, Page, 1908.
The Romance of a Plain Man. New York: Macmillan, 1909.
The Miller of Old Church. New York: Doubleday, Page, 1911.
Virginia. New York: Doubleday, Page, 1913, Rpt. New York: Penguin, 1989.
Life and Gabriella. Garden City, NY: Doubleday, Page, 1916.
The Builders. Garden City, NY: Doubleday, Page, 1919.
One Man in His Time. Garden City, NY: Doubleday, Page, 1922.
The Shadowy Third and Other Stories. Garden City, NY: Doubleday, Page, 1923.
Dare's Gift and Other Stories. London: John Murray, 1924.
Barren Ground. Garden City, NY: Doubleday, Page, 1925, Rpt. New York: Hill and Wang, 1957; New York: Harcourt, Brace, Jovanovich, 1985.
The Romantic Comedians. Garden City, NY: Doubleday, Page, 1926, Rpt. Charlottesville: University Press of Virginia, 1995.
They Stooped to Folly. Garden City, NY: Doubleday, Doran, 1929.
The Old Dominion Edition of the Works of Ellen Glasgow. 8 vols. Garden City, NY: Doubleday, Doran, 1929–1933. Includes *The Voice of the People, The Battle-Ground, The Deliverance, The Miller of Old Church, Virginia, Barren Ground, The Romantic Comedians,* and *They Stooped to Folly.*
The Sheltered Life. Garden City, NY: Doubleday, Doran, 1932, Rpt. Charlottesville: University Press of Virginia, 1993.
Vein of Iron. New York: Harcourt, Brace, 1935, Rpt. Charlottesville: University Press of Virginia, 1995.
The Virginia Edition of the Works of Ellen Glasgow. 12 vols. New York: Charles Scribner's Sons, 1938. Includes *The Old Dominion Edition,* 8 vols.; *The Romance of a Plain Man; Life and Gabriella; The Sheltered Life;* and *Vein of Iron.*

In This Our Life. New York: Harcourt, Brace, 1941.

Beyond Defeat: An Epilogue to an Era. Ed. Luther Y. Gore. Charlottesville: University Press of Virginia, 1966.

Nonfiction

"I Believe." *I Believe: The Personal Philosophies of Certain Eminent Men and Women of Our Time.* Ed. Clifton Fadiman, New York: Simon and Schuster, 1938.

A Certain Measure: An Interpretation of Prose Fiction. New York: Harcourt, Brace, 1943.

"Ellen Glasgow to Lila Meade Valentine: Three Letters." Ed. Edgar E. Mac-Donald. *EGN* 21 (October 1984): 5.

The Woman Within. New York: Harcourt, Brace, 1954, Rpt. Charlottesville: University Press of Virginia, 1994.

Poetry

The Freeman and Other Poems. New York: Doubleday, Page, 1902.

Collections or Editions of Works by Ellen Glasgow (in alphabetical order)

The Collected Stories of Ellen Glasgow. Ed. Richard K. Meeker. Baton Rouge: Louisiana State University Press, 1963.

Ellen Glasgow's Reasonable Doubts: A Collection of Her Writings. Ed. Julius Rowan Raper. Baton Rouge: Louisiana State University Press, 1988.

Letters of Ellen Glasgow. Ed. Blair Rouse. New York: Harcourt, Brace, 1958.

Secondary Works

Baedeker, Karl. *Great Britain.* 3 vols. 1887. Freiburg: Baedeker, 1966.

Bigelow, Gordon E., and Laura V. Monti, eds. *Selected Letters of Marjorie Kinnan Rawlings.* Gainesville: University Press of Florida, 1983, 1988.

Blain, Virginia, Isobel Grundy, and Patricia Clements, eds. *The Feminist Companion to Literature in English: Women Writers from the Middle Ages to the Present.* New Haven: Yale University Press, 1990.

Bond, Tonette L. "'A Thrilling Sense of Friendship and Sympathy': The Correspondence of Ellen Glasgow and Marjorie Kinnan Rawlings." *EGN* 16 (March 1982): 3–6.

Carroll, Roger Hunt. "Ellen Glasgow and Rockbridge County." *EGN* 9 (October 1978): 3–13.

Cella, C. Ronald. *Mary Johnston.* Boston: Twayne, 1981.

Cook, Martha E. "Miss Ellen and Miss Lucy: The Richmond-Nordhausen Connection." *EGN* 30 (Spring 1993): 13–14.

Duke, Jane Taylor. "Golfing with Genius." Preface Ray Bonis. *EGN* 35 (Fall 1995): 3–4.

"The Eyes of the Sphinx: Selections from Rebe Glasgow's Travel Journal of 1899." Ed. Mark Lurie and Shanon Wilson. *EGN* 35 (Fall 1995): 1, 7–10; 36 (Spring 1996): 3, 9–15; 37 (Fall 1996): 3, 5–9.

Godbold, E. Stanly, Jr. *Ellen Glasgow and the Woman Within.* Baton Rouge: Louisiana State University Press, 1972.

Goodman, Susan. *Ellen Glasgow: A Biography.* Baltimore: Johns Hopkins University Press, 1998.

Jones, Anne Goodwyn. *Tomorrow Is Another Day: The Woman Writer in the South, 1859–1936.* Baton Rouge: Louisiana State University Press, 1981.

Jones, Howard Mumford. *Howard Mumford Jones: An Autobiography.* Madison: University of Wisconsin Press, 1979.

Karl, Frederick R. *Joseph Conrad: The Three Lives.* New York: Farrar, Straus and Giroux, 1979.

Kelly, William W. *Ellen Glasgow: A Bibliography.* Charlottesville: University Press of Virginia, 1964.

Kluger, Richard, with the assistance of Phyllis Kluger. *The Paper: The Life and Death of the "New York Herald Tribune."* New York: Knopf, 1986.

Longest, George C. "A Deep and Loving Heart: The Letters of Amélie Rives to Ellen Glasgow." *EGN* 13 (October 1980): 3–4.

MacDonald, Edgar E. "Anne Virginia Bennett: Confidant and Catalyst." *EGN* 52 (Spring 2004): 5–9.

———. "Lellie: Ellen Glasgow and Josephine Clark." *EGN* 4 (March 1976): 11–17.

———. "'Remembering Ellen Glasgow'—and Elizabeth Branch Bowie." *EGN* 32 (Spring 1994): 1, 3, 6–7.

Matthews, Pamela R. *Ellen Glasgow and a Woman's Traditions.* Charlottesville: University Press of Virginia, 1994.

Parent, Monique. *Ellen Glasgow, Romancière.* Paris: A. G. Nizet, 1962.

Raper, J. R. "The European Initiation of Ellen Glasgow." *EGN* 5 (October 1976): 2–5.

Rappaport, Erika Diane. *Shopping for Pleasure: Women in the Making of London's West End.* Princeton: Princeton University Press, 2000.

The Reader's Encyclopedia. Ed. William Rose Benét. New York: Thomas Y. Crowell, 1948; 1998.

The Reader's Encyclopedia of American Literature. Ed. Max J. Herzberg et al. New York: Thomas Y. Crowell Co., 1962.

Scura, Dorothy M., *Ellen Glasgow: The Contemporary Reviews.* Cambridge: Cambridge University Press, 1992.

Scura, Dorothy M., *Ellen Glasgow: New Perspectives.* Knoxville: University of Tennessee Press, 1995.

Symbols of American Libraries. 14th ed. Washington, D.C.: Library of Congress (Cataloging Distribution Service), 1992.

Taylor, Welford Dunaway. *Amélie Rives (Princess Troubetzkoy).* Boston: Twayne, 1973.

———. "Ellen Glasgow in Woodcuts." *EGN* 43 (Fall 1999): 1, 3–15.

———, and George C. Longest, eds. *Regarding Ellen Glasgow: Essays for Contemporary Readers.* Richmond: Virginia State Library, 2001.

"Tea and Metaphysics: Excerpts from Mary Johnston's Diary." Ed. Mary P. Edwards. *EGN* 19 (October 1983): 2–9.

Tickner, Lisa. *The Spectacle of Women: Imagery of the Suffrage Campaign 1907–1914.* Chicago: University of Chicago Press, 1988.

Tutwiler, Carrington C., Jr. *Ellen Glasgow's Library.* Charlottesville: Bibliographical Society of the University of Virginia, 1967.

———, ed. *A Catalog of the Library of Ellen Glasgow.* Charlottesville: Bibliographical Society of the University of Virginia, 1969.

Van Doren, Carl. *Three Worlds.* New York: Harper, 1936.

Watson, Ritchie D., Jr. "Sara Haardt Mencken and the Glasgow-Mencken Literary Entente." *EGN* 20 (April 1984): 6–17.

Wheeler, Marjorie Spruill. Introduction to *Hagar* by Mary Johnston. Charlottesville: University Press of Virginia, 1994.

Index

Calendared letters are indexed separately only for infrequent correspondents.

Adams, Alya, 167, 194, 198, 275
Adams, Henry, 148
Adams, J. Donald, xliii, 132, 157, 167, 184, 194, 197-99, 208, 275, 282, 287
Adams, Mary, 197, 198
Adam's Breed (Hall), 103, 104, 110, 284, 285
Adirondacks, xxvii, xl, 29
African Americans, xvi, xvi, xvii, 61
Afro-American Old Folks Home (Richmond, Va.), 76, 78, 294, 300
Agglesby, Mrs., 275
Akermann, 275
Alderman, Edwin Anderson, 275
Alfred A. Knopf, Inc., 289
Alice, Princess, Countess of Athlone, 84
Alice B. Cookbook, The (Toklas), 296
Aller, SS, xl
Alsop, Joseph Wright, Jr., 160, 275
Alston, Mr., 49, 275
Amber Satyr, The (Flannagan), 130-31
Ambler, Betty (*The Battle-Ground*), 228, 229
Ambler, Va. (*The Battle-Ground*), 228, 229
Amelia (Fielding), 128
Amélie. *See* Troubetzkoy, Amélie Rives
American Academy of Arts and Letters, xxix, xliii, 286, 298
American Express, 3, 167
American Mercury, 69, 291, 292
American Museum of Natural History (New York), 286
American Tobacco Company, 293
American Woman's Association, 278
America through Women's Eyes (Beard), 162, 277
Anatomy of Criticism (Hazlitt), 138
Ancient Law, The (Glasgow), xl, xlv, 35-36, 38, 303
Andersen, Hans Christian, 186, 224-27
Anderson, (Colonel) Archer (cousin), 34, 276

Anderson, Henry, xli, xliv, 56, 79, 87, 88, 109, 119, 276, 285, 286
Anderson, James (cook), xvi, xliii, 76, 168, 170, 189, 215, 235, 236, 276, 277, 287
Anderson, Laura E., 259, 276
Anderson, Mary, 5, 9, 276
Anderson, Maxwell, 296
Anderson, Sally, 41, 270, 273, 276
Animal Rescue League (London), 99
Ann Arbor, Michigan, 126, 288
Anthony, Katharine, 74, 75, 276
Appledoor. *See* Horsey Place (Castine, Maine)
Archbald, General David (*The Sheltered Life*), 135, 240
Archbald, Jenny Blair (*The Sheltered Life*), 135, 136, 240
Argentina, 167, 299
Arrowsmith (Lewis), 70
As the Earth Turns (Carroll), 138, 139
Atherton, Gertrude, 258, 276
Atlantic City, N.J., xxvii, xlii, 27, 53, 64
Atlantic Monthly, 141, 179, 180, 181, 295
Atta Troll (Heine), 238
Audrey (Johnston), 295
Aunt Amity's Silver Wedding and Other Stories (Stuart), 296
Austen, Jane, 43, 219, 250
Austin, Tex., 126
autobiography. *See Woman Within, The*
Autobiography of Alice B. Toklas, The (Stein), 153, 296
"Autobiography of an Exile." *See Woman Within, The* (Glasgow)
A. V. *See* Bennett, Anne Virginia
"Ave ataque Vale" (Troubetzkoy), 133
Azores, the, 42

Baby McKee. *See* McKee, Benjamin Harrison
Baden-Baden, Germany, 180
Bagby, Ellen Matthews, 268, 276

Bagby, George William, 185
Bagby, Lucy Parke Chamberlayne, 185, 257, 260, 274, 276
Bagley, Miss, 260, 276-77
Balch, Edwin Swift, 280
Balch, (Mrs.) Emily Clark. *See* Clark, Emily
Baltimore, Md., xix, xlii, xliii, 2, 177, 187, 188, 286, 290, 291, 292
Baltimore Sun, 69
Balzac, Honoré de, 20
Bar Harbor, Maine, 208
Barnstable, Cape Cod, xlii
Barren Ground (Glasgow), xlii, xlv, 56, 67, 69, 128, 152, 161, 162, 207, 235, 240, 299, 303
Barrows (butler), 49, 277
Baskin, Norton, 213, 214, 277
Bath County, Va., 297, 299
Battle Avenue (Castine, Maine), xxviii, 277, 279
Battle-Ground, The (Glasgow), xxxix, xl, xlv, 1, 4, 14, 15, 16, 226, 228, 229, 295, 303
Beard, Mary R., 162, 264, 276
Bec, Aunt. *See* Glasgow, Rebecca Anderson
Becker, May Lamberton, 207, 208, 265, 277
Belgium, invasion of, 61
Bell, Mr., 20, 276
Belmont, August, 295
Belmont, Eleanor Robson. *See* Robson, Eleanor
Benét, Stephen Vincent, 150
Benjamin Franklin (Van Doren), 298
Bennett, Anne Virginia, xiii, xiv, xv-xvi, xix, xxvii, xxix, 56, 57, 67, 76, 79, 131, 133, 134, 139, 147, 170, 179, 183, 189, 204, 206, 208, 213, 234, 248, 250, 251, 259, 261, 262, 263, 265, 266, 267, 276, 277; letter from, 251; letters to, 87, 88, 93, 99, 101, 105, 109, 116, 118, 120, 121, 156, 157, 158, 167, 168; photograph of, *see illustrations gallery*
Bennett, Arnold, xli, 59, 277
Bent Twig, The (Fisher), 283
Berkshires (Mass.), xliii, 164
Bermuda, xxv, 44
Better Homes and Gardens, 284
Bettws-y-Coed, Wales, 43
Betty, Miss. *See* Patterson, Elizabeth Anne Duval

Beyond Defeat (Glasgow), xliv, 187, 219, 304
Bhagavad Gita, xxvi, 21, 233, 243, 245, 250
Bible, the, 43, 142, 152, 165-66, 171, 245
Billy (dog), xvi, xliii, 88, 94, 95, 99, 119, 121, 123, 131, 139, 158, 168, 277, 289; photograph of, *see illustrations gallery*
Biography of Manuel (Cabell), 118, 279
Bird, Robert Montgomery, 2
Birdie. *See* Richardson, Roberta
Birdsong, Eva (*The Sheltered Life*), 133, 136, 200, 201, 205, 240
Birdsong, George (*The Sheltered Life*), 201, 240
Birth of Venus (Botticelli), 237
Black Pup, The (Brooks), 160, 290
Blake, William, 122, 153
Bloomsbury (London), 100
Boehme, Jakob, 228, 229
Bolton Abbey (England), 85, 91, 109
Bonfire (Canfield), 140
Bonheur, Rosa, 99
Bonnibel (dog). *See* Bonnie
Bonnie (dog), 189, 197, 215, 277
Bookman, 72, 283, 291, 294
Book-of-the-Month Club, 160, 279
Borrow, George, 73
Boston, Mass., xvii, xl, 25, 27, 33, 44, 46, 138, 243, 292
Boston Adventure (Stafford), 243
Boston marriage, xvi
Botticelli, Sandro, 237
Bourland, Kathleen (Mrs. Albert), 277
Bowie, Elizabeth (Lizzie) Branch, 191, 209, 277, 289, 305
Bradley, 29
Branch, Beulah, 76, 83, 90, 95, 168, 169, 171, 276, 277, 278, 283
Branch, Blythe, 191, 278
Branch, David M., 293
Branch, Effie Kerr, 277, 278
Branch, John Kerr, 83, 277, 278, 283, 288
Branch, Margaret. *See* Glasgow, Margaret Branch
Branch, Mary Cooke, 292
Bread Loaf Writers School and Conference, xliii, 164
Bremen, SS, xl, 23
Brennerbad, Austria, 31, 32

Index

Brer Terrapin (Joel Chandler Harris), 90, 120, 196
Brickell, Herschel, 119, 184, 204, 250, 278, 286
Brimming Cup, The (Fisher), 283
British Museum (London), 4, 12, 100, 102
Bromfield, Louis, 139
Brooks, Anne, 160, 290
Brooks, Eleanor, xvii, xx, xliii, 206, 247, 278, 282
Brooks, Van Wyck, xvii, xliii, 206, 208, 247, 278, 299
Brothers in the West (Raynolds), 129, 130
Brown, Gertrude Foster, 258, 278
Brown, Lucy (Mrs. Arthur Page), 258, 278
Brown, Thalia Newton, 266, 278
Browning, Robert, 134, 230
Bryan, (John) Stewart, 119, 189, 278
Bryan, Ella Howard, 271, 278
Bryan, Winnie, 263, 278
Bryce, Carroll (domestic worker), 38, 278
Buddha and Buddhism, xviii, 19, 26, 173, 228, 229, 230, 244
Budrau (dog), 96, 98, 278
Buick, xlii, 75
Builders, The (Glasgow), 41, 56, 291, 303
Burden, Mrs. (Kesiah Agnes Watkins) (*They Stooped to Folly*), 246
Burgess, Gelett, 82, 278
Burnett, Frances Hodgson, 227, 229, 278
Burnham Beeches (England), 97-99
Burton, Isabel Arundell, 230, 231
Burton, Richard, 230, 231
Busman's Honeymoon (Sayers), 190, 191
Butcher, Fanny, 69, 278
Byland Abbey (England), 89, 91
Byron, George Gordon, Lord, 143, 144, 297

C., Dr. and Mrs., 279
Cabell, James Branch, xlvi, 68, 69, 73, 117, 118, 127, 157, 159, 160, 176, 178, 208, 210, 211, 213, 214, 279, 285, 294
Cabell, Mrs. Henry, 167, 279
Cabell, Priscilla Bradley ("Percie"), 113, 157, 214, 273, 279
California, xxvii, 62-63; San Francisco, xli, 62, 293; Santa Barbara, xli
"Call, The" (Glasgow), xli

Calvinism, xxvii, 122, 230
Cambridge, Mass., 81, 163, 164, 166, 178, 179, 180, 182, 288
Canby, H. S., 153, 163, 165, 172, 220, 238, 239, 279, 286
Canby, Marion, xxiv, xxviii, 172, 236-38, 239, 279
Canfield, Dorothy. *See* Fisher, Dorothy Canfield
Canopic, SS, 46
Canterbury (England), 59, 90, 93, 95, 97-99
Cape Cod, xlii, 76
Cardozo High School (Washington, D.C.), 209, 282
Carlyle, Mrs. John, 143
Caroline (domestic worker), 279
Carroll, Gladys Hasty, 139
Carroll, Lafayette, 3, 279
Caslon Old Face, 174
Castine, Maine, xix, xx, xxv-xxviii, xliii, xliv, 186, 190, 196, 197, 199, 203, 205, 208, 211, 215, 217, 218, 224, 225, 226, 230, 231, 232, 240, 242, 243, 245, 252, 276, 277, 278, 282, 283, 284, 289, 293, 295, 296, 298, 299
Castle Hill (Va.), 27, 33, 133, 279, 297
Castle Warden (St. Augustine, Fla.), 213, 214
Cat, The (Huidekoper), 287
Catalog of the Library of Ellen Glasgow (ed. Tutwiler), xlv, 13, 22, 33, 60, 67, 76, 116, 144, 154, 214, 239, 241, 244, 292, 298, 297, 306
cathedrals, English, 85, 88, 90, 108. *See also under individual names*
Catherine (domestic worker), 189, 279
Catherine the Great (Anthony), 74, 75, 276
Century, The (magazine), 77
Certain Measure, A (Glasgow), xliv, xlv, 16, 187, 225, 233, 242, 244, 304
Chamberlain, John, 241, 279
Chamberlain, Neville, 181
Chanler, John Armstrong, 41, 280
Chapel Hill, N.C., xlii, 81, 126, 183, 199, 288
Charles, Prince, of Denmark, 6, 8
Charlottesville, Va., xlii, 127, 130, 294
Chase City, Va., xl, 20, 21, 36
Chekhov, Anton, 66
Chère reine crosses (England), 97

Cherry Orchard, The (Chekhov), 66
Chestnut Hill (Pa.), 74, 280
Chicago, 69, 176; World's Fair (1933), 167
Chicago Tribune, 278, 294
Chigwell (England), 90, 93, 97
Children of God (Fisher), 191, 192
Chilmark, Mass., 225, 226, 233
Christianity, xxvii, 142, 168, 228, 230
Christian Science, 168, 250
Chronicles of Barsetshire, The (Trollope), 154
Chrysler, 75
Chummy (dog), 88-89, 280
Cindy (dog), 249, 280, 252
Claasen, Clara, 266, 280
Claridge's (London), 49, 280
Clark, Adele, 259, 280
Clark, Annette I., 272, 280
Clark, Annie Glasgow (sister), xiv, xix, xxix, 2, 11, 48, 64, 258, 276, 279, 280, 283
Clark, Dr. and Mrs., 99
Clark, Emily, 69, 73, 99, 118, 119, 126, 144, 183, 266, 276, 279, 280, 282
Clark, Frank Tarleton (brother-in-law), 280
Clark, Glasgow (nephew), 79, 117, 280
Clark, Josephine (niece), xiv, xxx, 47, 88, 119, 175, 253, 262, 271, 274, 280, 288, 305
Clark, Jubillant Mai, 271, 280
Clark, Mrs. Campbell, 119
Clark, Mrs. Meade, 119, 280
Clarke, Dr., 37, 280
Clay, Minerva (*In This Our Life*), 209, 219, 294
Clay, Parry (*In This Our Life*), 209
Clephan, Annie, 71, 280
Clifford, Lucy (Mrs. W. K.), 47, 280
Cloete, Stuart, 191, 192
Colcorton (Pope), 253
Coleman, Carrie. *See* Duke, Caroline (Carrie) Coleman
Coleman, Lucy Singleton, 39, 41, 78, 176, 280, 281, 290
Coleman, Mattie (domestic worker), 168, 189, 281, 290
Coleman, Mrs., 36, 176, 281
College of William and Mary, xliii, xlvi, 177, 189, 278, 289
Collier, Price, 300
Collier's Magazine, xli
Colman, Mrs., 260, 281

Colonial Dames, 41
Colorado, xxiv, xxvii, 49, 275, 277, 278, 287, 296
Colorado Springs, Colo., xxviii, xl, 50, 51, 282
Columbia University, xliii, xlvi, 137, 182, 216, 218, 290, 295, 298
Commager, Henry, 155, 174
Common Reader, The (Woolf), 141
Comstock, Lillian A., 266
Condemned to Devil's Island (Niles), 117
Confident Years, The (Brooks), 278
Congreve, Marjorie Glasgow. *See* Glasgow, Marjorie (niece)
Connecticut, xix, xliii, 148, 197, 202, 222, 223, 229, 233, 245, 249
Conrad, Jessie (Mrs. Joseph), 55, 98, 100, 102, 104, 106, 259, 281
Conrad, Joseph, xli, 59, 281, 305
Constantinople, xl, 48, 50, 143
Conti di Savoia (oceanliner), xliii, 279
Cooper, Page, 130-32, 263, 264, 281
Copeland, Mrs., 260, 270, 281
Cordelia (domestic worker), 156, 157, 281, 283
Cornell, Katharine, 200, 201, 205, 274, 281, 290, 291
Country Matters (Leighton), 173
Coxwold (England), 91, 92
Cranleigh (England), 100, 102, 106, 297
Crenshaw, Mrs. Dabney S., xl
Crescent Beach, Fla., 211
cricket (sport), 7
Crockett Springs (Montgomery County, Va.), xl
Cross Creek (Rawlings), xxvi, 211, 212, 214, 294
Cross, Mr., 281
Crutchfield, E. M., 169, 293
Crutchfield, Elizabeth Patterson. *See* Patterson, Elizabeth (Lizzie)
Current Literature, xli
Curtis, Mrs., 108, 281

Dahl, Mrs., 37, 281
Danes and Denmark, xiii, 6, 8, 227, 229, 235, 236, 241, 243, 244, 250, 297
Dare's Gift and Other Stories (Glasgow), xlii, 303

Darwin, Charles, 9, 142, 144, 228
Dashiell, Margaret, 261, 267, 268, 269, 270, 271, 272, 281
Dauban, Jeanne, 265, 281
David Copperfield (film), 195
Davis (table steward), 83, 281
Davis, Bette, xliii, 217
Davis, Mr., 145, 281
Dead Lovers Are Faithful Lovers Newman), 113
Dean, Elaine J., xvi, xvii, xxx, 209, 270, 282
Dearborn Independent, 299
de Havilland, Olivia, xliv, 217
Deland, Margaret, 260, 282
"Delivered of My Life" (Canby), 239
del Sarto, Andrea, 12
Democratic Convention (Roanoke, Va.), xxxix
Depression, Great, 146, 148
De Profundis (Wilde), 21-22
Descendant, The (Glasgow), xxxix, 1, 13, 14, 70, 176, 294, 300, 303
Descent of Man, The (Darwin), 144
Deutschland (oceanliner), xl, 23
Dickens, Charles, 42, 43, 52, 93, 97, 99, 195, 241
Dinwiddie (fictional), xli
Divine Fire, The (Sinclair), 20
Doctors Hospital (New York), xxv, xliii, 198-99, 282
dogs, xvi, xxvii, xxix, 30, 79, 88, 89, 94-95, 96, 98-99, 101, 102, 105, 106, 115, 122, 154, 156, 164, 215, 189, 190, 293. *See also names of individual dogs*
Donatello, 84
Dooley, Mr. and Mrs. James Henry, 290
Doubleday (publishers), xlii, 81, 131, 137, 145, 148, 162, 235, 241, 280, 281, 282, 290, 293, 289, 292
Doubleday, Frank N., 147, 148, 282
Doubleday, Nelson, 150, 151, 191, 282, 292
Doubleday, Russell, 104
Dresden, Germany, 221
Drums along the Mohawk (film), 195
Duke, Caroline (Carrie) Coleman, xxvii, xxxix, xlii, 34, 36, 41, 55, 63, 75, 76, 82, 83, 85-86, 90, 92, 93, 98, 103, 106-8, 111, 116, 118, 124, 134, 167, 177, 179, 181, 189, 190, 197, 206, 213, 214, 234, 236, 268, 277, 279, 281, 283
Duke, Jane Taylor, 99, 282, 304
Duke University, xliii, xlvi, 179, 283
Du Maurier, George, 176
Durham Cathedral (England), 84-87
Dwyer, Ada, 22, 282

Easby Abbey (England), 91
Eastern Europe, 192
Eckehart, Johannes, 228-31
Edgartown (Martha's Vineyard), 227, 229
Edinburgh (Scotland), 85, 121, 122, 123
Edmonds, Walter D., 195
Egypt, xxvi, xxvii, xl, 44, 85, 87, 92, 143, 153, 223
Eightfold Path (Buddhism), 228
"Elegy in a Country Churchyard" (Gray), 59, 94
Elemental Man (Hoffman), 166, 167
Ella (domestic worker), 37, 38, 282
Ellen Glasgow: A Biography (Goodman), xxx, xxxi, xxxii, 305
Ellen Glasgow: New Perspectives (ed. Scura), xlv, 24, 25, 27, 28, 33
Ellen Glasgow: The Contemporary Reviews (ed. Scura), xlv, 72, 77, 132, 208, 304
Ellen Glasgow and a Woman's Traditions (Matthews), xxx, 305
Ellen Glasgow Newsletter, xxxiii, xlv, 255
Ellen Glasgow Society, 297
Ellen Glasgow's Reasonable Doubts (ed. Raper), xlv, 226, 304
Ellsworth, Maine, 202, 208, 212, 282, 295
Ellwanger, Mrs., 50, 282
Ely Cathedral (England), 90, 92, 94, 95
Emmanuel Swedenborg, Scientist and Mystic (Toksvig), 224, 297
"Empty American Novels" (Glasgow), xliii
England, xix, xxvi, xxvii, xl-xlii, 3, 46, 50, 55, 58, 59, 61, 80, 81, 84, 86, 91, 92, 96, 111, 164, 172, 174, 181, 192, 193, 277. *See also individual place-names*
Englewood, N.J., xl
English Book Shop, 166
Epictetus, 13, 16
Epping Forest (England), 90, 93, 97

Equal Suffrage League of Virginia, xvii, xl, xli, 65, 280, 298
Essex (automobile), 75
Etruria (oceanliner), xxxix, 6
Europe, xxvii, xl, 1, 22, 32, 33, 49, 80, 84, 120, 143, 175, 181, 192, 193, 203, 228, 241, 281, 300, 305. *See also individual place-names*
Evans, Mr. and Mrs., 103, 112, 282
Evergreen Cemetery (Richmond, Va.), 76
Everitt, Raymond, 146, 282

Faderman, Lillian, xxx
Fadiman, Clifton, 180, 181, 226, 227, 228
Farm, The (Bromfield), 139
Farnsworth, Alice (Mrs. George James), 269, 283
Farrar (publishers), 283
Farrar, John Chipman, 72, 283
Fathers, The (Tate), 138
Faulkner, William, 139, 143, 144
Ferne Humanitarian Institute for Children and Animals, 285
Few, William P., 163, 283
Fichte, Johann Gottlieb, 29
Field Museum of Natural History (Chicago), 167, 286
Fiesole, Italy, xliii, 173, 237, 278, 283
films and film industry, xliii, 157, 158, 217, 287, 295, 297, 298
Fincastle, John (*Vein of Iron*), 156, 160, 161
Fisher, Dorothy Canfield, xlvi, 140, 155, 157, 264, 265, 279, 283
Fisher, Vardis, 192
Fitzgerald, F. Scott, 294
Flannagan, Roy, 130-31
Florence, Italy, xl, xliii, 36, 45, 46, 79, 168, 237
Florida, xxix, xlii, 71, 139, 177, 210, 211, 213, 277, 294
Flowering of New England, The (Brooks), 278
Flush (Woolf), 138, 139, 141
Forbes, Miss, 60, 266, 283
Ford (automobile), 175
Forster, E. M., 229
Forsyte Saga, The (Galsworthy), 283
Fountains Abbey (England), xxvi, 84-85, 86, 87, 91, 108, 109, 112, 122
Fourth Queen, The (Paterson), 293
France and French, xv, xxvii, xli, xlii, 43, 50, 51, 52, 71, 73, 91, 96, 134, 181, 209, 277, 281, 282, 285, 299. *See also* Paris
Frances (domestic worker), 168, 283
Francis of Assisi, Saint, 45, 46, 228, 237
Free (Niles), 117
Freeman (domestic worker), 37, 283
Freeman, Douglas Southall, 300
Freeman, Margaret, 127
French, Lillie Hamilton, 259, 283
Freud, Sigmund, 131
Friends of the Princeton Library, xlii
Frothingham, Cornelia, 73, 283

G., Hallie Belle, 168, 283
Gale, Zona, 82, 126, 261, 262, 278, 283
Galsworthy, Ada, 55, 58, 258, 283
Galsworthy, John, xli, 58, 59, 283
Gannett, Lewis, 129, 144, 283
Garden of Allah, The (Hichens), 20
Gardner, Mary Carter Anderson (Mrs. Charles S.), 272, 283
Garland, Hamlin, xxxix
Garst, Eleanor Hubbard, 264, 284
Gas Light and Coke Company (London), 300
Gause, Mrs., 191, 284
Gautama (Buddha), 230
Geffrye Museum (London), 98, 99, 105
George Gissing (Swinnerton), 297
Gerald B—— (*The Woman Within*), 17, 32
Germany and German, 3, 8, 61, 71, 129, 167, 180, 221, 230, 240
Geroni, P. G., 45, 284, 287
Gholson, Esther Cook, 89, 90
Gian-Luca (*Adam's Breed*), 83, 110, 284
Gibbet Tor (England), 107
Glasgow, Anne Jane Gholson (mother), xvi, xxi, xxii, xxxix, 1, 2, 75, 76, 142, 212, 216, 218, 219, 224, 230-31, 234, 284, 292, 294; photograph of, *see illustrations gallery*
Glasgow, Annie. *See* Clark, Annie Glasgow (sister)
Glasgow, Arthur Graham (brother), xxi, xxviii, xxxix, xl, xliii, xlv, 1, 3-12, 34, 37, 63, 75-76, 83-84, 90, 93, 95, 121, 133, 159, 165, 166, 174, 182, 215, 220, 276, 278, 284, 293, 297, 300
Glasgow, Betty, 34, 284

Index

Glasgow, Cary. *See* McCormack, Cary Glasgow

Glasgow, Ellen; apparel, 5, 6, 9, 10, 47, 58, 59, 64, 94, 157, 168, 236; books and reading (*see also individual titles*), 38, 42-43, 225, 240, 250; childhood, 1, 14, 55, 61, 62, 225, 230, 237, 242, 247; deafness, xxi, xxiv, xxix, 17, 48, 50, 218; domestic furnishings, xxix, 84, 88, 100-103, 108, 109; domestic workers, 34, 36-40, 156, 157, 167, 189, 224, 233; food and eating, 42, 45, 49, 96, 101, 108, 121, 190, 222; handwriting and typewriting, xxxiii, 226, 231, 252; health, xxvii, xliii, xliv, 40, 66, 85, 86, 123, 124, 126, 127, 136, 184, 186, 189, 190, 196, 200, 205, 208, 216-18, 220, 226, 229, 234-38, 240, 246, 250-52; heart attacks, xxvi, xliv, 196, 231; honorary degrees, 81, 170, 183, 278; as host, xxix; and nature, xxv, xxvi, 62, 86, 87, 97, 101, 104, 111, 128, 170, 172, 176, 191, 196, 199, 203, 208, 211, 215, 230, 231, 237, 240, 245, 252; photograph of, *see illustrations gallery;* sensitivity to suffering, xxii-xxiv, 193; stationery, xxvii, xxviii, 1, 158, 192, 193; works by (*see also individual titles*), xiii, xiv, xvi, xvii, xix, xxi, xxv, xxxix, xli, xliv, xlvi, 1, 13-17, 24, 25, 35-36, 38, 43, 55, 60, 67, 68, 72, 74, 79, 81, 112-14, 118, 139, 140, 144, 149, 151, 153, 155, 159, 162, 175-76, 177, 180, 184, 187, 203, 204, 207, 226-28, 230, 233, 235, 240, 248, 278, 281, 283, 286, 289, 291, 295-97, 299, 303-4

Glasgow, Emily. *See* Houston, Emily Glasgow (sister)

Glasgow, Francis T. (father), xv, xxi, xxii, xxvii, xxxix, xli, 5, 8, 21, 36, 37, 38, 39, 41, 48, 56, 142, 154, 160, 185, 218, 230, 276, 277, 284

Glasgow, Frank (brother), xxi-xxii, xl, 2, 4, 5, 7, 17, 32, 48, 49, 276, 283, 284

Glasgow, John McNutt (uncle), 284, 288

Glasgow, Joseph Reid (brother), xxxix, 284

Glasgow, Joseph Reid (uncle), 276, 284

Glasgow, Katherine McNutt (aunt), 297

Glasgow, Margaret Branch (sister-in-law), xl, 58, 59, 63, 82, 83, 84, 87, 90, 95, 102, 174, 175, 215, 261, 271, 277, 278, 281, 284, 290

Glasgow, Margaretta Gordon (aunt), 2, 284, 290

Glasgow, Marjorie (niece), 83, 152, 265, 269, 281, 284, 290

Glasgow, Mary Jane (aunt), 2, 284, 290

Glasgow, Rebe. *See* Tutwiler, Rebe Glasgow

Glasgow, Rebecca Anderson (aunt), xiv, xix, xxx, xxxix, 1, 2, 255, 284

Glasgow, Robert Arthur (uncle), 8, 295

Glasgow, Samuel Creed (brother), xxxix, 216, 281, 284

Glastonbury Abbey (England), 108, 109, 281

Glenn, Isa, xx, xxx, xxxiii, 125, 130, 137, 139, 263, 264, 277, 284

Glen Springs (Watkins, N.Y.), xl

Gloucester (England), 93, 96, 105, 108

Goddess of Reason, The (Johnston), 21

Golden Rose, The (Troubetzkoy), 170

Golden Vanity, The (Paterson), 293

Golden Wedding and Other Tales, A (Stuart), 296

Gone with the Wind (Mitchell), xx, 291

Goodman, Susan, xxx, xxxi, 32, 305

Gordon, Mrs. Howard S., 36, 39, 266, 285

Gore, Luther Y., 219, 304

Gorky, Maxim, 66

Goucher College, xliii, xlv, 177

Grace Avenue (Richmond, Va.), 20

Gray, Thomas, 59, 91, 92, 95

Great Meadow, The (Roberts), 143

Greece, xxvi, xxvii, xl, 85, 92, 143

Greenbrier County, W.Va., 299

Green Forest (Rockbridge County, Va.), 142, 174, 285

Greenslet, Ferris, 146-49, 285

Greyfriar's churchyard (Edinburgh, Scotland), 122

Greylock, Jason (*Barren Ground*), 70, 235

Grimms' Fairy Tales, 249

Growth of the American Republic (Morison and Commager), 174

Growth of the Soil, The (Hamsun), 73

Haardt, Sara. *See* Mencken, Sara Haardt

Hackett, Francis, 224, 229, 235, 241, 243, 247, 248, 249, 250, 279, 283, 285, 297

Haddon, Judge, 121, 285

Hadfield, Lady, 59, 110, 285, 299

Hall, Radclyffe, xiv, xix, xxiii, xxvi, xxxi, xxxiii, xlii, 80-81, 109, 222, 261, 262-66, 271, 284, 285, 288, 298; letters from, 103, 110, 115, 124, 220; photograph of, *see illustrations gallery*

Hamilton, Nina (Duchess of Hamilton), xvii, 83, 98, 100-101, 262, 265, 271, 285, 289

Hamlet Had an Uncle (Cabell), 214

Hamsun, Knut, 73

Hansen, Harry, 69, 285

Harcourt (publishers), xlii, 148, 205, 224, 285, 297

Harcourt, Alfred, xvii, 139, 146-51, 195, 201, 205, 275, 285

Harcourt, Ellen, xvii, 269, 271

Hard-Boiled Virgin, The (Newman), 292

Hardy, F. E. (Mrs. Thomas), 55, 261, 285

Hardy, Thomas, xli, 10, 11, 59, 70, 72, 102, 105-7, 112, 193, 194, 199, 251, 285, 289, 299

Hare, J. C. (*Walks in London*), 12, 13

Harper and Brothers, 13, 129, 294, 295

Harper Prize, 129, 192

Harper's Magazine, xli

Harris, Joel Chandler, 90

Hart, Antoinette (Mrs. Alan Lindsay), 265, 266, 286

Hartley, Mr., 96, 286

Harvard University, 81, 163, 197, 288

Harvie, Lu, 2, 286

Hasley (chauffeur), 94, 96, 98-99, 103, 107-11, 286

Hazlitt, Henry, 138, 144, 286

Heat (Glenn), 284

Heine, Heinrich, 237, 238

Helmsley Castle (England), 89

Hemingway, Ernest, 139, 294

Hemming, Mrs., 286

Hémon, Louis, 73

Henrico County, Va., 4

Henry VIII, King, 89, 91, 111, 112

Hergesheimer, Joseph, 69, 286

"Heroes and Monsters" (Glasgow), xlii

Herschel, John Frederick William, 9

Heth, Miss, 63, 286

Heyward, Du Bose, 144

Higbee Guards of Fort Worth, Tex., 41

High Mowing (Canby), 238-39, 279

Hinduism, 228, 231, 246

Hitler, Adolf, 192, 223

Hoffman, Malvina, 166, 167, 266, 270, 286

Hoffmann, E. T. A., 139, 143

Holden, Agnes Johnson, 266, 286

Holliday Bookshop, 241, 286

Holliday, Terence, 241, 286

Hollywood Cemetery (Richmond, Va.), xliv, 75, 76, 119, 224, 244, 286

Homeric, SS, xxviii, xlii, 117-20, 291, 299

Hopper, Katharine Baird, 61, 258, 286

Hoppner, John, 84, 96

horseback riding, 28, 39, 42

Horsey Place (Castine, Maine), xxviii, 196, 197, 209, 276, 279, 286, 299

Housatonic Valley, xliii, 164

Houston, Emily Glasgow (sister), xv, xxxix, xli, 2, 5, 36, 277, 282, 284, 286

Houston, Herbert Tedd (brother-in-law), 286

Howard Mumford Jones: An Autobiography (Jones), 183

Howard University, 209, 282

Howe, Mr., 52, 287

Howells Medal (American Academy of Arts and Letters), xxix, xliii

Howland, Marie, 263, 287

Huidekoper, Mrs. [Rush?], 13, 256, 287

Humphreys, Alexander Crombie and family, 3-10, 287, 293

Humphreys and Glasgow (London), 284, 287

Hurricane, N.Y., xl, 22, 29, 34, 287, 293

Hurst, Fannie, 260, 287

Huston, John, xliii, 217

Huxley, Aldous, 245

hyphenated words, 301

Hypothesis and Belief (Isherwood), 245

"I Believe" (Glasgow), xiv, 180, 181, 226-28, 304

I Chose Denmark (Hackett), 241, 244, 250

I Live in Virginia (Meade), 291

I'll Take My Stand (Twelve Southerners), 301

Imitation of Christ, The (devotional book), xxvi, 21

Imitation of Life (Hurst), 287

Imperator, SS, xli, 58, 59

"Impressions of the Novel" (Glasgow), 114

India, 230, 231

Indianapolis, Ind., 69

Innocence Abroad (Clark), 118, 127
In Pursuit of Laughter (Repplier), 295
Interlaken, Switzerland, xl
International Women's Council, 71
In This Our Life (film), xliii, 217
In This Our Life (Glasgow), xvii, xliii–xlv, 181, 185, 187, 188, 194, 198, 202, 207, 208, 209, 211, 217–18, 221, 222, 228, 229, 231, 282, 287, 291, 294, 304
Ireland, 100, 227
Irene (domestic worker), 224, 234, 287
Isherwood, Christopher, 246, 250
Italy, xix, xxvii, xl, 30, 42, 71, 86, 92, 133, 143; Assisi, xl, 44, 45, 46; Fiesole, xlii, xliii, 172, 173, 236, 237, 277, 283; Florence, 44–46; Italian Alps, 42; Milan, xl; Naples, xl, 45, 46; Padua, 45; Perugia, xl, 44–46; Porziuncola, 44, 45; Ravello, xliii, 173; Rome, 46; Tuscany, xxvi; Venice, xl, 46, 71. *See also individual place-names*

James, Henry, xli, 59, 138, 250, 287
James, The (Niles), 292
Japan, 12
Jay's Mourning Warehouse (London), 59, 94, 102, 287
Jefferson Hotel (Richmond, Va.), xli, 175, 247, 248, 282, 287, 291
Jeffrey, Mrs. Richard, 287, 290
Jerdone Castle, xxxix, 123, 282, 287, 293, 295
Jeremy (dog), xvi, xxii, xxviii, xlii, 78, 80, 88, 94, 99, 114–16, 118, 119, 120, 121, 123, 131, 287, 289; photograph of, *see illustrations gallery*
Jeroni, Padre. *See* Geroni, P. G.
Jesus, 228
Jim, 179, 212, 213, 287
Jo, 197, 287
Jock (pet), 97, 288
John Keats (Lowell), 76
Johns, Ann Page (Mrs. Frank), 271, 288
Johns Hopkins University, xlii
Johnson, Robert Underwood, 286
Johnston, Coralie, 18, 34, 36, 41, 42, 43, 44, 281, 288
Johnston, Elizabeth, 162
Johnston, Eloise, 19, 21, 23, 30, 42, 282
Johnston, Joseph Eggleston, 41, 288

Johnston, Mary, xvii, xix, xxv, xxvi, xxviii, xxx–xxxii, xlv, xlvi, 17, 18, 19, 32, 45, 46, 56, 80, 83, 162, 288, 290, 291; letters from, 114; letters to, 18, 20, 23, 26, 29, 30, 42, 43, 60, 162; photograph of, *see illustrations gallery*
Johnston, Mrs., 288
Johnston, Walter, 19, 288
Jones, Bessie Zaban, xvii, xix, xxiv–xxvi, xxviii, xxx–xxxii, xlii, xlv, xlvi, 81, 126–29, 216, 273, 288, 297; letter from, 126; letters to, 127, 128, 141, 142, 152, 155, 163, 165, 166, 173, 177, 178, 179, 180, 182, 184, 194, 196, 198, 199, 202, 207, 216, 218, 219
Jones, Howard Mumford, xvii, xlii, 81, 126, 128, 129, 180, 181, 183, 207, 286, 288, 297
Jones, Lizzie ("mammy"), xvi, xxiii, xxxix, 18, 35, 61, 76, 184, 232, 288, 289, 293
Jones, Llewellyn, 69, 288
Jordan, Elizabeth, 258, 274
Joy (dog), 34, 35, 43, 47, 288
Jude the Obscure (Hardy), 9–11, 285
Jürgen (Cabell), 285

Kaiser Wilhelm der Grosse (oceanliner), xl
Kant, Immanuel, 29
Karnak, Egypt, 86
Kauser, Alice, 258, 288
Kazin, Alfred, 220
Keats, John, 143
Kentore, Lady, 55, 60, 258, 289
Kerr, Sophie, 262, 289
Kibble, Rhoda, 289, 294, 295
Killman, Mr., 289
King, Blanche T., 264, 289
King, Mr., 3, 289
Knole (England), 111, 112, 295
Knopf, Alfred, 55, 74, 125, 289, 296
Knopf, Blanche (Mrs. Alfred), 55, 74, 75, 260, 274, 289, 296
König Albert (oceanliner), 44
Krock, Arthur, 69, 289

Lake country (England), 121, 123
Land Birds of Rockbridge County, Virginia (Murray), 292
Lankes, J. J., 82, 126, 289

Lark, The (magazine), 278
Last Puritan, The (Santayana), 165
Lavengro: The Scholar, Gipsy, Priest (Borrow), 73
Lawrence, D. H., 143, 148
Lectures in America (Stein), 154
Leighton, Clare, xviii, xx, xxiii, xxv, xxx-xxxi, xlv, 81, 188, 191, 199, 289; letters to, 164, 172, 187, 192, 195, 197, 198, 199
Leisy, E. E., 290
Lelia, 4, 289; photograph of, *see illustrations gallery*
Lellie, Aunt. *See* Glasgow, Ellen
lesbianism, xiii, xvi, xix, xxx, 80, 81, 285
Letters of Ellen Glasgow (ed. Rouse), xxx, xlv, 255, 304
Lewis, Sinclair, 70, 147
Lewis Rand (Johnston), 21, 44
Lexington, Va., xix, 172, 174, 176, 223, 249, 275
Liberty's (London), 47, 110, 289
Library of Congress, xxxvii, xlv
Life and Gabriella (Glasgow), xli, 56, 60, 289
Life of Hans Christian Andersen, The (Toksvig), 224-25, 227, 297
Life of Keats (Lowell), 75, 76
Life of Père Marquette, The (Repplier), 295
Life with Father (film), 297
Lightfoot, Amanda (*The Romantic Comedians*), 135
Lincoln Cathedral (England), 90, 92, 94, 95
Lind-af-Hageby, Emelia, 101, 102, 289
Literary Review, 69
Little Anne (dog), 88, 92, 96, 98, 276
Little Lord Fauntleroy (Burnett), 278
Littleplace (Castine, Maine), xxviii, xliii, 190, 191, 194, 279, 289, 298
Liverpool, England, xxxix, 3
London, England, xxii, xxviii, 3, 5, 8, 10, 13, 49, 58-60, 82, 85, 87, 93, 95, 100, 105, 108, 117, 123, 141, 174, 221, 295; Academy of Arts, 4; Bloomsbury, 100; British Museum, 4; Buckingham Palace, 6; Empire, the (music hall), 6; House of Commons, 8; Hyde Park, 3, 4, 6, 49; London Museum, 95; London Zoo, 4; Lords' (cricket grounds), 7; Lyceum, 5; National Gallery, 11, 12; Royal Academy, 5; Royal Academy of Arts, 5, 6; royal family, 6; St. James Park, 3; St. Paul's Cathedral, 9; Tower of London, 4; Trafalgar Square, 12; Victoria Gardens, 9; Waterloo Bridge, 9; Westminster Abbey, 3, 5, 8-9. *See also individual place-names*
Longfellow, Henry Wadsworth, 4
Longwell, Dan, 69, 114, 131, 144-46, 148, 150, 281, 289
Lorrain, Claude, 12, 13
Loti, Pierre, 134
Louisa County, Va., xxxix
Loveman, Amy, 264, 269, 271, 289
Lower Depths, The (Gorky), 66
Lucas, Elizabeth, 262, 290
Lucy (domestic worker), 36, 290
Luhan, Mabel Dodge, 148
Lutie, 36, 290
Lyell, Sir Charles, 9
Lyon, Dr. John Henry Hobart, xliii
Lyon, France, 133, 134
Lyon, John Henry Hobart, 182, 290

Mabie, Hamilton, 53, 290
MacDonald, Edgar, xxx, 304, 305
Mackenzie, Jean Kenyon, 264, 290
Macmillan, 162, 226, 300
Macy, Gertrude, 200, 290
Maggie, Aunt. *See* Glasgow, Margaretta Gordon (aunt)
Mahony, Mrs., 2, 290
Maine, xx, xxvi, xli, xlii, 62, 63, 120, 190, 197, 198, 200, 201, 202, 203, 208, 210, 212, 215, 219, 223, 224, 225, 226, 253. *See also individual place-names*
Malcolm, Miss, 20, 290
Manor, the (Castine, Maine), 191, 192, 295
Mansfield, Mrs. Damon, 62, 63, 290
Marcus Aurelius, 13, 143, 144
Maria (domestic worker), 37, 290
Maria Chapdelaine (Hémon), 73
Marsh, John, 204, 288, 290
Marsh, Margaret Mitchell. *See* Mitchell, Margaret
Martha's Vineyard, 225, 229
Martin, Helen, 173
Martin, Nathaniel (chauffeur), 76, 157, 290, 292

Martyrdom of Man, The (Winwood), 154
Mary (domestic worker), 39, 40, 290
Mary Ellen, 78, 290
Mary Magdalen, 237
Massachusetts Historical Society, xlv
Master of the House, The (Hall), 116, 125
Maud, Princess, of Wales, 6
Maule, Harry, 131, 138, 290
Maymont (Richmond, Va.), 189, 290
Maynard, Mrs., 189, 290
Mayo, Betsy Burke, 269, 290
McAfee, Helen, 112, 261, 262, 264, 272, 290
McClintic, Guthrie, 200, 201, 291
McCormack, Cary Glasgow (sister), xv, xxi, xxii, xxiv, xxvii, xxviii, xxxi, xxxix, xli, xlv, 3, 5, 8, 10, 11, 16, 17, 20-23, 28, 32-34, 36, 38, 39, 42-46, 51, 55, 65, 76, 87, 103, 224, 257, 258, 276, 279, 284, 290, 299; photograph of, *see illustrations gallery*
McCormack, Walter (brother-in-law), xxi, xxxix, 120, 290, 291, 299
McKee, Benjamin Harrison ("Baby McKee"), 121, 291
Meade, Julian R., 183-84, 291
Mellon Gallery (National Gallery of Art, Washington, D.C.), 237, 238
"Memorabilia" (Browning), 134
Mencken, H. L., 69, 124, 132, 135, 188, 197, 198, 286, 291
Mencken, Sara Haardt, xix, xlv, 124, 132, 135, 188, 263-65, 285, 286, 290, 291, 306
Men's League (Richmond, Va.), 54, 292
Merano Shoemaker, The (Hall), 222
Mercer, Mrs., 2, 291
Meredith, George, 47
Merrill, George F., 2, 291
metaphysics, 29, 160, 180, 306
Metropolitan Museum of Art (New York), 286
Meynell, Alice, 291
Meynell, W. B., 59, 60, 290
Middlebury College, xliii, 164
Midsummer Night's Dream, A (Shakespeare), 62
Mill, John Stuart, 9
Miller of Old Church, The (Glasgow), xli, 18, 162, 246, 303
Milton, Mrs. Marshall, 248, 291
Milton and His Daughters (Romney), 84

Miss Lulu Bett (Gale), 283
Mitchell, M. Jeannette, 259, 291
Mitchell, Margaret, xx, xxxi, 204, 270, 290, 291
Mitcoff, Elena, 271, 291
Moby-Dick (Melville), 141
Modern Language Association, xliii, 163-66, 288
Mona Lisa (Leonardo da Vinci), 125
Moncorvo House (London), 34, 82
Montague, Andrew Jackson (governor), 34, 292
Monte Carlo, 174, 175
Montréal, Canada, 29
Monty, Mary, 270, 292
Moody, Fluvanna (*Barren Ground*), 236
Moore, Anne Carsall, 119, 292
Morgan, J. Pierpont, 94
Morley, Frank, xliv, 238, 247, 283, 292
Mormons, 191
Morris, Miss, 40, 292
Morristown National Historical Park, xlvi
Morrow, Elizabeth C., 265, 292
Moulton, Louise Chandler, xviii, xix, xxx, xxxi, xxxvii, xl, 23-33, 256, 292, 297
Moulton, William U., 292
Mount Holyoke College, 299
Mr. Darlington's Dangerous Age (Glenn), 130, 137-38, 285
Munce, Mr., 54, 292
Munford, Beverley, 121, 292
Munford, Hunton, Williams, and Anderson (law firm), 292
Munford, Mary Branch, 292
Munford, Miss, 247, 248, 292
Munroe, Mrs. Vernon, 265, 292
Murray, Joseph J., 234, 292
Musselman, Eleanor, 188, 190, 193, 197, 282, 292
"My Last Duchess" (Browning), 230
mysticism, xvii, 17, 19, 21, 24, 178, 187, 220, 222, 224, 227, 228, 229, 231, 232, 245

Nantucket, xlii
Napanock, N.Y., xlii
Naples, Italy, xl, 45, 46, 101
Nation, 69, 70, 162, 298
National Gallery (London), 12, 96, 111

National Gallery of Art (Washington, D.C.), 238
National Institute of Arts and Letters, xxix
National Institute of Social Sciences, xli, 283
National Museum of Women in the Arts (Washington, D.C.), 286
National Portrait Gallery (London), 99
Natural History Museum (London), 111
"Nature Spirits of North America" (Toksvig), 244
Needham (Cumberland County, Va.), 292
Never Ask the End (Paterson), 136
Neville Screen (England), 87
Neville's Fields (or Cross), Battle of, 86, 87
Newark, Del., 291
New England, xlii, 81, 116, 139, 163, 173, 179, 181, 201, 202, 243, 246
New Jersey, xl, xlii, xliii, 38, 53, 158, 281, 290
New Left Review, 289
Newman, Frances, 69, 113, 262, 292
New Republic, 69, 244, 285, 297, 300
Newton, Isaac, 9
Newtown, Conn., 222
New York (city), xix, xxv, xxvii, xxviii, xli–xlii, 17, 24, 28, 36, 38, 39, 46, 49, 52, 53, 56, 59, 64, 68, 72–76, 81, 82, 112, 115, 117, 128, 134, 144, 147, 148, 153, 159, 160, 167, 172, 176, 181, 182, 184, 194, 196, 197, 202, 211, 234, 237, 246, 277, 292
New York Herald Tribune, 55, 157, 243, 275, 277, 281, 283, 293, 298, 305
New York Herald Tribune Books, xlvi, 69, 73, 113, 114, 118, 136, 139, 140, 155, 165, 180, 196, 208, 296
New York Public Library, xlvi
New York Times, 240, 241, 243, 248, 279, 284, 288
New York Times Book Review, 132, 157, 275, 279
New Yorker, 72, 299
Nicholls, Miss, 48, 292
Nicholson, Mrs. *See* Sackville-West, Vita
Niles, Blair Rice, 117, 277, 292
Nineteenth Amendment, 65
Ninth Wave, The (Van Doren), 77
Nirvana (Buddhism), 229
Norcross, Mr., 13, 293

Norfolk, Va., xix, 41, 57, 87, 291
Northwestern University, 296
Norwood (England), 8, 10, 293

Oakley, Dorinda (*Barren Ground*), 70, 72, 235
Oakley, Joshua (*Barren Ground*), 70
Of Ellen Glasgow: An Inscribed Portrait (Glasgow and Cabell), 178
Ogunquit, Maine, xli
Ohio State University, 209
Old Dominion Edition of the Works of Ellen Glasgow, xlii, 81, 115, 125, 150, 162, 303
Old Virginia Gentleman and Other Sketches, The (Bagby), 185
Olympic, SS, xlii, 88, 118, 281, 298
One Man in His Time (Glasgow), xli, 56, 303
"One Way to Write Novels" (Glasgow), 153, 162
One West 85th Street (New York), xxviii, xli, 293
One West Main Street (Richmond, Va.), xv, xxii, xxvii, xxix, xxxix, xl, xli, xlii, xliv, 133, 277, 280, 282, 284, 289, 293; photograph of, *see* illustrations gallery
On My Way (Canby), 172, 238, 279
On Native Grounds (Kazin), 220
On the Origin of Species (Darwin), 144
Orlando (Woolf), 295
Oxford, England, xxviii, 8, 9, 10, 11, 52, 93, 109, 111
Oxford University, 11, 111

Paddon, Mr., 4, 8, 9, 293
Page, Gabriella, 270, 293
Page, Walter Hines and Willa Alice, xxxix, 58, 293
Pal (dog), 158, 293
Pankhurst, Emmeline, 59
Paradise, Frank, xl, 34, 71, 283, 293
Paris, France, xl, 9, 25, 96, 103, 142, 235, 292, 297, 300
Pat. *See* Paterson, Isabel Bowler
Paterson, Isabel Bowler, 113, 114, 129, 135, 136, 144, 155, 264, 293
Patsy (domestic worker), 35, 36, 37, 293
Patterson, Elizabeth (Lizzie), xxii, xxiv, xxvii, xxxi, xxxiv, xxxix, xl, xlv, 1, 14, 16,

76, 169, 281, 294, 293; letters to, 14, 15, 46, 49, 50, 51, 52, 56, 57, 63
Patterson, Elizabeth Anne Duval (Miss Betty), 15, 46, 50, 57, 277
Patterson, Lucy Bramlette, 16, 256
Patterson, Miss, 161, 266, 293
Patterson, Mrs., 293
Patterson, Nita, 294
Patton, Mr., 13, 294
Pavlova Frieze (Hoffman), 167
Paxton, Gordon, 34, 294
Pedlar, John Abner (*Barren Ground*), 70
Pedlar, Nathan (*Barren Ground*), 70
Perkins, Maxwell E., 177, 182, 210, 294
Perkinson, Isabelle Holmes, 255, 293
Peter Abelard (Waddell), 142
Peterkin, Julia Mood, 68, 294
Petersburg, Va., xli, 296
Phases of an Inferior Planet (Glasgow), 1, 14, 303
Phelan, Senator James Duval, 62, 294
Philadelphia, Pa., xix, xlii, 2, 28, 32, 37, 67, 104, 144, 280, 283, 291, 294, 300
Philadelphia Ledger, 69
Phillips, George, 105, 106, 294
plagiarism, 226, 227
Play-House, the (Castine, Maine), 278
Plotinus, 26, 224, 226, 227, 245
Port of Refuge (Toksvig), 232-33
Powell, John H., 58, 291, 294
Poynter, Mr., 48, 294
Pratt, Mrs., 78, 119, 294
Pre-Raphaelites, 95
Presentation Medal of the National Institute of Social Sciences, xli
Preston, Edmund Myers, 176, 294
Prince Edward Island, 15
Prince of Wales, 6
Princeton University, 95
private collections (letters), 255
Prix Femina, 281, 292
"Problem, The" (Emerson), 141
Proctor, Adelaide Anne, 4, 5
Prohibition, 84, 120
provenance (letters), 255
Pulitzer Prize, xxix, xliii, 137, 138, 187, 216, 283, 289, 291, 294, 295, 296, 298
Pygmalion (Shaw), 58

Québec, Canada, xxvii, xl, 29, 30
Queenborough (fictional town), 240, 288
Quick or the Dead?, The (Troubetzkoy), 297

Raper, Julius R., xlv, 16, 304, 305
Rascoe, Burton, 114, 294
Rawlings, Marjorie Kinnan, xiv, xviii, xix, xx, xxvi, xxviii, xxx-xxxii, xxxiv, xxxvii, xlv, 139, 186, 277, 294, 304; letter from, 210; letters to, 188, 211, 213, 214, 253; photograph of, *see illustrations gallery*
Rawlings, Va., 2, 294, 299
Rebe. *See* Tutwiler, Rebe Glasgow
Rebecca of Sunnybrook Farm (Wiggin), 300
Reconstruction, 218, 250
Red Cross, xli, 276, 277, 282, 285
Reese, Agnes B., xvi, xvii, xxx, 170, 179, 212, 267, 271, 287, 294, 295
Reid, Mary, 71, 294
Rembrandt van Rijn, Paul, 99
Repplier, Agnes, xxxiii, xlvi, 55, 66-67, 73, 74, 259, 260, 283, 294
Return of the Native, The (Hardy), 9, 70
Reveille (Patterson home), 168, 169, 293, 294
Reviewer, xli, 126, 280, 296
Reynolds, Sir Joshua, 99
Richards, H. Grahame (pseud.), 227
Richardson, Roberta ("Birdie"), 170, 171, 179, 277, 294, 295
Richmond, Va., xix, xxii, xxiv, xxvi-xxvii, xxxix, xl-xliv, 46-57, 65-69, 74, 78, 88, 110, 112, 116, 121-35, 154, 159, 163-68, 180-88, 194, 195, 204, 207, 211, 216-24, 230-37, 241-51, 275-300
Richmond Castle (England), 89, 91
Richmond Female Seminary, 291
Richmond News-Leader, 113, 158, 300
Richmond Public Library, 278
Richmond Times-Dispatch, 43, 113, 115
Rievaulx Abbey (England), 89, 91, 109
Riggs, Mrs. (George). *See* Wiggin, Kate Douglas
Ringed with Fire (Campbell), 234, 235
Rives, Mrs., 295
Roberts, Elizabeth Maddox, 143
Robson, Eleanor, 19, 21, 22, 256, 277, 282, 295

Rockbridge County, Va., xlii, 285, 292, 304
Rock Castle (Rutherfoord home), 15, 16, 295
Rollins College (Fla.), xlii, 177
Romance of a Plain Man, The (Glasgow), xl, 18, 44, 303
Romantic Comedians, The (Glasgow), xlii, xlvi, 56, 113, 125, 153, 155, 159, 162
Romney, George, 84, 96
Roosevelt, Franklin Delano, 206, 222
Roosevelt, Theodore, xli
Rossetti, Christina, 20
Rouse, Blair, xxx, xlv, 30, 304
Rowe, Lelia Ann Munce, 289
Russian novels, 129
Rutherfoord, Ann Seddon Roy, 15, 16, 256, 295
Rutherfoord, John Coles, 295
Rye, Sussex (England), xix, 80, 124

Sabbath Glee Club (Richmond, Va.), 69
Sackville-West, Vita (Mrs. Harold Nicholson), xix, 80, 111, 112, 295
Safford, Miss, 212, 295
Sally (dog), 96, 98, 101, 295
Sanctuary (Faulkner), 143, 144
Sanford, Millie H., 267, 295
Sanskrit, 245
Saturday Review of Literature, xliii, 69, 118, 153, 162, 177, 178, 207, 277, 279, 289, 296
Saxton, Eugene P. (Gene) and Martha, xx, 134, 191, 264, 295
Sayers, Dorothy L., 190, 191
Scarborough, Dorothy, 137, 264, 295
Scarlet Sister Mary (Peterkin), 294
Schopenhauer, Arthur, 231
Scotland, xxvii, xlii, 5, 7, 8, 9, 10, 101, 121, 280, 285, 292, 294
Scott, Evelyn, 114
Scott, Mrs. Thomas, 191, 295
Scottish National War Memorial (Edinburgh), 122, 123
Scribner's, 173, 294
Secret Garden, The (Burnett), 278
Sedgwick, Anne Douglas, 147, 148
Selected Letters of Marjorie Kinnan Rawlings (Bigelow and Monti), 210, 304
Selfridge's (London), 87, 89, 95, 296
Sentimental Journey, A (Sterne), 91

Sergeant, Elizabeth Shepley, 262, 296
Shadows (Richards), 227
Shadowy Third and Other Stories, The (Glasgow), xli, xlii, 56, 303
Shakespeare, William, 71
Sheltered Life, The (Glasgow), xxviii, xlii, xliii, xlvi, 81, 128, 132-34, 135, 136-37, 153, 156, 162, 194, 195, 200, 201, 205, 207, 235, 240, 298, 303, 304
Sheltered Life, The (Turney), xliii, 200, 201, 205, 298
Sheltering Arms Hospital (Richmond, Va.), 289
Shepstone, Miss, 90, 296
Sherborne Almshouse (England), 105, 106, 294
Sheridan, Richard Brinsley, 6
Sherman, Stuart Pratt, 68-73, 78, 296
Short as Any Dream (Sergeant), 296
Short History of Julia, A (Glenn), 125
Signed with Their Honor (unknown), 234, 235
Silent Pool, the (England), 104
Simon (dog), 96, 98, 296
Simpson's in the Strand (London), 96, 98, 99, 296
Sinclair, May, xvii, xix, xl, 21, 47-48, 98, 100, 259, 261, 296
Sir Richard Burton's Wife (Burton), 231
Smart Set, 291
Smith (Cabell), 158
Smith, Mrs. Francis, 255, 296
Smith College, xliv, xlvi, 280
Smith-Rosenberg, Carroll, xxx
Society for the Prevention of Cruelty to Animals (SPCA), xxvi, xxxix, xlii, xlvi, 56, 57, 231, 277, 281, 290, 295
Sojourner, The (Rawlings), 253
"Some Literary Woman Myths" (Glasgow), 113, 114
Something about Eve (Cabell), 279
Sometime—Never (Leighton), 195, 196
So Red the Rose (Young), 140, 145, 152
South, the, xvi, xxiv, 81, 126-30, 134, 136, 143, 144, 174, 229, 236, 246, 247
South Carolina, 188, 294
Southampton (England), 83, 120
Southern Charm (Glenn), 284
Southern Methodist University, 290

Southern Women's National Democratic Committee, xliii
Southern Writers Conference, xlii, 127
South Moon Under (Rawlings), 139
South Poland, Maine, xlii
Speyer, Leonora, 271, 296
Spinoza, Baruch, 23, 26, 43
Spruce Knoll (Castine, Maine), 216-19, 279, 296
Stafford, Jean, 244
Stagg, Hunter, 157, 295, 296
St. Albans Cathedral (England), 97
Stallings, Mr., 74, 296
St. Augustine, Fla., 211, 213, 214, 253, 277
Stein, Gertrude, xvii, xlii, xlv, 80, 153, 154, 265, 296, 297, 299
Sterne, Laurence, 91, 92
Stevens, George, 177, 296
stock market crash of 1929, 146
Stoke Poges (England), 58, 59, 91, 97
Store, The (Stribling), 138
Strachey, Lytton, 142
stream of consciousness, 296
Stretch-berry Smile, The (Scarborough), 137
Stribling, T. S., 137, 138
Stuart, Ruth McEnery, 53, 258, 290, 296
Sully, Julia, xl, 34, 35, 36, 49-50, 52, 58, 69, 258, 287, 288, 296, 297
Swedenborg, Emanuel, 186, 224, 225, 297
Swinnerton, Frank, 98, 100, 102, 104, 106, 283, 297
Symbols of American Libraries, xxxvi, 305

Tate, Allen, 138
Tate Gallery (London), 95
Taylor, Bayard, 137
Taylor, Helen, 270, 297
Taylor, Henry J., 241
Taylor, Thomas (trans.), 226, 227
Teaching of Epictetus, The (trans. Rolleston), 13, 16
Tess of the D'Urbervilles (Hardy), 9, 285
theosophy, xvii, 245, 250
They Say the Forties (Jones), 166
They Stooped to Folly (Glasgow), xiii, xlii, xlvi, 81, 112, 113, 114, 116, 128, 153, 162, 246, 248, 279, 303
Thompson, Dr., 66, 297
Thoreau, Henry David, 187, 188
Thoughts of the Emperor Marcus Aurelius Antoninus, The, 13, 143, 144
Three Hills (Johnston home), 60, 162, 297
Three Sisters (Chekhov), 66
Thurman, Mr., 8, 11, 297
Timberlake, Asa (*In This Our Life*), 217
Timberlake, Roy (*In This Our Life*), 217, 228, 229
Timberlake, Stanley (*In This Our Life*), 217, 228, 229
Time (magazine), 145, 207, 208
Tintern Abbey (England), 89, 93, 96, 105, 108, 109
Titian, 12
Titus, Olive Glasgow, 266, 297
To Have and to Hold (Johnston), 288
Toklas, Alice B., xvii, 80, 153, 154, 296, 297
Toksvig, Signe, xiii, xiv, xviii, xxiv, xxv, xxvi, xxvii, xxviii, xxx-xxxii, xxxiii, xliv, xlvi, 173, 186, 187, 251, 278, 285, 297; letter from, 227; letters to, 222, 224, 225, 230, 231-33, 235, 240, 242, 244, 246, 249, 251; photograph of, *see illustrations gallery*
Tolstoy, Leo, 66, 72
Tom Jones (Fielding), 128, 129
Tommy (dog), 166, 297
Tomorrow (magazine), 242, 244
Torquay (England), 105, 107
To the Lighthouse (Woolf), 141
To What Dread End (Heberden), 234, 235
Towne, Charles Hanson, 234, 297
Treatise on the Gods (Mencken), 132
Tredegar Iron Works (Richmond, Va.), 276, 281, 284
Tricoby family, 9, 297
Trigg, Emma Gray, 157, 274, 297
Tristram Shandy (Sterne), 91
Trollope, Anthony, 21, 43, 155, 250, 251
Troubetzkoy, Amélie Rives, xiii, xviii, xix, xxvi, xxxi, xlv, 23-25, 33, 36, 55, 133, 168, 169, 173, 258, 259-60, 262, 270-71, 275, 279, 291, 297; photograph of, *see illustrations gallery*
Troubetzkoy, Prince Pierre, xviii, 169, 170, 294, 298
Troubridge, Una, xix, 80, 124, 222, 297
True Heart, The (Warner), 299

Trumbull, Miss, 191, 298
Tucker, Mrs. Alan, 190, 289, 298
Turkey, 49, 294
Turner, J. M. W., 12, 13
Turney, Catherine, xliii, 194, 195, 200-201, 205, 269, 270, 298
Turning Wheels, The (Cloete), 191, 192
Tutwiler, Carrington Cabell (brother-in-law), xl, 32, 35, 40, 45, 59, 62-64, 75, 78, 92, 176, 196, 234, 249, 298
Tutwiler, Carrington Cabell, Jr. (nephew), xlv, 75, 78, 95, 111, 117, 279, 298, 306
Tutwiler, Rebe Glasgow (sister), xiv, xix, xx, xxi, xxii, xxvi, xxvii, xxx-xxxi, xxxiv, xxxvii, xxxix, xl, xlvi, 6, 7, 8, 10, 11, 17, 19, 10, 21, 22, 23, 26, 27, 30, 32, 33, 35, 39, 41, 42, 47, 48, 56, 67, 79, 87, 88, 89, 92, 93, 95, 99, 102, 106, 109, 116, 121, 172, 182, 220, 224, 280, 284, 287, 288, 291, 293, 294, 298, 300, 304; letters to, 28, 32, 33, 34, 35, 36, 37, 38, 39, 40, 41, 44, 58, 59, 62, 63, 64, 66, 75, 78, 82, 84, 90, 95, 97, 104, 107, 108, 110, 119, 171, 174, 175, 181, 189, 190, 191, 196, 208, 212, 215, 223, 234, 248, 250, 252; photograph of, *see illustrations gallery*
Tweedie, Mr., 298
Two Wives, The (Swinnerton), 297

undated letters, xxxv, xlvi, 255, 273
Under Dispute (Repplier), 67
Under the Greenwood Tree (Hardy), 194
University of Florida, xlv
University of Illinois, 296
University of Iowa, xlv
University of Michigan, 126, 129, 288
University of North Carolina, xlii, xlvi, 81, 126, 182, 183, 278
University of Pennsylvania, xlvi
University of Richmond, xliii, 177
University of Rochester, xliii
University of Texas, xxxvii, xlvi, 126, 288
University of Vermont, xlvi
University of Virginia, xxxvii, xlvi, 127, 188, 255, 275, 296
University of Wisconsin, xliii, 177
University Publishing Company, 294
Unlit Lamp, The (Hall), 110
Upanishads, 29

Valentine, Ben, 54, 57, 65, 277
Valentine, Lila Hardaway Meade, 53, 57, 65, 258, 259, 277, 298, 304; photograph of, *see illustrations gallery*
Valley of Virginia, xl, 16, 21, 40, 142, 154, 160, 295
Vanamee, Grace D., 268-70, 298
Van der Hooy, Dr., 37, 298
Van Doren, Anne, 72, 73, 78, 207, 208, 275, 298
Van Doren, Barbara, 207, 276, 298
Van Doren, Carl, 65, 68-70, 73, 77, 113, 145, 152, 158, 276, 279, 298, 306
Van Doren, Dorothy, 143, 264, 298
Van Doren, Irita, xiv, xvii, xix, xxiii, xxv, xxx-xxxi, xli, xliv, xlv, 55, 148, 186, 199, 239, 298; letter from, 68; letters to, 65, 68, 70, 72, 76, 77, 113, 114, 117, 127, 129, 138-41, 144-48, 150, 151, 154, 158, 159, 183, 202-7, 238, 242, 252; photograph of, *see illustrations gallery*
Van Doren, Margaret, 159, 160, 207, 277, 290, 198
Van Doren, Mark, 158, 298
Van Vechten, Carl, xlii, 154, 279, 296, 299
Vedanta, 245, 246
Vein of Iron (Glasgow), xlii, xliii, xlvi, 81, 128, 139, 142, 145, 149, 152-53, 155-59, 160-61, 170, 221, 228, 283, 285, 303, 304
Ventnor, N.J., xlii, xliii, 156, 281, 290
Vermont, xliii, 164, 177, 179, 180, 181, 283
Veterans Hospital (Roanoke, Va.), 213
Victoria, Queen, 6, 84
Villa Marsilio Ficino (Fiesole, Italy), xliii, 172-73, 237, 278, 283
Villa Montalvo (Calif.), 63
Villard, Léonie, xlii, 134, 264, 266, 269, 299
Virginia (Glasgow), xli, 56, 161, 162, 303
Virginia Beach, Va., 28, 282, 288
Virginia Building (1915 World's Fair), 62
Virginia Commonwealth University, xlvi
Virginia Edition of the Works of Ellen Glasgow, xiii, xix, xliii, xliv, 81, 113, 173-75, 178, 180, 182, 187, 289, 303
Virginia Historical Society, xlvi
Virginia League for Woman Suffrage, xvii, xl, 298
Virginia League of Women Voters, 280

Index

Virginia Military Institute, 298
Virginia Quarterly Review, 72, 127, 128, 129
Voice of the People, The (Glasgow), xl, 1, 14, 176, 303
Voltaire, 44, 231

Walden (Thoreau), 188
Walker, Lily (Mrs. John Y. G.) (cousin), 4, 168, 202, 274, 299
Wallace Collection (London), 99
Walpole, Horace, 143
Walpole, Hugh, xli, 66, 69, 78, 96, 195, 286, 287, 299
Waltham Abbey (England), 93, 97
Waltham Cross (England), 97
war, xv, 23, 48, 55, 61, 92, 115, 122, 144, 181, 182, 183, 184, 192, 193, 203, 214, 219, 221, 222, 224, 225, 234, 236, 240, 241, 245–47, 249, 285, 292, 300
Wardwell, Ralph S., 208, 212, 276, 299
Warm Springs, Va., xli, 36, 38, 43, 63, 297, 299
Warner, Susan Bogert (pseudonym "Elizabeth Wetherell"), 2
Warner, Sylvia Townsend, 117, 299
Washington, D.C., 209, 237, 238, 281, 286
Washington Square (New York), 66
Watch for the Dawn (Cloete), 192
Waterloo bridge (London), 9
Waterloo station (Londona), 83
Watson, Va., 268, 299
Waves, The (Woolf), 141
Wear, River (England), 86
Webster, Mrs., 299
Weddell, Mr. and Mrs. Alexander, 167, 286, 299
Weird Tales (Hoffman), 139, 143
Welch, John (*The Sheltered Life*), 240
Wellford, Dr., 175, 299
Wellford, Judge, 9, 299
Wellford, Roberta (Berta), 34, 43, 45, 57, 58, 66, 121, 157, 169, 212, 277, 299
Well of Loneliness, The (Hall), 80, 285
Wessex (dog), 105, 106299
West, [Tanner?], 119, 299
West Cornwall, Conn., xliii, 148
Westminster Abbey (London), 3, 4, 5, 9, 82
Westover (Va.), 70

Wharton, Edith, 138
"What I Believe" (Glasgow), 162
What Is Remembered (Toklas), 297
What Price Glory? (Stallings), 296
Wheel of Life, The (Glasgow), xl, 18, 25, 178, 303
While the Sirens Slept (Dunsany), 244
Whistler, James McNeill, 96
Whitby Abbey (England), 86, 87
White, the. *See* White Sulphur Springs, W.Va.
White Sulphur Springs, W.Va. ("The White"), xxvii, xxxix, xl, 11, 12, 39, 42, 185, 299
Whiting, Elizabeth, 14, 256, 299
Whitman, Walt, 31, 32
Wickersham, Miss (Frances). *See* Hadfield, Lady
Wiggin, Kate Douglas, 48, 288, 295, 300
Wilde, Oscar, 22, 138
Willcox, Christine, 71, 280, 300
Willcox, Louise Collier, xxvii, xli, xlv, 36, 39, 45, 53, 70, 259, 260, 279, 289, 300
Willcox, Westmore, III, 299, 300
Willcox, Westmore, Jr., 71, 299, 300
Williams, Frances Leigh, 265, 300
Williams, Jane, 78, 290, 300
Williamsburg, Va., xl, xliii, 165, 182, 189
Willis, Dr., 37, 300
Willkie, Wendell, 202, 206, 242, 298, 300
Wilmer, Dr., 90, 93, 300
Winchester Cathedral (England), 104, 108
Wind, The (Scarborough), 295
Winter, Mr., 35, 58, 300
Wisdom of Solomon (Book of Wisdom), 28
Wister, A. L. (Annis Lee), 3
Witch, The (Johnston), 60
"Woman of To-morrow, A" (Glasgow), xxxix
Woman's Home Companion, xli
Woman Within, The (Glasgow), xiv, xvi, xix, xxi, xxv, xxx, xlii, xlii, xliv, xlv, xlvi, 1, 17, 32, 55, 56, 79, 81, 145, 148, 156, 159, 177, 187, 216, 238, 293, 294, 299, 300, 304
women, 4, 5, 7, 17, 40, 55, 56, 61, 80, 81, 136, 170, 172, 185, 209, 244, 247
Women's Political and Social Union, 59

women's suffrage, xvii, xxi, xl, xli, 17, 54, 57, 58, 59, 65, 280, 288, 289, 292, 296, 298, 306
Woodall, Corbet, and family, 5, 7–8, 300
Woodlanders, The (Hardy), 9, 194
Woodland Park, Colo., xl, 275, 287
Woods, Katherine, 244, 272, 300
Woolf, Virginia, xvii, 80, 96, 100, 138, 139, 141, 251, 261, 295, 300
word division, 301–2
Wordsworth, Dorothy, 143
Wordsworth, William, 92, 143
Wye Valley (England), 108, 109

Yale Review, 113, 290
Yale University, xlv
Yearling, The (Rawlings), 188, 214, 215, 294
York, Duke of, 6
York Minster (England), 86, 87, 90, 94, 97, 108
Young, Stark, 140, 144, 155, 168, 296, 300